Praying with Saint Matthew's Gospel

Daily Reflections on the Gospel of Saint Matthew

Edited by Father Peter John Cameron, O.P.

MAGNIFICAT®

F o r e w o r d

Father Peter John Cameron, O.P.

T OWARD THE CONCLUSION OF THE SERMON on the Mount, Jesus turns his gaze on all those who are willing to listen to his voice, and he speaks these words:

> "Do not worry and say, 'What are we to eat?' or 'What are we to drink?' or 'What are we to wear?'... Your heavenly Father knows that you need them all. But seek first the kingdom [of God] and his righteousness, and all these things will be given you besides." (Mt 6: 31-33)

Usually when someone tells us not to worry, the first thing we do *is* worry. But there is something different about the way that Jesus says it. It is not just counsel, advice... certainly not a warning. Rather, it is a *promise*. The care of the Father has come to us in the flesh: "Emmanuel, God is with us" (see Mt 1: 23). When Joseph was worried about taking the expectant Virgin Mary as his wife, this was the consoling assurance that the angelic messenger of God the Father gave to the distraught Joseph so that he would become the foster father of the Son of God.

The whole of the Gospel of Matthew is a plea to heed this pledge. The Someone whom our heart seeks – the Someone who was able to draw the Magi (Mt 2: 1-12) from the safety and security of their far-away homes and lead them to the improbable "throne" of the manger – is calling us forth from all our concerns. God has come close to us. To seek his kingdom is to desire the closeness he longs to share with us. To seek his righteousness is to say yes, again and again, to the way that Jesus wills to be one with us in our need, healing our resistance, our doubt, our inner division with his presence.

Matthew himself experienced the glory of such obedience through his self-surrender to the Lord's two simple words: "Follow me" (Mt 9: 9). Somehow he sensed in that seconds-long exchange that the Everything he had always sought – and that had always evaded him – was being given to him in a way he had never imagined: in the face of a friend who would never leave his side: "I am with you always, until the end of the age" (Mt 28: 20).

Seek first the Father's kingdom, the Father's righteousness. We find it in the companionship of his Son who foresees our resistance, anticipates our needs, and undoes our every alibi. With the entire tenderness of heaven he begs,

> "Come to me, all you who labor and are burdened, and I will give you rest. Take my yoke upon you and learn from me, for I am meek and humble of heart; and you will find rest for yourselves. For my yoke is easy, and my burden light." (Mt 11: 28-30)

The Gospel of Matthew is a living testament that we are not alone in our struggles, we are not left to ourselves in our trials. *Everything* will be given to us when we live from the certainty that we belong to the Father. That Belonging is who we are! Even if we come late to this awareness, the Father "pays" us with a wage of love equal to what our aching hearts crave (Mt 20: 9). Even if we have lived our life in a slavery of fear, the Father will stoop to the most ingenious ways to hand over his Son to us to transform us into his sons and daughters. Jesus is the "talent" the Father entrusts to us so that we will invest in his own desire for us to "share the Master's joy" (see Mt 25: 14-30).

How to use this book

Praying with Saint Matthew's Gospel is designed to help you in your life of faith in many ways. You can follow along each day of the year by reading the entry that corresponds to the day's date. Or you can begin your reading with that section of the book that matches the Church's reading of the Gospel of Matthew in the lectionary for Sunday Mass. For this purpose a handy table has been included on the inside front and back cover of the book that links the Gospel texts with each Sunday of the liturgical year. In this way, *Praying with Saint Matthew's Gospel* serves as an ideal way to prepare for the Sunday liturgy. Another idea is to read *Praying with Saint Matthew's Gospel* with a group of friends, studying the Gospel chapter by chapter and letting this book accompany you as a guide. In whatever way you choose to use *Praying with Saint Matthew's Gospel*, your *lectio divina* (prayerful sacred reading) of the Scripture with the help of this volume will lead you to seek the kingdom of the Father and to see how, through his Son, he generously gives us everything we need.

INTRODUCTION
Surrender at a Glance

Simeon Leiva-Merikakis, O.C.S.O.

As Jesus passed on from there, he saw a man named Matthew sitting at the customs post. He said to him, "Follow me." And he got up and followed him. While he was at table in his house, many tax collectors and sinners came and sat with Jesus and his disciples. (Mt 9: 9-10)

Such is the stark record that the evangelist Matthew has left us of what was surely the most memorable event in his life: Jesus' sudden irruption into his self-satisfied and worldly existence, when with one piercing glance and two well-placed words the Lord turned the greedy entrepreneur into a zealous apostle.

A great deal of the meaning of Matthew's Gospel may be read in this one scene. The way that Jesus, unbidden, mysteriously enters the space of Matthew's self-centered existence corresponds precisely to how the eternal Word of the Father unexpectedly slipped into our world, searching out what was lost (10: 6). With him he brings the light that enables us to see ourselves for the first time as we really are, the light that reveals both the deeper neediness and the deeper longing concealed just beneath the surface of all our busy ambitions and so-called successes.

In any other circumstance this sudden unmasking of a person's sham existence by Jesus' mere glance would surely hurl most of us into resentful denial. But in this one baffling instance we, identifying with Matthew, feel urged to embrace our exposure with humility as a saving truth. There can be only one reason for this unaccountable reaction: the sublime power of Jesus' person and presence. Rather than lash back with insolence or run away with shame, Matthew simply takes Jesus up on his invitation and follows him. Somehow, basking in the company of Jesus, all of our personal sins, infidelities, and fears can gladly become exposed before the world, because we sense the power of God at work here, healing us.

A painful revelation that without Jesus would be reason for endless shame becomes a way of purification leading to new life. Forgiven shame becomes a source of constant joy. We will never cease marveling at the superhuman magnetism that must have flowed from the arresting beauty of Jesus' face and voice for two little words, "Follow me," radically to have changed on the spot the course of a very ambitious man's life.

Clearly, this vocation story constitutes the very pattern of how anyone, by encountering Jesus, can become a Christian, which is to say an intimate disciple of the Son of God. Henceforward all the hope and energy that fuel Matthew's life derive from this one moment of encounter, when the inscrutable freedom of the gracious God visited the dark recesses of Matthew's life to lift him up to life eternal. In time he writes his Gospel with only one goal in mind: to make available to us his own encounter with the living Word so that we too may become glad disciples of Christ.

Light in Our Darkness: God Is with Us

Now, even though Jesus says to Matthew, "Follow *me*," in the very next scene we see Jesus seated at table in *Matthew's* house, dining with "many tax collectors and sinners." When the Pharisees object to his rubbing elbows with sinners in this way, Jesus retorts: "Those who are well do not need a physician, but the sick do… I did not come to call the righteous but sinners" (9: 12-13). Surely this is shockingly good news – that considering oneself righteous *disqualifies* one from being called by Jesus!

This penchant of Jesus for sharing his table and very life with sinners is at the core of his conflict with the religious authorities, and the clash will eventually climax in his death. We know that God's self-emptying descent into the heart of human darkness, to fill that void with light and love, will not be without severe consequences for the Savior. We may say that at Matthew's table we have a foreshadowing of both the conviviality of the Last Supper (26: 20-29) and the agony of the cross (27: 33-50). Since the earliest kernel of the Gospel narrative is the concluding story of the Lord's passion, death, and resurrection (26: 1–28: 20), we can already see the cross casting its shadow backward on every earlier scene in the Gospel. No word or action of Jesus makes any sense without its reference to the cross (10: 38; 16: 24).

Jesus' presence at Matthew's house as natural consequence of his call also reminds us of the awesome exchange that takes place between God and man in Jesus: God gives us his divinity and all its bliss in exchange for our humanity and all its misery. If God has come to invite us to share his divine life through all eternity, the process begins when Jesus first comes into our own time and space to dwell within our shabby lives and hearts – sinful, worldly, self-preoccupied, and yet full of the hope that his teaching, touch, and presence will gradually transform us into radiant children of God.

The utterly unfailing, challenging, and transforming way in which God abides with us in the person of Jesus Christ is the very heart of this Gospel. The whole text is structured around this truth. Early on, Matthew quotes the messianic prophecy of Isaiah: "'Behold, the Virgin shall be with child and bear a son, and they shall name him Emmanuel,' which means '*God is with us*'" (1: 23). And then, in the very last sentence of the Gospel, the risen Jesus makes this promise: "Behold, *I am with you* always, until the end of the age" (28: 20). Between these two "beholds" there unfolds the story of Jesus' life as the unbelievable passion of the Heart of God to share in all the joys and sorrows of our ordinary human life so as to make them his own and so raise them to his glory.

Law Becomes Light: The Shape of Matthew's Gospel

Matthew's Gospel is by far the most Jewish of the four. It contains many times over the number of Old Testament quotations found in the other three. One of the first is from Isaiah (Is 9: 1-2), which Matthew uses to show Jesus as the historical embodiment of the "light" the prophecy promises: "He left Nazareth and went to live in Capernaum by the sea... that what had been said through Isaiah the prophet might be fulfilled:... 'The people who sit in darkness/ have seen a great light,/ on those dwelling in a land overshadowed by death,/ light has arisen'" (4: 13-14, 16).

Unique to the first Gospel is a formula that Jesus repeats no less than six times in chapter 5: "You have heard that it was said to your ancestors... But *I* say to you..." (5: 21-22, 27-28, 31-34, 38-39, 43-44). In this way Matthew portrays Jesus as eager to show how his own life and teaching fulfill the revelation of the Old Testament by wondrously surpassing it. He presents himself, to the scandal of many, as God's living, enfleshed Torah, the law now become life-giving, personal Presence.

Torah ("instruction," "law") comprises the first five books of the Bible, perhaps the reason why Matthew structured his Gospel symbolically into five major sections, each ending with a demarcating formula ("When Jesus finished these words..." [19: 1], or something similar). Before the first section we have Jesus' family tree and the story of his infancy (1: 1–2: 23), and after the fifth section we witness the culmination of the Gospel in the narrative of the Easter events (26: 1–28: 20).

Each of the five major parts (3: 1–7: 29; 8: 1–10: 42; 11: 1–13: 52; 13: 53–18: 35; 19: 1–25: 46) in turn consists of a *narrative of episodes* in Jesus' life, followed by a *teaching segment* that normally presents a commentary on the meaning of the events just witnessed. This arrangement stresses the primacy of Jesus' person and deeds over anything he may teach. In other words, we are saved by the self-sacrificing, indwelling love of a divine Person, and not by abstract teachings.

In the Church: Where Our Burden Is Light

Matthew's is the only Gospel in which the word "church" appears (16: 18; 18: 17). He stresses the communal nature of our encounter with God, the fact that no one goes to God alone but only as a member of the Church Jesus built on the foundation of Peter's faith (16: 18). Matthew writes his Gospel with the new consciousness and enthusiasm of one who, having been "fished" out of his darkness by Jesus' powerful hand, has now in gratitude himself become a "fisher of men" (4: 19). The only ambition left him is to be God's tireless servant, ushering as many guests as possible into the joy of Christ's wedding feast in the kingdom (22: 10).

And the irresistible "hook" that this divine fisherman uses was nowhere better exposed than in Jesus' tender summons at Mt 11: 28-30, which Matthew alone transmits. Its seductive words reveal the full force of God's desire for us and are surely the precious pearl of Matthew's Gospel and an echo of his own calling, now extended to all:

> "Come to me, all you who labor and are burdened, and I will give you rest. Take my yoke upon you and learn from me, for I am meek and humble of heart; and you will find rest for yourselves. For my yoke is easy, and my burden light."

An Invitation to Saint Matthew's Gospel
Reading as Eating: Savoring the Word of God

Andrew Matt

For many of us the prospect of reading an entire Gospel can seem as daunting as scaling the face of a mountain. Don't you need to be an expert for that sort of thing, with a lot of free time to boot? Don't you need all kinds of specialized knowledge of ancient languages and scientific methods, like a professional mountain climber with a backpack full of intricate grappling equipment who treks off into the heights for weeks at a time?

Absolutely not. The beauty of the Bible, and of the Gospels in particular, is that Scripture ultimately reveals the Father's beloved Son, who has "come down" from the mountain, so to speak, to reveal to us his loving face. By embracing our humanity and speaking to us in the everyday language of his chosen people, Jesus communicates an intimate friendship that is accessible to each and every person on the planet. This event of Love become flesh has been received and recorded by the Church in a special way in the four Gospels, which is why the Gospel proclamation and the celebration of the Eucharist go hand in hand together at every Mass. As Saint Ambrose reminds us, "the body of the Son is the Scripture transmitted to us."

Reading Eucharistically

While it is very true, then, that the more we come to know and love the incarnate Lord, the more we will want to learn about the "bodily" dimensions of his divine Word, namely, the literary and historical forms through which he chose to communicate himself, it is even more fundamental to experience his concrete personal love. Biblical knowledge, Pope Benedict XVI observes, is "not the result of an ethical choice or a lofty idea, but the encounter with an event, a person." This means that we do not need to be intimidated by reading a Gospel from start to finish, worried about how we could ever comprehend it all. No one can. Or rather, the only way to understand the Gospel in its fullness is to read it eucharistically.

The Fathers of the Church were fond of saying that just as every fragment of the Eucharist contains the fullness of Christ's presence, so every individual word of Scripture mysteriously contains the whole Word. Thus, a single verse or two from the Gospel, one bite-sized morsel, is often all it takes to be seized suddenly with gratitude or with an acute sense of contrition; to be jostled out of a complacent place or infused with deeper commitment and zeal; to be permeated by a profound peace and abiding joy. Whatever particular form the fruit of such *lectio divina* may take, as long as we humbly "chew" each word slowly, attentively, and with an attitude of thanksgiving, then we are encountering Jesus already.

Reading in the Church

The present volume has been designed with a practical page-a-day format so as to facilitate this sort of intimate eucharistic encounter in the midst of one's busy schedule. Because it's often hard to savor the "taste" of a Scripture passage all by oneself, a verse or two from Matthew's Gospel is presented in communion with the insights of a gifted spiritual writer – in the "we" of the Church, as it were. In this way, eucharistic reading becomes simultaneously a fruitful form of ecclesial listening, which in turn often triggers a dynamic response in our lives.

Reading with Mother Teresa

I can still remember, for instance, my most pivotal encounter with the New Testament, which took place on a bus. I was a freshman in college and had just begun taking my faith seriously. For some reason I was thumbing through Matthew's Gospel on the local bus when – bang! – Jesus' words suddenly took my breath away: "Do not store up for yourselves treasures on earth… [S]eek first the kingdom [of God]… and all these things will be given you besides" (Mt 6: 19, 33). As a teenager these and similar passages had washed over me dozens of times at Mass, barely making a ripple in my life. What made them stick now?

Three months earlier I heard Mother Teresa speak at Harvard's commencement. I couldn't hear her very well. What I could hear well was the curious reaction of the audience. Some booed, others hissed. I had never experienced people hissing before. By the end though, everyone applauded politely.

Later I tracked down a copy of her speech and realized what the booing and hissing was about. Mother Teresa had evidently struck a nerve when she spoke about the destruction of the unborn as "one of the greatest poverties. A nation, people, family that allows that," she said, "they are the poorest of the poor." Clearly not the best way to endear yourself to a Harvard crowd.

It became clear as I read the speech, however, that her overarching theme was "the terrible hunger for love" that afflicts rich and poor alike. To satisfy this hunger, she said, God came close to us, God became man, he "made himself the Bread of Life for us," and "to make it easy for us, to help us to love, he makes himself the hungry one, the naked one, the homeless one." She gathered these statements together with a verse from the Gospel of Matthew: "Whatever you do to the least of my brethren you do to me" (25: 40). When I finished reading, it was as if Mother Teresa's words had stuck to my ribs.

Back on the bus, the impact of Jesus' words upon me reverberated with the echoes of Mother Teresa's speech. And from then on I knew with clarity that no treasure on earth was worth anything unless it also possessed value in the kingdom of heaven.

What makes words like Mother Teresa's so fruitful is that they themselves have sought and received such nourishment from the Word that they become powerful Bread-bearers to a famished world. This is the eucharistic mission of the Church, giving joyful witness to a Word that hungers to be eaten.

Say But the Word...

Monsignor James Turro

The book of the genealogy of Jesus Christ, the son of David, the son of Abraham. Abraham became the father of Isaac, Isaac the father of Jacob, Jacob the father of Judah and his brothers.
(Mt 1: 1-2)

In the history of mankind Abraham stands out for his ready submission to the will of God. When God comes to Abraham to say: "Go forth from the land of your kinsfolk and from your father's house to a land that I will show you" (Gn 12: 1), it was a large acquiescence that God was asking of him. In those times, to risk relocating oneself and one's possessions was a tall order. Yet Abraham's response to God's express will was swift and full – no mulling over, no hesitation whatever: "Abraham went as the LORD directed him" (Gn 12: 4).

Yet another instance of Abraham's unhesitating deference to God's express wish is found in God's extraordinary request that Abraham sacrifice his son Isaac. "Take your son Isaac, your only one, whom you love, and go to the land of Moriah. There you shall offer him up as a holocaust"(Gn 22: 2). Abraham's response was full and unhesitating. The next morning he set out with his son and two servants to carry out God's will. Abraham was well rewarded for his prompt assent to God. "The LORD said to Abram: 'Look about you, and from where you are, gaze to the north and south, east and west; all the land that you see I will give to you and your descendants forever'" (Gn 13: 14-15).

When we forge ahead to New Testament times we find Jesus every bit as disposed and prompt to carry out the will of the Father. "Not what I will but what you will" (Mk 14: 36). We have to conclude that Jesus' profound readiness to execute the will of the Father was foreshadowed by his ancestor, Abraham. The lesson for us to learn is that we would do well to cultivate a prompt acquiescence to God's will in every situation that enfolds us.

Dear Father, in every contingency of life, bitter or sweet, I pray for the strength to say: Here I am, I have come to do your will.

Share the Wealth

Monsignor James Turro

Judah became the father of Perez and Zerah, whose mother was Tamar. Perez became the father of Hezron, Hezron the father of Ram, Ram the father of Amminadab. Amminadab became the father of Nahshon, Nahshon the father of Salmon, Salmon the father of Boaz, whose mother was Rahab. (Mt 1: 3-5)

It is inviting to look for and find in the lives of the earthly forbears of Jesus parallels in Jesus' earthly life. The behavior of Boaz who is mentioned in the genealogy of Jesus could serve as an example.

There was a law, set down in the Book of Leviticus, that specified the obligation of the rich man toward the poor. "When you reap the harvest of your land, you shall not be so thorough that you reap the field to its very edge, nor shall you glean the stray ears of your grain. These things you shall leave for the poor and the alien. I, the LORD, am your God" (Lv 23: 22).

As recounted in the Book of Ruth, Boaz most cordially allowed Ruth to glean in his fields. Such deference to the poor and unfortunate as Boaz displayed is matched and surpassed in the life of Jesus as recounted in the Gospels. Boaz exhibited the generosity of spirit and the genuine concern for the welfare of one's neighbor commended by Jesus and exhibited by him.

The Gospels speak eloquently of Jesus' sensitive regard for the poor and unfortunate. As is noted at the very outset of Matthew's Gospel, "they brought to him all who were sick with various diseases and racked with pain, those who were possessed, lunatics, and paralytics, and he cured them" (Mt 4: 24).

But there are also the specific instances where the mercy and compassion of Jesus are detailed. First off, think of the beatitudes which exude profound concern for the poor in spirit, those who mourn, the meek. But perhaps the apex of tolerance and mercy is reached in Jesus' requirement that one love one's enemies: "I say to you, love your enemies, and pray for those who persecute you" (Mt 5: 44). The application to our own lives and behavior is only too obvious: as he was toward friend and foe, so must I be.

Arouse in me, O Father, a love for the poor, so special and dear to your heart. Inspire me to do for them as I would do for Christ your Son.

Give and It Shall Be Given to You

Monsignor James Turro

Boaz became the father of Obed, whose mother was Ruth.
Obed became the father of Jesse, Jesse the father of David the
king. David became the father of Solomon, whose mother had
been the wife of Uriah. (Mt 1: 5-6)

Combing through the genealogy of Jesus one comes upon all sorts of interesting persons. One of the most engaging is Ruth. A native of Moab, a country to the east of the Dead Sea, she was married to Mahlon, a son of Naomi. Early on in her marriage Ruth was widowed. The Book of Ruth gives a moving account of her devotion to her mother-in-law, Naomi. Widowed and childless, she insisted on accompanying Naomi when Naomi decided she had to return to her native Bethlehem. It was there that Ruth met and married Boaz, a wealthy landowner and one of Naomi's relatives. In time, Ruth gives birth to Obed, who was destined to become David's grandfather.

Ruth stands out as a model of fidelity. She could easily have stayed on in her native Moab and lived in the style of life she had known and followed from her childhood. Naomi had urged her to do just that, but Ruth's sense of loyalty was hard and fast. We have to conclude that the good fortune she eventually enjoyed – marriage to a wealthy man, the birth of a healthy boy – all this came to her as a reward for her fidelity and exquisite kindness to Naomi.

Sometimes people are too swift to conclude that the rewards of virtuous living are to be enjoyed only in the next life. God in his infinite wisdom and for his unfathomable purposes does at times permit us to reap the rewards of virtuous living in this life as well. There was, to be sure, also a long-range honor that accrued to Ruth. She would in time become the ancestor of the great hero King David and, farther along, the ancestor of the Messiah, no less.

Such blessings materialize not only in the lives of great figures in world history but also in the lives of devoted and virtuous people living in the here and now.

Loving Father, I desire to love and serve you, as the saints loved
and served you, without the expectation of any reward.

One's Wealth and Talent Used for the Glory of God

Monsignor James Turro

Solomon became the father of Rehoboam, Rehoboam the father of Abijah, Abijah the father of Asaph. Asaph became the father of Jehoshaphat, Jehoshaphat the father of Joram, Joram the father of Uzziuh. (Mt 1: 7-8)

To this day Solomon is remembered as an icon of wealth and power. He lived "large" and was celebrated, as well, for his wisdom. The Old Testament makes much of that wisdom. It tells of Solomon's shrewdness in determining which of two women was a child's true mother (1 Kgs 3: 16-27). It credits his ability to respond to difficult questions posed by the queen of Sheba. "King Solomon explained everything she asked about, and there remained nothing hidden from him that he could not explain to her" (1 Kgs 10: 3).

Jesus made a passing reference to Solomon's wisdom: "At the judgment the queen of the south will arise with this generation and condemn it, because she came from the ends of the earth to hear the wisdom of Solomon; and there is something greater than Solomon here" (Mt 12: 42).

Two lessons emerge that a modern-day Christian can derive from Solomon. First, Solomon's most illustrious descendant according to the flesh, Jesus of Nazareth, is the ultimate font of wisdom. This is a fact that was clearly recognized by his first disciples: "To whom shall we go? You have the words of eternal life" (Jn 6: 68).

Second, one can take a cue from Solomon in his moment of profound piety, the dedication of the temple in Jerusalem, when he readily acknowledges God's greatness and his goodness: "Solomon stood... and stretching forth his hands toward heaven, he said, 'LORD, God of Israel, there is no God like you in heaven above or on earth below; you keep your covenant of kindness with your servants who are faithful to you with their whole heart'" (1 Kgs 8: 22-23).

Paradoxically, for all his wisdom, Solomon was not a paragon of virtue. His life and work point up the need for God's grace. It is not enough to know better. We have a profound need for God's help – his grace – in order to live a virtuous life.

Loving Father, in your loving kindness, grant me to appreciate your grace above wealth, wisdom, and everything else.

Serving God to the Best of One's Ability

Monsignor James Turro

Uzziah became the father of Jotham, Jotham the father of Ahaz, Ahaz the father of Hezekiah. Hezekiah became the father of Manasseh, Manasseh the father of Amos, Amos the father of Josiah. Josiah became the father of Jechoniah and his brothers at the time of the Babylonian exile. (Mt 1: 9-11)

In most trying times, Hezekiah the king stood firm and loyal to God: "He put his trust in the LORD, the God of Israel; and neither before him nor after him was there anyone like him among all the kings of Judah" (2 Kgs 18: 5). Among other things, Hezekiah sought to unify the worshiping community by closing down local worship sites which are referred to in the Scriptures as "high places." He was concerned to focus the worship life of the people on the temple in Jerusalem. This move was aimed at fostering a tighter union among the faithful, especially in their prayer life. He understood that forms of common prayer serve to create community, as well as to join people of one generation with foregoing generations. Hezekiah seems to have had a sharp awareness of God and of one's duty to reverence him. Unlike modern man, the ancients took the worship of God most seriously.

Hezekiah's achievements take on a special meaning and value when one considers that he labored under a disabling circumstance. Like his father Ahaz before him, he was a vassal of Assyria – a fact which must have restricted a good bit of what he would have wanted to accomplish. Even though hobbled by that disadvantage, he was nonetheless able to make a mark on his times. Hezekiah eventually broke with Assyria, but his efforts were no match for Assyria's superior forces. He went down in defeat.

Though Hezekiah's life and tenure ended in failure at the hands of the Assyrians, the good he achieved lived on as happens at times in worldly situations. Worldly success does not come invariably to virtuous people. And that ought not dishearten one. A person cannot be sure of getting his just deserts in this life, but certainly in the next life the scales of justice are balanced.

Father, let me be always at the ready to serve you, in fair weather and foul. Whatever the cost I will pay it with love.

God Is My Shield

Monsignor James Turro

After the Babylonian exile, Jechoniah became the father of Shealtiel, Shealtiel the father of Zerubbabel, Zerubbabel the father of Abiud. Abiud became the father of Eliakim, Eliakim the father of Azor, Azor the father of Zadok. Zadok became the father of Achim, Achim the father of Eliud, Eliud the father of Eleazar. (Mt 1: 12-15)

Shealtiel – a curious sounding name that has not survived as designating a masculine identity. The word can mean "God is a shield" or "God is victor." Each of these etymologies is consoling and declares a very comforting fact. Let us investigate the first meaning of Shealtiel: "God is a shield."

In biblical antiquity, an ample shield was the best guarantee that a foot soldier could have for surviving a battle. The poor soldier could only count on a small hand-held shield with which to parry the enemy's spear thrusts. The wealthier soldier could sport a longer and wider shield that would guarantee his survival.

In ancient times, the foot soldier put his trust for survival and success in a sturdy shield and a good marching song. Hence, "the LORD is my strength and my shield" (Ps 28: 7) One cannot beat that for guaranteeing one's survival and success on the field of battle. Shield and song – the best tools for success a soldier could count on.

To say "God is my shield" is to say that God is my sure protector. It is this conviction that emboldens heroic souls to this day. The foreign missionary who leaves familiar environments for days and nights in a rank jungle trusts that he can survive all this strangeness – God is his shield. Will the people he encounters be open to his message or be enraged by it – to the point of personal hostility toward him? Not to worry, God is his shield.

One need not conjure up such extraordinary images. Even in the everyday flow of life, in the office, the school, the factory – wherever it is one works – it is there that one is frequently and formidably challenged. All need not be lost. One need only recall: God is my shield.

Into your hands, Father, I commend my life. In your supreme goodness watch over and protect me.

Jesus, My Brother

Monsignor James Turro

Eleazar became the father of Matthan, Matthan the father
of Jacob, Jacob the father of Joseph, the husband of Mary.
Of her was born Jesus who is called the Messiah. (Mt 1: 15-16)

Jesus' genealogy tells us that God is most earnest about becoming like us. He did not drop down from heaven in some magical way, having no human antecedents. Clearly he wanted to become as genuinely human as he was genuinely divine. After all, every human being has a genealogy – it's part of being human. Now with his genealogy Jesus resembles us in every way except sin. His humanity is deep-going – authentic, not a mere tincture. Abraham and all the others in the line-up contributed their genes to the humanity of Jesus. How interesting that God made himself beholden in this wise to all the persons in the genealogy. He took their genes.

It is inviting to think that just as the individuals in Jesus' genealogy were blithely unaware of the high purpose they served in life and in eternity as ancestors of the Messiah, so there are individuals today who all unawares are serving some long-range purpose of God.

In practical terms every Christian should construe his or her role in life as ushering Christ into the lives of the people that surround them. Let something of Christ – if only the thought of him – come to people through something we say or do. One has to wonder if anyone in the slate of Jesus' ancestors had any intimation of being employed by God in this exalted way – serving as a human antecedent of Jesus. This could lead one in our day and age to speculate whether perhaps God may be using him or her to serve some noble purpose, which is yet to materialize in the far-off future, just as he used Abraham.

There is a suggestion in all this of a deeper meaning to one's human existence, a meaning of which one may be totally oblivious. Who can say? All of which can lead one to wonder yet again how inscrutable are God's ways.

Into your hands, Father, I place my life, present and future.
Make it serve just as the human ancestors of your Son served:
as conveyers of you to many.

Generously I Have Received, Generously I Give

Monsignor James Turro

Thus the total number of generations from Abraham to David is fourteen generations; from David to the Babylonian exile, fourteen generations; from the Babylonian exile to the Messiah, fourteen generations. (Mt 1: 17)

When one stops to think of it, everyone of us is caught up in a genealogy. We are like links in a chain. There are links (persons) that precede us and links that follow us. We normally think of the genes and the culture that travel down through the generations to reach us and enhance our existence. In one respect, certainly, we should have to say we have been richly endowed by those who have gone before us. We have very likely received the true faith from them – our parents and grandparents who carefully nurtured it so as to hand it on to us. Even before we think of making out our will so as to pass on to our posterity what we have labored to earn, we must bethink ourselves of the grave obligation we have of handing on to those who come after us the best gift of all: the true faith. If they are keen minded they will be eternally grateful to you. Think of the great pains one takes – insurance, savings accounts – just to insure a comfortable inheritance for those we leave behind. Think of how assiduous, even insistent, we are to press upon our heirs a superior education. How much more fervidly must we act to safeguard the future of the faith that we leave behind for our descendants.

When one stops to think how earnest we are to shape the thinking and the lives of our offspring in matters of etiquette, for example, how much more intense should be our effort to prop up their faith. What more enduring, more munificent gift than faith can we bequeath to our heirs? It is inviting to think that one's influence in the matter of shaping the spirituality of the next generation can prevail beyond our times to future generations untold.

Loving Father, richly have I received from my forbears. They have handed on the true faith to me. Grant me the grace to do as much for my descendants.

Remaking the World

Anthony Esolen

*Now this is how the birth of Jesus Christ came about. When his
mother Mary was betrothed to Joseph, but before they lived
together, she was found with child through the holy Spirit.*
(Mt 1: 18)

In a dusty village in the troublesome province of Judea, a young
girl is found to be with child. No fire rains down from heaven,
no graves give up their dead. It seems an unfortunate but all
too ordinary occurrence. But a new world has begun.

When God made the world in the beginning, we are told that his
Spirit was brooding above the waters. In the silence of the world's
non-being, God said, "Let there be light," and there was light, most
glorious of creatures. Now the Spirit comes again, into the shelter-
ing darkness of the womb of Mary, who was as open to the will of
God as were the waters of the uncreated world. There, in a miracle
of smallness and silence, Jesus is conceived, who will be the true
light of the world, taking flesh to dwell among us. When on the
sixth day of creation God made man, he did for Adam what he had
not done for any other creature. The beasts were brought forth from
the earth, but God himself breathed the breath of life into the dust
of Adam, and he became a living soul. So now the new Adam breaks
into the world by a breath, by the Spirit of God, so that all who
unite themselves with the death and resurrection of Jesus will be
new creations, and will have true life within them.

When man makes idols, he makes them big; but God is infinitely
greater than our idols, not just because he holds the world in his
palm as a grain of dust, but because he permits a grain of dust to
hold him. We make ourselves great in pride, and God makes himself small, in the might of the Spirit of love. And for months the
only person who knew of this miracle was Mary, the unknown girl
of Nazareth, treasuring it in her womb.

*Father, teach us to shelter within our hearts the smallness of your
Son, who came to us in utter quiet to return us to your glory and
majesty. We ask this through the same Christ, our Lord.*

Righteousness and Mercy Meet

Anthony Esolen

Joseph [Mary's] husband, since he was a righteous man, yet unwilling to expose her to shame, decided to divorce her quietly.
(Mt 1: 19)

Joseph was an upright man. We can search the psalms to learn what that means. He stood straight with the Lord. He dealt evenly with his neighbor. He took no bribes. Far from squeezing an advantage from the less fortunate, he lent his ear to the pleas of the widow and the fatherless. In him to be just and to be merciful were one and the same thing, for justice and mercy are both the daughters of the God he loved with all his heart and soul and mind and strength.

Then he learns that Mary, his betrothed, is with child. He may indeed have been the first to learn of it. Mary has perhaps told him of what the angel said to her; we can doubt that she spoke of that miracle to all her neighbors. What Joseph made of it, we are not told. What would we make of it? Mary must be lying, we might think, or mad – for it must have been hard to imagine Mary telling a lie. In either case, Joseph in all righteousness wants to divorce her. But, pitying the reproach she would suffer, not to mention the strict penalty of the law, he plans to do it quietly, so that Mary and the family might make provision for the birth of the child, out of the sight of the neighbors.

It is not to be. In our day, among people impossible to shock, it is hard to imagine the greatness of Joseph's sacrifice. He will wed the young girl, and raise the child that is not his. It will be an act of righteous mercy – on the part of God, who will use Mary and Jesus to make of Joseph far more than a Jewish man who followed the law. For Jesus fulfills and transcends the law – and Joseph, upright and humble, will be his foster father.

Father, build up in our hearts the righteousness and the mercy of Joseph, that we too may be made into a fit dwelling for your Son, through the same Christ, our Lord.

Saved, from Whom?

Anthony Esolen

Behold, the angel of the Lord appeared to [Joseph] in a dream and said, "Joseph, son of David, do not be afraid to take Mary your wife into your home. For it is through the holy Spirit that this child has been conceived in her. She will bear a son and you are to name him Jesus, because he will save his people from their sins." (Mt 1: 20-21)

The angel of the Lord appears to Joseph in a dream, addressing him by the royal title "son of David." How ironic that is. No doubt as I write this there is a construction worker somewhere in England who can trace his lineage to the Plantagenets, or a woodcutter in France whose great-uncle twelve times removed was Saint Louis le Roy. Such is the decline of a family name. But a royal messenger comes to the carpenter Joseph with a message: "Fear not!"

What should Joseph not fear to do? If he is David's son, perhaps he will be asked to follow David's example. That king never feared to go into battle, for even as a boy he cried out to Goliath that the battle is the Lord's, and that the Lord had already delivered the uncircumcised dog into his hands. Or we might remember that King David was the leader of the people in their worship of God, dancing before the ark of the covenant as it was brought into Jerusalem. David dreamed of building the great house of God that his son, Solomon, would complete.

No battle to fight, no temple to build for Joseph. Or are there? His son will be called Jesus, whose name means "salvation," for he will save his people. David saved his people from the Philistines and the Moabites, but Jesus comes to save us from enemies even closer than those, enemies we harbor within our hearts. He comes to save us from our sins. The Jews built their temple to make atonement for their sins by sacrifice. But Jesus, the carpenter's son, will himself *be the temple* of atonement, and the place where the fullness of the Father dwells.

How much of this did Joseph understand? Probably little. But one thing he knew: he was to exert the royal virtue of courage. He did not fear.

Father, breathe into our hearts your Spirit of courage, that we like Joseph may fight the battle of our King, and bow before him as he enters his house in glory, through Christ our Lord.

God with Us

Anthony Esolen

All this took place to fulfill what the Lord had said through the prophet:/ "Behold, the virgin shall be with child and bear a son,/ and they shall name him Emmanuel,"/ which means "God is with us." (Mt 1: 22-23)

Recently, taking part in a faculty seminar, I encountered one of the demons of our age. This demon, through the writings of those who hate our faith, whispered into my ear, "Only matter exists. There is no meaning to the world. You are only a bundle of chemicals." And I saw the things of beauty I love, from the flowering quince in the backyard, to the stars above, to the faces of my wife and my children, through the terrible distorting lens of the demonic worship of Nothing.

It is all a lie. When my head cleared, I remembered that God is not simply a distant creator, but the Father so great that he submits to his own creatures, giving man the freedom to love him, and therefore the freedom to reject him. He withholds his glory, because he wants us to be like him, to be great by loving freely; but in withholding that glory he draws nearer to us than we are to ourselves. That is why he gives us his Son, to be with us in the flesh on earth, eating and drinking with us, praying with us, laughing with us, mourning with us, suffering with us, and dying for us. And even when Jesus ascends into heaven, he tells his disciples that he will be with them always, to the end of time; most intimately in the sacrament of the altar, coming down to us by raising us up to him and to the wedding feast of heaven.

Know, in the darkest and most wintry times, that Jesus is Emmanuel. He is with us; on our side; correcting us in love; cheering us in love. We adore a God who became a little babe, wholly dependent upon our love, so great was his love for us. We can put to flight the lies of darkness, for Light and Truth became flesh, and he has overcome the world.

Father, let us feel at every moment of our lives the abiding presence of your Son, by your indwelling Spirit of love. Let us never lose heart, but go forth in confidence, for the battle is yours, and you are at our side, through the same Christ our Lord.

Who Is Like God?

Anthony Esolen

When Joseph awoke, he did as the angel of the Lord had
commanded him and took his wife into his home. He had no
relations with her until she bore a son, and he named him Jesus.
(Mt 1: 24-25)

We are used to seeing angels portrayed as slim young ladies with flowing hair, flitting about and singing. That is hardly how they are portrayed in Scripture. These are beings of tremendous power, like the sword-wielding Michael. They are soldiers in the armies of heaven. They obey God, who yet gives them the freedom to execute his commands by their best judgment. Sometimes they are but messengers of God's Word, as here, when the herald comes from heaven to speak to Joseph in a dream and to tell him what to do.

How noble is a hierarchy of obedience! The angel hears God, Joseph hears the angel; then Joseph takes Mary into his home as her human protector, and Mary gives birth to Jesus, who would obey his mother and father in all things. Did Joseph abase himself by obedience? Far from it. I recall my own good father, whom it was no humiliation to obey, because he himself obeyed. When your father grounds his heart in the word of God, then to obey him is to be raised up, to share in his authority, and to gain a measure of the freedom that God desires for us all. When Joseph obeyed the angel, he gained a grace that the angel himself could but look upon with awe, for it was Joseph and not the angel who would be the foster father of the Word made flesh. When Mary submitted to Joseph, she became the pattern for all wives, and Joseph in turn could only look upon her with awe, knowing himself unworthy to dwell under the same roof with a woman so holy.

Then we have the child, whom Joseph names, in obedience to the angel. Jesus will obey Joseph and Mary, giving us proud human beings a lesson about godliness. Who among us is most like the Father? The one who is most like that child Jesus.

Father, grant us the grace to grow in wisdom and understanding,
as the child Jesus did, so that as he humbled himself to take on our
frailties, we might humble ourselves to take on his divinity, through
the same Christ, our Lord.

Coloring Outside the Lines

Father Lawrence Donohoo, O.P.

When Jesus was born in Bethlehem of Judea, in the days of King Herod, behold, magi from the east arrived in Jerusalem, saying, "Where is the newborn king of the Jews? We saw his star at its rising and have come to do him homage." (Mt 2: 1-2)

Balaam, the pagan diviner hired to curse the Israelites upon their arrival in the Promised Land, was constrained to bless them. Looking into the horizon, he saw Christ: "I see him, though not now;/ I behold him, though not near" (Nm 24: 17). These words also belong to the pagan Magi who, like Mary Magdalene in the garden, know who they are looking for but do not know where to find him. They see him in a star, but the closer they come, the more he eludes them. They arrive in Herod's palace because it is the abode of kings and because kings are in the know. "Someone dressed in fine clothing? Those who wear fine clothing are in royal palaces" (Mt 11: 8). But he is not there.

Our heavenly Father gives us stars as well, with enough light to guide us through the night in enough darkness to obscure where they might shine. Following these stars is a lengthy journey. The Magi have been long underway, trudging through the season of Advent. Theirs is the hope of this sacred season that learns to envision but also to remain supple. Habakkuk teaches us that "the vision still has its time" (Hb 2: 3), and so just as we draw carefully, yet so must we sketch lightly. If hoping involves imagining what we do not yet have, imagining includes holding already in some way what we hope for. We can paint our hopes in impressionist strokes, letting God fill in the details and work outside our lines. Keeping our expectations low, but our hopes high, we can follow the Magi's lead in letting God's entrances in our lives take their final form in his own way. The star, the prophecy, the adventure – Matthew teaches us that God is not a sheer realist, but a dreamer and idealist as well. He wants us looking for his stars and following their destination, and he wants our help in landing them beyond our horizon.

God, our heavenly Father, you give us glimpses of your Son along the journey of life. Help us to chase this light that we might see him as you see him and find him where he is waiting for us.

If You Can't Beat Him

Father Lawrence Donohoo, O.P.

When King Herod heard this, he was greatly troubled, and all Jerusalem with him. Assembling all the chief priests and the scribes of the people, he inquired of them where the Messiah was to be born. They said to him, "In Bethlehem of Judea."
(Mt 2: 3-5)

The obvious piece missing in Herod's calculations is the star. It shines the truth that the newborn King is anointed by the Lord of hosts. "When I see your heavens, the work of your fingers, / the moon and stars that you set in place" (Ps 8: 4), I should recognize the divine handwriting on the walls of the world and the stable. But Herod, stopping at mid-sentence, prefers the role of desperate murderer because his faith stops short. He believes the baby-king is in the neighborhood; he does not believe the Divine Regent will protect him. Herod believes in God's plan; he does not believe he is in it. He has faith in divine power, but not divine love. What a pity. Like the apostles, King Herod could have kept his crown and sat next to the King in glory. As with us, Jesus came to redeem Herod and give him his royal blood.

Accepting the divine plan is much easier when I believe that God is on my side. It is much more difficult when I take Providence halfway – when I imagine that God's plan has his own interest in mind and forget that his own interest is mine. Each time I blame him for forgetting me and my sufferings, I effectively assume his plans are meant only for himself and others. But if everyone is right in thinking this way – and we do – then all beneficiaries would be excluded from the divine policy. The truth is that no one is left out, beginning with the infant in swaddling clothes in the manger in the cold. Herod himself should join the trek to Bethlehem. By taking on manger and danger from the start, Jesus reminds me that he is Providence suffering with me in every moment of my life. It is about me because God is for me. That is why Love lies in wait in a stable.

Heavenly Father, I need your reminder that your plan of salvation includes even me. I don't need a backup emergency plan because I can't save myself anyway. I'm your problem.

I'm So Glad You Called

Father Lawrence Donohoo, O.P.

Then Herod called the magi secretly and ascertained from them the time of the star's appearance. He sent them to Bethlehem and said, "Go and search diligently for the child. When you have found him, bring me word, that I too may go and do him homage." (Mt 2: 7-8)

Herod knows better than God what's best for Herod. That's the reason for all this finagling, craftiness, and double-dealing. Herod is looking for God in his search for the Anointed One, but for the wrong reason. What he forgets is that he's up against a basic disadvantage: God can see Herod's deck of cards, but Herod can't see God's. Talk about unfair! The Psalmist recognizes there is no escape from the all-seeing Eyes: "If I ascend to the heavens, you are there;/ if I lie down in Sheol, you are there too" (Ps 139: 8).

I know that God knows me through and through, but do I always believe it? All right, I concede that God knows me better than I know myself, but don't I have a better plan for my life than he? OK, let me further admit that God's plan for my life is better than mine, but don't I know better how to get from here to there, how to deal with my weaknesses, and how much patience is required? Fine, I grant that God knows best how I can safely arrive, overcome my weaknesses, and the patience required for this. So I've nothing left to protect from him. Like Job, I am reduced to silence. I lose.

My loss is God's gain, but it's also mine! Isn't God really more patient with me than I am with myself? Doesn't his strategy for dealing with my weakness offer a far greater chance of success? Doesn't his map increase my chances of a safe arrival? So thank God I'm under divine surveillance. That's why the Psalmist continues: "If I fly with the wings of dawn/ and alight beyond the sea,/ even there your hand will guide me,/ your right hand hold me fast" (Ps 139: 9-10). God, who has already found us, is found by those who seek him for the right reasons and give him landing rights in the core of their being.

My heavenly Father, help me to open up to you the last strongholds of my heart armed with the illusion that I must protect myself from you. Take over and show me you are my best defense.

Now You See It

Father Lawrence Donohoo, O.P.

After their audience with the king [the magi] set out. And behold, the star that they had seen at its rising preceded them, until it came and stopped over the place where the child was. They were overjoyed at seeing the star, and on entering the house they saw the child with Mary his mother. (Mt 2: 9-11)

The Magi visit Herod because the star abandoned them. They need him to provide guidance to the newborn king. Perhaps they are naïve in neglecting the possibility of royal envy; perhaps they simply decide it's a risk worth taking. In any event, these readers of the sky are certainly humble enough to accept down-to-earth counsel. And Herod, for the darkest of motives, obliges and charts their course. They need him for the big picture; he needs them for the details. The Magi's visit to Herod keeps them on track but derails the oldborn king. Once again underway, they find the wayward star back on course and arrive at the infant Jesus and his Blessed Mother. God can write good with evil lines. The road to Bethlehem passes through Jerusalem.

We have all been given a star – a graceway that leads us to Christ on a unique road. The star is our life's work, but it is more than work. It is a revelation of God and his kingdom specially granted to each of us. Some see this star quite early in life; others glimpse it later. It brightens and dims at different times in our lives, but it is always there. When it appears, our path is clear. When it hides, we search for it. It is then we seek counsel, whether in palaces or huts, among the wise or feeble, among the powerful or weak. Yet I avoid those who deny the existence of stars in general or mine in particular. I will not climb every mountain, but only those that offer a broader sweep of the horizon. I may meet others with stars in the same galaxy as mine, but even here no two stars are alike. They will come bearing different gifts. My star, this light upon my path, is the Holy Spirit's unique gift to me, leading me onward to my home where Jesus and Mary have been waiting for my arrival.

My Father, your star is a lamp for my feet, a light for my path. You grant me a unique journey to Jesus and Mary. Give me the strength to stay on this path and to serve as a beacon for others.

Just What He Needed

Father Lawrence Donohoo, O.P.

[The magi] prostrated themselves and did him homage.
Then they opened their treasures and offered him gifts
of gold, frankincense, and myrrh. (Mt 2: 11)

Let's focus on the myrrh – the odd gift out, the gift that keeps on embarrassing. There's no problem with gold: it symbolically heralds the divine king. Similarly with the frankincense used by those in sacred orders: "you are a priest forever" (Ps 110: 4). But myrrh? In antiquity it was used to heal but also to embalm – to sustain the living and to preserve the dead. In either case, it is a worthy if difficult gift for the infant Jesus. He will be the healer of the nations, the one who "makes the deaf hear [and] the mute speak" (Mk 7: 37). It is he who is sent "to proclaim liberty to captives/ and recovery of sight to the blind,/ to let the oppressed go free" (Lk 4: 18). But note here that healing is now taken in a wider sense: salvation involves proclamation and intervention. The healer in the fullest sense is also the prophet who is anointed with a sacred oil that is mostly comprised of myrrh. And the prophet is mostly the truth-teller whose life is marked for death. This reinterprets the other gifts. The gold is for a king who is the servant; the frankincense is for a priest who is the sacrifice. And the myrrh is the symbol of the One who gives life through death.

Might we too see everyone who makes a mark in our lives, whether for weal or woe, as gift-giver? Though we need not accept everything from everybody, the "gift" is often deposited at our doorstep without our knowledge or consent. If I truly believe that no actions escape God's Providence even if they escape his will, then every gift has a place in my life. The challenge is to turn the dross into cross, the myrrh into gold. I can look back and note how many such gifts have bent my life in new directions. Indeed, are not these gifts I demur at receiving the most valuable of all?

Heavenly Father, help me to receive the myrrh – the more difficult gifts from others that you may not have ordered in the first place but can order in my life so that I am richer for having them.

There Are No Crooked Lines

Father Lawrence Donohoo, O.P.

And having been warned in a dream not to return to Herod,
[the magi] departed for their country by another way.
(Mt 2: 12)

The Magi had set out to find the newborn king, but the fickle star required an unplanned stopover at Herod's. Revision number one. In Jerusalem the king instructs them to stop by again on their way home so he can render homage. Revision number two. But now a dream commands them to revise their travel plans again. We're not told who precisely had the dream. The leader? The majority of the Magi? All of them? In any event, there is no indication in the Gospel that they wrestled with the evidence since you generally ask for a clear sign before you disobey a king. Revision number three.

Not all of our dreams are so clear as the Magi's, nor are the various signposts that indicate revisions in our itinerary of life. We know the general rule that it is prudent to look for clear evidence before shifting course lest we submit to the capricious whims of our hidden desires. But it is also possible out of sheer obsessive-compulsive stubbornness to resist these unmistakable revisions that the Lord offers us, whether in dreams, the "coincidences of life," the words of a trusted friend, or the actions of a consistent foe. Even more troubling, we can look upon these corrections as detours, always holding up our original plan as the standard, always trying to make our way back to the main highway as we have known it.

But that was then and this is now. The Lord did not give us an unalterable blueprint from the start. He gave us the Good Shepherd as our guide who has good reasons for not always sharing the map. The real itinerary is the one with the changes. We can throw out Plan A. The corrected version that only appears after we've been there, seen that, is the one to use for future markings. And markings they are, no less, no more. Sufficient for the day is its own direction.

My God and Father, help me to stay on the straight and narrow,
just as I recognize that your many revisions of my understanding
reshape the direction that Christ is walking with me.

From Egypt, into Egypt

Anthony Esolen

When [the magi] had departed, behold, the angel of the Lord appeared to Joseph in a dream and said, "Rise, take the child and his mother, flee to Egypt, and stay there until I tell you. Herod is going to search for the child to destroy him." Joseph rose and took the child and his mother by night and departed for Egypt.

(Mt 2: 13-14)

When the children of Israel came from Egypt, the Psalmist says, what rejoicing there was, with the braying of trumpets! In the Old Testament, that escape from bondage to freedom is the miracle of miracles: God brought Israel from Egypt to the Promised Land, while the chariots of Pharaoh were shattered and their riders drowned in the sea. Yet now we see that journey reversed. The Son of God is born among us, to lead us from the Egypt of sin to the freedom of the children of God. But because of the envy of King Herod, Joseph his foster father must take the child far away, even into Egypt.

Egypt, as a haven! There is some precedent. When the Babylonians grew weary of the upstart Jewish, Nebuchadnezzar sacked Jerusalem and razed the temple, dragging half of the people into Babylon and captivity. A few Jews remained, and some of these, with the prophet Jeremiah (who had in vain urged them to make peace with Babylon), set off for Egypt. They slew Jeremiah along the way. So the Holy Family now leaves the land that murders its prophets and quite a few of its kings to boot, to hide in Egypt, the land of beast-gods and the fertility cult of the Nile.

That should not surprise us. Where has anyone ever lived but in the land of sin that we have made for ourselves? On our own we can never escape it, no more than we can escape ourselves. Wherever we go, Egypt is there, with her snaky idols. As a little baby, Jesus must hide among idolaters to avoid the murderous designs of the supposed believer on the throne of Judea. Then, as a man, he will preach among sinners, eating and drinking with harlots and tax collectors, that is, with people like us, and because he does so the people who suppose themselves righteous, who do not know that they live in Egypt, will fail to see who he is.

Father, lead us as you led Saint Joseph, so that we will no longer wander in a land of sin, but journey always toward your Son, through the same Christ our Lord.

Murdering the Child

Anthony Esolen

When Herod realized that he had been deceived by the magi,
he became furious. He ordered the massacre of all the boys
in Bethlehem and its vicinity two years old and under, in
accordance with the time he had ascertained from the magi.
(Mt 2: 16)

We know that Jesus comes to redeem the world. It's harder for us to remember that the world, old in sin, does not especially want to be redeemed. Herod seeks to murder the child, and when Jesus is a grown man and preaches the kingdom of God, the successors of Herod will crucify him. Jesus' death is present at his birth: in the myrrh the kings bring to anoint his body, in Simeon's prophecy that a sword will pierce Mary's heart, and in the slaughter of the innocent children at the bloody hands of Herod.

But it may be hardest of all to consider that Jesus never did leave his childhood, even though he grew to manhood and came, in a human sense, to an ever clearer understanding of what he must do. We grow old and, alas, leave our childhood behind. Not Jesus. He through whom all things were made was swaddled up in the manger, unable to move a hand; the Word of God became speechless, learning from the lips of Mary and Joseph. Yet as he grew in wisdom he still lay in the bosom of the Father, relying wholly upon him, boasting nothing of his own. Jesus could well say that unless we become as little children we should not enter the kingdom. He himself, in his single-hearted trust and obedience to the will of his Father, even unto the loneliness of the cross, was as a little child.

The world has no use for children, unless to make them old – to make them useful to a Herod, whatever the regime may be. The world murders innocence, because it suspects that the hand of a little child comes to batter down its walls. It fears those eyes that come from beyond. Herod held to his purposes, pursuing them by his own strength. The child Jesus held to the purposes of the Father, and triumphed.

Father, give us the grace in the most difficult trials to be as
children, loving you for your own sake, and wishing only that we
might never be parted from you, through the mercy of your Son,
Jesus, our Lord.

The History Written in the Book of Life

Anthony Esolen

When Herod had died, behold, the angel of the Lord appeared in a dream to Joseph in Egypt and said, "Rise, take the child and his mother and go to the land of Israel, for those who sought the child's life are dead." He rose, took the child and his mother, and went to the land of Israel. (Mt 2: 19-21)

Herod is dead. Had there been newspapers at the time, that might have made the front page, above the fold. Herod the Great had rebuilt the walls of Jerusalem. He had been a friend of the great Marc Antony. He had ruled Judea with a ruthless efficiency. None of that matters to Saint Matthew, the former tax collector for the Roman regime. Matthew had precedent for not caring about the worldly success of kings. The Old Testament tells us of kings of Israel who managed to avoid being assassinated – not easy in those times – and who ruled for many a year over a prosperous land. The verdict on their reigns is always the same: Omri or Manasseh or Ahab did that which was evil in the Lord's sight; Asa or Hezekiah or Josiah did that which was right in the Lord's sight. Nothing else matters.

There's the history of the world that we know, wherein a coldhearted assassin like Augustus Caesar figures prominently, and then there's the history of the world as it is written in the Book of Life. Who knows, in that book, what the story really is, and who the Great Ones are? We have a hint of it in Scripture. Everyone knows Herod, but his death is of no importance whatsoever, except as it brings back from Egypt a certain carpenter of royal lineage, his young wife, and their little Son. To Joseph the messenger of God appears, and not to Herod.

And what of us? We teach our young people to follow the way of Herod, seeking prominence in the world; but in a century, who in this world will care or even remember that someone was a vice-president of a bank or a principal or a professor? In the history of the world as it really is, only holiness counts: Joseph, not Herod, is kingly.

Father, whose Son entered human history and overcame the world, teach us to see in our daily lives the true and only story, that of your salvation from eternity, through the same Jesus Christ, our Lord.

Can Anything Good Come from Nazareth?

Anthony Esolen

*[Joseph] went and dwelt in a town called Nazareth, so that what
had been spoken through the prophets might be fulfilled,
"He shall be called a Nazorean." (Mt 2: 23)*

That's what the apostle Nathanael asked, when he heard where Jesus came from. And Nazareth does fare poorly in the Gospels. When Jesus returns to his village, the people do not want to hear the good news that the blind will see, the deaf will hear, and the captives will be set free. All they can see in Jesus is the man they think they have known for many years, the man whose holiness was so complete and so natural to him that, unless he should perform wondrous signs, no one would notice it.

Matthew is punning on the town's name when he says that Jesus will be called a "Nazorean." A Nazirite, in Jewish custom, was a man separated from other people, dedicated wholly to the Lord, as were Samson and Samuel in the Old Testament. The mothers of those two judges had been barren and had prayed earnestly to the Lord to give them a son. Hence they consecrated their children to God. Mary does not need to do that for Jesus, however – since he is the Son of God, who instead has consecrated his mother Mary and his foster father Joseph to himself. Yet though Jesus dwells among his kindred and his fellow Nazoreans, he was set apart from them, too, precisely by his complete submission to the will of the Father. And in his humbling himself to live in so lowly a place as Nazareth, he sets himself apart from all those whom the world considers great.

Yet that should cheer us mightily, because Nazareth is where most of us live, thanks be to God. Consider that when you walk among your fellow Nazoreans there are those specially favored by the Lord, exalted in grace above the rest of us, whose goodness we overlook, because we are too familiar with it.

Father, open our eyes to the blessings you have showered upon the Nazareth where we live, that we may not miss your Son the Nazorean who preached the good news in that village long ago, through the same Christ, our Lord.

To Begin, Repent

Helen M. Alvaré

In those days John the Baptist appeared, preaching in the desert of Judea [and] saying, "Repent, for the kingdom of heaven is at hand!" It was of him that the prophet Isaiah had spoken when he said:/ "A voice of one crying out in the desert,/ 'Prepare the way of the Lord,/ make straight his paths.'"/ John wore clothing made of camel's hair and had a leather belt around his waist. His food was locusts and wild honey. (Mt 3: 1-4)

The admonition to "repent," spoken by John the Baptist, is the first message we receive in connection with the public ministry of Jesus Christ in the Gospel of Matthew. The message is so important that the prophet Isaiah foretold that John would bring it. John has devoted his life to it, wearing nothing but rude clothing and eating nothing but "locusts and wild honey." He comes to us as a "voice of one crying out in the desert." Today, we understand all too well what this means. John's message is hard. At first, it seems a long shot that it will reach beyond the desert into the cities and elsewhere.

And yet it makes perfect sense. In order to receive the Lord, we must start with a "clean up." We have to face things we have buried, things we know we should not have done, or really ought to start doing. Day to day, these "live" in us. They swim up to the surface of our minds now and again before we firmly shove them back into mental files marked "too embarrassing," "too hard to change," or "too upsetting to the people I love." Yet we know from ordinary experience that nothing beautiful or worthwhile gets done without "grunt work," without attention to details, without overcoming our laziness. Even when performing a menial task like cleaning the garage or sorting out a messy teenager's room, there is no substitute for grabbing every dirty, cobwebbed object, dragging each one into the light of day, and deciding what to do with it. The alternative is to leave them there, but this signals defeat.

Often we put off a full examination of our minds and hearts for decades. We fill the time rationalizing our behavior or distracting ourselves. Our guilty secrets obstruct our view of God and of one another. Saint John the Baptist invites us to let the hard work, and our new life in Christ, begin!

Dear Father, please give me the courage to face my faults and my past sins. Help me to reconcile with you, with myself, with those I have hurt.

The Power of Truth

Helen M. Alvaré

At that time Jerusalem, all Judea, and the whole region around the Jordan were going out to John and were being baptized by him in the Jordan River as they acknowledged their sins.
(Mt 3: 5-6)

Onlookers are often surprised at the power of Christianity to continue to attract adherents in the midst of modern life. The world offers potent attractions. Yet the religious orders practicing radical self-denial and equally radical service to the most vulnerable members of the human race flourish, like the order founded by Mother Teresa of Calcutta. Easter Vigil celebrations around the world welcome thousands of new Catholic Christians into the Church each year, even while the Church is denounced by the world outside for her teachings about marriage, family, or human life. We should cease being surprised at the power of the Christian call. Saint Matthew tells us about its power from the very beginning. He tells us that following John the Baptist's early preaching, "all Judea, and the whole region around the Jordan were going out to him and were begin baptized by him." Further, during their baptism they "acknowledged their sins," which is no small act of humility.

God's power to attract the human heart even with the most challenging calls should remind us to avoid despair. Even more, it should remind us to speak God's truth with a hopeful heart both in season and out, even when we know our words contradict the prevailing "wisdom" in the world today. God has invested truth with power. We cannot forget that we and all our fellow human travelers are made by God, and therefore made to respond to him. We were made to be happy when in union with him. No one is surprised when Jesus preaches, "Blessed are the meek of heart," and the meek jump on board. We should be no less surprised when John the Baptist tells people to "repent, for the kingdom of heaven is at hand," and an entire "region around the Jordan" signs on!

Loving Father, strengthen my will to speak your Truth. Open the hearts of your people to listen.

You Can't Fool Jesus

Helen M. Alvaré

When [John] saw many of the Pharisees and Sadducees coming to his baptism, he said to them, "You brood of vipers! Who warned you to flee from the coming wrath? Produce good fruit as evidence of your repentance. And do not presume to say to yourselves, 'We have Abraham as our father.' For I tell you, God can raise up children to Abraham from these stones."
(Mt 3: 7-9)

John the Baptist "talks tough" in this passage from Matthew. Perhaps he is making use of a colorful insult of his times when he calls the Pharisees and Sadducees a "brood of vipers." Why is he so mad? It seems he believes that the Pharisees and Sadducees, who claim to want baptism, are seeking it only as a sort of "escape-the-coming-wrath-for-free" card. He insists bluntly that they should rather "produce good fruit" as a means of showing that they have sincerely repented of their sins. Without missing a beat, John then blocks off the Pharisees' and Sadducees' next likely escape route. He tells them that their blood or religious affiliation with Abraham is something God made from nothing, and can discount to nothing. It would seem that God is not the least bit impressed or moved by meaningless formalities or important family alliances. He wants real repentance and *then* (not instead) good works as evidence of our new heart.

A meditation on this encounter between John and the Jewish leaders could well frighten us. Have we convinced ourselves that even though it's been ages since our last reconciliation, we can approach God in the sacrament of the Eucharist because, after all, we're a regular church-going member of our parish? Do we let outsiders ascribe holiness to us simply because we are active in our children's Catholic school, or count ourselves a "practicing Catholic"? How often at Mass – our personal encounter with God – or in our encounters with those we call "loved ones," are we simply going through the motions? Apparently, God holds this kind of behavior in particular contempt. We would do well to heed this kind of specific advice. John the Baptist heralded Jesus with the admonition to "repent." He urges us to put repentance first on our "to do" list for building a real relationship with Jesus.

Merciful Father, help me to be honest with myself and with you about what I have done and what I need to do, in order to be Catholic in deed and not only in name.

When the Hyperbole Is True

Helen M. Alvaré

"Every tree that does not bear good fruit will be cut down and thrown into the fire. I am baptizing you with water, for repentance, but the one who is coming after me is mightier than I. I am not worthy to carry his sandals. He will baptize you with the holy Spirit and fire." (Mt 3: 10-11)

Despite John the Baptist's relatively brief appearances in the Gospels, he manages to make a big impact and convey a lot of crucial information. Furthermore, he certainly can't be faulted for failing to "give it to us straight." He tells us that human beings who fail to bear good fruit will be "thrown into the fire." Beginning with himself, he compares human beings to Jesus, by saying that we are so low that we are "not worthy to carry [Jesus'] sandals." He calls Jesus "mighty," a word that we moderns still associate only with superheroes.

It's "good for the soul," as perhaps our grandmothers used to say, for us to reflect on the sheer authority and power of God, as John the Baptist has insisted we do. It might help when we are tempted to give too much credit – or to respond with too much fear – to the antics or threats of self-important human beings in the world. They are no more and no less children of God than ourselves, and no more worthy to carry his sandals than anyone else! It certainly helps when we are tempted to inflate our own self-importance in the world, or when we imagine that God doesn't really concern himself with our "slighting" him by forgetting to pray, or ignoring the needs of the most vulnerable people he has placed in our path. If these are our "fruits," then what will become of us?

At the very same time, however, like John the Baptist, we are God's voices, and arms, and legs here on earth. What a mystery! The Holy One – so infinitely above us that we cannot fully imagine his power – has charged us to help him. It does no good to say we are incapable, because God has ordained otherwise. We have no choice but to live in this mystery, both granting God's glory and his ardent wish that we offer the humble doings of our lives to his service.

Loving Father, help me to direct my talents toward service to you. Help me neither to overrate myself, nor to dismiss the gifts you have given me.

Knowing Our Place with God

Helen M. Alvaré

*Then Jesus came from Galilee to John at the Jordan to be
baptized by him. John tried to prevent him, saying, "I need to be
baptized by you, and yet you are coming to me?" Jesus said to
him in reply, "Allow it now, for thus it is fitting for us to fulfill
all righteousness." Then he allowed him. (Mt 3: 13-15)*

Jesus travels from Galilee to see John the Baptist at the Jordan
and to receive baptism at John's hands. John is rightly amazed.
That Jesus would make the journey to him! John, of all men,
"knows his place" even to the point of trying to prevent Jesus from
submitting himself to this ritual. Do we have in us anything resembling that barometer of sacredness? Do we recognize the good, and
love it and submit to it as John did?

This question assumes a good deal of importance considering
the culture in which we are immersed. It is often overflowing with
things that are loud and ugly, even depressing. But the world around
us is also full of people and places and events which reflect sacred
origins and sacred destinies. It is important to maintain our ability to recognize them. Or how will we come even to glimpse God's
beauty?

You probably know the thrill that goes through you when you
grasp how much a fiancé, or spouse, or parent, or friend really loves
you. Perhaps this happens when you see them take up some truly
selfless behavior on your behalf. Now think of what it means to
have this kind of place in God's heart. We could meditate for hours
on the fact that he could love each of us, billions of us, through history, but one by one, to the point of his suffering what he did to
draw us closer to him. Only God could be so infinitely superior to
us, yet also as near to us as our own heart. Whether meditating on
his greatness or his blessed condescension, we should take as our
model the example of John the Baptist, who experienced both first
hand.

*Almighty and loving Father, help me to be sensitive to your
magnificence always and to give thanks for your willingness to come
to me all the same.*

Submission: Not a Dirty Word

Helen M. Alvaré

After Jesus was baptized, he came up from the water and behold, the heavens were opened [for him], and he saw the Spirit of God descending like a dove [and] coming upon him. And a voice came from the heavens, saying, "This is my beloved Son, with whom I am well pleased." (Mt 3: 16-17)

Jesus had just subjected himself to a ritual that human beings could witness and understand as a willingness to die to self and be born again for religious purposes. He condescended to being "blessed" by the man – John the Baptist – who was the merely human herald of Jesus' divine coming. God crowns Jesus' submission in the most spectacular way, by sending the Holy Spirit and uttering words full of love, such as any of us would melt at hearing: "This is my beloved Son, with whom I am well pleased." God is blessing an act on the part of his Son that can only be called humble. This is even more interesting when we consider all that Jesus did in his "career" on earth. He performed so many miraculous cures. Think of Lazarus walking in his death bindings out of the tomb where he had been buried. Think of blind men made to see and of lepers made clean. But it is not at any of these moments that Scripture announces "Behold," the heavens are opened, and God speaks words of loving praise.

God marks the beginning of Jesus' mission with special praise. He gives his Son strength for the journey. But surely it is also true that God is marking, for all to see, the special nature of Jesus' public act of submission to his Father's heavenly will. Apparently, this type of act is particularly pleasing to God. He is proud of his Son for doing it. This is a feeling every human person can understand.

Whatever our station in life, whatever our usual daily work or chores, there are things we have perhaps subconsciously marked off as "beneath us" or perhaps simply as embarrassing. This passage from Matthew instructs us that seeking out occasions to perform this type of work, in humble service to our Father in heaven, could very well be especially pleasing to him.

Heavenly Father, help me to remember that you are God and I am your creature. Help me to submit to your will, as Jesus did.

Docility to the Spirit's Promptings

Father Joseph W. Koterski, s.j.

Then Jesus was led by the Spirit into the desert
to be tempted by the devil. (Mt 4: 1)

There is no aspect of human nature that the Divine Word did not take upon himself in becoming man. His identity as the beloved Son of God has been made clear by the voice of the Father after John baptized him in the Jordan. Here he shows us what it is to be led by the Holy Spirit and how to face trials and temptations. And all this comes before he begins his public life. These forty days of solitary retreat and prayer to his Father strengthen him for the task.

The Spirit does not lead him to a place of comfort and ease, but to the desert. The desert, of course, stands for the place where spiritual battles must be fought. The very fact that the devil will tempt him in this place of battle with such comforts as food, power, and possessions is already a sign that these suggestions come from the dark power. His readiness to dwell for a time in the bleak and barren desert is to embrace a different path: complete abandonment of himself to the providence and mercy of his Father, who will indeed send his angels to minister to Jesus, but only after the period of trials is finished.

The scene gives important directions for all of us as called by God to live out our vocations, as the adopted children of God, and all the more so for those with a religious or priestly vocation. We too need to go to the desert, to abandon ourselves to God, and to be led by the Spirit. Temptations will come wherever we are, but we must take God for our strength, not just our native abilities and possessions. We must learn not to accept easy remedies for our crises if they would compromise our vocations. Fasting from the answers that the world offers, we must wait in silent prayer for the Holy Spirit to lead us.

Heavenly Father, make us more and more like Christ, docile to the stirrings and promptings of the Holy Spirit, ready to embrace your divine assistance, and ever vigorous in rejecting the temptations of the devil.

God's Word, Our True Food

Father Joseph W. Koterski, S.J.

[Jesus] fasted for forty days and forty nights, and afterwards he was hungry. The tempter approached and said to him, "If you are the Son of God, command that these stones become loaves of bread." He said in reply, "It is written:/ 'One does not live by bread alone,/ but by every word that comes forth from the mouth of God.'" (Mt 4: 2-4)

The hunger that the devil tries to tempt Jesus with is hunger that comes from a long fast. But in his stern reply to the tempter we learn that Jesus had been nourished on something else during this long retreat. "Every word that comes forth from the mouth of God" had been his food, and this is what strengthens him to resist the temptation.

This first temptation is curious in many ways, for there is nothing sinful about eating bread, especially when one is hungry. It is not so much that the devil is putting some obstacle before Jesus or enticing him to do something wicked. Rather, the temptation here is more in the nature of putting him to the test, a trial designed to get him to reveal just who he is. Hence the devil's first words: "If you are the Son of God."

Perhaps Satan thinks that he has found a chink in Jesus' armor: bodily weakness after his prolonged fast. The defeat that cast Satan out of heaven had made it clear that he could not defeat God himself, but to Satan this apparently human Jesus must have seemed vulnerable. Or, perhaps, Satan was not entirely sure whether this was a divine Person, so thoroughly had our Lord taken on a human nature. Why not ask him for the miracle of transforming a stone into bread? If he can do it, it will be clearer just who it is he is dealing with!

Without yielding to the devil's effort to pry information out of him, Jesus shows what feeding on the Word of God brings. His answer is short and crisp. There is a lesson for us here about not getting into fancy arguments that the devil can cleverly use to weave some new trap for us. We need always to remember what we need beyond our ordinary bread: the Word of God that feeds us in Scripture and in the Eucharist.

Heavenly Father, nourish us on your holy Word and strengthen us by the bread of the Eucharist, that we may have the strength to resist the temptations that come to us.

How Not to Quote Scripture

Father Joseph W. Koterski, S.J.

Then the devil took [Jesus] to the holy city, and made him stand on the parapet of the temple, and said to him, "If you are the Son of God, throw yourself down. For it is written:/ 'He will command his angels concerning you'/and 'with their hands they will support you,/lest you dash your foot against a stone.'"/ Jesus answered him, "Again it is written, 'You shall not put the Lord, your God, to the test.'" (Mt 4: 5-7)

Since Jesus has quoted from the Scriptures in dismissing the first temptation, the devil tries to support his second testing of Jesus by also using a verse of Scripture (from Psalm 91: 11f.). But there are quotations, and there are quotations. When Jesus answers, he will speak with an authority that far surpasses the devil's command of the Scriptures.

It is curious that the devil takes Jesus up to the top of the temple for this verbal duel. Since Jesus has refused the temptation to use his divine powers to create some bodily nourishment, the devil carries his hungry antagonist to a place where one might perhaps expect to receive scriptural nourishment, the temple. Does he somehow expect Jesus to be impressed by his power to transport him bodily to such an unusual place? Is the magic supposed to give his quotations more credence?

"If you are the Son of God" sounds more like a taunt this time, especially when accompanied by the supernatural ability to transport him. By daring Jesus to throw himself down and to summon angels to catch him, it is as if he wants to engage Jesus in a magician's duel. He would rather not have us notice that the crisis is one that he has manufactured, and he wants to put Jesus into the position of forcing his Father into some observable miracle.

The line with which Jesus counters him is from Deuteronomy (Dt 6: 16). It lets him distinguish between authentic and inauthentic forms of faith. This portion of Deuteronomy chastises one who demands visible signs from God as lacking in faith in divine Providence. Those of real faith know that God truly knows the needs of those who believe, even prior to their request. They will never provoke a crisis to test God's reliability in the way the devil does here. God is not a puppet or toy for us to manipulate.

Heavenly Father, give us a sturdy faith and a wise heart, trustingly ready to call upon you in our needs, but ever reverent before you. We praise you as master of the universe, and we thank you for your constant care for us.

Recognizing Our Temptations

Father Joseph W. Koterski, s.j.

Then the devil took [Jesus] up to a very high mountain, and showed him all the kingdoms of the world in their magnificence, and he said to him, "All these I shall give to you, if you will prostrate yourself and worship me." At this, Jesus said to him, "Get away, Satan! It is written:/ 'The Lord, your God, shall you worship/ and him alone shall you serve.'" (Mt 4: 8-10)

When one strategy does not work, the devil can shift to another. If Jesus will not bite at the lure of invitations openly to declare his divinity, the tempter now changes his tactics. Maybe, he thinks, he can get the information he needs by offering his victim riches in return for an act of worship. We should notice the way in which Jesus calmly but firmly refuses to disclose what the devil so badly wants to know. Without giving his opponent any data for drawing an inference, he brings to bear one of the commandments of the Decalogue. What is more, this time he calls the devil by name – "Satan" – and thereby shows that he knows precisely who his antagonist is. His antagonist can only conclude that he has met his match and must withdraw, unsuccessful at getting any certitude about the nature of his opponent.

We might wonder why the devil thought that this temptation might seduce Christ, until we reflect on how many times we have given in to temptations for far less than this. There is a madness in thinking that all the kingdoms of the world were his to give anyway, but it is not surprising – empty promises are as easy to make as to break.

The lesson for us is not only to turn to the Scriptures as Jesus does, for clarity in our responses to the temptations that assail us, but to be direct and simple in denouncing the tempter. All of revelation is given to us for our salvation, but the commandments are especially clear and always binding. We do well to review these fundamental truths of our faith when we examine our consciences, and to practice clearing away the rationalizations and excuses that disguise our real intentions. In fact, we would do well to pray for God's light when we begin an examination of conscience and never treat that practice as if it were some self-help technique.

Heavenly Father, shine your light in our lives. Help us to see what you want us to see, and to recognize temptations for what they are, the better to avoid them, and to appreciate your mercies, that we may rely on you in everything.

Light for Lands of Darkness

Father Joseph W. Koterski, s.j.

[Jesus] left Nazareth and went to live in Capernaum by the sea, in the region of Zebulun and Naphtali, that what had been said through Isaiah the prophet might be fulfilled:/ "Land of Zebulun and land of Naphtali,/ the way to the sea, beyond the Jordan,/ Galilee of the Gentiles,/ the people who sit in darkness/ have seen a great light,/ on those dwelling in a land overshadowed by death/ light has arisen." (Mt 4: 13-16)

Long before the time of Christ, Isaiah was given a prophecy about certain places in northern Palestine where the Messiah, the suffering servant, would preach (Is 8: 23). In this passage, Jesus brings this prophecy to its fulfillment by moving from Judea to Galilee. His cousin, John the Baptist, has been caught up in the net that Herod Antipas, the son of Herod the Great, has cast. But these efforts to quash the sharp-edged preaching of the Baptist and others like him ironically serve God's plan. They bring the light of Christ to the land of Galilee, as Isaiah had foretold.

The Gospels speak to every age, but this prophecy has special bearing for our own age. As Pope John Paul II called it, our age is marked by the culture of death, and countless millions live in darkness, mistakenly labeling grave injustices like abortion, infanticide, and euthanasia as human rights. Confronting the culture of death by preaching the Gospel of Life is part and parcel of the mission of Christianity today. In this way we can join in the work of bringing light to darkened consciences and defending the lives of such vulnerable human beings as the unborn and the aged. In another place, the Lord assures us that the truth will set us free, and thus we are never to be afraid.

Giving witness to the truths of divine revelation on the life issues may well require a courage like that which John the Baptist showed in speaking the truth to Herod. It may well require the sacrifice of our lives and our liberty, for the culture of death shows increasing signs of readiness to use violence against its opponents and to trample on the rights of conscience. But like John the Baptist, we can have faith that in his own time Christ will bring light to lands overshadowed by death and illumine those who live in darkness.

Heavenly Father, Lord of all life, give us your grace always to respect human life, from its beginnings in the womb through the moment of natural death. And grant us, we beg you, the courage to bear witness to the Gospel of Life and to work to protect the vulnerable.

Repent!

Father Joseph W. Koterski, S.J.

From that time on, Jesus began to preach and say,
"Repent, for the kingdom of heaven is at hand."
(Mt 4: 17)

The initiative here passes from John the Baptist to Jesus. The message, however, remains the same, and the very first word that Jesus speaks displays the profound continuity between him and his forerunner: "Repent!" The difference is a shift from living in a time devoted to getting ready ("prepare the way of the Lord") to living in the time of fulfillment ("the kingdom of heaven is at hand").

The baptism that John had preached made profound use of the symbolism of the washing away of sins. Much as we need water to wash away dirt from our bodies, we need divine grace to cleanse the soul. With the actual coming in Christ of the kingdom that John had foretold, we are carried to a wholly new level: a baptism that makes one a member of his kingdom, that brings us a share in his divine life, and that truly effects what its sacred waters signify – the complete washing away of our sins.

What remains necessary from the individual is a response of faith and repentance. Crucial as it is to give even the youngest of children the advantages that the sacrament of baptism confers, the commonness of infant baptism in our day can perhaps obscure the need for the free assent of faith to join the kingdom of Christ. He will not save us without our cooperation. What the free assent of parents does for their children, adults must do for themselves. And this personal commitment that is faith in Christ is not just assent to the truth of what he says, but a willingness to change our ways. Hence, his summons then and now is, "Repent, for the kingdom of heaven is at hand." It is a summons that continues to challenge every single one of us until our dying day: we must turn away from anything that keeps us from living as citizens of his kingdom.

Heavenly Father, with gratitude for the new life that came to us in our baptism, we beg you now for the grace to live our lives worthily of your gift. And give us a missionary zeal to lead others to the saving waters of baptism by our words and our example.

Fishers of Men

Father Joseph W. Koterski, S.J.

As [Jesus] was walking by the Sea of Galilee, he saw two brothers, Simon who is called Peter, and his brother Andrew, casting a net into the sea; they were fishermen. He said to them, "Come after me, and I will make you fishers of men." At once they left their nets and followed him. (Mt 4: 18-20)

The immediate response that Peter and Andrew make to the summons of Jesus indicates their hunger for such a master. If they had been indifferent, it is hard to imagine that they would have been willing to abandon their nets and to follow so quickly. And it is presumably his awareness of their keenness to be obedient that explains why he chose them. It beggars the imagination to suppose that these were simply two fellows he happened upon by chance. Eager to remedy the long patterns of disobedience in the world, he sought disciples who would be ready to give their obedience gladly, just as he was engaged in obeying the will of his Father.

There is no hint here that he gave them any explanation of his teaching, let alone a political program, a philosophical vision, or even a specific project or course of action. He simply calls them to himself. If they had already heard his preaching, we are not told this here. They are to obey him simply because of who he is ("Come after me…") and because of the promise that he makes ("and I will make you fishers of men").

In this passage we find not just a clever play on words, for fishermen are now to become fishers of men, but the profound way in which the divine call takes up what we already are and powerfully transforms us. Later theologians like Thomas Aquinas coined a helpful phrase for expressing this point by saying "grace perfects nature." We can well imagine that Christ saw in the hard work, the disciplined lives, and even the simple patience of these fishermen something that he could craft into his first apostles. Reading the stories of their vocations should prompt us to ask what gifts and talents we have cultivated in our own lives and can place at his disposal.

Heavenly Father, you know us intimately and have called us to be the followers of Christ. Give us hearts like those you gave to Peter and Andrew, to obey the call of Christ promptly and generously.

Answering the Lord's Call

Father Joseph W. Koterski, S.J.

[Jesus] walked along from there and saw two other brothers, James, the son of Zebedee, and his brother John. They were in a boat, with their father Zebedee, mending their nets. He called them, and immediately they left their boat and their father and followed him. (Mt 4: 21-22)

The very next set of disciples whom Jesus calls turns out to be a second pair of brothers who practiced the same trade as Peter and Andrew. The scene here portrays them hard at their work, mending their nets. In rushing off to follow Jesus, they abandon not just their boats but their father! We have to hope that he had some hired hands.

Their designation as "apostles" comes later on in the Gospel (ch. 10), but there is no mistaking the urgency of the calling recorded here. As many a person who has perceived the summons of a vocation will testify, waiting for a suitable break in the normal rhythms of life could easily mean putting off the vocation indefinitely. Doing so also risks trying to crib, cabin, and confine God to a comfortable place in our schedules. As C. S. Lewis writes of Aslan, the lion who is the Christ-figure in *The Chronicles of Narnia*, this is not a tame lion.

And yet to grant the urgency of a vocation is not the same thing as to allow impetuosity or imprudence. When the Lord makes the calling perfectly clear, as in these cases or when Saul (later Paul) was struck from his horse, there is nothing to do but obey. In many cases, however, the calling consists more of a gradual but steady attraction. Sometimes there is evidence for and against that needs to be sifted by careful discernment. In cases like these, the counsel of a wise spiritual director is invaluable.

In none of these instances, however, is free choice removed. Even in the case of the Blessed Mother herself, when the archangel Gabriel came to announce that it was her vocation to be the Mother of the Savior, her *fiat* was indispensable. Whether one feels blessed, invited, challenged, or even confronted by the summons of a vocation, the individual needs to make a decision – hopefully with the abandon of the sons of Zebedee.

Heavenly Father, we beg you to send us many holy vocations, and to help those given such callings to respond freely, generously, and faithfully. May their self-offerings and consecrations offer you fitting praise.

Charity and Healing

Father Joseph W. Koterski, S.J.

[Jesus] went around all of Galilee, teaching in their synagogues, proclaiming the gospel of the kingdom, and curing every disease and illness among the people. His fame spread to all of Syria, and they brought to him all who were sick with various diseases and racked with pain, those who were possessed, lunatics, and paralytics, and he cured them. (Mt 4: 23-24)

Teaching, proclaiming, and curing are listed as the main activities of Jesus in his Galilean mission. Throughout Matthew there is considerable emphasis on the mission of Jesus to proclaim that the kingdom of heaven is at hand in his very person. His teaching of what this kingdom means often takes the form of parables. But the power displayed in his healings of the sick is clear testimony to his divine identity.

The words "all" and "every" are emphasized in these verses. He visits *all* of Galilee and his fame spreads to *all* of Syria. His power to cure extends to *every* sort of disease and illness, and they brought to him *all* who were sick. There is no special criterion that needs to be met to deserve his attention. The same universality of scope is characteristic of his charity: it goes forth to anyone in need, simply because of need and not for any merit of the recipient.

To understand this point it is helpful to compare charity and our natural loves. We human beings spontaneously tend to love what strikes us as good, whether it be good food, interesting people, lovely artwork, informative books, or what have you. In the normal course of things, we are more mature in our loves when we learn to make good assessments about what really deserves our love and what does not. And there is nothing wrong with this basic orientation, for this is the way God made us.

And yet such love is not yet charity, for charity does not arise from a goodness already in things, but looks to put the goodness into things. Like the two greatest acts of divine charity (the creation and the redemption), it is not a case of goodness already there but of goodness that needs to be given by God. So too here in these healings and curings, Jesus shows his charity in his acts of mercy.

Heavenly Father, we thank you for the wondrous charity manifest in the very person of Jesus your Son. We beg you to make us more and more like him, that we may give you honor and praise.

Scrub Mission

Father William M. Joensen

When [Jesus] saw the crowds, he went up the mountain,
and after he had sat down, his disciples came to him.
He began to teach them. (Mt 5: 1-2)

In a world where many seek to be king of the mountain, Matthew presents a God who draws others up with him, who sits with them on the scrub and claims the whole world as his platform. Jesus does not exalt the powerful, clever, and beautiful; he commends the meek, simple, and those who risk rejection for righteousness' sake. The beatitudes chart the mission of a God who never ceases blessing persons who meet him on the slopes of mercy and justice.

Some individuals have experienced the odd sensation of driving through the mountains and occasionally losing track of whether they are going uphill or downhill – a phenomenon that is disorienting. Perhaps a similar sense arises when we try to fix our location among the beatitude invitations to blessed intimacy with God. Does Jesus propose an upward or downward path: from poverty of spirit to mourning; from peace to persecution? The tropes of blessing defy power rankings, or attempts to be "best" or "most": the eminently meek, the prizewinning peacemaker, the fiercest insulted. But lest we lose our bearings entirely, there is an unfolding participation in the perception and plan of God, a progression of familiarity that is extended to many, grasped by some. For, unlike the hijacked sense of blessing that looks at the enjoyment of wealth, health, and physical satisfaction as the metric of God's favor, Jesus declares a state of blessedness that is sustained no matter how lofty or lowly our lives seem to be. Persons on the brink of beatitude envision being with God in the way that God chooses to be with us: sitting with us on the scrub; planted at the lowest point projecting upward so that his voice will carry to every human soul; and finally, perched on a hill, elevated high enough to be considered king of the mountain – except that the corporate ladder employed to achieve his reign is the cross.

Holy Father, you are the author of all blessing. You appeared to our ancestors in the faith upon the mountain that your presence made holy. May your Son draw us to you by teaching us the way of blessed intimacy.

Admitting Poverty

Father William M. Joensen

*"Blessed are the poor in spirit,/ for theirs
is the kingdom of heaven." (Mt 5: 3)*

Persons on a journey these days can usually expect to pass through some sort of security checkpoint. While they may not gladly divest themselves of their clothing, their devices, and privacy, they do so for the sake of getting where they want to go: a destination that – even if proposed by another – they have embraced as their own.

It is no accident that Jesus sets "poverty of spirit" as prior among the complement of blessings God tenders to us. Spiritual poverty is the precondition for anything else God might give us; we cannot look to our own worthiness, our good behavior, or even our desires for comfort, satisfaction, mercy, or peace as the credentials evoking God's favor. Poverty of spirit will remain foreign soul territory to which we cannot pass over unless we divest ourselves of the spoils of practical proficiency, tired nostrums, and token recognitions to which we fall back for hollow reassurance that we are pleasing in God's sight.

We approach the Mediator of the new covenant aware of our radical inability to turn wholeheartedly and embrace the dependency that will part the tepid sea of our own spiritual self-sufficiency. We acknowledge the "poverty" of our own self-jurisdiction, our inability to secure the peace and happiness that seem to represent the purpose and fulfillment of life.

No pioneer of beatitude peace and justice starts from scratch; the Jesus who preaches blessedness himself ascends a mountain in a land in which God and God's people already dwelled. His own poverty of spirit is radically instructive; his authority and example beckon us to shed the protective layers that keep us from coming face-to-face with the living God lurking in persons whose poverty is before us. We see the poor God and claim our own poverty, approaching the beatific destiny that is rich recompense for citizens of the kingdom of heaven.

Loving Father, you are our hope of heaven. Favor us by freeing us to release the layers that we cling to that would keep us from sharing your Son's poverty, for only then will we be ready to receive your life.

Relief Cycle

Father William M. Joensen

"Blessed are they who mourn/ for they will be comforted."
(Mt 5: 4)

When death and other losses have wrenched loose someone, something from human lives, persons can feel as though they are being carried by a great wave of grief that threatens to cast them upon a rocky-sandy beach. There they are successively pounded by other waves of anger-sadness-apathy-confusion-listlessness-frustration-despair. The effects of mourning threaten to leave individuals forlornly unattended like so much detritus on the shore, or to prompt their sodden retreat into the rinse cycle of emotion that never drains, never allows us to touch bottom. It is tempting to believe that since life in a relationship previously known will never be restored, we ought to jettison hope and the help God affords.

Before we succumb to despair, God seeks to buoy us up with the living spring of Spirit, enabling us to be gathered into the boat of the Church with others. Shared presence and pain help establish a new rhythm of life oriented toward resurrection, even as each of us must still pull his or her own oar. Ultimately, God draws us to the farther shore where consolation and peace enfold us as the Gentle Master, Jesus, releases his beatitude comfort into our hearts. But first, he installs us by the cross where Mary and other women and men of sorrows are mysteriously still stationed. Sometimes the cross seems simply to cast shadows; at other moments, it becomes a yardarm to which we fix the sail that catches the Spirit of hope – perhaps carrying us to the point where we can sense the mourning lighten, if not lift. We are comforted by the simple recognition that we do not ride the waves of grief alone. And we become capable of tendering this same mercy to others, imitating Mary and so many disciples who have discovered that when we extend Christ's consolation to those who grieve, our own groans and tears are eased, and we, too, find solace.

Merciful Father, grief sometimes submerges me. I do not want to flee the sorrow that attends my love, but I do ask that your Spirit would raise me to the surface so that I may be enfolded by your comfort.

Landing Patterns

Father William M. Joensen

"Blessed are the meek,/for they will inherit the land."
(Mt 5: 5)

Our earth is now well mapped out and available for viewing on our favorite website. Matthew's Gospel calls for a reconfiguration of the coordinates by which we measure distance, duration – and ourselves. The land promised to the meek is not some physical location to which Jesus scurries, a cosmic cottage with manicured lawn, fluffed cushions, and a chocolate resting upon the pillow. The land Jesus promises is a state of being to which one must pass over now that the access road has been plowed open by the cross. Jesus' sense of the land is the dynamic, undying form of presence that is natural to God, but into which we must be born, re-formed, purified, set free.

Place is possible within God because of the poverty of the Son who wholeheartedly, unconditionally welcomes the self-communication of the Father. Poverty is a prelude to fullness: of love, joy, peace. God is full. This located fullness is anything but suffocating or exclusive. There is no neon "No Vacancy" sign illuminating the divine in-dwelling. The self-emptying Son takes his lead from the Father who hands all over to him. The meek are surely among the first candidates for full communion that the Son gives back to the Father.

Jesus knows how best to approach us and draw us to himself. He prefers to rely upon the meek among us, proceeding gracefully, unassumingly, without condescension. Meekness is neither faint-heartedness nor is it a fawning attempt to bend God's ways to our own preferences. Rather, the meek person is constantly led by the Lord with great docility and charity. Our lives are obviously filled with comings-and-goings, out-and-back along the same streets, the same routine, but imitating our meek and humble-hearted Savior, all along the way we help one another bear our yokes and land upright.

Though you are beyond space and time, Father of the universe, place me where you will this moment, this day, so that your Son's meekness might become my own, and I might be found within your communion of life.

Still Right Desire

Father William M. Joensen

"Blessed are they who hunger and thirst for righteousness,/for they will be satisfied." (Mt 5: 6)

God promises to relieve our gnawing appetite for relationships to be made whole by the surfeit of Spirit that unites Father and Son. In preparation for the great communal feast of beatific friendship, God first allows that Spirit to course through our lives and awaken the same hunger and thirst that Christ experiences. Jesus' longing for us leads him to the cross, where he meets the Father who pines for him and for all humanity. Their reunion releases the Spirit anew. The Source of all holiness traverses the bleak terrain introduced when humans brought the original curse upon themselves and tragically expelled themselves from the Garden where all was rightfully ordered to God.

Where chaos reigns in the human estate, the Son takes our curse upon himself and exchanges it for the blessed assurance that righteousness is within our grasp. God's justice no longer incites servile fear among persons who allow God to do more than monitor their public transactions. God's beatifying Spirit counsels and guides our innermost desires so that we, too, are stirred in our baptismal call to become prophetically like Christ. We intrepidly call things by their proper name; we shed the veneer of longstanding arrangements that exclude others from having richer possibilities of bread and bounty; we are no longer content with popular respect and social ease as the measure of having made it in life. We willingly embrace the perpetual restlessness that accompanies having superficial satisfactions set aside and are converted to the righteousness that remains God's prerogative to grant. In our newfound favor, we perceive that the cross is like a royal scepter extended to us, drawing us into God's kingdom company where, though mountains may fall and chaos collapse upon itself, hunger and thirst are no more, and glory is ample fare for God's elect.

The cross of your Son convicts me, O just and saving Father. Awaken my appetite for your righteousness, and strengthen my resolve to witness to what is holy and true.

Show-Me State

Father William M. Joensen

"Blessed are the merciful,/ for they will be shown mercy."
(Mt 5: 7)

Mercy is the decision of Love that the world is not to be left alone. Mercy is the balm poured upon the chasm between utter human self-reliance and abject resignation that laments there is nothing more to be done. Mercy is the love of Christ refracted in persons who sense acutely: who see, hear, sniff out the truth of our predicament, and know what is at stake. Merciful disciples flow where they need not necessarily go; their blessedness consists in their willed proximity to suffering that allows them reverently to anoint the spiritual Body. The merciful recognize where blind justice cannot mend the wounds visited upon human souls. They perceive the suffering of Christ manifested both in those who are afflicted, and in those who have afflicted them – without overlooking the distinction between the two. They reveal the visage of the God whose unflinching gaze from the cross continues to haunt us until we allow ourselves to be enveloped by his burnished, comprehensive kindness.

God's merciful ones include Rosa, who lived with gracious forbearance with her own adult son Johnny for some twenty-five years after Johnny, a mentally disturbed man, had killed Rosa's own mother in a moment of raging violence. Johnny's medication brought him some measure of sanity and peace, but his cognizance of his senseless act would have swallowed him in self-recrimination had not Rosa's own resolve to remain with him, to forgive him and love him prevented him from yielding to despair. Rosa long suffered with a solicitude that refused to define their relationship by the death-dealing terms Johnny had drawn up. She understood that it is a blessing to bear violence and rejection to the heart of Christ, approaching the threshold between earth and heaven toward which love urges us, and beyond which God's mercy will not forsake us.

You have shown us your face, merciful Father, in the features of your suffering Son. Draw close and bestow the balm of your loving kindness so that we may show mercy to others.

Seeing, I, God

Father William M. Joensen

"Blessed are the clean of heart,/ for they will see God."
(Mt 5: 8)

Persons of faith recognize that if we are to peer deeper, farther, and become more comprehensive in our awareness of the world, there are some things we cannot supply, but must rely on God to initiate and activate. The God who says, "Let there be light," does not make humans the only animals who can see, but he does make us the only species who can see God, who can produce goodness and righteousness and truth, and are thus worthy of being called children of light. A clean heart is a heart that receives and reflects the light without the filters of sin, prejudice, or partiality. The Spirit purifies our hearts and perfects our senses. The clean-hearted person is able to perceive and point to the Son who is light from light.

Jesus enlists us, though our personal account certainly includes our own forms of blindness, our need for healing. He longs to restore our sense that we are worthy of working with him as witnesses to what we have seen and heard. God wants to share with us the night-vision goggles that would allow us to scrutinize the darkness in our own hearts. Our voluntary fasting from food and drink, from profanity and pornography, from excess in anything but prayer, will help us begin to perceive with the heart and mind of Christ. We become attuned to the dynamic current of Spirit that passes between divine and human persons. We no longer kid ourselves or cheat others of the opportunity to see us as we really are and to share our mutually graced perspectives, calling things by their proper name. Live-streaming discipleship continues to seek the course that reveals our true selves. In the process, our once senseless hearts are brought fully to life. The Spirit enables us to realize the very purpose for which we were created: to see the God who sees his own reflection in us.

To see you, glorious Father, is beyond my own power, but it is the graced hope you have awakened by your Son. Please give me a heart that is clean, so that I may realize this greatest of hopes.

Child's Play

Father William M. Joensen

"Blessed are the peacemakers,/ for they will be called children of God." (Mt 5: 9)

We embrace the kingdom Christ creates when we regard one another as God's children. We are agents of peace by blessing and building others up in hope, and in the process our own childhood is perfected. Peace on earth is possible only because God has visited his people in the person of the Son. Yet the disruption of childhood development preventing the play of nature and grace as God intends is undoubtedly one of the greatest stumbling blocks to peace in every sphere of human life: personal, familial, ecclesial, and political. Far greater than any physical disability is the handicap of our own sensibilities and the limits we impose upon the kingdom. Our blueprint for the heavenly Jerusalem can start to resemble the Emerald City, removed from reality. Our power to make peace is not predicated upon denying our vulnerability, even as the temptation to overprotection against the insults, toil, and pain of life is amplified by technological wizardry. The deterioration of cultures and cities results when the truth of human dignity splendidly revealed by God – inscribed in the most genuine human, Jesus Christ – is not at the center of civic order.

God is pleased to call us his children as we place our humanity at his disposal. Parents and persons in society who welcome, love, and nurture children with disabilities are agents of kingdom peace. We are blessed by God when we receive our own flesh and blood with the generosity supplied by the Spirit, and regard the dependence and disability of another as a vital element among God's elect. We look expectantly to the time when we might behold those who seemed in this life to be dysfunctional and disfigured serving as ambassadors welcoming others into the company of the blessed, where nobody holds anyone back from being called to Christ's embrace – the birthright of every child of God.

Father of all dignity and life, enable us to befriend our own spiritual childhood, to make peace with the play of our humanity and your grace, so that we might cooperate with your Son in bringing your kingdom to birth.

Enduring Insult

Father William M. Joensen

"Blessed are they who are persecuted for the sake of righteousness,/ for theirs is the kingdom of heaven./ Blessed are you when they insult you and persecute you and utter every kind of evil against you [falsely] because of me." (Mt 5: 10-11)

Matthew's kingdom of heaven is the ultimate society where God's people are fully themselves. Jesus communicates himself to us most perfectly in our wholehearted reception of every form of relationship that poses to us the possibility to bless and build up. This dynamic is real even if, in the course of seeking better things for others, we receive something less than a blessing in exchange for our efforts. We do not succumb to the temptation to curse those who curse us.

When King David is forced to flee from his own son Absalom, already he feels the insult inflicted by his own flesh and blood (see 2 Sm 16: 5-14). While in flight, he happens to cross paths with Shimei, who heaves sticks and stones and vile words his way. David might have flexed his regal force and flicked this pesky persecutor into the abyss; instead, he allows Shimei his day. "An eye for an eye" is not his emblem; in suffering Shimei, he manifests hope for his own son to come to his senses and once again seek to live in right relationship. Though David is ultimately thwarted in his hopes to find peace with his son, the Son Jesus takes up what remains to be reconciled with the Father on this side of the veil and sustains those who suffer in God's sight for the sake of righteousness.

Beatific prophets do not add insult to the injury caused by persons who would rather remain aliens than risk opening themselves to the merits of incarnate Love. Persecuted prophets willingly suffer evil for the sake of bearing witness to the truth of Christ, and this truth saves them and the world. The kingdom of heaven comes to be reality only because there are luminous souls in our midst who ceaselessly risk extending the righteousness that loves, forgives, befriends, and blesses without prospect of return.

Rather than recoiling from the prospect of rejection, keep me steadfastly turned to your Son, Blessed Father. To bear insult for the sake of his name is consolation enough; free me to love regardless of the cost.

Salt of the Earth

John Janaro

"You are the salt of the earth. But if salt loses its taste, with what can it be seasoned? It is no longer good for anything but to be thrown out and trampled underfoot." (Mt 5: 13)

In the Gospels, Jesus uses common experiences of the senses in order to convey the meaning of Christian life. When we put a little salt on our food we are trying to highlight and render more vivid the flavor of the food itself as well as adding the savor of salt to stimulate our sense of taste.

If we ponder this simple practice, we can begin to see how important is the role of Christians in the world. We are, says Jesus, the salt of the earth. Jesus has come to reveal and communicate the true flavor of life, and to open up our capacity to taste the goodness of his grace, which he communicates to us in the reality of our everyday circumstances.

Each Christian is called in turn to communicate the flavor of life in Christ to those around him or her. We are the "salt" of the world's banquet. This humble image conveys a grand and all-encompassing possibility for life and for all our relationships. Our task is to extend the love of Christ into the environment in which we live, to let love give a new taste to circumstances of the lives of others, awakening them to the true flavor of reality and to its Source and Purpose.

"But if salt loses its taste...'? Everything that the Christian person is and does presupposes and draws vitally from his or her relationship with Christ. Although the metaphor of salt does not lend itself easily to this connection, Jesus nevertheless emphasizes that it is essential. Salt without flavor is nothing and can do nothing. Without Christ we are nothing and can do nothing. The taste of the true life for which each person has been created is the love and mercy of God given to us in Christ. What is life without God's love, for me or for any other person?

Eternal Father, you have made us – in Christ your Son – the salt of the earth, the instruments through which the flavor of your love touches the lips of the world. Grant us ardent hearts that others may taste your goodness.

Light of the World

John Janaro

"You are the light of the world. A city set on a mountain cannot be hidden. Nor do they light a lamp and then put it under a bushel basket; it is set on a lampstand, where it gives light to all in the house. Just so, your light must shine before others, that they may see your good deeds and glorify your heavenly Father."
(Mt 5: 14-16)

Light is often used as an image for the impact of Christ's grace upon the world. It echoes back to the dawn of creation, when God began to shape the mysterious forces he had set in motion into a coherent universe by speaking the words, "Let there be light" (Gn 1: 3). Jesus has come to bring the light of salvation into the darkness of sin and death. The whole of the Sermon on the Mount emphasizes the new event of divine initiative and power that is the coming of Jesus into the world, and the divine authority with which Jesus speaks.

Let us try to appreciate the image itself. Go into a dark and unfamiliar room full of strange objects and you will find yourself disoriented, unable to appreciate the significance of the things around you, and unable to travel freely about the room. Turn on a lamp, however, and the room becomes a coherent place where you can identify things and find ways to pass from one end to the other.

Or consider the city on the mountain. Travelers in Jesus' time depended on landmarks, and they sought out towns especially for water, provisioning, and hospitality. A city set firmly and visibly was "light" for a journey: a landmark, and an invitation for needed rest, or perhaps the destination itself.

So also we are the light of the world. In John's Gospel, Jesus identifies himself as "the light of the world" (Jn 9: 5), so it is clear that our light depends upon his presence in our midst, and this light cannot be hidden. God has revealed himself for all to see in Jesus, and we share in this light insofar as we – in Christ – are conformed to the Father. Our "good deeds" are not performed for show, but they are – inevitably – luminous by their very nature, and will guide those who seek a way through the darkness.

Most merciful Father, you sent your Son Jesus into the world so that human beings might be freed from the darkness of sin and enter into your light. Grant that we might reflect this light of Christ in all our actions.

Fulfilling the Law

John Janaro

"Amen, I say to you, until heaven and earth pass away, not the smallest letter or the smallest part of a letter will pass from the law, until all things have taken place. Therefore, whoever breaks one of the least of these commandments and teaches others to do so will be called least in the kingdom of heaven. But whoever obeys and teaches these commandments will be called greatest in the kingdom of heaven." (Mt 5: 18-19)

In order to understand this text, one must look at the verse immediately preceding it, where Jesus says, "Do not think that I have come to abolish the law or the prophets. I have come not to abolish, but to fulfill" (Mt 5: 17). We ought to consider what such words must have sounded like in the ears of a first-century Jew. "The law and the prophets" was a phrase that indicated the whole of the Torah and the rest of the Scriptures with their great prophecies of the restoration of Zion and the coming of the Messiah.

And here is this rather young rabbi from Galilee, who has no status among the learned men of Israel, speaking in absolute terms about *his own significance* with regard to the whole of the covenant. He is not going to abolish it (does that imply that he thinks he could if he wanted to?). He is going to *fulfill* it. His hearers do not fail to grasp the implications of such claims: this man does not comment on the Scriptures like their scribes; he speaks *with authority* (see Mt 7: 29).

Thus Jesus goes on to emphasize that it is his authority alone that fulfills the law, and that no one else may presume to tamper with the smallest part of it. The law endures "until all things have taken place" in him. This leads us to reflect on the significance of "the law" in Christian life. The ceremonial law of the old covenant is fulfilled in the Paschal Mystery of Christ. But the commandments of the moral law remain as the foundational indications of what it means to be conformed to Christ. The moral law does not "pass away" because the commandments indicate the basis of relationship between God and man. Life in Christ, however, is more than mere adherence to a moral code. It is, in essence, a path of growth in love.

Father of all goodness, your Son Jesus reveals the meaning and brings about the fulfillment of your law of love. Grant that we might always be conformed to him in fidelity to your will and growth in love.

A Greater Righteousness

John Janaro

"I tell you, unless your righteousness surpasses that of the scribes and Pharisees, you will not enter into the kingdom of heaven."
(Mt 5: 20)

The scribes and the Pharisees convinced themselves that pleasing God meant observing all the ceremonies and external moral precepts of the law with scrupulous attention. In doing this, they were in a way making idols out of the precepts of the law, observing them in order to assert their own self-righteousness and to conjure God's approbation rather than as *means* to open themselves up to a relationship of love of God. They looked upon the law as a kind of limit – "This (and no more) is how much I have to give to God" – rather than as the entrance into a relationship of love that knows no limits, because we can never love the infinite God "enough."

What if a man, in proposing marriage to a woman, were to say, "I am not interested in having a relationship with you. But I love myself, and therefore I want to feel that I am being a good husband. So please write a list of all the things you expect me to do, and I will do them." Most of us would not advise the woman to marry this strange, egotistical man. Yet this was the kind of game that the scribes and Pharisees were trying to play with God.

Jesus tells us we must go beyond such games. Do we? Perhaps we say to God, "Tell me what the rules are. What do I need to do to keep you from sending me to hell? I'll do that. The rest of my life *belongs to me*." Jesus wants to tell us that this strategy will not work. No one gets to the kingdom by doing it their own way, according to their own plan. We must follow God's plan, which is to love him. Maybe you don't feel much love for God. But do you at least *want* to love him? This is a beginning. It is already more than the scribes and Pharisees.

Father, we pray that we may not fall into the trap of self-satisfaction. Through your Son Jesus, make us always aware that love for you is the fulfillment of true righteousness.

Offering with a Pure Heart

John Janaro

"If you bring your gift to the altar, and there recall that your brother has anything against you, leave your gift there at the altar, go first and be reconciled with your brother, and then come and offer your gift." (Mt 5: 23-24)

Jesus refers here to the ceremonial law of the old covenant, and yet we can easily see how it applies to ourselves. We are called to offer spiritual sacrifices – the content of our daily lives – in union with the once-for-all sacrifice of Jesus, whose redemptive offering on the cross is re-presented daily on the altars of our churches in the Holy Sacrifice of the Mass.

Whether we participate in the Mass by our physical presence or through the desire of our daily self-offering, we are asking the Holy Spirit to purify our self-sacrifice and to conform it to the perfect offering of the heart of Jesus to the Father for the salvation of the world. We are thereby consecrating the circumstances of our lives and the environment in which we find ourselves each day, bringing therein the love of Christ for the Father in the Spirit.

Yet how can this communication of Christ's love be effected if our hearts are at war with the very human persons – our brothers and sisters – to whom God wills to give himself through us? Or how, as Saint John remarks, are we to love the God whom we cannot see if we do not love the brother whom we can see (see 1 Jn 4: 20)?

How often do we approach the altar of God in a state of enmity with our neighbor? How often do we receive the Eucharist, ignoring or suppressing the divisions, anger, slander, cruelty, partisan spirit, or simple lack of attentive love that characterizes our common life? If it be due to grave sin on our part, we know the sacramental path of contrition, confession, and reparation that we must travel in order to restore the purity of our relationship with God. Yet how often we say, "It is the other's fault. I am blameless." Is this really true? Are we seeking reconciliation with the fullness of our hearts? What does God expect of us?

Father in heaven, source of all love and unity, through your Son Jesus grant that we might be truly reconciled with you and with our brothers and sisters, that we might offer you worthy sacrifice and praise.

Jesus Is God!

John Janaro

"You have heard that it was said, 'You shall not commit adultery.' But I say to you, everyone who looks at a woman with lust has already committed adultery with her in his heart."
(Mt 5: 27-28)

I magine that you are driving through a town, following the 35 mph speed limit sign that just passed in plain view. You reach a stop sign and I approach your car. You roll down your window and I begin to speak to you: "You saw that sign that said '35 mph'? But *I say* to you that the speed limit is 25 mph!"

Perhaps you would think I was some sort of crank. The state establishes the speed limit; who is this guy who thinks he can change it on his own authority? "If you have the authority to change the speed limit, show me a policeman's badge or something," you might say, "otherwise get out of my way, please."

This example may help us to understand what it felt like for many pious Jews when Jesus began speaking this way in the Sermon on the Mount. "It was said to you…." By whom? By the Lord, the God of Israel. Moses did not invent the commandments; he spoke as the Lord instructed him. So also did all the prophets after him. At this moment Jesus does something completely unique: he follows a statement of the law not with commentary, not even with prophecy "from the Lord," but with a further statement on *his own* authority: "But *I say to you…*"

It is worth pausing at this momentous declaration. By implication, Jesus is claiming to have authority over the law equal to that of the Lord God himself. There can be no mistake: no mere religious teacher worthy of respect would ever claim such authority. In order to speak this way, Jesus must show divine "credentials." If he speaks like God he must be able to *act like God*. Thus the essential role of the "signs" – the miracles – which even the Sanhedrin cannot deny (see Jn 3: 2). Let us worship the New Lawgiver.

Father, you sent your Son Jesus in the fullness of divine authority to bring to perfection your law of love. Grant that in him we may always adhere to its precepts in deeds, thoughts, and heart.

The Holiness of God's Name

John Janaro

*"Again you have heard that it was said to your ancestors, 'Do not
take a false oath, but make good to the Lord all that you vow.'
But I say to you, do not swear at all; not by heaven, for it is God's
throne; nor by the earth, for it is his footstool; nor by Jerusalem,
for it is the city of the great King. Do not swear by your head,
for you cannot make a single hair white or black." (Mt 5: 33-36)*

The tendency to idolatry comes in many subtle forms. The
way we speak can reflect our attitude toward God, the degree
to which we recognize that he is real, and that his name is
worthy of reverence.

In this saying, Jesus is not intending to abolish the invocation of
God that accompanies the grave necessity for the truth in judicial
proceedings, or of commitment on the part of those assuming public responsibility. He is appealing for humility in common speech
and deportment – a humility that corresponds to the status of the
human being before God.

The created human person is completely dependent on God for
his or her very existence in each and every moment. From the
omnipotent God comes every good thing: the breath of life, the
ground under one's feet, the joy of the heart – everything that makes
up the circumstances of each day and the passage of time. The very
name of the Source of all being and goodness is holy. Indeed his
goodness to us is a revelation of his own inner majesty and glory.
At the same time the Infinite One has revealed himself to us, and
given over to us (as it were) his name, because he wants to enter
into a relationship of love with us.

Idolatry can pervert this relationship, not only by turning us to
false gods, but also by giving us the illusion that God's revelation
somehow subjects him to our power. Because of his love, he has
taken this "risk" – that we might speak of him and of sacred realities linked to him not in reverence and awe but frivolously and
thoughtlessly. We toss the name of God about as an emphatic assurance of our own self-affirmation, or even to punctuate our anger
and frustration. Thus we reduce God's holiness to something under
our control – we who cannot even account for the hairs on our head!

*Holy Father, grant us a deep reverence for your name and the name
of your Son Jesus, that we may speak of you in prayer and love,
recognizing that we are creatures who depend on you and are called
to share in your glory.*

Simplicity of Speech

John Janaro

"Let your 'Yes' mean 'Yes,' and your 'No' mean 'No.'
Anything more is from the evil one." (Mt 5: 37)

What a beautiful and tender world it would be if everyone spoke the truth from the heart. We would all stand humbly before one another. We would be willing to take the risk of being transparent, of admitting our deficiencies and failures. We would accept and benefit from charitable correction, and be able to render it to others in turn, conscious of our common weakness and smallness in the eyes of a merciful God. We would accept one another, console one another, encourage one another, and never be embarrassed by anything.

We would be simple Christians: profound, wise, and at peace with all things. Jesus reduces it to basic terms: "Let your 'Yes' mean 'Yes' and your 'No' mean 'No.'"

This is not the world we live in. We live in a world of lies, which come from the father of lies, the evil one. The lies of our world stem from pride, vanity, fear, treachery, and deceit. It is not difficult even for those who propagate them to recognize their wickedness.

But what about us Christians? We are committed to the Truth. Why do we fall so short of the ideal of speaking the truth from the heart? Does our yes mean yes and our no mean no? All too often not. Gossip and rumor seep into our conversation, and skew our view of each other. No wonder we have so little trust in one another, and so little willingness to help one another. At best we avoid the overtly wicked lies of the world. But most of us prevaricate, exaggerate ourselves and minimize others, tailor the truth to our convenience, or just plain fib when "necessary" for self-promotion or at least to get out of a jam. Our yes and no, alas, are not simple. We are weak Christians – let us at least tell this truth in simple terms. And let us beg God for mercy and conversion.

Heavenly Father, free us from the fear that makes us hide behind false images of ourselves and fail to see others as they truly are. Form our speech and actions according to the "Yes" of your Son Jesus Christ.

Progress on Our Journey

John Janaro

"Offer no resistance to one who is evil. When someone strikes you on [your] right cheek, turn the other one to him as well."
(Mt 5: 39)

Many of the sayings of the Sermon are called "counsels of perfection" by the tradition, and it is right that they should be distinguished from the fundamental requirements of the moral law. The moral law is the essential foundation for a right relationship with God, and provides the basic framework for the development of that relationship. But the living relationship with God through Christ in the Spirit is more than a matter of observing; it is above all a matter of growing in love. Life in the Spirit is a trajectory that reaches its fulfillment in self-abandonment and perfect communion with God himself.

Our relationship with God is dynamic, and is continually challenged to grow through the circumstances that God gives us each day. The images of "journey" and "pilgrimage" are apt, and the "counsels" – although they may not bear the mark of immediate moral obligation – are signs and indicators of how our journey must progress, how our hearts must expand to meet the arduous nature of life's circumstances, and above all the nature of the perfection that is eternal life: our destiny of being transformed in Christ, sharing in the divine life, living a new creation.

If I never buy flowers for my wife, I have not violated the marriage covenant. But I must wonder whether my love for her has begun to grow cold. So too, if I give no attention to these counsels, what is to be said of my love for God? Am I attending to his voice? Am I allowing him to prepare me for the trials that lie ahead?

For the present saying, we note that sometimes we can and even must resist an evil person. But to fight is to arouse passions that pose a risk to love. God therefore calls us always to a readiness to humble ourselves, a readiness to forgive, a readiness that counters the worldly wisdom of war.

Loving Father, lead us along the path of the journey to you. Open our hearts to give more and more of ourselves every day as you transform us in your Son Jesus Christ.

Going the Extra Mile

John Janaro

"If anyone wants to go to law with you over your tunic, hand him your cloak as well. Should anyone press you into service for one mile, go with him for two miles." (Mt 5: 40-41)

This counsel is often interpreted (and with good reason) as an exhortation to do more than is strictly required, to show a generosity of spirit in giving one's time and energy to a necessary task. The theme of the second part of this counsel has passed into our common speech: when we say that someone is willing "to go the extra mile," we mean that they are willing to make additional effort, to throw themselves into a project, to labor and struggle courageously, in an extraordinary fashion, above and beyond the call of duty.

We certainly have here a call to active love and willing service. It is love that moves us to excel and grow beyond our immediate limitations. When I get a job, it has a specific job description that delineates my duties and responsibilities. If I carry these out with due diligence, I am rightly considered successful and dependable in my work. But if I put in longer hours, make further creative contributions, and expand the scope of my usefulness to the company, I will be specially commended and perhaps even considered for promotion. It is always love of one kind or another (even if only the self-love of ambition) that motivates me to "go the extra mile."

But Jesus' exhortation entails love for our neighbor, even when our neighbor does not have our personal benefit in mind. Hence this counsel calls us not only to go beyond the call of duty, but to let love be the measure of our whole response to our neighbor. We are being counseled to give more even when the burdens being laid upon us are unjust. In this fallen world, service will often be *demanded* from us beyond what is required and/or against our freedom and inclinations. The invitation contained in such circumstances is to give even more of our love for God, and thereby to expand the capacity for that love.

Eternal Father, increase the love in our hearts when we face burdensome circumstances. May we joyfully advance further along the road of the cross in union with your Son Jesus.

Give to Those Who Ask

John Janaro

"Give to the one who asks of you, and do not turn your back on one who wants to borrow." (Mt 5: 42)

Again Jesus exhorts us to give what is asked of us, to be generous to others. The terms "giving" and "asking" indicate that here again we are in the realm of love and freedom. If you ask me to give you a hundred dollars in order to buy something legitimate and worthy (but not necessary for your survival), I am perfectly within my rights to say no. I prefer to keep the money for a legitimate purchase of my own. I have violated no law. I have committed no injustice.

But what kind of a life would I be living if I attempted to apply nothing more than the rigorous standard of strict justice to every circumstance in which something was asked of me? In my fallen condition, such a calculated, pharisaical resolution would surely breed selfishness and result in my falling short even in the order of justice.

But beyond this consideration, our fundamental vocation is to grow to the perfection of charity, which means more than just being a "good person" in the purely human sense. God's plan for us is something greater: he wills that we be transformed in his likeness, that we become "good" according to his measure, not our own. This means that we must grow in love; we must ask God to give us this growth – which he will do because it corresponds to his loving plan for us.

If our aspiration is to grow in love, we will look upon those who ask for our generosity as instruments of Christ, inviting us to give of our means and ourselves more and more in abandonment to him. We will grow in the inclination to think less of our own desires (even our legitimate desires) and more toward the possibility of bringing joy to others. Moreover, our eyes will be opened to see them as persons loved by God, and ourselves as ambassadors of that love.

Loving Father, give to us the aspiration to grow in love by giving of ourselves to others, recognizing in them the presence of Jesus your Son.

Who Is My Enemy?

John Janaro

"You have heard that it was said, 'You shall love your neighbor and hate your enemy.' But I say to you, love your enemies, and pray for those who persecute you, that you may be children of your heavenly Father, for he makes his sun rise on the bad and the good, and causes rain to fall on the just and the unjust."

(Mt 5: 43-45)

"Love your enemies." In our affluent culture, this saying is in danger of being reduced to a pious sentiment that evokes warm feelings about the noble teaching of Jesus, but has very little to do with our own lives. We live superficially, and an artificial film of "niceness" obscures many of our genuine dispositions. When I hear "love your enemies," I am tempted to react by saying, *"but I don't have any enemies."*

My imagination wanders to images of scar-faced men in cloaks, wielding daggers behind my back. Nope. The people I know are all "nice" people, just like me. I get along with everybody.

This is an illusion. As the Lord's Prayer makes clear, Jesus takes it for granted that we "trespass" against one another all the time. Any person or group that acts in a way that is contrary to what is truly good for me is at enmity with me, and vice versa.

How we hurt one another with our voices! When we speak about one another disparagingly, without due credit, or falsely, we create the poison of dissension. It is not easy to love someone who slanders you, to pray for someone who puts you down verbally. For us, the persecutors that Jesus wants us to love actively may be people we consider our friends, or members of our own household.

Then we must consider the enemy that is the culture surrounding us: the individuals and groups that tempt us to sin. The adage "love the sinner, hate the sin" is more difficult than it may seem. The sinner, insofar as he or she seeks to draw us into sin, is a real enemy, a persecutor of our soul. Here love cannot reduce itself to sentiment: we must resist sin firmly, without bitterness, but rather with ardent prayer for the conversion of sinners.

Father of all, enable us to make peace with our brothers and sisters, and to resist temptation and pray for the conversion of sinners through the mercy of your Son Jesus.

Turning Enemies into Friends

John Janaro

"If you love those who love you, what recompense will you have?
Do not the tax collectors do the same? And if you greet your
brothers only, what is unusual about that?
Do not the pagans do the same?" (Mt 5: 46-47)

One of the reasons why I may feel like I have no enemies is that I avoid my enemies and surround myself only with friends – or perhaps I should say, with people who make me feel good about myself. It is only natural to want to avoid unpleasant realities. But God calls us to be more than "natural" – as the verses surrounding this saying indicate, he calls us to be like himself.

Still, our transformation in Christ into the Father's likeness is not a contradiction of the fundamental intuitions of our human nature. On the contrary, it brings to fulfillment every human hope. And one of the core human desires is friendship.

God does not want us to love our enemies *because* they are our enemies. Rather he wants to use our love to change our enemies, so that they might become our friends. God is patient with the unjust, and showers goodness upon them, because he longs for their conversion. He wants us to enter into this desire, which is the desire of Jesus on the cross, who forgives his enemies – forgives all of us whose sins put him on the cross. Love of enemies and prayer for persecutors is a supernatural reality, which is possible because – in Christ – our enemies can be converted into friends of God and of us.

This is important to remember when we experience the enmity of the surrounding culture. Everywhere we are surrounded by violence perpetrated against human life and the human spirit. We must protect our purity and oppose this violence, but we cannot shut our hearts against the persons who carry it out. We must not conform to their ways, but we must meet them with generosity, pray for them, and sacrifice for them, that they might be converted to the way of divine friendship.

Father in heaven, help me to love those who oppose you and who seek to hinder your kingdom of love. Through your Son Jesus, fill my heart with genuine forgiveness of my enemies, so as to lead them into your company as friends.

How Can I Be Perfect?

John Janaro

"Be perfect, just as your heavenly Father is perfect."
(Mt 5: 48)

Here we have a fundamental statement of Jesus' whole teaching about our destiny and the path that leads us there. We are called not simply to be "basically good people" – we are called to the perfection of love, to participate in God's own life and love. This is why each of us was created and it is the meaning of our lives and of the circumstances that confront us each day.

The message "Be perfect…" might cause us to wilt. How can I be perfect even as a human being, much less "as the Father is perfect" – the Infinite, Omnipotent God whom I cannot see, whom (it seems) I know only from a distance? This is an impossible vocation! Indeed it is… if I am relying only on my own efforts. This is why a Gospel reduced to mere human moralism is always either oppressive or watered down to a purely human proposal.

The true Gospel – the *Good News* – is not simply that we must become perfect but that we *can* become perfect, not by our own power but by the supernatural grace of God in Jesus Christ. It is because Jesus Christ is God that we are able, in him, to become "like God." If Jesus were merely a human moral teacher, he could do nothing for us. As Redeemer and Lord, he can transform us if we remain in him. This is what Christianity means.

And I am a Christian. Still, I am far from perfect. I often feel overwhelmed by the whole thing. But God's grace takes the initiative and puts the desire for perfection in my heart. If I open my heart to his grace, I find more and more that I do want to be like him. But how? Desire turns to prayer, and I beg God to make me holy. I am not alone on this journey to perfect love. Christ is with me and his grace bears my desire and answers my prayer.

All perfect Father, you have called us to share in the perfection of your infinite life. Grant that we might desire you, seek you, and find perfect conformity with you through your Son Jesus.

Wanting to Be Seen

John Janaro

"Take care not to perform righteous deeds in order that people may see them; otherwise, you will have no recompense from your heavenly Father. When you give alms, do not blow a trumpet before you, as the hypocrites do in the synagogues and in the streets to win the praise of others. Amen, I say to you, they have received their reward." (Mt 6: 1-2)

I admit it. If I do something good, I am often motivated by the desire to win the praise of others. I want to be admired. I am a theologian, and theologians often fall into the trap of thinking that they are "professional" Christians. It is my *job* to talk (especially) about Christianity in a coherent and attractive way, and I appreciate a pat on the back for doing a good job, thank you very much.

Maybe in itself this is not so bad. Perhaps I am seeking not so much praise as encouragement. And I do want to do the will of God. Still this text provokes me to examine my heart. Where is my heart's desire when I perform good deeds? Often it is divided.

It is only by God's grace that many of us are not completely sunk in the complacency of the hypocrites. Why do we want to be seen, when Jesus so clearly tells us that our true reward is in the hiddenness of our relationship with God? Why do we become petulant or even resentful when our good deeds are not appreciated? Why do we not rejoice when human beings ignore us or misunderstand us and God alone sees the good?

It is because we are weak and frail. We believe in God's Word, but our contemplation of divine realities is small. We are so stingy with God even as he waits to pour out his mercy into our hearts. Human respect seems so real and tangible: we can see it with our eyes and hear it with our ears, and our disordered emotions jingle so sweetly to the tunes of flattery and praise. But what is human opinion, ultimately? It changes like the wind. Those who praise us are as complex and as frail and as much in need of God's love as we are.

And so we must go to that Love and beg to grow in faith, hope, and charity, and the gifts of the Spirit that will enkindle in our hearts the desire to please God.

Father, source of all good, deepen our faith that we might seek reward in you through your Son Jesus, rather than the vanities of this world.

The Joy of Serving God

John Janaro

"When you give alms, do not let your left hand know what your right is doing, so that your almsgiving may be secret. And your Father who sees in secret will repay you." (Mt 6: 3-4)

There are various stories about saints or holy people who were well known during their lifetimes, and who perhaps had access to a fair amount of the goods of this world. After the death of such a person, those who knew him or her are amazed by multitudes of hitherto unknown poor people who appear at the funeral procession, each with a story about how the deceased had supported him or her in distress. The hidden benefactor of many knew ever during his or her life the spiritual joy of serving God in secret.

For there is abundant fruit in the service of God, not only in heaven, but even now – in this life. Saint Catherine of Siena said, "All the way to heaven is heaven." She was merely expressing the truth that grace and the supernatural life are already the beginning of eternal life in us, and the signs of that life are abundant and sustaining for those who abandon themselves to God with a depth of faith and trust.

We are stingy with God because we lack faith. But God is not stingy with us. We struggle and find Christian life burdensome because we refuse to see the world and ourselves as they really are. We want to give ourselves to God in a minimal way – enough to obtain salvation – while we hold on to the rest of our lives for our own self-directed enjoyment.

This is not real life! Real life is the path that God gives us to lead us to him. Abandonment to his way, to walking in his steps, is the only way that I can truly experience joy and peace in the living of my own life. Even in the midst of trials, God provides the secret sustenance of an inner life that sustains me in the vocation he has given me, which is the only real life I will ever have. This secret of the saints is discovered by prayer; I must beg God to open my eyes and my heart.

Father in heaven, our only true hope for life is union with you through your Son Jesus. Open our hearts to discover the secret joy that comes from abandoning ourselves to you.

Conversation with God

John Janaro

*"When you pray, go to your inner room, close the door, and pray
to your Father in secret. And your Father who sees in secret will
repay you. In praying, do not babble like the pagans, who think
that they will be heard because of their many words.
Do not be like them. Your Father knows what you need
before you ask him." (Mt 6: 6-8)*

If our life is relationship with God, then prayer is its language.
Jesus does not intend here to deny the value of liturgical prayer
in public, or common prayer among Christians. The whole of
the Gospel testifies to the communal and public nature of Christianity. Here, however, Jesus is emphasizing an essential element of
prayer: its penetration to the core of the particular Christian as a
person.

"Go to your inner room" and "close the door." This can be understood in a literal sense (when possible) but it also serves as an image
for that special "inner place" where the person holds himself in
freedom, disposes of himself in intent and self-awareness, and
therefore stands "alone" with himself – alone, that is, before God.
For God is with us in this, the deep recess of our *heart*.

The human heart is the place of the special creative and self-giving love of God, where he offers himself personally and in a
unique way to every human being. It is God's presence – the
presence that says, "this is a person, created, redeemed, and
destined for eternal glory" – that ultimately measures the dignity
and inviolability of every human being. Thus the human person is
a "sanctuary" and must be treated with reverence, and never
profaned by external or internal violence.

This sanctuary where the human being meets God in his own
freedom is the irreplaceable place for prayer. Only here can the person hand him- or herself over to God in freedom, turn to God in
conversion, implore his mercy, meet him in the self-abandonment
of that "yes" that enables God to enter in and work miracles of love.
Every Christian must continually return to that "inner room," where
his own encounter with the Father is nourished and made fruitful
for his brethren.

*Father, you offer your love personally to each of us in the depths of
our own hearts. Give us the courage to go to that "inner room" to
seek your presence through your Son Jesus.*

The Lord's Prayer

John Janaro

"This is how you are to pray:/ Our Father in heaven,/ hallowed be your name,/ your kingdom come,/ your will be done,/ on earth as in heaven./ Give us today our daily bread;/ and forgive us our debts,/ as we forgive our debtors;/ and do not subject us to the final test,/ but deliver us from the evil one." (Mt 6: 9-13)

The Lord's Prayer: what a tremendous gift! Perhaps we are too familiar with it through so many thoughtless repetitions. Let us resolve to make it a subject for meditation, to say it – as best as we can – consciously and from the heart. For these are the words of Jesus, the only Son of the Father, who became human to redeem us with the whole offering of his life, death, and resurrection. Here he offers us the very words that can shape our heart's offering to God. The Lord's Prayer is an instruction that is intended to shape the whole of our interior life as well as the communion of the Church. It teaches us that, in Christ, we must make room in our hearts for love of our neighbor. We pray the Lord's Prayer in the first person plural: *Our* Father… give *us*… forgive *us*… deliver *us*.

The Lord's Prayer begins with praise and adoration – "hallowed be your name" – and leads to petitions for his glory, our need for sustenance and forgiveness, and our total dependence on him in the face of evil.

It has always struck me that there is one place in the Lord's Prayer where our own activity is specifically highlighted: the part that refers to our "debts" – our sins, or (in the traditional form of the prayer) our "trespasses." *Forgive us our trespasses as we forgive those who trespass against us.* Several facts are implied in this petition: (1) we are sinners in need of forgiveness; (2) others *are* going to sin against us – it is not a question of if, but when others will disappoint us, abuse us, neglect us, fail us, or otherwise stand in need of our forgiveness; (3) we are *asking God* to treat us with the measure of mercy we show to others. In praying the Lord's Prayer, I stake my very salvation on my attitude of forgiveness toward others. God's mercy toward me and my mercy toward others are thus central to the providential plan of my life.

Father in heaven, your Son Jesus has given us the perfect prayer. Give us the grace to pray these words with devotion to you and mercy for our brothers and sisters.

Treasure in Heaven

John Janaro

"Do not store up for yourselves treasures on earth, where moth and decay destroy, and thieves break in and steal. But store up treasures in heaven, where neither moth nor decay destroys, nor thieves break in and steal. For where your treasure is, there also will your heart be." (Mt 6: 19-21)

It is worth noting that Jesus has a great deal of common sense. For many of us in these times, the first part of this text has been an unfortunate personal experience. We have seen our earthly treasure suddenly diminish or vanish entirely, and have learned how misplaced our former confidence in it had been.

Jesus appears simply realistic when he declares that moth, decay, and thieves are permanent features of our economy. Why, then, are we so anxious about earthly treasure?

Once again, it is our lack of faith. Our faith is weak because we do not give Jesus the time to open our minds and hearts to what "treasures in heaven" really entail. And so, we are tempted to think that earthly things, with their immediate, empirical usefulness, are the only things that "really" exist. "Treasures in heaven" seem like an abstraction, while the things "at hand" seem to promise immediate enrichment and enjoyment.

This attitude reveals that we understand neither heavenly things nor earthly things. The human being is made for Infinite love. That is reality. Even if there were no moths or thieves – even if we could possess finite realities for ever – they could never make us happy. God has made us for himself, and we will never find the real treasure that he is by limiting ourselves to finite things.

To understand earthly realities as *creatures*, however, implies a different attitude. Creatures are *signs* that reveal the Truth, Goodness, and Beauty of the Creator. They are not meant to be "stored up," but to be *used* as aspects of the journey toward the enduring treasure that is the love of God – a love that grows as we use earthly things for his glory.

Heavenly Father, our true Treasure, help us through your Son Jesus Christ to use the treasures of this world as steps on the road that leads us to you and to the enduring joy of dwelling with you for ever.

The Liberating Power of Serving God
Michele M. Schumacher

"No one can serve two masters. He will either hate one and love the other, or be devoted to one and despise the other. You cannot serve God and mammon." (Mt 6: 24)

God did not save the Israelites from slavery in Egypt so that they might become slaves again by bowing down to the golden calf in the desert. Nor has he freed *us* from the slavery of our sin so that we might bow down to the work of our own hands or to any other creature, including ourselves and our own desires. Strange as it might seem, we are not really free when we consider ourselves the masters of our own lives. From precisely that standpoint, we quickly fall into the trap of serving someone or something else: our self-images, our bosses, our spouses, our corporations, our tyrannical two-year-olds or teenagers, our homes, our cars, our portfolios, our social statuses, our egos, and the list goes on and on.

When, however, we seek to serve God, we soon learn that we thereby allow God to serve us. He wants our hearts precisely so that he might reign there: more as servant than as king. It is he who sets the table before us, who washes our feet, waits upon us, and invites us to eat of his own body. As servant, he not only nourishes us, however; but he also liberates us from inordinate attachments that both weigh us down and enslave us. He does not merely liberate us from without, by removing obstacles that would hinder his coming into our hearts. He also and more profoundly liberates us from within; for once we have received him, he begins making order within us, freeing us from all that prohibits us from the interior freedom that characterizes the children of God. He will not allow any competition for his love; for all other loves will enslave us if they are not ordered to him, who alone can render us free.

Heavenly Father, grant that I might know the freedom of a child of God by serving you alone and all others for love of you.

Letting God Be God

Michele M. Schumacher

"Do not worry about your life, what you will eat [or drink], or about your body, what you will wear. Is not life more than food and the body more than clothing? Look at the birds in the sky; they do not sow or reap, they gather nothing into barns, yet your heavenly Father feeds them. Are not you more important than they?" (Mt 6: 25-26)

How strange it is that we, who have not fashioned our bodies nor brought them life, so quickly fall into the illusion that we are capable of sustaining ourselves in existence! If, however, we recognize – as every Christian should – that it is God who provides for our needs, then our work most properly consists in responding to his gifts, and our basic disposition is one of gratitude and receptivity. This certainly does not mean that God condemns us for providing for ourselves and others, for looking after our earthly needs: it is he who has given us the power to sow and reap and to gather into barns. It is he who blesses our labors by sending the rains and giving growth to the seeds we plant. Despite all of his bounty, however, we much too easily place our trust in our storehouses rather than in his daily providential care for which we petition him in the Our Father.

That is why he invites us to look to the birds. "They do not sow or reap, they gather nothing into barns." No accumulation of wealth weighs them down, and indeed, they soar into the heavens. This they do not simply in virtue of their light-heartedness, nor merely by the power of flight that God has given them. Without denying the importance of all of this "natural" endowment – which is also God's gift – we might remark that they are lifted up and move forward by the wind that he provides beneath their wings. For this reason, they do not work themselves to exhaustion by frantically flapping their wings; their "work" consists most especially in allowing themselves to be lifted up, that is to say, of letting God work for them. While they are soaring in the heights, he provides for their needs. He feeds them. And how much more surely does he feed us! Are we not "more important than they"?

Heavenly Father, grant that I might confidently abandon myself to your loving providence this day and every day.

Clothed in Faith

Michele M. Schumacher

"If God so clothes the grass of the field, which grows today and is thrown into the oven tomorrow, will he not much more provide for you, O you of little faith? So do not worry and say, 'What are we to eat?' or 'What are we to drink?' or 'What are we to wear?' All these things the pagans seek. Your heavenly Father knows that you need them all." (Mt 6: 30-32)

Just shortly after we are introduced to the Lord's Prayer (6: 9-14), wherein we are instructed to address God as "our Father" and confidently to petition him for "our daily bread," we are further reminded that this "heavenly Father" knows our needs: that we must eat and drink and be clothed. God is not only all-knowing, however; he is also all-loving. We can therefore be certain that he will provide for our every need. He will not give us a rock or a scorpion when we seek bread or fish from him (see Mt 7: 9-10). Nor, however, will he give us a scorpion when it is indeed a scorpion that we seek! Although we, in other words, might well be misled in the discernment of our "needs," he sees beyond our stray desires to grant what we most earnestly need and desire.

The conviction of this truth is characteristic of the Christian. What most obviously distinguishes the believer from the non-believer ("pagan") is certainly *not* that God cares more for the former. If he "clothes the grass of the field," he certainly provides for all his children, whether or not they have accepted his love and acknowledge him as Father. No, what distinguishes the believer from the non-believer is the confident assurance called "faith" that God is providing for our every need – even in the midst of the most difficult trials and tribulations, including the apparent absence of his loving intervention in our lives. This conviction (faith) is also his gift: we trust him because he is indeed trustworthy – he has proved this to us in innumerable ways – but also because he has placed this conviction (faith) in our hearts. He gives it to us every time we pray for "our daily bread," for the gift of faith is as essential to us as the bread that we eat.

Heavenly Father, grant that I might faithfully allow you, in confident trust, to provide for my every need, as you know best.

Hungering after Righteousness

Michele M. Schumacher

*"Seek first the kingdom [of God] and his righteousness,
and all these things will be given you besides. Do not worry
about tomorrow; tomorrow will take care of itself.
Sufficient for a day is its own evil." (Mt 6: 33 34)*

Not unlike the verses surrounding it, this passage reads as a commentary of the Lord's Prayer. We pray therein that God's kingdom may come and even specify – as if to give concrete meaning to that petition – "your will be done, on earth as in heaven" (6: 10). This passage further concretizes the meaning of the kingdom and the fulfillment of God's will on earth: "Seek first the kingdom [of God] and his righteousness." And, just as the Lord's Prayer joins these two petitions (for the coming of the kingdom and the fulfillment of God's will) with those of our earthly needs, these verses also insist upon their conjunction, even to the point of recognizing a causal effect of the first upon the second: it is in seeking the kingdom and the righteousness of God that we can be assured that our own earthly needs will be met.

It is too superficial to say that if we look after "God's business," he will look after ours. God does not bargain with us, like a desperate employer; but he does invite us to participate in his own "hunger" for righteousness. This is possible only when we – like Christ – recognize our greatest need as consisting in the fulfillment of the Father's will: "My food is to do the will of the one who sent me and to finish his work" (Jn 4: 34; see Jn 6: 27, 38). And the will of the one who sent him is, Jesus tells us, that he give us life – his life – so that we might live (see Jn 10: 17-18). Seeking the kingdom first means, therefore, that we hunger and thirst for this life, not only for ourselves, but also for the world. It means employing the entire strength of our minds and bodies to bring this life to the world: not tomorrow, but today; for "sufficient for a day is its own evil."

Heavenly Father, grant that I might hunger for your kingdom and for the righteousness that characterizes your children.

Judgment that Condemns and Judgment that Saves

Michele M. Schumacher

"Stop judging, that you may not be judged. For as you judge, so will you be judged, and the measure with which you measure will be measured out to you." (Mt 7: 1-2)

God does not "measure" us with our own measuring devices, so as to judge us as we judge others. Rather, our judgment of others hardens our hearts and prevents us from receiving his merciful and forgiving love. This love is manifest in God's definitive judgment over sin, for he condemned it in the flesh of his Son: "For our sake he made him to be sin who did not know sin" (2 Cor 5: 21; see Gal 3: 13; Mt 8: 17). This means that Christ bore all of sin's consequences and, in so doing, he revealed not only the weight of our sin – its terribly destructive force manifest in the crucifixion – but also the depth of God's merciful love, which both spurs us to conversion and invites us to be merciful in turn. God's judgment is liberating, healing, and empowering. It changes sinners into "ambassadors" of Christ and instruments of reconciliation (2 Cor 5: 20). It invites us to participate in his saving judgment.

It is not God's saving judgment, then, that is addressed in these verses, but rather the condemning judgment of the sinner: the judgment of one who would justify his own sin by pointing to the sins of another. Such, for example, is the judgment of those condemning the woman found in adultery (Jn 8: 1-11). Unlike Jesus, who invites her to conversion – "Go, and… do not sin anymore" (v. 11) – they seek to condemn her. Because she willingly receives Christ's saving judgment, the woman is saved. We hope the same for her accusers, for Christ's judgment has revealed to them their own sin: "Let the one among you who is without sin be the first to throw a stone at her" (v. 7). These are words of conversion, which invite each of us to move beyond our own self-justification and condemning tactics in regard to others, so as to recognize our need for salvation.

Heavenly Father, grant that your saving judgment might so penetrate my mind and heart that I might participate therein, as your instrument of reconciliation.

The Objective Regard Born of the Cross
Michele M. Schumacher

"Why do you notice the splinter in your brother's eye, but do not perceive the wooden beam in your own eye? How can you say to your brother, 'Let me remove that splinter from your eye,' while the wooden beam is in your eye? You hypocrite, remove the wooden beam from your eye first; then you will see clearly to remove the splinter from your brother's eye." (Mt 7: 3-5)

As our Lord points out in this passage, we tend to be less "objective" in our judgment of ourselves than we are in our judgment of others. Seeing the "splinter" in their eyes, we fail to see the "wooden beam" in our own. On the other hand, what we find most abhorrent among the faults and sins of our neighbors is often that which most resembles our own. If we are impatient, we probably will not easily tolerate the impatience of our neighbors. If we are possessive, we will likely find repugnance in their possessiveness. If we are intemperate, we will detest their intemperance. And so on. We are thus capable of recognizing the objective wrong of human fault and sin – perhaps even that of passing judgment on others – but we often fail to acknowledge our own weaknesses vis-à-vis sin's objective weight and thus also our need of a Savior. Instead, we tend to concentrate on what appears objective to us: the sins of our neighbors.

Thankfully, however, God is constantly moving us to conversion; for he will not tolerate that those whose debts have been pardoned should fail to pardon their neighbors (see Mt 6: 12). On the other hand, we must avoid thinking that breaking from sinful judgment is simply a matter of a stoic diversion of our regard. Removing our "wooden beams" and overlooking our neighbor's "splinters" requires, in fact, that we concentrate neither on ourselves and our sinfulness nor on our neighbors and their sin. We are to focus, instead, upon the Lamb of God who bears the sin of all – our own and those of our neighbors – so that we might really see sin for what it is, recognizing its objective "value" – its whole weightiness and destructive power. It is only through Christ that we are able to break free from sin's power over our lives (remove the wooden beam) and to forbear our neighbor's faults and sins.

Heavenly Father, grant that I might so focus on your loving act of redemption that I might constantly be moved to conversion and patiently bear with the faults of others.

The Seeking of God that Allows Him to Come

Michele M. Schumacher

"Ask and it will be given to you; seek and you will find; knock and the door will be opened to you. For everyone who asks, receives; and the one who seeks, finds; and to the one who knocks, the door will be opened." (Mt 7: 7-8)

Perhaps my first introduction to prayer was presented in the form of a story: that of a child who asked his father to fix a broken toy. The father, as the story goes, was slow to act, so the child's simple request turned to a bitter plea and eventually to an outburst of frustration. Ever so calmly, the loving father responded: "How can I fix your toy, my child, if you do not let go and give it to me?"

If our Lord – not unlike this patient, capable, and loving father – commands us to ask, to seek, and to knock, surely this is not so as to prove his mastery over us or otherwise to show off his strength and power. Rather, he who created us to live and love freely will not force upon us what we will not possess; nor will he reveal what we will not see. Nor still will he force open the door to our hearts. Knowing all our needs before we ask him (see Mt 6: 8, 32), God so respects our freedom that he will not gather up from our hands what we have not willingly surrendered to him. If, on the other hand, we do indeed surrender our needs, desires, fears, and worries to him – if, that is to say, we ask, seek, and knock – we can rest assured that he has already responded. He – the good shepherd in search of the one sheep gone astray, and the father of the prodigal, whom he perceives from afar and runs out to meet – is, in fact, always the first to ask, the first to seek, and the first to knock. With neither coaxing words nor manipulative tactics, he humbly comes to us with gifts for the taking. Our seeking is, therefore, more accurately expressed as an allowing of ourselves to be found.

Heavenly Father, grant that I might willingly surrender all my worries, fears, hopes, and desires to you, in confident assurance that you are ever looking out for my good.

Letting God Decide
for Our Neighbor's Good

Michele M. Schumacher

"Do to others whatever you would have them do to you."
(Mt 7: 12)

Once we have removed the "measure" from our hearts which we have used to judge one another (see Mt 7: 1-2), we are invited to introduce a new "measure" in our relations with one another. Rather than a measure based upon an objective standard of justice – "an eye for an eye and a tooth for a tooth" (Mt 5: 38) – Christ proposes one based upon our own subjective desire for justice: "Do to others whatever you would have them do to you." Because, however, we are often mistaken in our subjective desires, we do well to confide both our neighbors and ourselves to God, trusting that he will provide for our needs, which he knows better than we. It follows that the so-called "golden rule" of doing to others as we would have them do to us is realized in the submission of our wills to God's will (see Mt 6: 10).

Doing God's will "on earth as in heaven" is, moreover, revealed in all of its objective value in the "new commandment," which requires that we love one another *as he has loved us* (see Jn 13: 34). His, more specifically, is a love which is not self-centered, but radically other-centered: a love which seeks one's own good precisely *in the other's good.* This is why the Gospel command to love "your neighbor as yourself" (Lk 10: 27) is followed by a presentation of the good Samaritan who is recognized as a "neighbor" to the victim beaten by robbers precisely because of his mercy (see v. 37). All of us are victims in need of merciful love, and all of us are – in virtue of the empowering love of Christ – capable of providing merciful love to the least of our brothers and sisters with whom Christ identifies himself: "Whatever you did for one of these least brothers of mine, you did for me" (Mt 25: 40).

Heavenly Father, grant that I might always look to you to provide not only for my own happiness, but also for the happiness of my neighbor.

Good Fruit Born of the One True Vine

Michele M. Schumacher

"Just so, every good tree bears good fruit, and a rotten tree bears bad fruit. A good tree cannot bear bad fruit, nor can a rotten tree bear good fruit. Every tree that does not bear good fruit will be cut down and thrown into the fire. So by their fruits you will know them." (Mt 7: 17-20)

With these words our Lord provides us with an important principle for discerning our intentions: the quality of the fruit arising from our actions bespeaks the value of the intentions that conceived them. Similarly, he instructs us: "Nothing that enters one from outside can defile that person; but the things that come out from within are what defile" (Mk 7: 15; see Mt 15: 11). As a case in point, he explains: "Everyone who looks at a woman with lust has already committed adultery with her in his heart" (Mt 5: 28). The medicine for this evil is as radical as the diagnosis: "If your right eye causes you to sin, tear it out and throw it away" (v. 29). This can only mean that God wills to purify us of everything that is not life-giving within us, everything that might be considered among what Saint Paul calls "works of the flesh," namely: "immorality, impurity, licentiousness, idolatry, sorcery, hatreds, rivalry, jealousy, outbursts of fury, acts of selfishness, dissensions, factions, occasions of envy, drinking bouts, orgies, and the like" (Gal 5: 19-21).

Thankfully, God assists us in cultivating our inner garden, as it were, by removing all that hinders a fruitful harvest. "Every plant that my heavenly Father has not planted will be uprooted" (Mt 15: 13), Jesus explains. "My Father is the vine grower. He takes away every branch in me that does not bear fruit, and everyone that does he prunes so that it bears more fruit" (Jn 15: 1b-2).

God does not only weed our garden and prune us, however. He also plants his "seed" – his Word and his Spirit – within receptive hearts: hearts that are "rich soil" (see Mt 13: 8). Hence, our good fruits ultimately stem from him as from their source, so as to be properly rendered "the fruit of the Spirit": "love, joy, peace, patience, kindness, generosity, faithfulness, gentleness, self-control" (Gal 5: 22-23).

Heavenly Father, grant that I might always bear good and lasting fruit for the kingdom by remaining deeply planted within your Son and moved by your Spirit.

The Obedience of Heaven's Child

Michele M. Schumacher

*"Not everyone who says to me, 'Lord, Lord,' will enter
the kingdom of heaven, but only the one who does the will
of my Father in heaven." (Mt 7: 21)*

It is not lip service that our Lord seeks of us, but obedient action. Nor is it enough, Jesus teaches, to accomplish the law as it is presented in the Old Testament, for example: to follow the commandments and to live according to the precepts laid out in the Scriptures. In this there is still lacking "one thing" (see Mk 10: 21). What our Lord asks of us – what he presents as the key to heavenly glory – is purely and simply that we embrace the Father's will as his children: as, that is to say, Christ himself embraced it, and even to embrace it *in Christ*.

To be sure, this does not mean that we might turn our backs on the ten commandments or on natural law ethics. "Do not think that I have come to abolish the law or the prophets," Jesus says. "I have not come to abolish but to fulfill" (Mt 5: 17). Indeed, it is precisely because the whole law is so perfectly fulfilled in and by the person of Christ that we, in turn, are called to accomplish its precepts by embracing Christ and following him (Mk 10: 21) and by doing, as his Mother suggests, "whatever he tells you" (see Jn 2: 5).

It is not surprising, then, that it is precisely in contemplating the person and mission of Christ that we are moved to obedience: not as to a king who lords his authority over us, but as to one who is himself supremely humble and obedient; one who can do nothing on his own (see Jn 5: 19, 30) and who does not speak on his own authority (see Jn 12: 49; 14: 10); one, in short, who does not seek to fulfill his own will but only the will of the Father who sent him (Jn 5: 30). We do well, therefore, to submit ourselves to his school of discipleship, for Christ is himself the most obedient of heaven's children.

Heavenly Father, grant that we might partake of your Son's loving obedience to you and his confident abandonment to your fatherly care, so as also to share in the peace and joy that comes from being your children.

Building on Love

Michele M. Schumacher

"Everyone who listens to these words of mine and acts on them will be like a wise man who built his house on rock. The rain fell, the floods came, and the winds blew and buffeted the house. But it did not collapse; it had been set solidly on rock. And everyone who listens to these words of mine but does not act on them will be like a fool who built his house on sand. The rain fell, the floods came, and the winds blew and buffeted the house. And it collapsed and was completely ruined." (Mt 7: 24-27)

Here again the Lord commands us *to listen*: to allow his word to so penetrate our hearts that it might become the source, or motivation, of our actions; that which impels us to act. We are not far from the parable of the sower and the seed: some of which fell on rocky soil so as to be scorched by the sun, some of which fell among thorns so as to be choked away, and some of which fell on rich soil so as to produce abundant fruit (see Mk 4: 1-9). In both cases, it is the word of God which is underscored: the word which is, as the Letter to the Hebrews expresses it, "living and effective, sharper than any two-edged sword… and able to discern reflections and thoughts of the heart" (Heb 4: 12).

This portrayal of God's word as active and discerning serves as an invitation to enter into its rhythm: to discern thereby the sense-lessness of our selfish projects whose motivating force is nothing but vainglory or the futile accumulation of wealth. All of this we are invited to surrender to the power of this same word, allowing it to destroy all that is superficial in our efforts and actions, all that is motivated by self-interest or mistaken ideologies, as flood waters destroy all that is not firmly established upon a solid foundation.

In its stead, we are invited to construct a lasting edifice of charitable works: not by our own power, but by the strength supplied by an on-going meditation of the word. It is this word that employs us, when we so allow it, to achieve its lasting purpose: the glory of God that is – as Saint Irenaeus presents it – "the living man." This is why there are only three things which remain in the end: faith, hope, and charity, "but the greatest of these is love" (1 Cor 13: 13).

Heavenly Father, you have given us your word: the word, which was fulfilled in the coming of your Son, who is your Word. Help us to receive this Word, that our every action might be thereby motivated by it, to your glory and the world's salvation.

The Authority of Love

Michele M. Schumacher

When Jesus finished these words, the crowds were astonished at his teaching, for he taught them as one having authority, and not as their scribes. (Mt 7: 28-29)

The authority of the scribes and the Pharisees rests upon the fact that they "have taken their seat on the chair of Moses" (Mt 23: 2). For this reason, Christ instructs his disciples to "observe all things whatsoever they tell you, but do not follow their example. For they preach but they do not practice" (Mt 23: 2-3). They obey the law; Christ obeys the Father. Everything he does is motivated by love. For precisely this reason, he brings to fulfillment – both in word and act – all that is promised in the law of Moses, the prophets, and psalms (see Lk 24: 44). As one "mighty in deed and word" (Lk 24: 19), his words give meaning to his actions, and his actions testify to the truth of his words; and both serve the Father's revelation and the coming of his kingdom.

This unity of word and deed is particularly striking in the healing of the paralytic. "Which is easier, to say," Jesus asks, "'Your sins are forgiven,' or to say, 'Rise and walk'? But that you may know that the Son of Man has authority on earth to forgive sins" – he then said to the paralytic, "Rise, pick up your stretcher, and go home" (Mt 9: 5-6). Here, as throughout the Old Testament, God reveals himself in his saving actions. What is unique to New Testament revelation, however, is the fact that Christ *is* revealed as the Father's Word: "In times past, God spoke in partial and various ways... through the prophets; in these last days, he spoke to us through a son... through whom he created the universe,... and who sustains all things by his mighty word" (Heb 1: 1-3). Never does this Word speak so powerfully of God's saving love, however, as in the silence of the cross. In this supreme act of obedience, we come to know that "God is love" (1 Jn 4: 8).

Heavenly Father, you have sent your Son to manifest your love in all that he said and did. Grant that this same love might inform all that I say and do, so that through him, with him, and in him, I might be an instrument of your saving revelation.

The Good Under Construction

Father Romanus Cessario, O.P.

A leper approached, did [Jesus] homage, and said, "Lord, if you wish, you can make me clean." He stretched out his hand, touched him, and said, "I will do it. Be made clean." His leprosy was cleansed immediately. (Mt 8: 2-3)

Leprosy supplies one biblical image for spiritual disfigurement. Contrariwise, one can observe something recognizably human about the person who exhibits the virtues of the Christian life. More than human, there is something beautiful. Divine grace overflows into the human body. It makes us somehow resemble Christ and the saints. The Christian tradition refrains from speculating about the physical appearance of Christ. However, the generally held view supposes that the humanity of Christ is perfectly formed. There is nothing disfigured in his soul or body. What Solomon remarks of divine wisdom, the Christian says of Christ: "I have become enamored of his beauty" (see Wis 8: 2).

The encounter of the leper with Jesus brings together two extremes: the bodily disfigurement that symbolizes the vicious deformation sin introduces into the human race, and the Son's luminous splendor that perfectly reveals what human nature can become. The leper is not only a victim of social prejudice that Christ exposes by approaching an outcast. The leper is us. The leprous man exhibits the first movement of divine grace. He does Christ "homage." Already, the drama of salvation unfolds. Still, observe the tentativeness that marks the leper's initial approach to Christ. "If you wish, you can make me clean." The leper expresses himself in the conditional. The Source of all goodness is never bound by human conditions. So the Lord responds with an immediacy that should console the most tepid among us lepers. "I will do it," says Christ. No conditions. No hesitations. No preparations. It would be easy to think that Christ's encounter with the leper represents a once and for ever life-changing experience. It does not. The truth is that throughout our lives we must return to Jesus. Each time, we must ask him to make us beautiful. Beautiful and ready for heaven.

Heavenly Father, thank you for showing us the beauty of your Son. Make me steadfast before the luminosity of his visage so that one day, in the place where your beauty is revealed, I may contemplate him with all the saints for ever.

Jesus under Our Roofs

Father Romanus Cessario, O.P.

When [Jesus] entered Capernaum, a centurion approached him and appealed to him, saying, "Lord, my servant is lying at home paralyzed, suffering dreadfully." He said to him, "I will come and cure him." The centurion said in reply, "Lord, I am not worthy to have you enter under my roof; only say the word and my servant will be healed." (Mt 8: 5-8)

Among the best known verses of the New Testament, the words of the centurion rank high on the list. "Lord, I am not worthy to have you enter under my roof…" Catholics repeat these words each time they approach the reception of Holy Communion. It is easy to forget that these words first were spoken by a military officer in charge of one hundred soldiers. That is, by a man who only dimly glimpsed the dignity of the Person whom he addressed. One personal encounter with Jesus leads this centurion to make a very bold request. It is customary therefore to observe the humility of this Roman officer who, though he enjoyed no documented access to divine revelation, was willing to ask a favor of Christ. A stranger reveres the incarnate Son of God. A pagan hopes for some form of divine intervention on behalf of a paralyzed servant.

Perhaps we should rather think of his boldness instead of his humility. There runs a thin line between boldness and folly. Each time that we approach the reception of Holy Communion we mark out a path midway between the bold and the foolish. Not human foolishness. Divine foolishness. The Catholic who approaches the Real Presence makes bold to consume the body of the Lord. Unless Christ himself had commanded this sacramental practice, whoever would have thought of a mere mortal saying, "Lord, I am not worthy to receive you, but only say the word and I shall be healed"? Who could have imagined that God would have arranged a sacramental means for this divine visitation to occur? Not once, as happened with the centurion. Rather, again and again throughout the ages. French spiritual authors rightly remind us of this folly of God. Who but an all-loving God would have stooped down to care so intimately for a creature? Only the God who inspired a centurion to approach his Son with a request for a sick slave.

Almighty Father, you send your Son into our lives under the form of bread and wine. Make us worthy hosts of such a divine guest. Keep the house of my soul and body a fitting place to welcome the King of Glory.

Too Much Freedom

Father Romanus Cessario, O.P.

When Jesus heard this, he was amazed and said to those following him, "Amen, I say to you, in no one in Israel have I found such faith." (Mt 8: 10)

People ordinarily identify personal freedom with human autonomy. Autonomy means that I do what I want within certain reasonable and agreed upon limits. Many today fear that the only alternative to preserve autonomy is to submit to the authority of another. This alternative the modern world considers undignified, at least. Pope John Paul II's encyclical letter, *Veritatis Splendor*, offers a way out of the dilemma. "Human freedom and God's law," the encyclical states, "meet and are called to intersect, in the sense of man's free obedience to God and of God's completely gratuitous benevolence towards man" (no. 41). The centurion who asked Jesus to cure his slave enacted this kind of freedom. In effect, he submitted himself to the divine benevolence. Although deprived of the instruction that the Old Testament provides, this Roman soldier still recognized that human freedom must confront its own limits. His servant was at home "suffering dreadfully" (Mt 8: 6). If we are attentive to the little signs that God places before us, we can easily recognize when our human freedom runs out of possibilities. For those without faith, these limits oftentimes provide the occasion for deep anguish. Christ praises the faith of the pagan centurion. He esteems it unparalleled among those whom he has encountered from his own nation. This comparison should give moment for pause to those who have become infatuated with autonomy. Faith in Jesus Christ promises much more than even the boldest expression of human freedom can attain. In the end, only faith saves. Only faith lays hold of heaven.

Almighty God, your divine power offers us more than we can provide for ourselves. Give us the grace to trust in the utter gratuity of your benevolence, so that we may come one day to behold you face to face.

Direct Giving

Father Romanus Cessario, O.P.

And Jesus said to the centurion, "You may go; as you have believed, let it be done for you." And at that very hour [his] servant was healed. (Mt 8: 13)

The healing of the centurion's servant points to the efficacy of the sacraments. Among its effects, each sacrament, in its own way, heals man of the wounds of sins. Baptism removes Adam's sin that excluded him and his posterity from communion with God. The original sin. Confirmation strengthens us for living the Christian life, and so heals the timidity that would inhibit us from standing up for what we believe. The bishop once placed a light blow on the cheek of the one confirmed. Penance forgives sins committed after baptism and, through the penances that we perform, heals the wounds that these sins leave in us. Even the Eucharist, sacrament of unity and charity, heals us of our daily venial weaknesses against these primordial gifts of the divine gratuity. Marriage traditionally is said to heal the concupiscence of the flesh, according to the saying of Saint Paul, "it is better to marry than to be on fire" (1 Cor 7: 9). Holy Orders heals men of the natural inclination to pursue human affairs instead of devoting themselves completely to divine things. Lastly, Holy Anointing heals the remnants of sin in those who fall ill, and so prepares them for the Beatific Vision. This sacrament may even heal the bodily illness that brings the Catholic to the point of death.

The sacraments accomplish these various forms of healing. The ministers and the visible rites of the sacraments remain indispensable. These link the sacrament to Christ and his Church. However, the real efficacy of the seven sacraments comes from God himself. Only God cleanses, strengthens, forgives, unites and inflames, binds, consecrates, and in the end restores health to the sick person. These great mysteries of faith find their foreshadowing in the anonymous slave of an equally anonymous Roman centurion who mustered the boldness to approach Jesus.

Merciful Father, your Son Jesus Christ introduces divine power into our world. Grant us the grace to frequent the sacraments of the Church, and to cherish the new life that each of them brings to your chosen people.

What Mothers Do

Father Romanus Cessario, O.P.

*Jesus entered the house of Peter, and saw his mother-in-law lying
in bed with a fever. He touched her hand, the fever left her,
and she rose and waited on him.* (Mt 8: 14-15)

A touching biblical expression of divine power appears in the
two verses that recount the healing of Peter's mother-in-law.
Jesus enters, and he sees a sick woman. He touches her hand.
The fever disappears. The mother begins to do what mothers do.
She cares for the friend of her son-in-law. She cares for Jesus in the
way that expresses quintessentially the maternal instinct. She feeds
him. What else would one expect? The mother-in-law of Peter
instantly becomes the patron saint of the ordinary. This woman
initiates a pattern that recurs throughout the Christian ages. Once
healed by Jesus, she returns to do, with renewed vigor, the things
that she had been accustomed to doing. By faithfully accomplishing these ordinary, everyday things, Christians still find their salvation. They discover how to express their devotion. It is significant
that a woman provides a model for the Church's everyday existence.
Peter's mother-in-law displays the charity that should inform the
world. God bestows the gift of divine charity. Christ and his ministers mediate the grace that underlies divine charity. A feverish
woman of first-century Palestine whom Jesus relieves of an inhibiting distress models the reception of this divine gift. This enactment
takes the form of her waiting on Jesus.

We find ourselves thinking about the gesture of charity that
Christ himself will enact on the night before he died. In the Upper
Room, the apostles, including Peter, discover the pattern that
distinguishes divine charity from all the forms that human loving
can take. Recall that Peter hesitates when Jesus comes to wash his
feet, that is, to wait on him. Perhaps he found it odd to see Jesus do
for him what his mother-in-law had done for Jesus. Then Jesus
makes clear the significance of this action. "Unless I wash you, you
will have no inheritance with me" (Jn 13: 8).

*Eternal Father, we delight in the charity that your Church creates
in the world. Make us eager to surrender ourselves to the commandments of love as these are taught in your Church, so that we will
reach the banquet table of heaven.*

Miracles by the Dozen

Father Romanus Cessario, O.P.

When it was evening, they brought [Jesus] many who were possessed by demons, and he drove out the spirits by a word and cured all the sick, to fulfill what had been said by Isaiah the prophet:/ "He took away our infirmities/ and bore our diseases."
(Mt 8: 16-17)

As much as it is possible for a God-Man to assume the conditions common to all men, Christ embraced those very conditions. He ate. He drank. He slept. And so forth. Those who encountered Jesus discovered someone whom they considered like them in all things but sin. One sign of this appears in his approachability. The New Testament includes many incidents where common people flock to Jesus. Sometimes they follow him because they have received bread and fish to eat. Other times they seek him out because they have witnessed his miracles of healing. And still other times, they congregate to hear Jesus' teaching. Exorcisms and physical cures appear repeatedly throughout the pages of the New Testament. One cannot get through reading Saint Matthew's Gospel, let alone interpret it, without some convictions about these extraordinary occurrences. Those who accept only what they can figure out for themselves easily find some way to explain away the miracles. Saint Matthew was not a rationalist. We must conclude that these two verses report a scene that was common to behold during the Lord's public ministry. He cured people.

The Church still looks for divine cures of physical disease and other human infirmities. The most obvious example is found in the extensive efforts made by the Church to verify miracles of healing at the intercession of a holy person proposed for sainthood. The miracle lends support to the Church's proclamation that the intercessor enjoys a privileged place before the glorious Christ. Of course only God can heal someone. Even so, those close to God can pray for others who seek relief from suffering. When they do, we benefit. We receive inspiration and help to lead a Christian life. And the Church discovers anew the significance of the prophet's words, "He took away our infirmities and bore our diseases."

Loving Father, you sent your Son to heal a world wounded by sin and infirmity. Grant us what we need to remain steadfast in the Catholic faith, and to participate fully in the sacramental life that communicates your divine power.

Love Comes First

Father Romanus Cessario, O.P.

Another of [his] disciples said to [Jesus], "Lord, let me go first and bury my father." But Jesus answered him, "Follow me, and let the dead bury their dead." (Mt 8: 21-22)

When Jesus instructs a potential follower, "Let the dead bury their dead," the Lord of the living and of the dead gives notice that the Christian religion should not succumb to sentimentalism. What more non-sentimental thought can one imagine than to instruct someone to follow Christ rather than to attend a family funeral? We know from what the Church teaches about burying the dead that she does not interpret this passage as a divine command to omit what is required. In fact, the Catechism teaches the opposite of what one might superficially adopt as the meaning of this text: "The burial of the dead is a corporal work of mercy (cf. Tb 1: 16-18); it honors the children of God, who are temples of the Holy Spirit" (CCC 2300). All the more does the obligation to bury the dead apply to one's parents.

What then does Jesus mean? He clearly wants to teach us that the pursuit of divine holiness takes precedence over honoring even the legitimate wishes of a human family. Christ wants to ensure that his disciples get their priorities straight. In the ordinary course of events, no conflict should arise between loving God and honoring parents. Still other persons can make competing claims on our charity. The Lord's reminder that loving God always comes first in our lives forestalls a false sentimentalism.

What distinguishes authentic charity from sentimental altruism? The answer is simple: God's goodness. How can we ensure that our choices follow the priorities of charity and not what we imagine to provide the most comfort to the neighbor? The answer again is clear: Choose the course of action that will ensure that the neighbor grows in his love for God. First, however, make sure that what you do also increases your own love for God and his Son, Jesus Christ.

Omnipotent God, you are the Creator of all that exists. Only in your life and love do we discover the source of our living and our loving. Draw us close to your incarnate Son who is Lord for ever and ever.

Yet You Are There

Anthony Esolen

[Jesus] got into a boat and his disciples followed him. Suddenly a violent storm came up on the sea, so that the boat was being swamped by waves; but he was asleep. They came and woke him, saying, "Lord, save us! We are perishing!" He said to them, "Why are you terrified, O you of little faith?" Then he got up, rebuked the winds and the sea, and there was great calm. The men were amazed and said, "What sort of man is this, whom even the winds and the sea obey?" (Mt 8: 23-27)

Fishing is still one of the most arduous and dangerous occupations in the world, and it was all the more dangerous in the time of Jesus, when there were no outboard motors, no life preservers, no helicopters, and the only thing you could do when the violent storms swept across the Sea of Galilee was to pull down the sail, hang on, and pray.

Why then does Jesus rebuke his disciples? Some of them were fishermen, and Jesus was but a carpenter. Any ordinary carpenter would have been of no use in the storm, but these fishermen wake Jesus precisely because he is their "Lord." They do not yet understand just how fitting that title is, but that is what they call him, hoping that he will do something, anything, as the waves crash over the little boat.

So their calling upon Jesus is an act of faith. He does not say that they lack all faith; only that their faith is little. What should they have instead? Think of the faith of Jesus, sleeping like a child through all the turmoil about him. He is like the ship's boy up on the crow's nest, untroubled by the swaying and the rocking, trusting that the mast will always right itself. Jesus more than any man can know anguish of heart, and sorrow, as we find when he weeps at the tomb of Lazarus, or as when he sweats blood in Gethsemane. But so often we see in him that childlike and wise shake of the head, as if to say, "Now what is it that you are worried about?"

Jesus is always with the Father, and *that* is the faith he wants to give us, a faith that looks upon storms and is not moved, because the Father knows what we need, and will not try us beyond our strength.

Father, when storms overtake us, grant unto us the sweetness of Jesus' sleep, the confidence of his rebuke, and the faith in you by whom all things are possible, through the same Christ, our Lord.

We Are Not Alone

Anthony Esolen

*When [Jesus] came to the other side, to the territory of the
Gadarenes, two demoniacs who were coming from the tombs met
him. They were so savage that no one could travel by that road.
They cried out, "What have you to do with us, Son of God?
Have you come here to torment us before the appointed time?"*
(Mt 8: 28-29)

I f we heard on the news that a lion was prowling about the neighborhood, seeking whom to devour, we would shut our doors and huddle inside, waiting for the police. Or some of the more reckless among us would reach for a rifle. The last thing we would do would be to wander off into the coverts of the woods, thinking, "The lion will never see me here."

Yet a lion is prowling about, ravenous, filled with hatred for us and for God; a murderer from the beginning; the father of lies; yet possessed of an intelligence that far outstrips our own. So what do we do about it? We wander off into the coverts of the woods, thinking, "No one will see me here," and "God does not really care," and, "There is no such thing as a devouring lion."

Here Jesus is met by two wild men who dwell in caves. Their minds and bodies are taken over by demons, who bellow, impudently, "What have you to do with us!" The demons know who Jesus is, and they guess that the time of Jesus' great battle is drawing near, but is not yet. If we were traveling in that area, we would avoid those caves. We would, that is, if the demons were so kind as to make themselves manifest. Otherwise we might walk right by, or right in – to buy the latest item from Beelzebub's Boutique.

But the battle is engaged, all round us, and we are soldiers in it, or traitors, or foolish prey, ignorant as to what is going on. How clever a ruse by the enemy! God's great revelation is "I am who am," but Satan's, to the sophisticated people of our day, is "I am not." No matter, when the caves are so richly decorated!

*Father, send forth your Spirit upon us that we may discern the lies
of the ancient enemy, and keep from his path, through Jesus Christ,
our Lord.*

Leave Us Our Swine!

Anthony Esolen

Some distance away a herd of many swine was feeding. The demons pleaded with [Jesus], "If you drive us out, send us into the herd of swine." And he said to them, "Go then!" They came out and entered the swine, and the whole herd rushed down the steep bank into the sea where they drowned. (Mt 8: 30-32)

Jesus cures the demoniacs by casting their demons into a nearby herd of unclean animals – swine, which the Jews were forbidden to eat or to touch. We might ask, "What was the herd of swine doing there, then?" Maybe the Gadarenes do not follow the law of Moses. Maybe they raise swine to sell to their Roman overlords. Whatever the case, it must have been with mighty braying and squealing that the swine stampeded over the edge of the embankment to drown in the sea.

I've always assumed that the demons drove them over on purpose to make the ungrateful people tell Jesus to leave their turf alone. And perhaps they did. But the Gospel does not make that clear. Maybe the swine themselves, unclean though they were, went mad, unable in their animal nature to endure the presence of the demons. If that's so, it's to the credit of the swine. The Gadarenes by contrast do not come off so well.

They, after all, have grown used to the arrangement. We don't see *them* rushing about madly in the presence of evil. What profit would there be in that? So long as the swine are fed and the demoniacs stay near their tombs and the Romans buy pork, the Gadarenes are content. It does not even occur to them to pray for their possessed brothers, or to thank Jesus for the cure.

What would it be, to watch a herd of swine hurl themselves headlong into the sea? If it happened now, would we cheer? Would we welcome our brothers back from the tombs? Or would we miss that comfortable and profitable filth in our midst? Consider how far from Jerusalem this place must have been, where the possessed were living among corpses and swine's flesh was raised for meat. Let us draw closer than that to the kingdom of God.

Father, create in us a clean heart, and renew in us a right spirit, that we may reject the filth of sin and be prepared to welcome Jesus into our midst, through the same Christ, our Lord.

Which Is the Greater Miracle?

Anthony Esolen

[Jesus] entered a boat, made the crossing, and came into his own town. And there people brought to him a paralytic lying on a stretcher. When Jesus saw their faith, he said to the paralytic, "Courage, child, your sins are forgiven." (Mt 9: 1-2)

Jesus' words to the paralytic are directed to us all. "Courage!" he cries. "Be not afraid, my child!" For though we walk about our daily business, when it comes to advancing in love and righteousness we are like that man lying helpless on his pallet. We may, on our own, thrash about a bit, throwing out a hand or a foot, but without the grace of God we cannot even raise ourselves to sit upright, let alone run the race of faith to the finish.

I wonder then what the paralytic expected when his friends brought him to Jesus, and whether he was surprised or disappointed or abashed when he heard Jesus say that his sins were forgiven. What sins can a paralytic commit? All of them: he can do what he can, by daily acts of selfishness, to harden his heart and darken the days of those who must care for him. His limbs are stiff, not because of sin – but they are a fine image of what sin does, as it turns the heart to stone.

This man came to be healed of his malady, and Jesus the physician, gratified by the faith of the man's friends, peers into his soul and speaks the words we should all long to hear: "Take heart! Don't worry! Your sins are forgiven." That is more than a statement of fact. It is an enactment of grace, a miraculous healing, right before our eyes! Before the man rises from his pallet, his soul stands upright, stretching its long-useless limbs, ready to live again. It is the greater miracle of the two, the miracle that really matters. The prophet Elisha could raise the widow's son from the dead. But only God can raise the soul from its sinful tomb. Why, then, should we take that wonder for granted?

Father, grant us the courage to seek the healing of our souls by faithful prayer and frequent confession of our sins, that we may rise, and join the ranks of your saints, through Christ, our Lord.

Who, Me?

Anthony Esolen

As Jesus passed on from there, he saw a man named Matthew
sitting at the customs post. He said to him, "Follow me."
And he got up and followed him. (Mt 9: 9)

The Pharisees were surprised that Jesus numbered among his apostles Saint Matthew, who had cooperated with the Romans by squeezing his fellow Jews for tax money. Not as surprised, I daresay, as Matthew himself.

God loves us with a boundless love, vast as the heavens above. So great is his love for us that in ways we can hardly understand he has made himself subject to us, giving us the freedom to love him in return or to reject his love. We look at ourselves in the mirror with some approval, and can believe this about God. What gives us pause is the notion which we seldom entertain, that God showers that same infinite love upon the irritating person next door, upon the atheist with his stony mind, the prostitute working the alley, the murderer in prison waiting for his apparently pointless life to end.

But God wants us, and each for a unique and unrepeatable purpose. It is more than that we are all called to be saints. There is no such thing as a generic saint. The more closely we look at the lives of the saints, the more they seem to enjoy a wild communion among one another, yet the more sharply distinct they are from one another, more themselves, in the bright and joyful colors of holiness. God knows us and calls us each by name. "Matthew!" says he, with a commanding look. "You over there with your accounts! Come let me tell you of a master who gives a profit of a hundredfold and more!"

And Matthew, the Jew rejected by his fellows, will write of the King of the Jews, as the gift to the Gentiles. In the transforming power of God, his sins are burned away, yet the man and his history remain, like refined gold. Who knows what particular sainthood God has in mind for each of us?

Father, send your Spirit down into the alleys and the coverts where we hide, so that we may become the saints you mean us to be, which is no less than to become ourselves, through Christ, our Lord.

Mercy, Not Sacrifice

Anthony Esolen

While [Jesus] was at table in [Matthew's] house, many tax collectors and sinners came and sat with Jesus and his disciples. The Pharisees saw this and said to his disciples, "Why does your teacher eat with tax collectors and sinners?" He heard this and said, "Those who are well do not need a physician, but the sick do. Go and learn the meaning of the words, 'I desire mercy, not sacrifice.' I did not come to call the righteous but sinners."

(Mt 9: 10-13)

There are two kinds of people: sinners who know that they are sinners, and sinners who don't. When the Pharisees narrow their eyes at Jesus and accuse him of consorting with the wrong people, Jesus replies by teaching them something they should know about God, and about themselves.

But why does God not desire sacrifice? Won't Jesus sacrifice his life for sinners? That is true, but then sacrifice is an act of love, a giving of oneself, and not what it is among the heathen and among the hardhearted who think they know the true God. For them, sacrifice is part of an economic arrangement. I slaughter the ram in the temple to secure good harvests for my family. This makes me "righteous," as a businessman who keeps up his end of a bargain. What that view of sacrifice forgets is our entire dependence upon God, for we sacrifice to him nothing that is not already his. It is a wonder that he should take thought for us, and love us, and want us to dwell in his house for ever. We can do nothing to earn such favor; rather, what we earn by our sins is disgrace, alienation, and affliction.

So the true sacrifice that God loves, the one that makes us most like him, is mercy. In mercy we regard the harlot or the tax collector, as they acknowledge their sins and try to amend their lives, as beloved by God, who looks with kindness upon the brokenhearted. God did not need to create a world. He did not need to make man in his image. He did not need to dwell among us in the flesh, so that he might redeem us. In all these things he goes forth from himself in love and mercy. It is exactly what Jesus is inviting the Pharisees to do, that they too might be healed.

Father, give us a heart to rejoice in the abundant mercies you have shown us, so that we in turn might give mercy freely to others, through the merciful Jesus, our Lord.

Divinity Shown through a Cure

Father Joseph Koterski, S.J.

*An official came forward, knelt down before [Jesus], and said,
"My daughter has just died. But come, lay your hand on her,
and she will live." Jesus rose and followed him, and so did
his disciples. (Mt 9: 18-19)*

Fresh from a contentious encounter with certain Pharisees over the failure of Jesus' disciples to keep the expected fasts, Jesus now meets a synagogue official. The death of his daughter has broken the man's heart. From the man's position, we can imagine that Judaism's rituals about purity, sickness, and mourning have been observed, but – in some contrast to the argumentative Pharisees – he conducts himself with humility. The painful reality of this death brings him to seek out this unusual rabbi, whatever the practices of his disciples.

The word used here for "official" is *archon*, one who "keeps order" in the synagogue. In maintaining order for everyone else, he would surely have known well the Jewish policy against giving such homage to any creature and reserving it for God alone, lest the object of one's reverence be thought an idol. Yet he kneels before Jesus, in the posture of a beggar, mindful of his reputation for having powers to cure the sick and even to raise the dead. Jesus agrees to go with him.

Throughout the Gospels, miracles like the one about to unfold here are testimony to Jesus' divinity. He does what no human being can do. In fact, the vast numbers of Jews who came to belief in Christ in the earliest age of the Church would provoke a crisis of enormous proportions in Judaism. Acknowledging Jesus as truly divine – something hinted at in this gesture of adoration – seemed to threaten the dearly cherished and long preserved doctrine of Jewish monotheism.

Our Christian faith does acknowledge the distinction of persons: Father, Son, and Holy Spirit. Yet we insist that the three persons of the Blessed Trinity are one God. The power that Christ will momentarily exhibit over life and death comes from the fact that he is "one in being with the Father," as the Nicene Creed puts it. We do well to follow him to this miracle, as his disciples did.

Heavenly Father, we bless you for the power that you manifest in your divine Son, our Lord Jesus. Grant that we might have, like this synagogue official, an ever deeper trust in him.

Only to Touch His Cloak

Father Joseph Koterski, S.J.

A woman suffering hemorrhages for twelve years came up behind [Jesus] and touched the tassel on his cloak. She said to herself, "If only I can touch his cloak, I shall be cured." Jesus turned around and saw her, and said, "Courage, daughter! Your faith has saved you." And from that hour the woman was cured.
(Mt 9: 20-22)

Before Jesus reaches the home of the synagogue official, a woman long suffering from hemorrhages waylays him. Apparently she doesn't even expect to attract his attention, but simply hopes to receive a cure from touching the tassel of his cloak. If we are right to notice certain differences between the Pharisees and the synagogue official, not only in regard to observance of Jewish ceremonial laws but in regard to propriety and humility, the present scene takes on yet new meaning by virtue of her condition. The very nature of her sickness renders this woman ritually unclean according to Mosaic law, for blood is the very sign of God's gift of life, and so, strictly speaking, she should not touch anyone while blood is flowing out from her, lest she render them impure.

Where the Gospel of Mark gives us the added details about Jesus asking who touched his cloak and his disciples' amazement at the question in view of the crowd pressing around Jesus, the Gospel of Matthew presents the story more simply. But, as always in stories about the healings of Jesus, what is crucial is the presence of real faith. Sometimes Jesus works the miracle to elicit faith in those who do not yet share it. In cases like this one, Jesus testifies to the faith the woman already has and urges her not to be afraid.

While this particular action of Jesus has not been the source of a liturgical ritual in our sacramental practice, one of the most moving experiences I have ever witnessed is connected to this story. Once at a retreat for women, the sisters sponsoring the retreat asked me to wear the humeral veil while carrying the Blessed Sacrament slowly up and down the communion rail. Kneeling at the altar rail, those retreatants who wished could imitate this woman by clinging for a few moments to the humeral veil and praying for the healing they needed.

Heavenly Father, origin of all life and source of all healing, we thank you for the gift of your Son and we beg for your healing, for ourselves and for those whom we know to be in need. In all things we trust you.

Power over Life and Death

Father Joseph Koterski, S.J.

When the crowd was put out, [Jesus] came and took her by the hand, and the little girl arose. And news of this spread throughout all that land. (Mt 9: 25-26)

At the home of the synagogue official, the first thing Jesus does is to remove the crowd from the house. It is not that he simply needs room to work. What he found there were flute players and the crowd "making a commotion" (v. 23). They "ridiculed him" for claiming that he will wake the girl from her sleep (v. 24). In contrast to the faith that brought this distraught father to plead before Jesus, these people presumably lack such faith. But worse than that, they mock him by their laughter, entirely too confident that no one has power over death.

Like the miracle of having Lazarus rise from the grave, the miracle here shows Jesus to be one with his Father, the very author of Life. Lazarus' four days in the tomb may give special evidence that he was not simply unconscious, but in this story too there is no reason to suspect that the girl had not truly died. Jesus' declaration that she is only asleep should not be taken as if this were not a case of someone truly being raised from the dead. Rather, it is testimony that in the sight of God, death is no more an obstacle to his will than slumber.

The author of Life blew life into the clay of Adam. He can restore it to the beloved daughter of a mournful father who humbly asks that she be restored to life. In a way, the man is an image for one of the beatitudes, for Jesus consoles him who truly mourns by this miracle. But like Lazarus, she too will need to die again, and like the rest of us, await the resurrection of the dead. For us, consolation from the Lord will be a gift that comes from our faith that he is the judge of the living and the dead and has plans for our purification, so that someday we may be with him eternally.

Heavenly Father, master of all life, we thank you for the gift of life and we beg you for the grace to reverence it from conception to natural death. Strengthen our belief in your dominion over life and death, and direct us in the use of the life you have given us, for your honor and glory.

Jesus, Son of David

Father Joseph Koterski, S.J.

As Jesus passed on from there, two blind men followed [him], crying out, "Son of David, have pity on us!" When he entered the house, the blind men approached him and Jesus said to them, "Do you believe that I can do this?" "Yes, Lord," they said to him. Then he touched their eyes and said, "Let it be done for you according to your faith." And their eyes were opened.

(Mt 9: 27-30)

Isaiah prophesied that the Messiah would make the lame walk, the blind see, the mute speak, and the deaf hear (Is 35: 4-7). In Matthew we see Jesus doing all these things. After eliciting a confession of faith from two blind men who were following him, he touches their eyes and restores them to sight.

Just imagine blind men trying to follow anyone. They can detect the direction of a sound, and perhaps walk more easily in that direction if they can hold on to someone leading them. But if we've ever played Blind Man's Bluff, we can begin to imagine the hesitation of trying to walk where we cannot see. In chasing after Jesus whom they cannot see, they are a model for what it is to have faith. We cannot see God, and yet in faith we do well to raise our voices in prayer as they did.

Why call him "Son of David"? From the genealogy at the beginning of Matthew, we know Jesus to be a descendant of David (Mt 1: 1-16). This greeting evokes the memory of the promise God had made to David and his descendants: "I will make his royal throne firm forever. I will be a father to him, and he shall be a son to me… I will not withdraw my favor from him… Your throne shall stand firm forever" (2 Sm 7: 14-16). There may even be a political overtone here, for the king then reigning could not claim such ancestry. But even if these blind men are innocent of political allusion, the claims about Jesus as the Messiah rest both on the truth about Jesus as the Son of God and on the truth of his descent from King David (see also Rom 1: 3).

What they ask for is his mercy. We echo their request often in the liturgy – in the *Kyrie*, for instance, and in the *Agnus Dei*. We do well to make those prayers with the same kind of trust.

Heavenly Father, we believe – help our unbelief. Give us, we beg you, a faith like that of these blind men, to ask for what we need in a way that is simple and without reserve. Deliver us from what holds us back from you.

An Exorcism

Father Joseph Koterski, S.J.

A demoniac who could not speak was brought to [Jesus], and when the demon was driven out the mute person spoke. The crowds were amazed and said, "Nothing like this has ever been seen in Israel." But the Pharisees said, "He drives out demons by the prince of demons." (Mt 9: 32-34)

The hardness of heart of some of those who witnessed the miracles of Jesus can sometimes seem even more astonishing than the miracles themselves. Admittedly, real belief in Christ can prove difficult, and the very power to believe is a gift from God. We can well understand and even sympathize with those who do not find themselves able to believe when they have not seen God's power for themselves. But to witness it and still to disbelieve suggests something deeply wrong. The problem could be an intense sort of rationalism – an insistence on making reality conform to one's own categories rather than to open one's mind to what is real.

For many in our age, there is complete skepticism about the reality of the devil. They dismiss references to demonic possession like this one as merely naïve superstition. They think that the Gospels are too simplistic to believe on this point, and thus are doubtful in general. On the other hand, there are some who are all too fascinated by talk about exorcism. They like it in the way that they like exhibitions of magic, but without any sense of the danger to souls and the suffering of the possessed.

Stories like this one show us not only the power of Christ to drive out demons but also his profound unity with the Father in his care for people. In the account of the creation of Adam and Eve in Genesis, we learn that human beings are distinct from all other creatures by being made in God's image and likeness. It is hard to conceive of a state farther from that status than a case of demonic possession, when one's reason and will are rendered inoperative. Here the demoniac has been deprived of speech, that most human of faculties. Despite the Pharisaic reaction, Jesus with joy delivers the man from his bondage and restores the fullness of God's image within him.

Heavenly Father, we praise you for making us in your likeness and we beg you for your mercies. Restore that image, we beg you, when it is damaged by sin, and send your healing especially on those whom the devil tries to steal. Lord, we trust you in all things.

Preaching in the Synagogue

Father Joseph Koterski, S.J.

Jesus went around to all the towns and villages, teaching in their synagogues, proclaiming the gospel of the kingdom, and curing every disease and illness. At the sight of the crowds, his heart was moved with pity for them because they were troubled and abandoned, like sheep without a shepherd. (Mt 9: 35-36)

From the Sermon on the Plain, or the Sermon on the Mount, we might get the impression that Jesus preached largely out of doors, but here we learn that he preached regularly in synagogues. Presumably this would have been less an occasion for oratory and more an occasion for study, and thus an opportunity for his critics to scrutinize his doctrine. It would have been a time to persuade his listeners that the one who was reputed for so many healings and such inspiring words was truly authentic – not a revolutionary in religion or in politics, but one who knew the traditions of Israel better than anyone else and who claimed to be the fulfillment of messianic prophecies.

The passage also speaks to us of the feelings within Christ's own heart: a compassion that moved him deeply. What he saw was wounded and chaotic, as confused as shepherdless sheep. The image of Israel as sheep without a shepherd comes from earlier within the Bible. Moses, for instance uses it (Nm 27: 15f) when begging God to raise up a leader. Ezekiel employs it to describe his own times (Ez 34: 5). Moved by a similar feeling about a people deeply in trouble, Christ takes the role of shepherd upon himself.

Romantic as the life of a shepherd may seem to those who don't really know the trade, the reality is quite different. Guiding and guarding a flock in all sorts of weather, running after the strays, and confronting those who would kill or steal will take the bloom off the rose fairly quickly. Yet the choice of this work runs deep in the history of revelation: Abel, Abraham, Moses, David, and countless others. By its very nature, the work suggests the providential care of those in need, and so the foster son of the carpenter makes it his own.

Heavenly Father, we praise you for the redemption your Son won for us by his suffering and death. In your mercy, keep us ever faithful.

What's in a Name?

Father Joseph Torchia, O.P.

*Then [Jesus] summoned his twelve disciples and gave them
authority over unclean spirits to drive them out and to cure
every disease and every illness. The names of the twelve apostles
are these: first, Simon called Peter, and his brother Andrew;
James, the son of Zebedee, and his brother John; Philip and
Bartholomew, Thomas and Matthew the tax collector; James,
the son of Alphaeus, and Thaddeus; Simon the Cananean,
and Judas Iscariot who betrayed him.* (Mt 10: 1-4)

In the course of his earthly ministry, Christ fully empowers
his disciples to carry on his redemptive work. He gives them
everything they require to be his ambassadors. This includes
the ability to bring healing to people in body, mind, and spirit. But
we can focus so much on the disciples' immediacy to Christ that
we lose sight of the fact that they are flesh and blood individuals:
simple men – talented, to be sure – but small in the eyes of the larger
world, and for all their goodness, men with failings and limitations.
The disciples are real people like us, fully in touch with the realities and struggles of life. As Matthew's account reminds us, they
have names, and with those names, life histories.

Christ calls his disciples by name, on a personal basis. He sees in
them a potential that others could easily overlook. He draws them
into his service with all the baggage of their pasts. Notice what is
highlighted here. There's Matthew the tax collector – the one
despised by his own people. And then, there's Judas Iscariot, the
one who will betray Christ to his enemies. No, the Gospels are by
no means oblivious to the pervasiveness of sin. And what else lies
between the lines? There's Simon, the one Jesus renames as Peter,
who will deny him three times, but who will go on to become the
rock on which the Church is built. And there's Thomas, the great
skeptic, whose initial expression of faith requires tangible proof of
Christ's resurrection. The whole panoply of human existence is
here, exposed to the world's scrutiny.

Like the disciples, Christ calls us by name. He chooses us as
the persons we are, with all our own weaknesses, for his special
purposes. He takes us like so much unformed clay and reshapes us
to do his work in spreading the kingdom of God on earth. How
shall we respond?

*God, my Father, you know me to the inner core of my being.
Take me as I am, with all I can offer you, and put me to good use
in the service of your Church.*

Close to Home

Father Joseph Torchia, O.P.

Jesus sent out these twelve after instructing them thus, "Do not go into pagan territory or enter a Samaritan town. Go rather to the lost sheep of the house of Israel. As you go, make this proclamation: 'The kingdom of heaven is at hand.' Cure the sick, raise the dead, cleanse lepers, drive out demons. Without cost you have received; without cost you are to give." (Mt 10: 5-8)

How often we've heard it said, "Charity begins at home." We hear that aphorism, but easily forget its implications, and how we ourselves might fail to heed it. Even the most charitable individuals have a tendency to overlook the needs of those closest to them, from friends and neighbors to members of their own families. This doesn't necessarily bespeak a neglect on our part. Rather, our very familiarity with people sometimes lends itself to taking them for granted.

Christ takes no one for granted, especially those most in need of his saving care. His proclamation of the kingdom of God will eventually encompass the people of all nations. But as his words to his disciples attest, he begins his redemptive mission with those closest to home, the people of Israel themselves, the ones chosen by God for implementing his plan of redemption. This initial phase of ministry becomes the springboard for spreading the net of evangelization over the entire world.

Are we attuned to the needs of those in our midst? Let us follow the disciples' lead and spread our nets of Christian service over a wide area. But let us not neglect those closest to home. Because there are many people in desperate need of the healing of Jesus Christ and the transforming power of his word. These people are all around us. Perhaps they live next door. Or like the wounded Lazarus, they might be lying on our own doorstep and so get easily overlooked in our daily travels to and fro. We must reach out to them, not only in response to their physical needs, but to their spiritual hunger as well, in all the ways this impoverishment manifests itself. We do it with the generosity of Christ himself, without any strings attached or expectations. We give in the way we have received from him, free of charge.

God, my Father, grant me the clarity of vision which will enable me to recognize the needs of those closest to me. Help me to give freely and without reservation in your name.

Traveling Light

Father Joseph Torchia, O.P.

*"Do not take gold or silver or copper for your belts; no sack for
the journey, or a second tunic, or sandals, or walking stick.
The laborer deserves his keep. Whatever town or village you
enter, look for a worthy person in it, and stay there until you
leave. As you enter a house, wish it peace. If the house is worthy,
let your peace come upon it; if not, let your peace return to you.
Whoever will not receive you or listen to your words – go outside
that house or town and shake the dust from your feet."*
(Mt 10: 9-14)

I'm often amazed by those able to pack for a long journey at a
moment's notice, with only the barest necessities. They know
exactly what they'll require in advance. Christ's words to his
disciples encourage this very sort of economy. He expects them to
travel light: basic requirements are minimized. The very nature of
their task doesn't allow for anything that would distract them from
proclaiming the Good News.

But can we really live this way? Regardless of our state in life or
vocation, we must confront a hard-hitting fact about Christian discipleship. Jesus continually stresses the tension between the call to
follow him and an inordinate attachment to the things of this world.
What is it that we simply could not do without in order to be happy?
This is not a question about material possessions, or how much we
are willing to give up. It really concerns what we deem most essential. If we call ourselves followers of Christ, we must place him at
the top of our list of priorities. And that demands that we separate
ourselves from anything that impedes our relationship with him.

Once we recognize ourselves as the dependent beings we are, we
can rely completely upon the providence of God. What is such a
reliance but an imitation of Christ's own example, the one willing
to empty himself completely for our redemption? This is how we
stand in solidarity with the apostles as they went out on mission.
And with this comes a freedom from attachment to fleeting things
that are not crucial to who and what we are as persons, and most
importantly, as Christians. Because the greatest wealth we can ever
possess is found deep within, where we encounter the One in whom
we live and move and have our very being.

*God, my Father, help me to know where my priorities really lie, and
to recognize the true source of every good you have granted me.*

Survival Skills

Father Joseph Torchia, O.P.

"Behold, I am sending you like sheep in the midst of wolves; so be shrewd as serpents and simple as doves. But beware of people, for they will hand you over to courts and scourge you in their synagogues, and you will be led before governors and kings for my sake as a witness before them and the pagans. When they hand you over, do not worry about how you are to speak or what you are to say. You will be given at that moment what you are to say. For it will not be you who speak but the Spirit of your Father speaking through you." (Mt 10: 16-20)

In the chapel of the Dominican House of Studies in Washington, DC, there's a striking stained-glass window depicting Saint Dominic sending out the initial band of friars. It evokes a sense of the concern Dominic must have felt for them, the way parents feel when their children go to school for the first time, worried about what lies ahead. What lay ahead of the apostles was certainly challenging: rejection and persecution, and almost to the man, a martyr's death. On the surface, Christ's words imply that they don't stand a chance for survival, any more than sheep in the midst of ravenous wolves. That's why they must sharpen their own spiritual "survival skills." Christ wants his followers to be as resourceful as serpents in dealing with the many hazards of their missions – not in some deceitful or underhanded way, but with that single-minded devotion to God that mirrors his own divine simplicity.

Christ's words speak directly to us. How do we face the challenges of being Christians in today's world, especially when people are indifferent or even hostile to our message? These challenges are part and parcel of our special calling as followers of Christ: to be in the world as active participants with something unique to give, but not completely of that world; to witness to Christ and the truth of the Gospel in the concrete circumstances of our lives; to rejoice in the goodness of creation even as we affirm our spirituality and supernatural destiny. The inspiration to do these things and so much more can only come from God through the working of the Holy Spirit. This is our source of confidence: that we are not out here alone, stranded behind the lines, so to speak. Rest assured, God is with us, and he will instruct and direct us, just as he instructed his own disciples.

God, my Father, grant me the wisdom to discern my place in the world, the prudence to do whatever I must in your service, and the courage to witness to the truth of your Gospel.

Guilty as Charged

Father Joseph Torchia, O.P.

"You will be hated by all because of my name, but whoever endures to the end will be saved. When they persecute you in one town, flee to another. Amen, I say to you, you will not finish the towns of Israel before the Son of Man comes." (Mt 10: 22-23)

One of the greatest compliments people in authority can receive is that they don't expect anything from others they're not willing to sacrifice themselves. We might consider Christ's sobering words to his disciples this way. Before any of his followers experienced the world's rejection, he would receive the full brunt of its hatred, even unto death.

But why does a message of love, forgiveness, and redemption arouse such enmity? And why have so many people witnessing to the truth of the Gospel been victims of intense persecution through the centuries, from Roman times to our own age? Perhaps because those who follow Christ embrace a way of life that can easily put them at odds with secular values. And while Christians are committed to a spirit of toleration and fellowship, there's a critical point at which devotion to God simply doesn't allow for the easy road, or the luxury of fence-straddling. It demands that we stand and be counted for what we are as Christ's followers.

It shouldn't surprise us that those who are unabashedly Christian in their practice rarely make the covers of national magazines, or appear on mainstream talk shows, or win popularity contests for their beliefs. In a world so given to equivocation and compromise, in fact, those who actively live the Gospel might well find themselves objects of derision and reproach, like one of the Old Testament prophets (see Jer 20: 7-8).

But Christians possess a power far greater than hatred, and it proceeds from the example of Christ himself: "Love one another as I love you" (Jn 15: 12). This is how all will know we are his disciples, by the way we love friends and enemies alike. And if being a Christian were ever declared a crime (to paraphrase an old cliché), then the depth of that love will immediately convict us, proclaiming to the world, "Here I am, guilty as charged!"

God, my Father, show me how to love in the manner you love us. And help me to accept the costs of that love, including the hatred or disdain of those I love in your name.

Privileged Information

Father Joseph Torchia, O.P.

"Nothing is concealed that will not be revealed, nor secret that will not be known. What I say to you in the darkness, speak in the light; what you hear whispered, proclaim on the housetops."
(Mt 10: 26-27)

"Have I got a tip for you!" A statement like that makes people perk up and listen, especially if it comes from a source they can trust. In that case, they think they're receiving genuinely privileged information that provides an incentive to act and even take risks for the sake of success.

This is what the disciples receive from Christ: privileged information from the highest possible authority about the means to salvation. He teaches them what he himself has received from his heavenly Father. What they learn through parables on a gradual basis will assume increasing clarity in the course of their journeys of faith. And they in turn will pass on the Good News to others. This is precisely what Christ intends: to bring the truth of his saving message into the light of day. He doesn't want it confined to a select few or kept under wraps. When we consider what the disciples and the first Christians have to share, is it any wonder that they cannot keep quiet even under threat of martyrdom? Or that they are willing to go to the ends of the earth in serving Christ?

The responsibility to share God's Word falls to everyone who enters into fellowship with Christ. For those who gain access to the Good News, there's but one option: to communicate what we have received to others. We're simply not Christians in isolation or on a solitary basis. Nor can we rest content with locking our faith deep within. Now, this doesn't mean that we must all be public preachers. We can witness to the truth of Christ's teachings in many ways. We do it by the very quality of our lives and by the choices we make. May our lives and our choices attest loudly to our Christian vocations. And in that way, let's proclaim what we know far and wide, from the veritable housetops!

God, my Father, fill me with a generosity of spirit so that I freely share the joy of the Good News. Help me to be a Christian in the most public, visible way so that I may lead others by my example to your saving truth.

Many Sparrows

Father John Dominic Corbett, O.P.

"Are not two sparrows sold for a small coin? Yet not one of them falls to the ground without your Father's knowledge. Even all the hairs of your head are counted. So do not be afraid; you are worth more than many sparrows." (Mt 10: 29-31)

The world often looks like a cold place even in warm climates. That is to say, it sometimes seems like the world dwarfs us, shrinks us, cuts us down to size, reduces our thoughts and our hearts to our brains, reduces our brains to the laws of biology, chemistry, or physics, and reduces all of these to sheer chance. We are just a roll of the cosmic dice and at the end of the day we don't matter.

Politicians who breathe in this poisonous air sometimes translate this conviction into totalitarian regimes. Stalin is often quoted as saying, "One death in a traffic accident is a tragedy. One million deaths is a statistic." He was making fun of what he regarded as the unrealistic and sentimental view of human life characteristic of those who resisted the Communist Party's claimed right to totalitarian rule. History for him was the ruthless process which would bring the workers to rule and which would crush and trample underfoot any who stood in its way. He was willing to "liquidate" his opponents in the service of a history which would in any case and necessarily work its will.

I only cite Stalin to dismiss him. The Gospel teaches us that there are no finally ruling laws whether of physics or of history which bind, rule, and in the end crush the human person. Instead there is a Father who knows each of his children by name. He rules indeed, but he rules providentially, that is, with an eye to the true well being of each and of all. This does not mean that we do not suffer or die or seem to disappear without a trace. But it does mean that these appearances are only appearances. In the end we will see in even the most baffling events the care of our Father.

Father, teach us to trust that even in the most baffling moments of life, you are there present as our Father. Teach us to trust in your providence in all times and places.

Acknowledgment

Father John Dominic Corbett, O.P.

*"Everyone who acknowledges me before others I will
acknowledge before my heavenly Father. But whoever denies me
before others, I will deny before my heavenly Father."*
(Mt 10: 32-33)

When we acknowledge someone, we admit we have a relationship with that person. The relationship often enough involves indebtedness and so we publicly honor the person who has helped us. Depending on the relationship and on the favor received, acknowledgment can be merely correct, or warm, or be a testament of undying gratitude. It can be as informal as a nod or wink, as official as a letter of recommendation, or as fulsome and rambling as an after-dinner wedding toast. It is about what this person has meant to us and about what he or she has done for us, and it is a debt of justice as well as an expression of gratitude.

With this in mind, we can see that the whole of the Bible is about acknowledgment. It is about acknowledging God for the wonders of creation and of redemption and for the saving name of his Son Jesus Christ. We do this both as a Church when we celebrate the Eucharist and as individuals when we publicly thank God for the way he answered our prayers.

It is natural that we should acknowledge and confess our God. What is strange is the idea that God would ever acknowledge us. And yet he has said that he will do so.

Our persons are held in high esteem by him, our friendship is desired by him, and if we will acknowledge him as our Lord, he will acknowledge us before his Father.

How far he will carry this is seen in the case of Peter who once confessed him as Messiah and then who denied him three times. Jesus did not let this denial stand but led Peter to acknowledge him again, and then again, and then again on that beach. Then Jesus acknowledged him as head of the Church and as the one who, despite his denial, would in final acknowledgment of his Lord be crucified upside down.

*Father, teach us to confess your name before everyone we know.
May our lives as well as our words honor your name.*

Full Disclosure

Father John Dominic Corbett, O.P.

*"Do not think that I have come to bring peace upon the earth.
I have come to bring not peace but the sword."*
(Mt 10: 34)

But Jesus elsewhere says to his disciples, "My peace I give unto you." So the question becomes: How can Jesus bring both peace and a sword? Peace seems to mean not an undisturbed inner tranquility but a relationship from which nothing is missing. There is peace between Jesus and his disciples on Easter morning because Jesus' act of mercy on the cross and his rising from the dead leaves nothing missing between him and his disciples.

Getting to that point was another matter and, in fact, required the sword. Swords can stab and kill, but this is not what the Lord has in mind. What the Lord has in mind is the cutting function of swords. A sword can cut something in two. Cutting something has two effects. First of all it divides. Secondly, it reveals. If something is cut in two its inner core, an area normally unseen, is fully disclosed. One is reminded of the prophet Simeon's words to our Lady, "and you yourself a sword will pierce so that the thoughts of many hearts may be revealed" (Lk 2: 35).

So Jesus' words cut and divide. They reveal by cutting open the hearts of those who hear him. They force people to disclose what is in their minds and to take a stand with reference to him. He makes terrible claims about his own person and he will not allow those who meet him to escape with the cliché that he is a great moral teacher. He is either the Son of God and is therefore to be adored, or he is a lunatic who will accept no boundaries between you and him and who therefore must be resisted to the death if you are to preserve your autonomy and your control over your own life. There are those who accept his claims, and these are for ever divided and cut off from those who deny the claim. One must choose.

Lord Jesus, your claim on our lives is sometimes hard to understand. Help us to see that your words are able to cut us free from everything that would enslave us. Help us to see that the only freedom worth having is in belonging to you.

Zeal

Father John Dominic Corbett, O.P.

"Whoever loves father or mother more than me is not worthy of me, and whoever loves son or daughter more than me is not worthy of me; and whoever does not take up his cross and follow after me is not worthy of me." (Mt 10: 37-38)

This saying is harsh, but Jesus' harshest words are his most loving. How can this be? His harshest words are the ones which destroy the hidden barriers between ourselves and him. What keeps us from him? It is our sad habit of settling for less than what he wants to give us. We are told to love one another and so we do. If we have been blessed in our family lives we think we need look no further to understand what he means. We think he means felt affection within a perhaps enlarged family circle. Affection is given to those who are familiar to us. We love those who know us and love us. This is fine as far as it goes, but it doesn't go nearly far enough.

Perhaps thinking about what love is can help us to see why it doesn't. Knowing and loving move in different directions. Knowing brings the world to me. Loving brings me to the world. Knowing God makes God present to my mind. Loving God makes me present to God in a way that pushes me outside of myself and puts me in direct contact with his limitless goodness.

When I love something it is because I am like it. The more I go out of myself in love to something, the more I take on its qualities. If I love something dishonorable, I become dishonorable. If I love someone who is great, I begin to share, in however small a way, in that greatness. I become like unto and hence worthy of that which I love.

So it is with Christ. If we love him beyond all others, it is because we have come to see that he cannot be contained within our familiar world. Then we see we need to go out to him in preferential love and in doing this become like him. This is how we become worthy of him.

Holy Spirit, love of the Father for the Son and love of the Son for the Father, burn in our hearts so that, in the end, we settle for nothing less than yourself.

Losers Keepers

Father John Dominic Corbett, O.P.

"Whoever finds his life will lose it, and whoever loses his life for my sake will find it." (Mt 10: 39)

I f you are of a certain age and still watch the evening news, you are most certainly bombarded with ads for prescription drugs. These ads are both alarming and humiliating. They are alarming because they warn of the drug's possibly fatal, possibly merely permanently disabling side effects. They are humiliating because they imply that the advertisers are sure that we have no thoughts that are not about the preservation of our bodies.

Still, we take the advice and "talk to our doctors about" whatever promises to prolong our lives. Is this always a good thing? I'm not so sure. There is such a thing as hypochondria. It is possible to worry overmuch about one's health. It is possible to make ourselves sick by excessive self-concern. It is possible to place ourselves in danger because we are too concerned with our safety.

I remember a communion call I went on to a house in a wealthy neighborhood. The house had a gate. Behind the gate was a wall. Behind the wall was a triply electronically-secured door. Behind the door was a man. He was both secure and confined by fear to bed.

If we think that "prudence" means never to run a risk, then we shall never be prudent, for we shall be too prudent truly to live.

Where is our safety? We find it in Christ. He who was as invincible as God chose to become as vulnerable as a man. He put himself in harm's way when he left the ineffable peace of heaven for the war-torn and sin-scarred surface of the earth. He gave his life up in obedience to his Father who asked him to do so out of love for us who are always vulnerable both to the first and to the second death. We are disciples and are called to fidelity rather than to safety. We only truly find safety when we leave it behind by following in his footsteps.

Father, help us to fear you rightly. Teach us so to reverence your care for us that we would risk losing any good thing if such loss would join us fast to your Son who lives with you and the Spirit in glory for ever.

Simple Gifts for Simple People

Father John Dominic Corbett, O.P.

*"Whoever gives only a cup of cold water to one of these little ones
to drink because he is a disciple – amen, I say to you,
he will surely not lose his reward." (Mt 10: 42)*

W ho are the little ones? They are the believers who,
without too much fuss or bother, take Jesus at his word.
They are marked by simplicity of spirit which makes
them vulnerable to his promises. In a certain sense, they are like
children.

We are apt to misunderstand this. We tend to sentimentalize
little children because we regard them as innocent. We think they
are too young ever to have tasted the sad and dour dregs of moral
failure. Of course, the people who thus sentimentalize children have
probably never spent too much time at a playground. Anyone who
has had a close-up look at children knows that they are not innocent. They can lie, cheat, and bully each other. But children know
that they are not adults. They know that they cannot take care of
themselves, and so they have to trust someone else to do that for
them. What makes someone a child in this sense is not innocence
but incompetence.

The little ones are those who know that they cannot find their
own way to heaven. They know that they need to be led there.
And so, despite their sins, they are precious to Jesus because, unlike
the clever and learned, they are ready to take him at his word. This
is what thrills him. They welcome him. Since they welcome him he
dwells with them. He lives in their spirits and so the colors of their
lives begin to take on the hues of heaven. Their lives now begin to
resemble his. They welcome his word just as he welcomes the word
of his Father.

This welcome is so astonishing to him that he immediately
pledges to reward with eternal life anyone who is good to them for
his sake. This means that Jesus promises to share with the simplest
of his disciples a very great reward indeed – that of being one of
the reasons why the world was saved.

*Father, help us to give special welcome to those who welcome you.
Help us to see in them the glad evidence of your blessed presence
with us even now.*

The Truly Human Question

Father Vincent Nagle, F.S.C.B.

When John heard in prison of the works of the Messiah, he sent his disciples to him with this question, "Are you the one who is to come, or should we look for another?" (Mt 11: 2-3)

The ancient palaces in the Holy Land often had cisterns built under them to hold large amounts of rainwater, sometimes hewn from rock, or built with stone. And into these lightless depths, perhaps watery or muddy, or filled with the waste of previous occupants, the condemned were lowered down on a rope and disappeared from the sight of their fellow men.

It is a sign of the deep sanity of this great prophet that this gloomy misery has not effaced him. He knows who he is. Our Lord speaks of John as the one "of whom it is written, 'Behold, I send my messenger before thy face…'" He is the one waiting to encounter that face and who is to recall the people to their need to see it. And all the circumstances of his life, the harsh, long sojourn in the wilderness, and now his entombment in a fetid grave, are merely the conditions for him to live that longing, proclaim that desire, and prepare for that encounter. And thus he sends forth a message from his living death to say, "Are you the one?"

This is his greatness, and how much greater is ours, who are called to live the memory of our encounter with that face. Yet, how easy it is, almost "natural" for us, to think that our circumstances are our life, imagining that when they are good, we have a good life, and that when they turn against us, we have no life at all. How easy it is to forget what we truly long for, and thus lose our humanity. Christ makes it possible to live our humanity always, by offering his self as that presence and memory that tells us who we are and within all circumstances. Even in the confusion of loss and pain, we can still cry out not with John's question, but with that affirmation that unites us to the victory of Christ, "You are the one."

Father, do not let me be a slave of my circumstances, but let my belonging to you through your Son free me, and allow me to live in hope and love always.

Moved by a New Fact

Father Vincent Nagle, F.S.C.B.

Jesus said to [John's disciples] in reply, "Go and tell John what you hear and see: the blind regain their sight, the lame walk, lepers are cleansed, the deaf hear, the dead are raised, and the poor have the good news proclaimed to them. And blessed is the one who takes no offense at me." (Mt 11: 4-6)

It all went beyond just words for me one day when I was listening to a priest talk to a large group of young people whom he led through a Catholic youth organization. During my several years of study, prayer, and discussion, which had moved me toward the Catholic Church, I had been exposed to some very fine Catholic teaching. Taking in the words of this priest, I recognized a lot of what he was saying as more or less the ideas or concepts that I had already considered.

And yet there was something different that moved me greatly and, it seemed, also deeply moved the many other young people with me. At first I could not understand why what he was saying was not the same as what I had heard before. Then it hit me. It was that these words of his were describing what it is he actually saw among us, the life of Christ and holiness he observed in this person or the other, on that occasion or the other, in our midst. He was recounting what was moving him, and asking us to open our eyes and observe it around us.

The truth of Christ's claim to be he "who is to come" (Mt 11: 3) was, from that moment on, no longer an assertion that needed to be argued, but an evidence that needed only to be verified. More than twenty years later, I have never recovered from the power of that new way of seeing the world, of seeing Christ, of reaching certainty about his identity. And it all comes back to my reading the words that Jesus sends to John, "the blind regain their sight, the lame walk, lepers are cleansed, the deaf hear, the dead are raised, and the poor have the good news proclaimed to them." In other words, "What do you see, John? Answer your question."

Father, don't let me ever be more interested in my thoughts about you than I am in seeing and meeting you in your Son made flesh who dwells among us.

The Victories of Satan

Father Vincent Nagle, F.S.C.B.

"Amen, I say to you, among those born of women there has been none greater than John the Baptist; yet the least in the kingdom of heaven is greater than he. From the days of John the Baptist until now, the kingdom of heaven suffers violence, and the violent are taking it by force. All the prophets and the law prophesied up to the time of John. And if you are willing to accept it, he is Elijah, the one who is to come." (Mt 11: 11-14)

A third-world refugee in Italy, Wael, gave up his small business in order to move himself and his family to the United States and to help his brother, who had been begging that he come. His brother took advantage of this and drained him of his savings. Then an anonymous call brought the Immigration Police to Wael's door. When he and his wife were released to appeal for asylum, Wael found himself accused of having once touched his brother's daughter, and he was arrested again. He was found guilty, although another niece of his, daughter of the same brother, tells me that her father admitted to her that he had set Wael up.

In prison he was crippled from a suicide attempt and learned that when his time was up, he would be deported to his native country, where he would be arrested for having deserted the military. He said, "I blame God. If he had wanted he could have stopped my brother, or had that jury find me not guilty. But he did nothing, and he let me be brought here. And I only came to help my brother." But I suggested this to him: "God is giving you the opportunity to do what you set out to do. For it seems that nothing less will save your brother except that his innocent brother suffer everything for his salvation. Your prayer has been answered."

"The violent are taking it by force," says the Lord. Satan has his victories, the greatest being when he convinced men to crucify the Son of God. But as with Satan's victory on Calvary, these are, "if you are willing to accept it," only stepping stones for the victory of the kingdom of God. Satan may bear it all away, but if we share this "defeat" with the Lord, it serves only to defeat the enemy and fulfill Jesus' purposes, a passion for the salvation of sinners.

Father, do not let me become a slave through fear and hate, even when evil lifts its head in victory. Help me to love your Son on the cross and to live as a free man in the victory of the resurrection.

Listening to the Music

Father Vincent Nagle, F.S.C.B.

"To what shall I compare this generation? It is like children who sit in marketplaces and call to one another, 'We played the flute for you, but you did not dance, we sang a dirge but you did not mourn.' For John came neither eating nor drinking, and they said, 'He is possessed by a demon.' The Son of Man came eating and drinking and they said, 'Look, he is a glutton and a drunkard, a friend of tax collectors and sinners.'" (Mt 11: 16-19)

At a friend's house for dinner, at a certain point a few little girls, daughters of my friend and some of their little friends, decided to put on a ballet for us. They came out dressed in their tutus and the music began. All the girls were darling, but it was soon evident that one of the children stood out. The difference was not so much in physical coordination or gracefulness, but in the fact that, as they danced, there was just this one who was truly listening to the music and, with her whole self, answering. The others were perhaps concentrating on this catching move or that, on their pretty costumes or even on the reaction of the adults. But the beauty became apparent in the one who had been captured by the melody, the source, and then responded.

We want our lives to be a communication of something beautiful. The question, as with those little girls, is what we are listening to and to what or whom we are responding. In front of our colleagues and bosses at work, our friends and family, or the images we see in the entertainment that bombards us, the world is, as Jesus points out, always playing us different and contradictory tunes, expecting us to respond accordingly, and then shuns us when we do not. We end up acting one way at work, another at home, and still another with our friends. When that is the case, the unity of our lives, the beauty of our existence, the melody of our being is lost. In the end, we communicate nothing and lose ourselves.

It is only in the one come from God that we find a presence, a communication, that truly corresponds to our deepest being, our most profound and truest desires. It is in responding, then, to that communication that we are able to express our selves, the unique miracle of our lives.

Father, I get so distracted by so many things. Don't let me be manipulated by the false authority of this world. Let me be made complete by giving myself entirely to your Son, responding freely to his true love.

A Closed Door

Father Vincent Nagle, F.S.C.B.

Then [Jesus] began to reproach the towns where most of his mighty deeds had been done, since they had not repented. "Woe to you, Chorazin! Woe to you, Bethsaida! For if the mighty deeds done in your midst had been done in Tyre and Sidon, they would long ago have repented in sackcloth and ashes. But I tell you, it will be more tolerable for Tyre and Sidon on the day of judgment than for you." (Mt 11: 20-22)

When I was studying theology I was deeply frustrated by the opposition to the faith and teachings of the Church that often emanated from my Catholic teachers. My Russian Orthodox friends offered something of a safe harbor for me. They believed in Christ seriously. And they naturally enjoyed talking to me of their Church, and trying to show me the deficiencies of the Roman Catholic Church. It all came to a head one night when I asked one of them, "Since the purpose of being a Christian is to become a saint, and in the Catholic Church we have even living saints today such as Mother Teresa of Calcutta and John Paul II, then it is evident that by following this path I can become a saint. Why, then, should I leave and join the Orthodox Church?" My friend answered that he had asked his spiritual director that same question. The monk had answered that the saints in the Catholic Church were an illusion. "Do you believe that?" I asked. "Well, it is what my spiritual director said," he answered.

That ended the conversation for me, permanently, and with great frustration. With all the love in the world, where can a conversation go when people will believe neither their eyes nor those who point to what is happening? What frustration Jesus must have felt in front of those people that he loved, who would not let themselves consider the events taking place among them. There was nowhere to go from there. He will not force that door open. With tears, with human frustration, he waits for us to turn the knob. It is not indifference, as Jesus shows, crying out in agitation, "Woe to you!" Yet he will not put aside our freedom, but continually calls to it, suffers for it, and dies for it. He will not do it without us, for it really is us that he wants. Thus, painfully, he calls.

It is so easy for me to get caught up in defending what I understand of you, Father, and forget to look for your Son at work revealing you to the world. Let me be led by what he does, not by what I think.

The Light in a Child

Father Vincent Nagle, F.S.C.B.

At that time Jesus said [...], "I give praise to you, Father, Lord of heaven and earth, for although you have hidden these things from the wise and the learned you have revealed them to the childlike." (Mt 11: 25)

I accompanied the mother into the waiting room where her two young sons, one about ten and the other about six, had been waiting for her. She had bad news for them. Their father was dead of a heart attack. They knew something was up and were silent. She finally came right out and told them that their beloved dad was gone, dead. The younger did not understand, but the older one certainly did. "Dead?" he repeated quietly, as he searched his mother's face hoping for her to contradict him. I will never forget how he seemed visibly filled with pain, how his eyes seemed to change color before me, growing dark with suffering in a moment. I thought I saw a light going out.

What light is that? It is the curiosity to find out, discover, and see what lies around the corner, an expectation that things reveal themselves. It is that spontaneous movement of the soul, so natural in children and rare in adults, to follow after the promise of things – beauty, happiness, and life. And it is only to those with this light that Jesus can truly reveal himself.

It is our perceiving things under their aspect of promise that makes us young. What makes us old is to perceive things under their aspect of limit, no longer even perceiving the promise. This boy had met the ultimate limit, death. Jesus presents himself in a human form, limited. Who can see that he is the one who is fulfilling the promise of creation? Only the one in whom this light has not gone out, who is still asking for the fulfillment of the Father's creation, asking for happiness and life. This is the prayer that we must always go back to, asking to have the light rekindled, to remember what it is that we were expecting to discover, to return and be childlike and curious, by his grace.

Father, the fear of pain turns me away from discovering your grace at work in the world. Enkindle within me a desire to discover your truth and beauty in all that you send me through Jesus your Son.

Where Do You Come From?

Father Vincent Nagle, F.S.C.B.

"All things have been handed over to me by my Father.
No one knows the Son except the Father, and no one knows
the Father except the Son and anyone to whom the Son wishes
to reveal him." (Mt 11: 27)

What does God look like? How do you recognize him? Have you ever been walking down the street and had your eye caught by the striking looks of a person and said, "That guy looks like God?" Of course this is absurd. No one has seen God. So how does one recognize the Father in the Son? How does the Son reveal him?

The answer to that question first began to dawn upon me in a way I could articulate when one night, in my student days, a young couple from Italy, students as well, invited me to their home. They brought out four different courses for the dinner, a fine wine, and homemade desserts. I was flabbergasted. "Why would you do this for me?" I asked. "We barely know each other. Why have you chosen to treat me this way?" What could explain this behavior?

At first I asked what they might want from me. But as time passed they were not asking anything. And yet there was that extraordinary interest they showed in me. With time, though I saw their personal quirks as well, I noticed that there was also a striking depth to their minds, compassion in their hearts, and a limpid faith that judged everything with a simplicity that could not be gainsaid. Despite their limits, they seemed to me to be exceptionally human.

When they spoke of the community that they followed, I had no doubts but that this experience was from God. How did I know? I do not know what God looks like, but I do know something about humanity, and this human experience was more than just human. This is how the Son reveals the Father, through an exceptional humanity in front of which we must choose to accept where it comes from or abandon it. To accept this humanity is to accept the Son, and the one who sends him, his Father.

For your own purposes, Father, your Son has chosen to reveal to me his life with you. Let me keep saying yes to this choice, and offering this chance to others.

The Camel and the Donkey

Father Vincent Nagle, F.S.C.B.

"Come to me, all you who labor and are burdened, and I will give you rest. Take my yoke upon you and learn from me, for I am meek and humble of heart; and you will find rest for yourselves. For my yoke is easy, and my burden light."
(Mt 11: 28-30)

During my years in Morocco, I would take up jogging in the spring to work off my winter pounds. Thus I would spend many hours passing through the miles and miles of fields beyond my house, watching the farmers plow the fields for planting, lashing their animals forward. I noticed that the harnesses were always for two animals. And normally, they were not of equal size. I sometimes saw a tiny donkey yoked with an enormous camel. I understood then that this was done to encourage the larger animal, who carried virtually all of the weight, forward. The smaller one was yoked, but was not the one carrying the weight, or very little of it.

I understood then something of what Jesus is telling us when he encourages us to take up *his* yoke… *his*. We shrink back at the load pulled by this yoke. We feel our smallness, our incapacity to bear the weight. We gaze at the immense open field waiting to be plowed, and our hearts melt. But we are not yoked alone. It is *his* yoke, and we are but the small donkey, while he is the immense camel. He is not asking us to pull our fair share, but to be *with him* in our work.

Looking out ahead from beneath the yoke, of course, we do not see him – we only see the work, and how great it is. Again and again we are tempted to compare ourselves with the work, and to despair. But we have only to remember our yoking, our accepting to be harnessed *with* the Lord, to plow the fields of *his* Father. We have accepted to love with a love greater than our own, to face a mission larger than ourselves, because we have accepted to be yoked with his yoke, all easy and light.

Father, I am so tempted to shirk the weight of what you have asked of me. Don't let me miss the opportunity of being yoked with your Son, who is all light and compassion.

Seeing with the Eyes of Mercy
Helen M. Alvaré

"Have you not read in the law that on the sabbath the priests serving in the temple violate the sabbath and are innocent? I say to you, something greater than the temple is here. If you knew what this meant, 'I desire mercy, not sacrifice,' you would not have condemned these innocent men. For the Son of Man is Lord of the sabbath." (Mt 12: 5-8)

After the Pharisees censure Jesus and his apostles for plucking corn and eating it on the Sabbath (Mt 12: 1), Jesus calls to task their approach to the law. He reminds them, and us, what the law is *for*. It turns out, it does not exist to give full employment or a sense of superiority to the lawyers who make it or enforce it. It does not exist so that we can manufacture our own salvation. It points, rather, beyond itself to love of God, who among other things, is "Lord of the Sabbath."

How might we better understand how Jesus wants us to approach laws governing religious observance? In this passage from Matthew, Jesus offers a brief guide: "I desire mercy, not sacrifice." How might we faithfully understand this, since we are accustomed to thinking of sacrifice as an important part of the Christian life? It seems likely that Jesus is referring to a particular understanding of "sacrifice" in use during his time, i.e., the many rules and regulations about formal actions required or forbidden by religious law. How is this "sacrifice" different from mercy? Merciful behavior more likely begins with an encounter with another person and an effort to appreciate his or her situation. This encounter "moves" us. Mercy thus involves a predisposition to give more than justice strictly requires because we have been touched by another. In his encyclical *Caritas in Veritate*, Pope Benedict XVI passionately exhorts us to approach every human being in this merciful way. He writes that a willingness to give more than justice requires is the *sine qua non* of the Christian response to the experience of living alongside other peoples in the world. It begins in our families, but extends to the ends of the earth.

Merciful Father, nurture in me the ability to pay attention to others, to see others' needs, and to give generously.

Be Bold. Jesus Is Bold!

Helen M. Alvaré

"Which one of you who has a sheep that falls into a pit on the sabbath will not take hold of it and lift it out? How much more valuable a person is than a sheep. So it is lawful to do good on the sabbath." Then [Jesus] said to the man [with the withered hand], "Stretch out your hand." He stretched it out, and it was restored as sound as the other. (Mt 12: 11-13)

Would that each of us had the confidence in the truth that Jesus has! The confidence to say what is true, and then immediately to follow it up with action that indicates both our firm commitment to the truth, and the effectiveness of truth.

Jesus has just encountered the Pharisees who are claiming that existing religious laws about appropriate Sabbath activities forbid a wide variety of actions, even those easily classified as "doing good." Jesus not only verbally contradicts his accusers; he acts according to his conviction. He asserts that it is "lawful to do good on the Sabbath," then promptly says to the man with the one withered hand, "Stretch out your hand." Jesus miraculously restores the hand so that it is "as sound as the other."

Undoubtedly, in the course of your adult life, there have arisen moments when you knew the right thing to say or do, and it was contrary to the momentum swirling around you. But you demurred… said nothing, did nothing. Maybe you didn't believe your objection or observation could really change anything. Maybe you felt it would only inflame another person, and drive him or her further away from the truth. Either or both of these predictions might be true.

And yet… there is another factor that is perhaps too little weighed by many of us when considering whether to speak the truth in difficult environs. Have you noticed how bold people and advertisers and news outlets can be when they lie? I notice it all the time, and it doesn't concern just tiny matters either. They tell us that equality for women requires unlimited legal abortion. They tell us that the only way to "keep politics out of science" is to provide federal funds for embryo-destroying research.

Jesus' behavior counsels us to be bold when we speak the truth. And then to follow up on it with action. Apparently, this can make quite an impression.

Father, help me to know what is true, to speak it in season and out, and to act on it.

Where We Look for Hope

Helen M. Alvaré

This was to fulfill what had been spoken through Isaiah the prophet: "Behold, my servant whom I have chosen,/ my beloved in whom I delight;/ I shall place my spirit upon him,/ and he will proclaim justice to the Gentiles./ He will not contend or cry out,/ nor will anyone hear his voice in the streets./ A bruised reed he will not break,/ a smoldering wick he will not quench,/ until he brings justice to victory./ And in his name the Gentiles will hope." (Mt 12: 17-21)

Following Jesus' cure of the man with the withered hand and the Pharisees' subsequent decision to plot against Jesus' life, Matthew tells us that "this was to fulfill what had been spoken by Isaiah the prophet." Then he reports the prophecy referring to Jesus as a "servant" in whom God takes "delight," and a servant who "proclaims justice." Isaiah further promises that this servant will not operate in a dramatic or violent way; he will not show his strength even so far as to "break" a "bruised reed," or to "quench" a wick that is already "smoldering." Yet in Jesus, the "Gentiles will hope."

The recollection of Isaiah's servant prophecy at this point in his Gospel is unmistakably in tension with the events surrounding it. Jesus had just performed a miracle, curing a visibly withered hand before onlookers. After the prophecy is reported, Jesus cures a man who is both blind and mute (Mt 12: 22). This later miracle drives the Pharisees to even worse accusations. They now insist that Jesus' power is derived from the devil.

The confluence of all these events with the repetition of Isaiah's prophecy reminds us again that we should look to Jesus not on account of his splashy miracles, but because he has made himself the servant of all. This is a paradox to human beings. Our political, intellectual, and entertainment cultures are arenas in which actors contend loudly, even outrageously, for our attention. Temporary awards await those who take dramatic action and then claim credit for any results. Still, human beings come to understand over the long run who is worthy of honor. Even as we temporarily reward self-centered politicians or celebrities, we reserve a special place for the selfless servants: the Mother Teresa and Saint Francis figures. That the witness of such holy men and women is eventually acclaimed is a great sign of hope in the world.

Father, help me to remember where true hope lies, and to turn toward it for encouragement every day.

Seeing an Answered Prayer

Helen M. Alvaré

Then they brought to [Jesus] a demoniac who was blind and mute. He cured the mute person so that he could speak and see. All the crowd was astounded, and said, "Could this perhaps be the Son of David?" (Mt 12: 22-23)

My family and I helped set up a Catholic youth festival that happened to fall on the most glorious summer day imaginable, even though it took place in the middle of the usually humid month of July. Instead, though, it was one of those days you couldn't consider warm or cool. Just perfect. The sun was bright but not hot. The sky was a magnificent blue. It was like a movie. The next morning, at Mass with the religious order that put the festival together, the priest asked all of us playfully during his homily whether we really thought that the unusually gorgeous day was a coincidence. Didn't you pray for such weather? he asked. Wasn't it just exactly what you needed to entertain eight hundred adults and children out of doors for eight hours?

I have thought about that homily often since then. Like many Americans during the recent economic downturn, we've suffered our share of unemployment, but the school tuition and mortgage bills just keep coming. I pray to God for help, and what do you know? "Unexpected" good fortune pops up – some rebate we forgot about, or an offer to take up some discrete task for pay. When this happens, I remind myself to remind myself more often that God has never let us fall over the edge. "If he's told you once, he's told you one hundred times," I say to myself, "He's got that angle covered."

During Jesus' time on earth, even after he performed a miracle, the onlookers still asked themselves whether he was perhaps special, even "the Son of David." Perhaps they were worried because evil has its powers too, even the power of performing miracles. Yet even when Jesus was using his power to destroy demons – an unambiguously good sign – they held back their trust. Apparently, that tendency hasn't died in two millennia.

Loving Father, give me the eyes and the heart to recognize your work in my life. Thank you for listening to my prayers.

Hatred and Unreason

Helen M. Alvaré

The Pharisees [...] said, "This man drives out demons only by the power of Beelzebul, the prince of demons." But [Jesus] knew what they were thinking and said to them, "Every kingdom divided against itself will be laid waste, and no town or house divided against itself will stand." (Mt 12: 24-25)

The Pharisees unleash quite an accusation: Jesus "drives out demons only by the power of Beelzebul." They have nothing resembling proof for this slur. More likely, they arrive at their decision because Jesus has violated the script that forms the basis of their authority: the rules for Sabbath behavior. Furthermore, they probably conclude that if Jesus "gets away with this" then their power will be diminished and his increased. Their jealousy and anger overflow to the point where they insist Jesus must be in league with Satan himself. Perhaps their choice of words reflects a usage of the day. Yet in any day, to accuse another of channeling Satan is certainly an extreme charge.

While we can't imagine launching such an attack ourselves, we probably can imagine being driven to unbecoming or even irrational behavior on account of jealousy and the fear of loss of position. It seems that we human beings are quite an insecure lot. This is true whether we are talking of international political figures – posturing to convey a false strength – or of our own tendency to try to impress others by dropping names or dollar figures. This is apparently so common that one popular comedian has developed a skit in which an astronaut at a dinner party waits until everyone else has exhausted their travel stories before beginning to say: "When I first landed on the moon…"

We might then pity these Pharisees, while at the same time granting the wisdom of Jesus' rebuke. In their jealousy they are driven to irrationality (why would Satan help to drive out a demon?). They also refuse to see what is before their eyes: Jesus restores a sick body to beautiful health. God is reasonable and has made us in his image. God wills human good including bodily wholeness. The Pharisees' blindness and irrationality need to be called to task, as do ours.

Father of Truth, help me to recognize and submit to truth and to your authority, no matter how difficult this can be.

Evil and Beauty in the Present Kingdom
Helen M. Alvaré

*"If Satan drives out Satan, he is divided against himself;
how, then, will his kingdom stand? And if I drive out demons
by Beelzebul, by whom do your own people drive them out?
Therefore they will be your judges. But if it is by the Spirit of
God that I drive out demons, then the kingdom of God
has come upon you."* (Mt 12: 26-28)

God drives away evil. If we believe this, then "the kingdom of God has come upon [us]." There is an enormous amount of evil in the world, and we cannot fail to notice it. From individual acts of greed, theft, and violence, to whole systems and structures which – whether by design or merely as an indirect result of pursuing other goals like efficiency or profit – operate to oppress, or cheat, or exploit human persons. Short of evil, there is also the plague of uncertainty that can wear us down: the failing health of a spouse or a child or a parent, job instability, and relationship difficulties.

Our God attends to both body and soul. He calls on us to make our lives beautiful, beginning with the cleansing of repentance. He shows us with Jesus' physical cures throughout the Gospels that he really cares for our bodies. Our restored bodies further symbolize his beautiful kingdom.

It's too easy to spot that ugliness and sin are all around us. Sometimes I joke with friends that my constant struggle against dust and disorder in my own home is proof enough for me that this earth is just a way station on the path to a perfect (not to mention, more orderly) heaven. None of us is alone in finding it harder to see that the "kingdom of God has come upon [us]" than to know that evil exists. Still, we pray at every Mass that "heaven and earth are full of your glory." We sincerely believe Jesus when he tells us that he came "so that they might have life and have it more abundantly" (Jn 10: 10).

Despair is not an option for Christians. At the very least, then, we are required to submit our wills and our intellects to the Lord's gifts to us of beauty, wholeness, and happiness.

*Father, in dark times and in ordinary times, help me to understand
your beautiful will for your human creatures, and to cooperate with
you to communicate this to others.*

Yes to Doubt and Even Ignorance; No to Despair and Atheism

Helen M. Alvaré

"Whoever is not with me is against me, and whoever does not gather with me scatters. Therefore, I say to you, every sin and blasphemy will be forgiven people, but blasphemy against the Spirit will not be forgiven. And whoever speaks a word against the Son of Man will be forgiven; but whoever speaks against the holy Spirit will not be forgiven, either in this age or in the age to come." (Mt 12: 30-32)

There is no doubt that an average Christian can be forgiven for struggling over Jesus' sayings in this passage. On the one hand, Jesus is "firm," to put it mildly, when he says that "whoever is not with me is against me." We are also told bluntly that there is no prospect of forgiveness "either in this age or in the age to come" if we utter "blasphemy against the Spirit" or "speak against the holy Spirit." Jesus comforts us, though, with the prospect of forgiveness for "sin and blasphemy" or if we "speak... against the Son of Man."

One possible reading of this difficult material, from within the history and tradition of the Church, would be to understand that Jesus is issuing an authoritative call to open our minds and hearts to the truth of his divinity, his teachings, and to God's continuing action in history. At the same time, he is promising forgiveness if we have not had an opportunity in our lives to come to know Jesus Christ. I am thinking here in particular of people who are born into families and cultures divorced from Christianity.

Today the presence of over two billion Christians in the world testifies to the naturally attractive power of the person and word of Jesus. The Catholic popes, by their words and deeds, have earned the status of "world leaders." Still, many continue to deny God's existence. Fortunes are made from books decrying religion, and from research meddling with God's designs for the human being. The gift of human intellect, authored by God, is all too often used today as it was during the "early days" in the Garden – as a tool for trying to replace, or second-guess, God's authority. Yet Matthew reminds us that while humans may doubt and falter occasionally, those who have come to know God must continue to acknowledge his sovereignty, and the continuing action of the Holy Spirit in history.

Father, help lead me away from the temptation to pride, and to despair, and to pray rather, "Holy Spirit of truth, guide me."

A Hearts and Minds Campaign

Helen M. Alvaré

"From the fullness of the heart the mouth speaks. A good person brings forth good out of a store of goodness, but an evil person brings forth evil out of a store of evil. I tell you, on the day of judgment people will render an account for every careless word they speak. By your words you will be acquitted, and by your words you will be condemned." (Mt 12: 34-37)

Parents in particular know that when choosing what to stress with children – given the limits of time and patience on this side of heaven – you stress what goes into their hearts and minds, versus what goes into their stomachs or onto their backs. Because it's only the former that will help determine what comes out of their mouths and their lives as they grow up to be mature adults themselves. As a first-time mother, I grew upset when my toddler daughter gravitated to sequined t-shirts and junk food. I wanted her to look like the genteel, Victorian-curled baby of her grandmothers' dreams! Eventually I came to see the time that was getting chewed up during these battles and adopted instead a philosophy my husband and I came to summarize as: "If it won't land her in jail or in hell, it's OK." She soon grew out of her "junky" tastes, and I learned that we had made the right decision to invest the lion's share of our time into simply loving her, and guiding her when it came to the really crucial matters of faith and morals.

Jesus speaks directly about this. He says that we are what we have put into our hearts, to the point that we have to render an account for "every careless word" we speak.

So how do we get better results from our hearts and our mouths? Forming our hearts and minds is a formidable task if we think about its importance, but it's also a discrete and even ordinary matter of putting one foot in front of the other every day. It's choosing to pray, to spend time quietly with Jesus, to put beautiful spiritual reading on our agenda, to talk about the "things that matter" with admirable people. These are some of the continuous small decisions and improvements which, over time, help to purify us.

Father, help strengthen my will so that I might make a habit of reading, listening to, and learning about what is good and true.

A Parent's Love

Helen M. Alvaré

Some of the scribes and Pharisees said to [Jesus], "Teacher, we wish to see a sign from you." He said to them in reply, "An evil and unfaithful generation seeks a sign, but no sign will be given it except the sign of Jonah the prophet." (Mt 12: 38-39)

"If you misbehave, I'm going to lavish far more attention on you so that you know just how much I love you and want you to be good!" This is probably something only a devoted and experienced parent could utter to their child. Parents know that their children are only so mature, and that they often "act out" to secure their parents' attention. Parents thus feel that if they could do more to express their solidarity with the child's trials and tribulations, or do more to model good behavior, then their child might be significantly less likely to "act out." My husband and I received this advice from a fairly eminent pediatric doctor when we were very inexperienced and anxious new parents. To our shock, it worked like a charm!

Jesus' retort to the Pharisees recalls this wisdom to mind. When they demand a sign from him, and make him angry (as in Jesus' remark: "An evil and unfaithful generation seeks a sign"), Jesus promises "no sign" except the "sign of Jonah." Scripture scholars tell us that this reference to the prophet Jonah's three days and nights in the belly of the whale is meant to foretell Jesus' own death and resurrection. In other words, Jesus is promising us his own excruciatingly painful death, on a cross, for us, followed by his triumph over death with the resurrection. So this is "all we're getting," huh? This can only be explained by God's perfect parental devotion! This is not to underestimate the difficulty of understanding the full meaning of Jesus' death and resurrection. Many will have trouble seeing it as the answer to their cry for attention and for perfect love. This is true and God knows this. Still, this sign becomes increasingly comprehensible as human beings move through life and grow to understand that what every child of God really wants more than anything else in life is just that kind of attention and love.

Father, help me to understand, even a little, the size and strength of your love, and to show love like that to my own children, my own family, and the human family.

God's Way Is Wherever We Are

Helen M. Alvaré

"Just as Jonah was in the belly of the whale three days and three nights, so will the Son of Man be in the heart of the earth three days and three nights. At the judgment, the men of Nineveh will arise with this generation and condemn it, because they repented at the preaching of Jonah; and there is something greater than Jonah here." (Mt 12: 40-41)

One hears many stories recounting individuals' differing paths to faith. We know the story of Edith Stein who was moved to the Catholic faith by the writings of Saint Teresa of Ávila and the example of some Catholic friends. There is also the story of Mother Veronica Namoyo LeGoulard, P.C.C., recorded in her autobiography, *A Memory for Wonders*. Raised far from Catholic influences as a result of her parents' firm desire to raise her an atheist, she was conclusively turned to God by a little picture of Jesus on the cross that she spotted in the jewelry section of a catalogue. And then, of course, there is Thomas – "doubting Thomas" – who refused to believe in Jesus' resurrection until he could touch the evidence personally.

Jesus reminds the scribes and Pharisees of his time how the "men of Nineveh" repented and turned back to God due to the warning of Jonah alone. He tells them ominously that these righteous men will "condemn" those who refuse to believe, even when "something greater than Jonah" is right before their eyes!

What did it take for us to believe? Or, for some of us, what might it take to have a firm faith? What got us started on the path, and what helps to move us along the way, closer and closer to friendship with God? We all have our stories. One story might begin with the wonderful example of Catholic parents, or a friend, or role model. I have a friend, though, who says the opposite! It began for her with the *absence* of caring parents. This convinced her that she must have a Father as well as a Mother in heaven, as she had too little of either on earth! The variety of these stories, all by itself, tells us quite a bit. An infinite God will find ways as unique as we are to reach our hearts. Thank God for that!

Reach me, Father, wherever I am, and let me be reached by you!

Satisfying Our Longing for God
Helen M. Alvaré

"When an unclean spirit goes out of a person it roams through arid regions searching for rest but finds none. Then it says, 'I will return to my home from which I came.' But upon returning, it finds it empty, swept clean, and put in order. Then it goes and brings back with itself seven other spirits more evil than itself, and they move in and dwell there; and the last condition of that person is worse than the first." (Mt 12: 43-45)

When it comes to belief in God, it seems human nature abhors a vacuum. When people have God taken out of their upbringing, or their education, or their social life, or even their experience of national identity, they often fill that space with something or someone else. The outcomes are not pretty. I'm thinking of a couple I met whose children were deliberately denied the practice of any particular faith because of the father's feeling that religion was for poor, uneducated families (his past) rather than for well-off, educated people (his present and his future). Each of the children has migrated toward either a religiously-styled cult, or toward education involving the study of one of the major world religions. Sometimes political systems or discrete social groups exclude God from their ways of understanding human beings and the events of history. What often results? The elevating of another thing or person – money, or environmental consciousness, or human physical or intellectual accomplishment, or a particular political figure – to the role usually filled by God or by religious practices.

Jesus instructs us about this phenomenon in his story about the person who is cleansed of a demon which had previously possessed him. When the demon returns to observe his former "home," he finds it "empty" and proceeds to occupy it again along with "seven other spirits more evil than itself." This, of course, doesn't just happen to others, but also to ourselves as we travel through the stages of our lives. At different times, we are more or less mindful of God, more or less devoted to spending time with him in quiet companionship, more or less able to see the world through the lens of our faith. But if God is not within us, we can be sure something else will fill the space, and it just won't be – can't be – nearly as wonderful.

Father, let me be mindful of you, and let me see the world and the people in it as you see them. Fill my heart and soul.

Obedience as Freedom

Helen M. Alvaré

While [Jesus] was still speaking to the crowds, his mother and his brothers appeared outside, wishing to speak with him. [Someone told him, "Your mother and your brothers are standing outside, asking to speak with you."] But he said in reply to the one who told him, "Who is my mother? Who are my brothers?" And stretching out his hand toward his disciples, he said, "Here are my mother and my brothers. For whoever does the will of my heavenly Father is my brother, and sister, and mother."
(Mt 12: 46-50)

Jesus is not denying his love for his family, as the world understood "family," but rather emphasizing the outsized importance of "doing the will of [his] heavenly Father" when he says to the crowd, "Who is my mother? Who are my brothers?" He is reminding us that if we do his will, we are as family to him.

But wait, what do we make of the expression "do his will"? This is not a commonly heard phrase today. In fact some parenting "experts" tell us that it's downright harsh for a parent to tell a child: "Because I said so." Other observers assert that "doing another's will" generally leads to the oppression of the weak. Isn't the ruling idea today that obedience is "out" and freedom (read: license) "in"? "Thinking outside the box," "breaking all the rules," "doing it my way"? Don't advertisers and technology gurus insist that without these experiences, there is no freedom or innovation?

In short, modern culture wrongly conveys the idea that there's never a good time to toe the line. It's not hard to see how this notion gets extended into the realm of faith; but it's a terrible fit. For it is the Father's will that we should live in his image and likeness, in love and for love, while exercising our gifts of intellect and free will. It is his will that we should imitate him through his Son, Jesus, in every way possible, by living in loving communion with God and with all who are "given" us as our nearest neighbors. As anyone who has aged wisely will tell you, these are the only lifestyles sure to bring true freedom to the human person. It's not about me and my will. That way leads to frustration and loneliness. It really is about God and his will for us. Shockingly enough for Americans, this is great good news.

Father, help me to do your will, and to know the real freedom to be had as a child of God.

Sowing the Field of Prayer

Father Kevin Kraft, O.P.

[Jesus] spoke to them at length in parables, saying: "A sower went out to sow. And as he sowed, some seed fell on the path, and birds came and ate it up. Some fell on rocky ground, where it had little soil. It sprang up at once because the soil was not deep, and when the sun rose it was scorched, and it withered for lack of roots. Some seed fell among thorns, and the thorns grew up and choked it. But some seed fell on rich soil, and produced fruit, a hundred or sixty or thirtyfold." (Mt 13: 3-8)

In the Andes Mountains, where the *campesinos* plant seeds one by one in furrows and painstakingly cover each one with soil, the "broadcast" method of planting seeds described in today's Gospel sounds extremely wasteful, not to mention downright foolish. But the point of this parable, taken globally, is that this method of sowing still "pays off": even if only a quarter of the seed falls on good, productive soil, it bears such abundant fruit that it repays the labor of the farmer. So too, the work of God, even when it is (apparently) not very "efficient," and suffers frustration in many quarters, still "pays off." When people truly open themselves to God's action, God's grace is "superabundant," making them tremendously fruitful – enough to make up for all those who don't produce anything.

When we pray, are we not like the farmer in today's Gospel selection, where our poor efforts at times are scooped up before they even germinate, and other times are too superficial, and their joy is short-lived and fragile? At other times our prayers are squelched by anxieties and concerns, by attractions and false "needs," and produce no fruit in our lives. But sometimes, just sometimes, our efforts at prayer somehow fall on rich and fertile soil, free of pecking birds, stones, and weeds, and then our perseverance more than "pays off" in fruits of grace in our lives. However, in reality it is not our efforts that "pay off"; it is God who rewards our poor efforts with his disproportionate generosity. Thus, such moments make up for all the sterile or fruitless attempts at prayer that we've experienced. Knowing that not all of our prayers will produce life-giving fruits, but aware that sometimes they will – and in great abundance, let us continue to sow in the field of prayer trusting in a harvest which will more than repay our efforts.

Loving Father, repay our poor efforts to cultivate a life of prayer with an abundant harvest, that we might grow in your grace and come to know you face to face.

Use It or Lose It

Father Kevin Kraft, O.P.

"To anyone who has, more will be given and he will grow rich; from anyone who has not, even what he has will be taken away."
(Mt 13: 12)

Some twelve years ago when I was in Latin America, a United States friar who's an internet whiz came to put our studentate on-line and help us move into the twenty-first century. A friend of his came along to set up the hardware, while he mostly taught us how to use it. He also gave a one-week crash course on how to construct web-pages. I was twenty years older than the students learning the same task – a distinct disadvantage as far as computer knowledge goes – but I still managed to hold my own and learn the tricks of the trade. By week's end, I could do just about everything the students could. But unlike them, over the next five to six years I never had occasion (or sufficient time and interest) to apply the knowledge and to practice creating web-pages, whereas they put the same know-how into practice immediately. When, six to eight years later, I finally had the desire to elaborate a web-page, I discovered I'd forgotten everything I'd learned on that score. I'd lost it because I'd never used it. As in many other areas of learning, the rule seems to be: use it or lose it!

So too in the spiritual life: we must "use" what we have, or else lose it. What we have received we must "give away" if we are to keep it. Our faith becomes stronger when we share it; our understanding grows more acute when we teach others; our courage more real as we strengthen the faint-hearted. This is perhaps the secret of missionary dynamism: faith "given away" becomes more vital. I was always amazed at the Scripture reflection groups there, where barely literate ladies with a very elementary understanding of the Scriptures nevertheless put me (with my years of theological training) to shame, in their readiness and zeal to share with others something of the riches of God's Word which they had discovered.

Father God, teach us how to be generous as you are generous, and how to remain in your grace by sharing your love with those around us.

Blessed Your Eyes That See!

Father Kevin Kraft, O.P.

"'Gross is the heart of this people,/ they will hardly hear with their ears,/ they have closed their eyes,/ lest they see with their eyes/ and hear with their ears/ and understand with their heart and be converted,/ and I heal them.'/ But blessed are your eyes, because they see, and your ears, because they hear. Amen, I say to you, many prophets and righteous people longed to see what you see but did not see it, and to hear what you hear but did not hear it." (Mt 13: 15-17)

Many of us have said about a deceased loved one on a very special occasion: "Oh, I wish Dad were here; he'd love to witness this day!" or "If Grandma could only see her granddaughter graduate from medical school!" We are often intensely aware of how key people in our lives died before seeing the fruition of their dreams and hopes.

So it is too with the Church and the kingdom of God. Many centuries of believers before Christ awaited the day of redemption, the coming of the Messiah, but did not see it. They longed to hear the words of God, not from a prophet's mouth but spoken by God himself, but never heard it. We Christians have seen and heard, touched and felt the Word who is life. Yet even among the followers of Christ, there were many Christians of past generations who longed to see the day when Christians would seek unity among themselves, when the liturgy would be in the language of the people, when popes would travel around the world to visit their flock, when pastors would be courageous in denouncing social injustices (and humble in recognizing the sins of Church members, beginning with the clergy), when the handicapped would be accepted into the priesthood, when the laity would "come of age," and married people be recognized as saints… Yes, many prophets and religious people among Christian believers have longed to see and hear things that only we of the latter twentieth and early twenty-first centuries have seen and heard.

Gracious Father, Lord of history, thank you for allowing us to live in this blessed, graced, privileged time! We praise you for the period of human history in which you have placed us!

Satan the Pigeon

Father Kevin Kraft, O.P.

"The seed sown on the path is the one who hears the word of the kingdom without understanding it, and the evil one comes and steals away what was sown in his heart." (Mt 13: 19)

The "evil one" comes not only "prowling around like a roaring lion looking for [someone] to devour" (1 Pt 5: 8), as a wolf in sheep's clothing (Mt 7: 15), as an astute, deceitful serpent (Gn 3: 1), or a grotesque, seven-headed, ten-horned dragon (Rv 13: 1). Satan also appears as apparently innocuous, fluttering little birds – sparrows, perhaps, or pigeons, such as flock in parks to peck at seed scattered by bird-lovers – a telling comparison! He can just as easily frustrate the saving power of the Word in our lives by distracting us as by terrorizing us in direct confrontation. All he needs to do is gobble up the Word before it enters into our understanding!

Imagine! Robbed of a precious treasure before we realize the value of what is taken from us! An unopened gift not yet discovered disappears from under our nose! Through lack of understanding we may be unconcerned about preserving the Word we hear: careless, distracted listeners… If even priests can be distracted in the liturgy, how much more those who simply "attend" Mass and do not prepare the readings: "In one ear and out the other!"

Let us prepare our hearts and minds to receive the Word in private reading and liturgical celebrations. The key to assimilating the Word is – according to today's Gospel text – understanding it. Without understanding, the readings easily "escape" us. They take no root in us. Try memorizing something you don't understand! (Very difficult, because you can't "master" the text until you understand it. It's better to get the drift of a text first, and then memorize it.) So too, by striving to understand the Word of God that comes to us in the daily liturgy (taking time to read, study, and pray over the Mass texts), we can much more easily conserve them in our hearts and minds. Only then will the Word sown in us be able to mature and bear fruit.

Father of the Word incarnate, help us to understand and value the words of Christ your Son, that they may take root, grow within us, and bear abundant fruit in our lives.

No Roots, No Authentic Joy

Father Kevin Kraft, O.P.

"The seed sown on rocky ground is the one who hears the word and receives it at once with joy. But he has no root and lasts only for a time. When some tribulation or persecution comes because of the word, he immediately falls away." (Mt 13: 20-21)

This is one of the few biblical texts in which *joy* is a counter-sign. Here it is a superficial joy, a "light" view of the Gospel message: happiness at the Good News without readiness to commit oneself to it. In today's reading, "receives it at once with joy" suggests an unreflected embrace of something one may later throw off because of not having deliberated enough. It bespeaks a lack of serious purpose (not measuring one's strength and determination against the rigors of one's goals, not preparing oneself for sacrifices ahead). Someone may be enthusiastic about marriage, having children, a professional career, religious life or priesthood… but may not have faced up to the demanding aspects these life choices involve: a "fair-weather friend."

"At once" sounds very generous, even exemplary (as in Abraham, Isaiah, Mary, Joseph, and Matthew's prompt response to God's call). Prompt obedience is indeed a saintly attitude, provided it is founded on a deep commitment to God's will. What is that "deep commitment"?

In biology, roots are key to a plant's nourishment. "No root" means no nourishment, and, once the seed's nutritional content has been exhausted, it means death. Cut branches thrust into the earth will not survive, even in rich potting soil with regular watering… unless they develop roots very quickly… In fact, any plant will soon wither and die if it lacks an adequate root system! So too, in our life of faith we need "roots" to grow stronger through the assimilation of vital elements… We can tap the riches of our Catholic tradition through adult catechesis (e.g., ongoing Bible study), diverse types of prayer, approaching the sacraments, reading spiritual works, Church history, and lives of the saints… Together these constitute a "root system" for our ongoing spiritual nourishment and the gradual development of a truly joyful Christian life.

Father, ground and source of our life, help us to assimilate the incredible riches of our faith so that, well-nourished by your manifold gifts, we may bring forth fruits according to your will.

The Strangler Fig

Father Kevin Kraft, O.P.

"The seed sown among thorns is the one who hears the word, but then worldly anxiety and the lure of riches choke the word and it bears no fruit." (Mt 13: 22)

Plants, and even large trees, can be strangled by other plants! The "strangler fig" is a case in point. It is an unusual tree which begins its life's journey as an "epiphyte": a plant-parasite living off the air, water, and sunlight, nestled in the branches or crevices of another tree. Later it sends down roots to the earth below, and when it touches earth, it begins a process of rapid growth, enveloping the "host" tree and eventually strangling it, reducing it to a simple pedestal for its own growth. The strangler fig may not actually kill the other tree, but may render it sterile, or at least sickly and of pathetic production.

Our mission is to "go and bear fruit" (Jn 15: 16b). There are many ways to get strangled (not only with a pair of hands around your neck): one can be strangled by an addiction to the media (radio, television, internet, cell phones); strangled by the appetite for fashionable clothes, chic places, and spending money; strangled by the need to drop names, impress people, and maintain an "image"; strangled by an imperious need to drink (alcoholism); strangled by the urge to make ever bigger profits, and risk more and more in doing so...

Worldly cares and material riches are not bad in themselves, indeed a certain level of involvement in both is necessary for human life. What seems to be the problem here is a question of priorities. Putting material concerns ahead of one's relationship with the Lord is to "put the cart before the horse." One must seek first the kingdom of God, "and all these things will be given you besides" (Mt 6: 33). Putting God absolutely first in our priorities will allow us to bear fruit and experience God's Providence in the provision of our material needs. "Cast all your worries upon him [God] because he cares for you" (1 Pt 5: 7).

Loving Father, do not let worldly anxieties and the lure of riches strangle us into spiritual sterility. Help us to seek first your kingdom, and trust you for our other needs.

Amazing Fertility!

Father Kevin Kraft, O.P.

"But the seed sown on rich soil is the one who hears the word and understands it, who indeed bears fruit and yields a hundred or sixty or thirtyfold." (Mt 13: 23)

A hundredfold! Nature is prolific, especially in the reproductive organs of plants and animals (milkweed seedpods, acorns, apple seeds, kernels of corn on a single ear, puffball spores, protozoa, anthills and beehives, rabbit reproduction, fish roe…). It more than suffices for the survival of species: it serves, rather, for its increase. Even if only 1 percent of the seeds produced germinate, or only 5 percent of the animals spawned survive, there would still be a net growth in the population of that plant, of that animal species. And so even though some members of the species remain sterile, or are cut off before reaching productivity, those organisms that do reproduce more than compensate for all the other losses.

The most enduring joy of teachers, preachers, counselors, and parents are one's protégés who have truly assimilated and understood one's message, who have benefited from one's services and guidance, and who in all likelihood will bear good fruit the rest of their lives. They make up for all the headaches and heartaches, all the failures and disappointments that orienting other people involves. Several years ago I worked in a religious formator's training program and was myself a formator in Lima, Peru. A massive number of young men and women, religious, and clergy were being formed for the consecrated life and ministry in the Church. It is my enduring joy to know that I had some part in the religious formation of so many young people who are serving the Church today. That joy is magnified when those I taught or guided as seminarians are ordained priests, when the religious I knew come to final profession and choose to say their definitive "yes!" to the Lord, or when others go off to the missions, and bear fruits of generosity and holiness.

How have you experienced the "hundredfold" in your own life, family, or Christian commitment?

Father of mercies, we praise you and bless you for the fruitfulness of our Christian lives which is your gift, and we ask you to multiply still more the workers in your kingdom.

Time-Delayed Scandals

Father Kevin Kraft, O.P.

[Jesus] proposed another parable to them. "The kingdom of heaven may be likened to a man who sowed good seed in his field. While everyone was asleep his enemy came and sowed weeds all through the wheat, and then went off. When the crop grew and bore fruit, the weeds appeared as well." (Mt 13: 24-26)

The "weeds" here ("bearded tares") are like counterfeit wheat, closely resembling the plant and young heads of true wheat, discernible only in the last stages of growth, and poisonous for human consumption. So too the scandal of false Christians in the midst of the Church: very difficult to distinguish, they appear in the midst of Christian activities, and seek to poison their works. Many of us believers have experienced the horror of discovering evil sown in our plans and programs, among our families and friends, our parishes and dioceses, especially at a mature point in time ("When the crop… bore fruit, the weeds appeared…"). When we think we know with whom we're dealing, living, and working hand in hand, then suddenly comes a rude shock and disappointment. We can only distinguish those who are not "of God" by their fruits (see Mt 7: 16-20), i.e., after the fact. Evil, in order to attract people to it, bears the appearance of good, and can only be "known" in its fruits, which reveal its innate perversity.

This parable speaks of a damaging growth consciously sown among the good crop by the hand of an "enemy." Satan indeed tries to "sabotage" God's choicest works, the most productive branches of the Church, and communities of striking holiness, by infiltrating people in his service (perhaps even unaware of being his instruments), in order to vitiate from the inside, if it were possible, the work of the Spirit. But God's plan is not so easily derailed nor spoilt. Jesus knows what is in the human heart, what we are capable of doing, how we may be misled without even being conscious of the wrong we do (see Jn 2: 24-25). Even if a particular part of the Church is marred or destroyed, or a given ministry or institution ceases to exist, God's purposes in the Church will never fail: "I am with you always, until the end of the age" (Mt 28: 20).

Lord of the harvest and Father of all believers, strengthen your Church to face the many scandals of our day without losing faith in your providential care for us.

The "Double Whammy"

Father Kevin Kraft, O.P.

"The slaves of the householder came to him and said [...], 'Do you want us to go and pull [the weeds] up?' He replied, 'No, if you pull up the weeds you might uproot the wheat along with them. Let them grow together until harvest; then at harvest time I will say to the harvesters, "First collect the weeds and tie them in bundles for burning; but gather the wheat into my barn."'"

(Mt 13: 27-30)

This parable speaks of the "double whammy" dealt to workers in God's kingdom. After the first scandal (discovery of the enemy's sabotage), there is a second: that of the Master's response to the problem (his order not to uproot at once the poisonous weeds). This can be a greater difficulty for believers than the discovery of evil in the Church. Well-intentioned workers in the Lord's plantation may espouse an ill-advised, premature judgment which could be disastrous for the very harvest they think to be serving by their offer to "go and pull up" the weeds. We cannot judge things rightly, and may do more harm than good.

The dividing line between good and evil runs through each human heart. The simplistic temptation to categorize human beings into "good" and "evil" is a fallacy, and can do great damage to the cause of good in the world by uprooting the wheat along with the weeds. (Here the comparison lags: weeds never turn into wheat, nor vice versa, but Satan's unknowing instruments may be won over to the kingdom of God, *and* true believers may one day fall into Satan's clutches.) It is an understandable but ultimately destructive tendency to want to deal with problems in the Church rapidly and according to human wisdom. Frustration with Church authorities who do not "act on" problems by taking decisive steps to rid the Church of scandals may be one manifestation of this tendency. The temptation to seek a "Church of the perfect" by policing one's ecclesial context and denouncing abuses to the bishop may be another. It is not a matter of making peace with such evil elements in the Church today, but of leaving the judgment to God and trusting that he will sift out the wheat from the chaff in due time.

This "double whammy" is really an invitation to enter more deeply into the mystery of the Church, human and divine.

When we do not understand your ways of working in the Church, wounded by sin and evil, help us, Father, to trust in the designs of your Providence, as obedient servants of your kingdom.

Subversive Mustard Seeds!

Father Kevin Kraft, O.P.

"The kingdom of heaven is like a mustard seed that a person took and sowed in a field. It is the smallest of all the seeds, yet when full-grown it is the largest of plants. It becomes a large bush, and the 'birds of the sky come and dwell in its branches.'"
(Mt 13: 31-32)

In 1975, when the Communists took over Vietnam after the fall of Saigon, they attempted to squelch discreetly the power of the Catholic Church, rather than risk an outright persecution (which, they had found, could be tremendously counterproductive for atheistic regimes). The government decided that only two organizations would be officially recognized and permitted in each Catholic parish: the choir and the Dominican Laity. Choirs existed solely to perform religious songs in Church services, and the Dominican Laity groups were at the time pious gatherings of old folks praying the rosary; both seemed innocuous enough to the Communist officials. No political militancy was to be feared from either quarter, and they were seen as apt groups to accompany the demise of a decadent Church of the aging generation.

Little did the government realize, the latter groups had within them the dynamism of the Gospel and a solid constitution based upon personal, contemplative, and liturgical prayer, ardent study of the Word of God, the truths of the faith, and signs of the times, hands-on experience of democracy in their fraternal community life, and a very broad, prophetic, evangelizing mission. Over the past thirty-five years (since the Communist policy designed to ease Catholics out of existence), Dominican lay groups have became the backbone of the Catholic Church in Vietnam, numbering now over one hundred thousand members with great cohesion, courage, and dynamism in their Catholic witness and action. An insignificant little group of old ladies praying the rosary turned out to be the germ of a mighty tree which gives shelter to the "birds of the sky"!

In our own experience, have we not at times discounted or even despised projects, groups, or people as being unfit, incompetent, "of no use," which are in fact God's chosen instruments for his mighty works?

Father, give us eyes to see the world with Gospel criteria, and let us rejoice to discover the mustard seeds of today growing into mighty plants of your kingdom.

Leavening Work

Father Kevin Kraft, O.P.

[Jesus] spoke to them another parable. "The kingdom of heaven is like yeast that a woman took and mixed with three measures of wheat flour until the whole batch was leavened." (Mt 13: 33)

Many years ago I lived in a small religious community where we baked our own bread. I was happy to learn and practice the art of bread-making. One of the things which never ceased to amaze and intrigue me was the slow, silent, hidden action of the leaven causing the warm dough to rise until the bread pan filled out and swelled up like the belly of a pregnant woman. I don't mean the comparison to be irreverent; rather it seems quite fitting: both are mysteries of hidden life growing slowly, well nigh imperceptibly, silently; both are a vital part of the daily life of women and men, a cause for celebration.

So too in the spiritual life, there are unseen, unnoticed, "invisible" contributions which uplift the entire mass of dough (a given group or environment, the Church or society itself). My mother observed in her parish pastoral team meetings an irksome phenomenon: a woman friend would offer creative suggestions which were rejected out of hand at the time, but which would resurface several months later, proposed this time by the pastor as his *own* "bright ideas," and *then* they would be implemented! Mom used to reason with this lady, chagrined by what she considered the "intellectual piracy" and male chauvinism of the pastor: first, it wasn't clear whether the pastor even remembered that these ideas had first been proposed by someone else, and second, the really important thing was that the bright ideas took root and were finally implemented, not who first suggested them. At least under that pastor, such preparatory contributions which germinated in silence, and finally reached fruition as the pastor's proposals were regular occurrences. This was "behind the scenes" work, like the leavening process: planting an idea whose authorship might be for ever unknown, unrecognized, but which eventually changed the face of the parish.

Father of life, teach us to be patient as your life is brought to maturity in us; let us humbly accept the processes and hidden contributions your kingdom asks of us.

Only in Parables

Father Kevin Kraft, O.P.

All these things Jesus spoke to the crowds in parables. He spoke to them only in parables, to fulfill what had been said through the prophet:/ "I will open my mouth in parables,/ I will announce what has lain hidden from the foundation [of the world]."
(Mt 13: 34-35)

Certain people in different ages and in various religions and cultures were notorious for speaking in enigmas and riddles. They would respond to questions with other questions, or sum up a complicated situation with a pithy proverb: Greek "oracles," Shakespearian characters, Jewish rabbis, traditional African elders, wise people in many illiterate cultures... It seems they were able to express *more* about reality that way (by having recourse to suggestive images, pithy statements, enigmatic expressions, and open questions) than by using conventional (conceptual, discursive) language.

A Dominican priest in Arequipa, Peru, Father Crispín Jiménez, for many years would spend all week long hammering out an intuition for his Sunday message and whittling it down into a catchy proverb or an amusing poem. Often, during community recreation, the other friars were the "guinea pigs" on whom he would try out his rough drafts. ("What do you think of this...?") When Sunday came, he would teach the finished product (no more than a few lines in length) to the people at Mass, drilling them on it until they could recite it by memory, and then "take them through it," explaining the significance of the poetic synthesis he'd elaborated. It was uncanny: he both annoyed people with his "memoristic" methodology and amused and enlightened them with his original insights. He managed to leave a lasting impression on them, and open to them new points of view, something like the Catholic Worker patriarch Peter Maurin's "Easy Essays" did (and still do) for generations of United States Catholics.

So, is Jesus' recourse to parables for the sake of hiding/limiting the revelation of the "mysteries of the kingdom" to his disciples, or is it not rather to *reveal* God's plan ("announce what has lain hidden...") in all the richness of its meaning to those who can accept it?

Father whose ways are shrouded in mystery, help us to live with the questions your Son raises for us until we also are capable of living the answers.

Jesus the Educator

Father Kevin Kraft, O.P.

*Then, dismissing the crowds, [Jesus] went into the house.
His disciples approached him and said, "Explain to us
the parable of the weeds in the field." (Mt 13: 36)*

When teaching courses in seminary, I'd begin each course with an exploratory survey, have a mid-term dialogue with the students on how the course was going, and end the semester with a post-examination student evaluation of the course, the teacher, and their own participation. Good pedagogy requires that learners be free to express doubts, questions, objections, and suggestions, and to receive adequate responses to their personal queries, desires, and complaints. It calls for educators to be constantly attentive to verify levels of understanding and difficulties the students may encounter in grasping key elements of the material.

Jesus was a great educator, as we can see in the confidence he inspired in his disciples, shown when they asked him questions, admitted their lack of understanding, and even disagreed with some of his teachings.

In today's Gospel the apostles simply didn't "get" the message of the parable! They were afraid to ask in public, but at least asked in private! (Even today workshop facilitators find that people are more willing to pose anonymous written questions or reveal their doubts in private, than to broach touchy questions publicly.) Here, the private question of the apostles is a new starting point which permits Jesus to pass to a second level: the application or explanation of the parable. We, too, ought to ask, question, and seek to *understand* our faith so that we can receive clarification, rather than remain in ignorance or doubt.

Now if even Jesus' teachings were not understood at first by his own disciples, how much more may Church teachings (considerably more complex and extensive than Jesus' original message) be misunderstood (given the much more diverse audience of Catholics around the world today) – unless there is an opportunity to ask questions, clarify things, and receive a synthesis of the teachings!

Father of our Lord Jesus Christ, open our hearts and minds to understand the teachings of Christ, your Son, and of his bride, the Church, that we may enjoy fullness of life.

Conflict in the Field

Father Kevin Kraft, O.P.

[Jesus] said in reply, "He who sows good seed is the Son of Man,
the field is the world, the good seed the children of the kingdom.
The weeds are the children of the evil one, and the enemy who
sows them is the devil. The harvest is the end of the age,
and the harvesters are angels." (Mt 13: 37-39)

This parable has a different focus from earlier ones dealing with seeds. Here *people* are the seeds, both good and bad. The emphasis is not on the diverse receptions of the Word of God (as in the parable of the sower), but on the origin and nature of the seeds sown. Those sown by Jesus are "good seed"; those sown by "the enemy" are "weeds." It sounds all "black and white," "cut and dried" (not true to the fickle, changeable nature and destiny of human beings), yet the point of this parable is the intermingling of two very different types of plants, and letting the two grow side by side until the harvest.

Some people are motivated and inspired by God's project (the kingdom of heaven), whereas – we must be realistic – others are motivated and take their cues from a contrary "project," the reign of evil. These latter are those who pursue corruption under cover of respectability: sexual predators, drug dealers, thieves big and small… the list could go on and on. As long as we remain naïvely optimistic, and consider everybody's project equally valid, we have our heads in the sand, and may be the victims of unscrupulous dealings by those directed by the devil. However, at "the end of the age" (Mt 13: 40) a judgment will be made "as a shepherd separates the sheep from the goats" (Mt 25: 32). This judgment, it should be noted, will not be entrusted to human beings. While recognizing the spiritual warfare that is taking place today on the world scene and in our own family, neighborhood, or place of business, we are not to judge others – only to distinguish healthy fruits of Christian living from the rotten fruits that betray sinful lives. That much we can and must do, but it is not ours to condemn others. Our task is to bear good fruit for God's kingdom.

Father and Lord of the harvest, help us to live with integrity and unwavering faith amid the ambiguities of this world, and so bring forth a harvest of good fruits.

The End of Scandals

Father Kevin Kraft, O.P.

"Just as weeds are collected and burned [up] with fire, so will it be at the end of the age. The Son of Man will send his angels, and they will collect out of his kingdom all who cause others to sin and all evildoers. They will throw them into the fiery furnace, where there will be wailing and grinding of teeth."
(Mt 13: 40-42)

What do we do with weeds? Innocuous ones are trampled underfoot, left on the pavement to die, or thrown on a compost heap. Dangerous ones (e.g., poison ivy, deadly nightshade) or particularly obnoxious ones (like brambles or nettles) are disposed of in such a way that they will neither cause havoc nor return to multiply. Such weeds may be dumped into a river, thrown out with the trash, or burned; one way or another, they are definitively "disposed of."

Dangerous elements in the Christian community are scandal-givers, those who "cause (induce) others to sin," doers of evil. I'm not speaking of those who succumb to sins of weakness but of true evildoers. These latter are not to be handled lightly; they are the really dangerous plants which can ruin the whole crop, like bearded tares whose grain *looks* like wheat, but whose kernels are poisonous for human consumption.

We are told that there will be an end to the scandals, there will be a judgment that is just, and we will see a separation of the wicked from the just. Must we await the end of time, Christ's return in glory? For the absolute, definitive judgment, yes, but even now we may be consoled to see anticipatory signs of God's judgment, as evildoers are unmasked, immoral practices corrected, and policies adopted which help people to be good. Even in human solutions to deeply rooted problems we can see something of God's just judgment anticipated.

Loving Father, who know better than any of us the ravages of sin in your Church, may we be helped by truly evangelical policies which lead us all to lives of greater holiness.

157

From the Ashes, Light

Father Kevin Kraft, O.P.

"Then the righteous will shine like the sun in the kingdom of their Father. Whoever has ears ought to hear." (Mt 13: 43)

Today's text suggests that the Church will shine more resplendently after repenting of sinful actions, being purified of harmful practices, and making amends for clergymen who unworthily exercised their ministry as Christ's ambassadors. So it happened in the Protestant Reformation, the French Revolution, and many other periods of conflict when Church members were judged, accused, and she herself painfully purified: from the ashes emerged new vitality, new expressions of holiness and mission, new credibility before the world.

Jesus promises that after judgment "the righteous will shine like the sun" (Mt 13: 43). This phrase recalls the Book of Daniel (12: 3) where the "wise" and those who "lead [others] to justice" will "shine brightly" and "be like the stars forever." This text suggests that the "righteous" in today's parable are not so much those who "have it all together" spiritually, those who have a self-contained holiness, but rather those who lead exemplary lives: catechists, parents, teachers, spiritual directors... These are the counterparts of the evildoers who "cause others to sin" (v. 41): *they lead others to holiness* by their example and encouragement, their witness of Christian integrity. Today many courageous and compassionate bishops and priests are plotting a new path, blazing a trail that other sectors of society could well follow in order to heal and amend their own wrongdoings. Whoever has ears to hear...!

Father, give us eyes to see and ears to hear the examples of righteousness in the people around us, in our own days, and to discover your goodness reflected in them.

Buried Treasure

Father John Dominic Corbett, O.P.

"The kingdom of heaven is like a treasure buried in a field,
which a person finds and hides again, and out of joy goes and
sells all that he has and buys that field." (Mt 13: 44)

Buried treasure isn't the sort of thing one usually finds in a field. Walking in a field one would expect to find weeds, tin cans, broken off bits of wooden platforms, rusted pipes, and so forth. But suppose you were going to be late for the bus one morning on your way to work and you decided to take a shortcut through the backyard of an abandoned home. Running to catch your bus you trip over something only just protruding from the surface of the soil. You mutter something unprintable and then notice that what you tripped over has a sort of glitter to it. Your curiosity is quickened and so you putter about and remove some more dirt. A beginning of a box appears. It looks solid. Now you have to check this out. You forget about work for that morning and you go to the hardware store to get a shovel. You dig. The box opens. Inside the box are diamonds and rubies and gold. What are the odds of that happening? There are no odds for something like that. This is the day that changes everything for you. This is the day of your life.

You rebury the treasure. You don't have much good credit so you sell everything that you have. Your friends think you are nuts for investing your last dime in an iffy property, especially with the housing market so unpromising. You don't care. You know what you have bought. You are joyful because you know that everything you give up to get that house and yard and treasure is nothing at all compared to what you receive.

The kingdom of heaven is like this. Except that you don't really find it by accident. It finds you. This treasure had your name on the box. It was a setup from the start. Finding it is the beginning and only the beginning of your joy.

Father, show us the kingdom of God that is already in our midst.
Help us to recognize the treasure you have placed within our
grasp. Help us to understand that you only want to enrich us beyond
our wildest dreams.

The Train Set

Father John Dominic Corbett, O.P.

"The kingdom of heaven is like a merchant searching for fine pearls. When he finds a pearl of great price, he goes and sells all that he has and buys it." (Mt 13: 45-46)

Graham Greene once wrote a short story entitled "A Hint of an Explanation," which I summarize here. David grew up as a Catholic in a small village in Scotland in which nearly everyone went to Church. The exception was a man named Blacker who was the village baker and the village atheist. He was widely known to detest the Catholic Church.

There was a toy shop in the town and in the window of that toy shop appeared a long and beautiful train. Blacker had had occasion to observe David looking into that window and obviously dying to have that set.

One day Blacker met David in the street and said that he had a deal to propose. If David would only pretend to receive communion one Sunday and to put the host in his pocket and later deliver the host to him, he would deliver the train set to his front doorstep the next morning. "It's got to be consecrated, mind. It's no good if it's not consecrated," Blacker said. "Why do you want the host?" David asked. "Never you mind. That's my business," said Blacker.

David actually started to do the terrible thing Blacker suggested. He took the host out of his mouth and placed it in his pocket and hid it in a napkin. And he spent one terrible day and one terrible sleepless night with what, he was becoming more conscious of by the hour, was the Blessed Sacrament, our Lord himself present in his divinity and in his betrayed, sacrificed, and risen humanity.

Morning came. Blacker appeared beneath his bedroom window. "Have you got it, boy?" "You can't have him," whispered David as he consumed the host.

It's only a story, of course. But it reminds us that we only grow in our appreciation of the real presence of the Lord as we are willing to sustain loss for his sake.

Lord Jesus, you are the pearl of great price. You who paid with your own blood the price of our redemption, help us to see and rejoice in the chances we get to share in this sacrifice.

Final Reckoning

Father John Dominic Corbett, O.P.

"The kingdom of heaven is like a net thrown into the sea, which collects fish of every kind. When it is full they haul it ashore and sit down to put what is good into buckets. What is bad they throw away. Thus it will be at the end of the age. The angels will go out and separate the wicked from the righteous and throw them into the fiery furnace, where there will be wailing and grinding of teeth." (Mt 13: 47-50)

Some years ago there was a Bible summer school production of the story of Adam and Eve in the Garden of Eden. One little girl was chosen to play Eve and naturally she was thrilled. So her parents were surprised and a little concerned when she came home from the first rehearsal frustrated and angry. "What's wrong, honey," they asked. "Oh," she said, fighting back tears, "the snake has all the lines."

It seems like that, doesn't it? On stage and on television the villain often seems by far the most interesting character. But this is only a surface impression. The only reason he seems interesting is that he is also in some way good. He displays power, ingenuity, raw animal courage, and a certain *panache*. All of these qualities would make him a good man, not a bad man.

What marks him as bad is not what he has. It's what he doesn't have. He doesn't have a good reason for what he does. (After all, there are no good reasons for bad actions.) He doesn't have any genuine empathy or compassion for anyone else. He doesn't have real friends. He doesn't have a place where he can be alone with himself in peace.

Jesus warns that these sad deficient humans are not going to make the grade. They will be thrown away. What is worse, Jesus warns us that such can happen to us. The kingdom of God is on offer, but just because it is on offer it can still be refused. Refusal of the kingdom means we who refuse it are, in our turn, turned down, turned away, thrown away. This warning should not panic us. It should, however, guard us against being too certain that God wouldn't finally respect our decision to get along without him. Actually, he might. If he does, we will discover what it means to stink like dead fish.

Lord Jesus, you will come to judge the living and the dead. Teach us always to hope in your mercy and also to have a salutary fear of your respect for our freedom.

The New and the Old

Father John Dominic Corbett, O.P.

"Every scribe who has been instructed in the kingdom of heaven is like the head of a household who brings from his storeroom both the new and the old." (Mt 13: 52)

It takes a long time really to get to know and trust someone. He might not say too much about himself at first. His actions might or might not fit in easily with what he says. After a while we see patterns in his activity. We get to know the things he does, and we get to know something of the reasons he has for the things he does. When what he does is of a piece with what he says, we finally are getting to know him as a man who is reliable and a man of his word.

This applies not only to what we know of our friend's past. It also applies to the future. We often can tell what our friend would do in similar circumstances in the future. We know how he would react because we know him. If he is both reliable and inventive, we know he will keep his word to us, but in new and unpredictable ways.

It is like that with God. The Bible tells us of what God did in the past for us. What he did in the past is a pretty good indication of the kind of thing he will do in the future. So the Bible talks about the first creation. And then it brings up a new creation. A first exodus is followed by a second exodus. A first King David will be followed by a new and even better King. What God did before he will do again. So Jesus is called the beginning of the new creation and the New Adam. God never does the same thing twice in exactly the same way. So we look to God's words to us, and we who are scribes in the new covenant look to see if we can guess the new and exciting ways that God is bringing us life again.

Father, you are the scribe who brings forth both old things and new. You bring forth the wisdom of your law and the fresh springs of your grace. Help us to live in your new creation with the freedom and joy of the children of God.

Native Son

Father John Dominic Corbett, O.P.

*[Jesus] came to his native place and taught the people in their
synagogue. They were astonished and said, "Where did this man
get such wisdom and mighty deeds? Is he not the carpenter's son?
Is not his mother named Mary and his brothers James, Joseph,
Simon, and Judas? Are not his sisters all with us? Where did
this man get all this?" (Mt 13: 54-56)*

In large cities where people come and go with such frequency,
it is rare to find a neighborhood where the residents have
remained and retained much of a common memory. But it
is different in smaller communities. Everyone knows everyone.
Everyone knows everyone's mother and father, and everyone
can tell stories about not only their own grandparents but also
everyone else's.

In Jesus' time, everyone would be able to recite everyone else's
family history, chapter and verse. They would know that if
Bartholomew's brother had a temper, it wasn't surprising since his
grandfather had had an even worse one. When people know your
family they think they know what they can expect from you.
When people think they know what they can expect from you, the
worst thing you can do to them is to turn out to be someone very
different.

This is why they are astonished at Jesus. His teaching illumines
everything and makes everything shine with the light of God. The
reports of his miracles are even more unsettling. How can this be?
They know where he comes from. They know his family. There isn't,
there just isn't, any hint of this in his (or anyone else's) background.
How can he pretend to all this? Just who does he think he is? How
dare he presume to instruct them about God?

Jesus is a native son. But he is a native son not only of Nazareth
but of heaven. Heaven has come to earth, the unearthly to the ordinary. It's scary when that happens, because it lets us know that our
routines are not the final arbiters of reality, and that one day a bit
of heaven could appear in our own native town, that one realm
where we are sure there are no surprises. And then we will have to
choose.

*Father, teach us both to recognize you in the ordinary providences
of our lives but also and most especially in those moments of crisis
to which our ordinary prudence is unequal. Do not abandon us
when everything depends on seeing you rightly.*

The Power of Faith

Father John Dominic Corbett, O.P.

They took offense at him. But Jesus said to them, "A prophet is not without honor except in his native place and in his own house." And he did not work many mighty deeds there because of their lack of faith. (Mt 13: 57-58)

"They took offense at him." Well, he took offense at them. They found in him the excuse to reject God's overtures. He found in them a stubbornness which, at least then and there, prevented him from doing the full will of God. To see how this could happen we need to look at what faith is.

What, after all, is it to have faith in someone? We have faith in someone when we believe what the person says. We have faith in someone when we believe what he says precisely because he says it. In a word, to have faith in someone is to be in a personal relationship of trust.

As Catholics, when we think about faith we place a premium on doctrine. We tend to emphasize content as though faith were mostly a way of accessing divinely guaranteed information about God. This way of approaching faith is fine so far as it goes, but there needs to be more to faith than that.

How so? When God communicates something to us he has a choice. He could make the truth of what he says so plain and so inescapable that we would have no choice but to accept it as true. The problem with this way of approaching us is that it leaves our freedom, and therefore our very persons, uninvolved. If God wishes to win us personally, he has to leave us free. When he tells us about his love for us, we are free to accept it or not. If we do, he has not only won the assent of our minds. He has won our hearts and our very selves. That was the whole point.

This is why he did not do many mighty deeds there. If their hearts were already closed against him, there was no point in performing signs to pry them open. He will only come in the front door if he is invited. He will not batter it down.

Father, teach us to have such faith in your Son that we will welcome his presence in any sign his love may deign to send.

A King without Faith

Father Donald Haggerty

At that time Herod the tetrarch heard of the reputation of Jesus and said to his servants, "This man is John the Baptist. He has been raised from the dead; that is why mighty powers are at work in him." (Mt 14: 1-2)

The importance of a personal encounter with Jesus is often stressed today. This exhortation to meet Jesus in a quite personal manner has great value, and it presumes ordinarily an effort of prayer. But what happens if a person does not bring an open spirit to an encounter with Jesus? The Gospel has many examples.

King Herod's first awareness of Jesus did not come from any personal contact with him. It was the result of secondhand reports of Jesus' miracles, and these reports only caused him fear and dismay. By this time he had beheaded John the Baptist in the palace dungeon cell. Upon hearing of Jesus' miraculous powers, Herod questioned whether it might actually be that John had returned from the dead and was performing these wonders. No doubt, late at night, Herod also anxiously agonized about what a "raised" John the Baptist might do next. A man like Herod, with a violent, paranoid history of eliminating his enemies, would not delay in presuming a desire for revenge from the man he had murdered.

This fear of Herod's, fed and magnified by guilt for his crime, can provoke a thought in us. Herod quickly embraced the possibility of a man coming back from the dead to revenge his murder – despite the absurd nature of such a threat. An observation pertinent to our own time of diminished faith can be made. Superstitious convictions often take hold in the absence of genuine religious belief. When people believe in nothing of true religion, they tend to put their faith in anything, easily succumbing to distortions of authentic faith. But a caricature of faith bears only a thin veneer of resemblance to Christian faith. Our faith is an assent to revealed truths proclaimed by the Church. It brings us into real contact with the truth of Jesus Christ, an encounter that arouses no fear, but rather a great attraction for the person of Jesus.

Father in heaven, grant to me a deeper conviction of faith, that I may know you as my Lord and see all things in life in the light of your providence and gracious will.

Prophetic Courage

Father Donald Haggerty

Now Herod had arrested John, bound [him], and put him in prison on account of Herodias, the wife of his brother Philip, for John had said to him, "It is not lawful for you to have her."
(Mt 14: 3-4)

It is always worth recalling that John the Baptist suffered imprisonment and execution for denouncing what might seem to a modern ear a moral violation of minor note. Herod had married his deceased brother's wife. Such a marriage violated the strictures of Jewish law in Leviticus. Today in the Catholic Church such a marriage, while unseemly in some cases, would be permissible as long as there were no other impediments to prevent the union. But John knew the Jewish law, and he was blunt and vehement in publicly confronting Herod with scandal. In this he certainly showed no diplomatic bent; discretion was not his preeminent virtue. Instead John exhibited the heroic fortitude of a saint, paying no mind to the risk of proclaiming a moral obligation to a man of power. And indeed Herod soon countered with a vicious act of vengeance.

Those serving the Church in any form of leadership ought to take note. The prophetic charism of the Church demands at times bold confrontations with public evils. The powerful of this world will always be capable of responding with aggressive hostility toward any prophetic defense of moral truth. And often their power of influence is aligned with the popular culture of a society. Indeed, Western societies have managed to enshrine under legal protection terrible offenses against the law of God. In many cases these triumphs of immorality arouse little opposition from the general population. All the more, then, do Catholics need to stand firm and united in defending moral truths affecting human life or the value of the family. John the Baptist, in that sense, is a forerunner of all the martyrs in history who have accepted death rather than compromise moral principles. We can recall in recent history, for instance, the thousands of men and women who shed their blood during the Nazi and Communist regimes rather than give any support to evil. May we learn from their examples of courage.

Almighty Father, grant me the courage to bear strong witness always to my Catholic convictions, and always to meet any challenge to my faith with steadfast fidelity.

A Link to Christ's Passion

Father Donald Haggerty

Although [Herod] wanted to kill [John the Baptist], he feared the people, for they regarded him as a prophet. (Mt 14: 5)

Herod's fear of the people kept him from promptly executing the Baptist after John's arrest. This is surprising, given Herod's reputation as a tyrant with little hesitation in shedding blood. Moreover, his outrage must have been great. He was not a man accustomed to being publicly embarrassed. John's denunciation of Herod's marriage was reason enough for an immediate death sentence. But John by this time was a man of unusual interest in Jewish society, respected by the crowds and appealing in his prophetic challenge. Herod is held back for the moment, afraid to damage his own standing among his subjects by killing John.

This initial tension at the time of John's arrest reminds us that John is a prophet not only by pointing to the Messiah in his spoken words. The circumstances of John's death also anticipate in a prophetic manner Jesus' passion. The parallels are notable. In Jesus' case the Jewish leadership desired to kill him long before Judas offered to betray him. Jesus was aware of these designs, and of the malice intensifying toward his person. His predictions of his passion do not arise simply from a knowledge of scriptural prophecy. They express a painful knowledge of men's hearts. Nonetheless, until Judas provided the convenient opportunity, the high priests were not ready to act. They too feared the people, aware as they were of Jesus' profound attraction.

These parallels might spark a thought for the current day. The desire for the demise of Christian influence in society is certainly a real threat in the West. But this opposition to Christianity may be only a hint of the hostility still awaiting the Church. If it is true that the Church mirrors in a mysterious way the life of Jesus Christ, perhaps we should prepare ourselves more realistically for the likelihood of greater persecution in days to come.

Heavenly Father, allow me to understand better that the truth your Son taught will not always be accepted, and that I must be ready to suffer for my faithfulness to him.

Morality and Character

Father Donald Haggerty

*At a birthday celebration for Herod, the daughter of Herodias
performed a dance before the guests and delighted Herod so
much that he swore to give her whatever she might ask for.
Prompted by her mother, she said, "Give me here on a platter
the head of John the Baptist." (Mt 14: 6-8)*

The occasional abject moral weakness of powerful men in
the world is usually concealed from the public eye. Their
diversions remain closed to view, and no doubt that is only
proper. As a result, however, we may be inclined to think that the
private behaviors of a man are inconsequential to the importance
of his public work. But dissolute tastes for sensual pleasure cannot
be separated from questions of character. Virtue and integrity are
issues of the whole man. A man weak in sensual indulgence, for
instance, is likely to lack moral fiber in public challenges that
demand resolute strength. The combination is not surprising, and
not just in prominent public figures. By a certain logic, immorality is bound to weaken one's sensitivity to truth; a tendency to
minimize real guilt increases as sin continues. The loss of a sense
of sin becomes in turn an insensitivity to God. Sooner or later this
withdrawal from God shows itself in external affairs.

In Herod we observe evidence of this effect of immoral living
on a man's judgment. In an hour of entertainment the king's
character is fully exposed. Delighted by the sensual dance of the
daughter of Herodias, Herod by his vow invites the girl to indulge
her whim in any extreme manner she may wish. And of course it
is likely that Herod is not simply rewarding her for a performance
but also has lustful intentions toward her in this promise. The
request of the girl after consulting her malicious mother is for John's
head. There is a lesson here not just in the irrational state of mind
that afflicts Herod under the strain of sensual desire. We are observing the longer effects of dissolute living upon a man's character.
This man remains powerful in his kingdom, but a vassal to a young
girl's caprice due to his corruption of character.

*Gracious Father, grant me always a great respect and esteem for
chastity, and the protection and strength of your grace to remain
unharmed by temptations against purity.*

Martyrdom's True Face

Father Donald Haggerty

[Herod] was distressed, but because of his oaths and the guests who were present, he ordered that it be given, and he had John beheaded in the prison. His head was brought in on a platter and given to the girl, who took it to her mother.
(Mt 14: 9-11)

King Herod's distress at the request by his stepdaughter for the head of John the Baptist provokes some wonder. Is it, again, because he fears the reaction of the Jewish people if he kills John, who accorded John the respect of a prophet? Or is it possible that Herod visited John during his imprisonment and discovered a mysterious appeal in this man? Did Herod question John about his purpose in the desert? Did John in their exchange cry out in some manner to the wilderness of Herod's soul and leave Herod discomforted as the door of the prisoner's cell closed behind him? In any case, no mere conversation was enough to change the character of Herod. Herod was a man long ruled and dominated by his weakness. If there was any shred of honest reluctance in Herod to take the life of John, it quickly evaporated at the dinner celebration. Herod could not bear being laughed at, and he gave way to a fear of embarrassment were he to renege on his promise. And so he orders the swift execution. The scene that follows is quite horrific.

A dinner party of distinguished guests and royal officials is treated to the sickening sight of a head carried in on a dinner platter, and perhaps, after an initial gasp, the hall simply filled with laughter. But this is the brutal ambiance of Herod's world. One can only wonder whether dessert and coffee were served next. The combination of gore and low frivolity that provide the setting for John's death reminds us that the reality of actual martyrdom has always been dreadful. The martyrs were all treated with indignity and disgrace, humiliated before what was often a laughing audience – laughing at their pain. In this we should remember that John is the prophet of the incarnate Son. And he is also the prophet of the martyrs who will follow him in Christian history.

Father, you have allowed many saintly men and women in history to suffer the ultimate price of giving up their lives in loyalty to your Son. Help me always to keep before my soul the desire to refuse you nothing.

The Example of Jesus' Prayer

Father Donald Haggerty

[John the Baptist's] disciples came and took away the corpse and buried him; and they went and told Jesus. When Jesus heard of it, he withdrew in a boat to a deserted place by himself. The crowds heard of this and followed him on foot from their towns. (Mt 14: 12-13)

When Jesus received the painful news of John's murder, he withdrew by boat to a deserted place to be alone. He must have been much distressed in hearing the details of John's death. Now he goes to mourn in solitude the cousin he had known many years before as a young boy, the man he once called the greatest among all living men.

But possibly there were other reflections during this brief interlude away from the press of the crowds. Jesus perhaps ruminated on the uncertainty and disquiet John experienced when he sent to Jesus from the darkness of his prison cell a question whether Jesus was indeed the anticipated Messiah. The thought of the fearless John confronting a doubt of his prophetic mission may have given pause to Jesus. Perhaps he realized a hint of the dark hour of anguish awaiting his own human soul in Gethsemane when he would ask his Father to remove from him the cup of suffering.

Ultimately we do not know what took place in the interior heart of Jesus when he was alone and in prayer. But the references in the Gospel to Jesus' desire for solitary prayer remind us of our own need to seek quiet and solitude. And sometimes that will entail a need to ponder the mystery of suffering in our lives. At times this will involve loss of loved ones, other times personal disappointment, and even periods of interior confusion or darkness. Prayer allows us to realize that these experiences cannot be separated from the greater truth of God's presence during times of trial. Even when we seem to be uncomprehending, we may recognize in a quite mysterious manner that God never forsakes the faithful soul. As we can expect John understood, the sacredness of our existence may reveal itself most acutely in the hour when we are most in need of God.

Father of all goodness, help me to turn to you in prayer at all times of my life, and most especially when I find difficulty, so that I may surrender myself always to your will.

Jesus on Sea and Land

Father Joseph T. Lienhard, s.j.

When [Jesus] disembarked and saw the vast crowd, his heart
was moved with pity for them, and he cured their sick.
(Mt 14: 14)

The sea and the land have clearly different meanings in the Gospels. When Jesus is on the Sea of Galilee, he is apart from the crowds, in a boat with his disciples. He sleeps through a storm on that sea. When a storm comes up, he stills it, to his disciples' amazement. He does not even need a boat: once he walks across the water to his disciples. The sea is a place apart. The land – the towns and villages of Galilee – mean something different for Jesus. There he finds crowds of his countrymen, people in need. The Gospel verse we are considering moves quickly through three key words: "disembarked," "crowd," and "pity." That the crowds are needy is nothing new. But in Jesus they have found someone wholly new, someone who can fulfill their needs. "And he cured their sick," the Scripture says, so simply; and yet who ever heard of someone curing the sick by a word or a touch?

And then, where do I see myself in this scene? As one of Jesus' disciples, on the sea, close to him, protected by him, yet not quite knowing who he is? Or as one of the people of Galilee, crowded along the lake shore, waiting for what I have no right to, what I dare not expect – to be cured of sickness? Perhaps I am both: the disciple in the boat, glad to be near Jesus and trying to understand who he is, and the Galilean on the seashore, waiting for the unexpected gift of grace. I can know Jesus on the sea, and I can know Jesus on the land; and I need Jesus both on sea and on land. I need to ask for his healing grace, as he steps out onto the land and reaches out to the crowds. I can know Jesus' power on the sea, and I can know his pity on the land.

Almighty God and Father, I call out to you for your healing grace;
make me, I implore you, a trusting disciple of Christ whom you
love, and bring me safely to the harbor of eternal life.

Give Them Some Food

Father Joseph T. Lienhard, S.J.

When it was evening, the disciples approached [Jesus] and said,
"This is a deserted place and it is already late; dismiss the crowds
so that they can go to the villages and buy food for themselves."
[Jesus] said to them, "There is no need for them to go away;
give them some food yourselves." (Mt 14: 15-16)

In a few phrases, Saint Matthew draws a sharp contrast between two settings. One is the wilderness: the people who come to Jesus to listen to him go to a deserted place. The day is drawing to a close, and darkness is falling. All these details are symbols of dependence, of helplessness. In a deserted place, there is no one to provide for me. At the end of the day, I grow hungry. Darkness falls, and I grow fearful; I need light. Light, food, companionship – they are not to be found here. At first, Jesus appears to provide no help at all: "Give them some food yourselves," he says. What do the disciples think when they hear these words? Where are they to get food? Jesus' command must seem impossible, absurd to them. It is better for the disciples to remain with what is familiar, what is known and trusted. There are villages that the crowds can walk to, and people there who can sell them food. That's the way we always do it.

Sometimes Jesus can tell us, too, "Give them some food yourselves." Perhaps Jesus tells us to care for a sick relative or an elderly parent. Perhaps he tells us to give money or time to a friend who needs it. Perhaps he tells us to offer our lives to the Church, as a priest or a religious. One thing is certain: the command will be startling. My first reaction will be, "What do you mean? I can't do this. My life is a desert, where it is late and dark. I can't even take care of myself – how do you expect me to provide for someone else? How do you expect me to do something extraordinary?" Jesus has an answer prepared, one that we could not anticipate, one that we could not even imagine. Do we sense what it is?

Eternal Lord of all things, open my heart to the voice of Christ your Son; may I always be ready to hear his call, and with the help of your grace, may I always have the courage to trust his trust in me.

The Sacramental Mystery

Father Joseph T. Lienhard, S.J.

*But [his disciples] said to [Jesus], "Five loaves
and two fish are all we have here." (Mt 14: 17)*

Pope Benedict XVI has written beautifully about the matter, or material element, of the sacraments. Water, used in baptism, is universal; every civilization, every human being, uses water. In contrast, wheat bread, and grape wine, and olive oil – the matter for the Eucharist and for confirmation – are the foods of the Mediterranean basin. The Gospels tell us of Jesus using some of these foods. He asks the woman at the well for a drink of water. He provides bread for the crowds. At Cana he changes water into wine. The Gospels do not mention Jesus using olive oil, but his title "Christ" means "the anointed one"; in the Old Testament, priests, prophets, and kings were anointed with oil. To these sacramental signs we might add one more food: namely, fish. After his resurrection, Jesus proves to his disciples that he is truly risen by eating a piece of fish, and later he cooks a breakfast of fish for his disciples on the shore of the Sea of Galilee. In these last instances, fish becomes nearly sacramental, a visible sign of invisible grace, as the pieces of fish mean so much more to the disciples than just food to satisfy physical hunger.

When words are used in the inspired Scriptures, they take on resonances that they do not have in ordinary speech. When loaves of bread and pieces of fish are mentioned in one place in Holy Scripture, they remind us of other places in the Scriptures, too, where these words are found. Five loaves of bread remind us of the manna given in the desert, the bread from heaven that God provided in abundance; and the two fish in this passage from Saint Matthew's Gospel stand in contrast to the superabundant catch of one hundred and fifty-three fish that Saint John recounts. The disciples begin with what is modest and small, five loaves and two fish; God gives his gifts in amazing abundance.

Almighty God and Father, you are the source of all that is good; give us, we ask you, the food of eternal life, which Christ your Son has promised to us.

Jesus: Guest and Host

Father Joseph T. Lienhard, S.J.

Then [Jesus] said, "Bring them here to me," and he ordered the crowds to sit down on the grass. (Mt 14: 18-19)

The Gospels often recount that Jesus was a guest at dinner. At Cana in Galilee he attended a wedding feast, with his mother. After Jesus called Matthew to follow him, Matthew prepared a meal for his friends, who were the tax collectors and the sinners; he invited Jesus, too, and Jesus came, despite the Pharisees' objections. Simon the leper, who lived in Bethany, invited Jesus to dinner but treated him rudely; an unnamed woman made up for Simon's bad manners, pouring ointment on Jesus' head. It was in Bethany, too, that Jesus came to a supper in the house of Martha, Mary, and Lazarus, after he had raised Lazarus from the dead – surely one of the most touching pictures of a meal in the Gospels; we can only imagine what the conversation was like.

At a few other times, Jesus is the host at a meal. In the passage we are considering, the meal seems to lack any proportion. The food at hand is five loaves of bread and two fish; the guests are five thousand men and uncounted women and children. Yet Jesus the host is utterly serene, and he does what any good host does: he invites his guests to sit down. There are no tables or chairs here; he invites them to sit on the grass. Jesus serves the meal, and everyone eats and is satisfied. After his resurrection, Jesus serves another meal, a much smaller one: he serves a breakfast of bread and fish to his disciples. There is one more meal, of course, at which Jesus is the host – that is, the Last Supper. Here is a meal that fulfills and transcends all others, for here the host not only serves the meal but offers himself as the food, the food of eternal life. In that wondrous meal, the old covenant is first fulfilled in the paschal lamb, and then the new covenant is established by the Lamb of God.

Eternal God and Father, you nourish us each day with food and drink, and provide us with the eucharistic food of life; satisfy all the hungry, we pray, and bring us to the fullness of life that the Eucharist promises, through Christ our Lord.

The Eucharistic Bread

Father Joseph T. Lienhard, S.J.

Taking the five loaves and the two fish, and looking up to heaven, [Jesus] said the blessing, broke the loaves, and gave them to the disciples, who in turn gave them to the crowds. They all ate and were satisfied, and they picked up the fragments left over – twelve wicker baskets full. Those who ate were about five thousand men, not counting women and children.
(Mt 14: 19-21)

"Looking up to heaven, he said the blessing, broke the loaves, and gave them…" "He took… blessed… broke… gave": these are the words of the eucharistic mystery. The miracle of the multiplication of the loaves and fish is the only one of Jesus' miracles that is recounted in all four Gospels, and Mark and Matthew each recount two instances of it. The same words that describe Jesus' actions, moreover, also narrate Jesus' institution of the Eucharist, as recounted in three Gospels and by Saint Paul in his first Letter to the Corinthians. What are the characteristics of this multiplication of loaves and fish? One is superabundance. Five thousand men are fed, along with women and children; and still, more food is left over than was there to start with. Further, everyone not only gets enough to eat, but more than enough. And note the striking phrase, "he looked up to heaven." The power to do this great work can come only from on high, just as the manna came in the desert, and as the heavenly food of the Eucharist comes.

One aspect of this Gospel passage merits further reflection. What do those thousands of people think? And what would we have thought, if we had been among them? Some, perhaps, do not bother to wonder about what has happened. They have plenty to eat, and that is enough for them. Others, as we know, think of carrying Jesus off and making him their king; I will allow anyone who satisfies my needs to rule over me. And some, finally, may come to faith, faith in the person of Jesus the Christ. For the miracle is a sign, and a sign is something known first that leads us to knowledge of something else. From the loaves and the fish, we come to recognize Christ as the Son of the living God.

Almighty Lord of all things, giver of all good gifts, lead our hearts, we ask you, beyond the things of earth to the unseen things of heaven, the only source of true happiness.

God's Mysterious, Wise, and Loving Plan
Douglas Bushman

*Then [Jesus] made the disciples get into the boat and precede
him to the other side, while he dismissed the crowds.*
(Mt 14: 22)

Jesus instructs his disciples to board the boat. He knows what
to do because he is one with the Father. He confidently gives
commands because he knows what it means to obey the Father:
"I do just as the Father has commanded me" (Jn 14: 31).

Jesus' initiative does not originate with him. Its origin is his
Father's plan of love: "I came in the name of my Father" (Jn 5: 43).
Jesus is never alone: "I am not alone, because the Father is with me"
(Jn 16: 32). This is why he says: "Whoever has seen me has seen the
Father" (Jn 14: 9). We must learn to see the Father, and the realiza-
tion of his loving plan, in all that Jesus says and does, and in what
he commands us to do.

By his loving obedience, Jesus makes the Father's will a reality on
earth, fulfilling the petition: "Your kingdom come, your will be
done, on earth as in heaven" (Mt 6: 10). The Father answers the
Son's petitions by fulfilling them in and through the Son! The commands Jesus gives us, then, are heaven's answer to our own petition that God's kingdom come and his will be done on earth.

If Jesus does not explain himself it is because we are unable to
comprehend the wisdom behind his commands. What does boarding a boat have to do with the coming of the kingdom? Like
teenagers, we want to know, now, what this means. If the apostles
had asked, how could Jesus have explained? We must learn to be
patient, and not to demand explanations. Only Jesus knows what
lies ahead. Our place is to trust him and to get into the boat, like
the apostles.

And because they do, they are precisely where they need to be in
order to witness a revelation of Jesus' glory. Such epiphanies await
all who faithfully obey what Jesus commands.

*Father, help me to see you in Jesus, and to believe that in obeying
Jesus even in very small things your plan will be fulfilled, your
kingdom will come on earth, and that Jesus will show me the glory
of what it means for him, and for me in him, to be your son.*

Christ Prays in Us, and We in Him

Douglas Bushman

[Jesus] went up on the mountain by himself to pray.
When it was evening he was there alone. (Mt 14: 23)

The first reason why Jesus dispatches his disciples and the crowds now appears: it is time to be alone with his Father. The Catechism teaches: "Christ enables us *to live in him* all that he himself lived, and *he lives it in us*" (CCC 521). What does it mean for Jesus to live this prayer-encounter with his Father in us, and for us to live it in him?

The mountain is the place of encounter with God. Jesus is at home there. If there is no record that he was transfigured, as he will be later, it is because there are no witnesses. What the transfiguration reveals, though, is already a reality here. Jesus is the splendor, the glory of the Father; yet, he must suffer and die to accomplish the Father's will. In Christ, prayer is always communion with the Father and participation in the Paschal Mystery, which fully reveals his love.

Jesus did not need to ascend the mountain to pray, and neither do we. His ascent teaches us, though, that to pray we must remove ourselves from distractions. We must rise above the preoccupations of daily life, if only to reflect on them in God's presence. Yet, by doing so we gain a new perspective, looking at things from on high, as God does. Prayer transforms daily preoccupations into revelations of God's will: crosses, trials, so many indications of God's plan of love for us. Prayer does not remove us from daily life, but allows us, in the midst of it, to be aware of God's presence, his loving plan, and the salvific power of suffering.

We do not live atop mountains. It is always necessary to descend and return to ordinary life. But there is nothing ordinary about life in communion with God, in fulfilling the vocation he has entrusted to us. Jesus will descend to embrace the cross. Having ascended with him, we must also descend with him.

Father, through the intercession of Saint Matthew, draw me to the mountain of aloneness with you, to pray, not just with but in your dearly beloved Son, Jesus, and may it be he praying in me.

177

In Him I Can Do All Things

Douglas Bushman

Meanwhile the boat, already a few miles offshore, was being tossed about by the waves, for the wind was against it.
(Mt 14: 24)

The contrast is imposing: Jesus on the mountain, alone with the Father, while the disciples are engulfed in the futile effort to cross the lake. In reality, though, they are not alone. He is with them, precisely because he is with the Father, for the Father watches over all his children. Not a sparrow falls to the ground without the Father's knowledge (Mt 10: 29).

Jesus' command does not cause his disciples any concern. Some are fisherman, making their living on boats, and fishing by night. No doubt they are confident. Crossing the lake is within their power. There is no need for special preparations, or even to pray.

Their motive is not worldly. They are obeying their Master. Would God allow something to thwart this mission? Only if he intends something greater, if he intends to bring some good out of this apparent futility. In the end, the apostles will make it to the distant shore. But they will be transformed by the events of this night. This night they face the power of the wind that is too great for them. In the divine plan it is the occasion to witness God's power that is greater than the wind.

This is no surprise to Jesus. Every mission that he entrusts to us is beyond us.

If sometimes it seems that we accomplish the tasks he gives us on our own, it is appearance only. A stormless crossing, an eventful day, may be an act of mercy because he knows we would crumble before a setback. We must learn what it means to rely on God's grace.

God calls us to the shores of heaven, to eternal life. Every storm and every calm sea is his providence for us, a detail of his plan of love. We may be more conscious of our need for Jesus when the seas are in tumult. In reality, even on placid waters we cannot reach heaven's shores without him.

Loving Father of Jesus, purify me of all presumption. Never withdraw your grace from me, and teach me to turn to Jesus even when the winds and waves are not threatening.

Do Not Be Afraid

Douglas Bushman

During the fourth watch of the night, [Jesus] came toward them, walking on the sea. When the disciples saw him walking on the sea they were terrified. "It is a ghost," they said, and they cried out in fear. At once [Jesus] spoke to them, "Take courage, it is I; do not be afraid." (Mt 14: 25-27)

Though on the mountain praying, Jesus is not distant from those he loved. It is because prayer is communion with the Father, and these disciples are precious to the Father's heart. Prayer is never withdrawal from others, but the truest approach to them. Prayer makes us share in God's closeness to those he loves.

Jesus comes to the disciples in their predicament. They might have learned from his healing a centurion's servant from a distance (Mt 8: 5-13), and trusted that his physical absence was no obstacle to his saving power. They might have remembered his teaching about the Father's solicitude extending even to sparrows, in order to reassure them of the Father's providential care for them, and the conclusion: "So do not be afraid; you are worth more than many sparrows" (Mt 10: 31).

What is left for man if he does not believe in God, or does not believe that God's love is concrete and effective? Only fear. The disciples display a fear rooted in what Pope John Paul II called practical atheism. It is not a considered denial of God, but living as if God does not exist, living as if we were alone in the world, as if we had to rely only on ourselves.

Lack of faith does not prevent Jesus from coming to them. Wind and waves do not impede him, and this shows that Jesus' love for his disciples is truly divine. No storm or lack of faith can prevent God from loving us. How else can we come to faith, unless he loves us first (1 Jn 4: 19)?

Jesus is the answer to all our fears. He comes to us in storms and impossibilities, when we cannot reach our destination by our own power. He draws close to us because he wants to say, "'Do not be afraid' but believe that nothing 'will be able to separate us from the love of God in Christ Jesus our Lord'" (Rom 8: 39).

Father, "I do believe, help my unbelief." Help me, in the midst of life's tumults, to believe in your love, in the presence of Jesus, and in believing, not to be afraid.

Save Me, Lord, from Lack of Faith

Douglas Bushman

Peter said to [Jesus] in reply, "Lord, if it is you, command me to come to you on the water." He said, "Come." Peter got out of the boat and began to walk on the water toward Jesus. But when he saw how [strong] the wind was he became frightened; and, beginning to sink, he cried out, "Lord, save me!" Immediately Jesus stretched out his hand and caught him, and said to him, "O you of little faith, why did you doubt?" (Mt 14: 28-31)

The contrast is clear. Jesus commanded the disciples to sail to the other side of the lake, and they could set off confidently. What need is there to pray about something within one's power? Then comes the wind that makes this ordinary task impossible. Now, the Lord commands Peter to do what is absolutely impossible, and he does it.

For a few miraculous steps, Peter is fearless. By faith he is drawn into the divine love that overcomes all obstacles. The Lord calls and, as though blinded by love to everything around him, Peter sets out to meet his Master. Then, becoming aware of his precarious situation, he becomes frightened. He is like the seed in the parable of the sower that, having started with impressive growth, becomes choked to death by worldly worries (Mt 13: 22).

Jesus calls us to have faith rather than to worry (Mt 6: 25, 31, 34; 10: 19). To worry is opposed to faith because to worry means to lack confidence in God's Providence: his wisdom, love, and power. Do we really believe that "all things work for good for those who love God" (Rom 8: 28)?

In the case of Saint Peter, worry leads to doubt Jesus' divine power (Mt 28: 17-18). Yet, such doubting does not prevent Jesus from reaching to us as we sink, as he did for Peter. How he longs to hear us say: "Lord, save me," for he is our Savior. Peter cried out to be saved from drowning, but we can cry out to be saved from what causes us to sink, namely, the lack of faith that leads to worry and doubt.

Peter will rise to a glorious profession of faith in Jesus, only to sink again due to fear, when three times he denies even knowing Jesus. It is not difficult to imagine with what intense humility Peter cried out to Jesus, after his denials, "Lord, save me."

Father, grant me the grace every day to respond to Jesus' call to come to him, and, through Saint Peter's intercession, may I always pray: "Lord, save me!"

The Bark of Saint Peter

Douglas Bushman

After [Jesus and Peter] got into the boat, the wind died down.
(Mt 14: 32)

The storm has subsided, the crisis has passed. Fear has been overcome, not by Peter's courage, but by the Lord's presence and power. The lesson of Christian virtue is that it is not ours. We do not forge it, we receive it. Left to ourselves we are weak and fearful. Only by God's power and love can we accomplish great things. Saint Peter has learned the lesson: "'My grace is sufficient for you, for power is made perfect in weakness'... for when I am weak, then I am strong" (2 Cor 12: 9-10). From which comes the imperative: "Whoever boasts, should boast in the Lord" (1 Cor 1: 31).

Catholics know the Church as the bark of Saint Peter. This naturally leads to thinking of Peter as the captain, the one in authority. While this is true, this authority presupposes something more fundamental, namely, Peter's faith. What is remarkable about this episode is that Peter boards this boat twice. The first time, he simply follows the Lord's command and jumps aboard. This first boarding is done as though it is Peter's own doing. The second time, though, is a supernatural boarding. It is entirely the Lord's doing. How true are the Lord's words: "It was not you who chose me, but I who chose you" (Jn 15: 16).

We board the ark of salvation, not by our own will and power, though we must of course desire it, but by the will and the power of God, through baptism. The authority of Saint Peter is entirely at the service of bringing people to faith and baptism, thereby reproducing Peter's experience of salvation by the power of God in Jesus. Peter's contribution to being placed on the boat was to cry out, "Lord, save me." In all of life's storms we can enter more deeply into the meaning of baptism and, in faith, relive being saved by Jesus and placed in safety on the ark of salvation.

Praise and blessing and thanks to you, heavenly Father, for sending your Son to save me in the Church. May I live and relive the graces of salvation by crying out in faith, "Lord, save me."

Behold God's Glory in Jesus

Douglas Bushman

Those who were in the boat did [Jesus] homage, saying,
"Truly, you are the Son of God." (Mt 14: 33)

Those making this act of faith are not called apostles. Right now their identity derives from where they are, in Jesus' presence, and how they respond, by worshiping him. Having witnessed Jesus' power, and finding themselves safe in the boat, they come to the conclusion of faith: Jesus is the Son of God. Apostles are first of all men of faith.

The miracle has served its purpose. Jesus' disciples have glimpsed something of his glory. The source of Jesus' glory is the Father. Having spent the night in prayer on the mountain, Jesus descended in order to reveal this glory by walking on water and saving Peter. Later, he will bring Peter, James, and John up the mountain, where he will be transfigured. They will rise up with him to the place of encounter with God.

God's glory is not confined to the mountain of the transfiguration, or the miracle of walking on water. It may be more readily perceived there, but faith allows us to perceive it in ordinary circumstances of daily life. Jesus has, so to speak, come down from the mountain of heaven in order to manifest his glory. Wherever Jesus is, there is the Father, and God's glory.

Miracles punctuate the Church's life. In them we readily perceive God's glory, as in the transfiguration. But miracles are not the Church's daily bread. The Eucharist is. Under the lowly appearance of bread and wine, faith perceives Christ's presence and thus God's glory as it was manifested in Christ's sacrifice. We might be tempted to think that we should live from miracle to miracle, in which case there would be no need for a boat. After Jesus and Peter walked on the water, and after Jesus rescued Peter, they completed their crossing in the boat. Let us welcome miracles when they come, and thank the Lord of glory for being present on our boat, the Church, in miracles, in sacraments, and in daily life.

Eternal Father, grant me faith to see your glory wherever Jesus is present, and in faith may I see him present everywhere.

Spread the Word: Jesus Is Here!

Douglas Bushman

After making the crossing, [Jesus and his disciples] came to land at Gennesaret. When the men of that place recognized [Jesus], they sent word to all the surrounding country.
(Mt 14: 34-35)

Obviously, the people of Gennesaret have heard of Jesus. They certainly know what to do. Their expectation is fulfilled. Jesus is present! Divine power and love are present! The great healer is among them. They have to let people know.

The whole purpose of Jesus' miracles is to bring people to faith, but they are not simply preparatory to faith. In Jesus' healings love is already revealed, and this means that God is revealed in them, since God is love. Yet, his love is not exhausted, it is not finished, nor can it rest until it gives much more than the restoration of health. God has more to give. He desires to give himself, but how many desire that "more"? How many are content to receive the gift of health but neglect the gift the Healer wants to make of himself?

Yet, Jesus is humble and begins with the real and true, but only partial, gift of restoring health. In the process of healing physical ailments, he reveals that he has the power to heal the deeper wounds of sin. He reveals a love that desires the restoration of spiritual health. All sin is in one way or another a lack of love, or disordered love, loving oneself or someone or something else too much. Jesus, Immanuel, God-with-us, brings divine love to fill the void of love in the world and in each person's life. He may begin by healing illnesses and infirmities, but this contact with him is the occasion for us to discover the depths of his love, that he has more to give.

What joy it must bring to him when we open ourselves to this greater gift, when we allow him to heal us spiritually! And when we have received this love, then the joy of having been loved is the most effective way to evangelize, to proclaim the good news that, in Jesus, God is with us.

Heavenly Father, through Saint Matthew's intercession, let me bring joy to Jesus' heart by asking him to give me what he wants to give, himself, and may my joy in being loved be an invitation for others to come to him.

Jesus Wants to Be Touched by Faith
Douglas Bushman

People brought to [Jesus] all those who were sick and begged him that they might touch only the tassel on his cloak, and as many as touched it were healed. (Mt 14: 35-36)

What faithful friends and family the sick in Gennesaret have, that they bring them to Jesus for healing! Evangelization is more than informing people about Jesus, or pointing out where he is. It is active service, and all service, if it is genuinely Christian, should bring people to encounter the love of God in Jesus.

Often it is Jesus who touches those he heals. He puts saliva-paste on the blind man's eyes, touches the bier of the widow's son, takes the hands of Jairus' daughter and Peter's mother-in-law, and lays his hands on the woman who has suffered for eighteen years. Jesus grasps Peter, too, to save him from sinking. Here, at Gennesaret, the people take the initiative. Jesus appears more passive, allowing them to touch his cloak, just as the woman with a hemorrhage does.

Of course, Jesus is not at all passive, for he is God, and God is love, and love is always giving, always communicating goodness and grace. He desires, though, that we come to him in faith. He wants to be touched by faith. This means that we approach him with awareness of our need, weakness, and sins, and with a firm conviction that in him God's love and power are present. This twofold truth, about ourselves and about Jesus, makes a saving encounter possible.

To all who come to him, touch him, and are healed, Jesus could have said what he says to the woman with a hemorrhage, "Courage, daughter! Your faith has saved you" (Mt 9: 22). We too can hear him saying this to us whenever we come to him in the sacraments. Faith is not the power to heal ourselves, but the gift to recognize the saving presence and power of God in Jesus Christ. Our faith is always a response to God's initiative. And, when we come to him to touch him in faith, it is so that he can touch us with healing love.

Heavenly Father, thank you for my parents, who brought me to Jesus to be baptized, and for all who have brought me to him. Thank you for the priests and bishops through whom he remains present in his power to heal.

Marching to the Beat of Another Drum

Monsignor James Turro

Then Pharisees and scribes came to Jesus from Jerusalem and said, "Why do your disciples break the tradition of the elders? They do not wash [their] hands when they eat a meal."
(Mt 15: 1-2)

From time to time, the prejudice which the religious leaders, specifically, the Pharisees, harbor against Jesus breaks through the surface. This is not unique. In fact it is a frequent occurrence during the public life of Jesus. The opposition dogs his steps and takes great pains to challenge Jesus and to warn people against him. This is one such instance.

To be sure, the followers of Jesus have continued to be challenged in various ways up to the present day. For instance, prevailing public opinion today insinuates that the followers of Christ and his teaching are beyond the pale of modernity and that, in their estimation, is bad. They (we) adhere to "benighted" opposition to numerous current practices that modern man seems to find in no way objectionable, but which by Christian standards of judgment must be held to be wrong. The question is, whom shall we permit to set the norms for our lives? Many contend for the honor. Who shall it be: fashion, public opinion, the media? Or as must be, the will of God. That will has been expressed to us in the Scriptures and translated for our everyday living by the Church. It will almost certainly cost us a price to stand by the Church's teaching against widely held opinions.

It all boils down to this: we must be willing and able to swim against the tide of prevailing public opinion when we find it to be in conflict with our Catholic conscience. All of which means we must dare to be different. And that is more easily said than done. It takes much courage. No one wants to be a maverick. It is more acceptable by far to run with the pack – to mix metaphors – than to stand out like a sore thumb.

Grant me the strength, dear Father, to stand my ground in defense of your truth – come what may. It will be an honor to suffer for your glory.

I Come to Do Your Will, O God

Monsignor James Turro

[Jesus] said to [the Pharisees and scribes] in reply, "And why do you break the commandment of God for the sake of your tradition? For God said, 'Honor your father and your mother,' and 'Whoever curses father or mother shall die.' But you say, 'Whoever says to father or mother, "Any support you might have had from me is dedicated to God," need not honor his father.' You have nullified the word of God for the sake of your tradition." (Mt 15: 3-6)

Pharisaic custom had served to nullify the clear-cut command of God in every instance to care for one's parents. A strange usage had been allowed to prevail, even though it served to obscure God's outright command to honor one's parents.

From time to time it does happen that one attempts to circumvent, to water down God's firm command. "God understands" – that is often the dodge that is thought to legitimize a clearly unacceptable action. It is a strange quirk that prompts a person to set aside a clear duty for some other more engaging project.

God would have us reverence those persons – our parents – who are the first of our fellow creatures toward whom we have responsibilities. But beyond that and more significant is the fact that our parents are representatives of God to us. As such these persons are to be revered and cared for unstintingly.

If one should ever be tempted to wonder why one's parents ought to be loved and obeyed, the reason is clear and strong: God requires it – this is the highest, most compelling reason. It appears to be a modern day aberration to exclude God from one's calculations and from one's life altogether. It's as if reference to God is an embarrassment. It is remarkable with what facility people manage to weasel out from quite patent obligations.

A little known fact of American history touchingly illustrates the love and concern one should have for one's parents. George Washington originally contemplated a career in the Navy. On the day of his induction, as he took leave of his mother before boarding the ship, he noticed the tears in her eyes. He straightaway had his servant remove his trunk from the ship on which he was to sail. He could not bear to see his mother's pain. "I will not go away to break my mother's heart." And thus he settled the matter.

Dear Father, thank you for my parents. They are your first and precious gift to me. You have blessed me most generously.

Going through the Motions...

Monsignor James Turro

"Hypocrites, well did Isaiah prophesy about you when he said:/ 'This people honors me with their lips,/ but their hearts are far from me;/ in vain do they worship me,/ teaching as doctrines human precepts.'" (Mt 15: 7-9)

Serving God ought not to be a mechanical process – producing what is called for but all the while lacking heart. What this kind of service to God may imply is that one is in a state of estrangement from God. Sincerity is absent in one's efforts to praise God. What is pathetic is that such a one who acts toward God in this fashion deludes himself into thinking that his situation of estrangement from God goes unnoticed. As if God could be unaware of the situation. But God will not be mocked.

Hypocrisy, it would seem, was rampant in those times and in that place. A certain rabbi – roughly in the New Testament period – was prompted to write: "There are ten parts of hypocrisy in the world, nine in Jerusalem and one in the rest of the world" (Rabbi Nathan, AD 160). Elsewhere in Matthew's Gospel one finds another searing denunciation of the hypocrisy of the scribes and Pharisees: "Do not follow their example" (Mt 23: 3) the reader is counseled. "In vain do they worship me" (Mt 15: 9) is a devastating assertion that exposes the emptiness of the hypocrite's efforts at prayer. That man is wasting his time. Nothing comes of his praying.

In dealing with one's neighbor as well as dealing with God one ought to be aboveboard. Setting aside any religious considerations, this makes practical good sense. Once a person is identified as a hypocrite, people tend to give that man a wide berth. And if circumstances compel one to be involved with a hypocrite, one is on the alert so as to avoid being done in.

In modern society as well, there is small tolerance for the hypocrite. He is viewed as a pathetic, deluded fool:

"May the man be damned and never grow fat
Who wears two faces under one hat."

With confidence I turn to you in prayer, O Father, and ask that you keep me from any taint of hypocrisy. You who hear the footfall of an ant will surely hear my prayer.

Create in Me a Pure Heart

Monsignor James Turro

[Jesus] summoned the crowd and said to them, "Hear and understand. It is not what enters one's mouth that defiles that person; but what comes out of the mouth is what defiles one."
(Mt 15: 10-11)

More important than what one actually does is what one thinks and feels, what one intends: the state of a man's heart and mind. Jesus took aim at a view of life which believes that it is the mechanical observance of rules and regulations – regardless of one's state of mind – that pleases God. Jesus saw religion in a man's intent, from which intent all manner of good acts could issue.

If religion were just a matter of observing certain specified regulations, it would lack real challenge. Religion goes beyond rules and regulations to involve a person in some massive challenges. Further, one might say that it is most important *why* we act. Man sees only the deed, but God sees the intention, and the intention is of the highest significance. A man can call himself good when he has acted with the best intention. That is, with the intention of serving God through this particular action just performed. "A man is defiled not from the food that enters his mouth but from the perverse thoughts of his mind which proceed from his heart. For the food we receive for eating was created by God to sustain human life." Thus wrote Chromatius, one of the early Church Fathers.

In the matter of human behavior, it is interesting to speculate on the motivation of modern man as portrayed by the media. "To get ahead in life" – obviously no thought is given to what lies beyond earthly life. And if as some believe there is no life beyond, then all one's exertions are an exercise in futility.

It is most important to understand that we are not helpless in the face of a temptation to sin. Fortified by God's assistance, his grace, there is firm hope for success in resisting sin.

Merciful Father, grant me your grace in abundance that I may successfully oppose sin in my life. "I can do all things in him who strengthens me."

To Grow in Love and Loyalty to Christ
Monsignor James Turro

Then his disciples approached and said to [Jesus], "Do you know that the Pharisees took offense when they heard what you said?"
(Mt 15: 12)

The complexities of life are such that even well-meaning people stray from the right path at times. These persons have to be made aware of their blunder and be set on the right road. Hence the corrections that Jesus makes. It would be unwarranted to hold that every last Pharisee was hypocritical and mean-spirited.

Let us not forget Nicodemus who, in spite of his Pharisee affiliation, eventually turned to Christ and did so in spades. There is a fascinating account in John's Gospel of his coming to Christ. At first he approaches Jesus timorously. He calls on Jesus at night – for fear of being seen by his confreres in the Sanhedrin, the Jewish governing body in Jerusalem (Jn 3: 2). Later on when Jesus' case is being considered by the Sanhedrin, Nicodemus, still not ready to throw caution to the winds and step forward to identify himself as an admirer of Jesus, plays the part of a casual, uncommitted bystander. He observes: "Does our law condemn a person before it hears him and finds out what he is doing?" (Jn 7: 51).

At the death of Jesus on Calvary, Nicodemus the Pharisee finally does throw caution to the winds and helps Joseph of Arimathea take down the limp corpse of Jesus from the cross and give it a respectful burial. It was a most courageous thing to do. Feelings were running high and there was the probability that having killed Jesus, the crowds would go after his followers, among them, Nicodemus.

Beyond all this it must be noted that the matter brought up by Jesus' disciples – namely, the offense taken by the Pharisees – may represent the shock treatment Jesus used on the Pharisees. He sought in a strong way to bring them to their senses, so to say, to open their eyes to his Messiahship.

How favored we are to have come to know Jesus the Messiah without having to struggle as did the Pharisees of old.

Father, let me draw strength from Nicodemus' example – to stand by your Son and his teaching, in fair weather and foul.

Without God There Is No Hope of Success

Monsignor James Turro

[Jesus] said in reply, "Every plant that my heavenly Father has not planted will be uprooted." (Mt 15: 13)

How prone people are to speak for God. They are so confident of the rightness of their pet notion that they impute it to God. And if that be so, that their assertion is from God, as they would have others believe, who would dare ignore it, much less oppose it? In biblical times the Pharisees brazenly presumed to do just that – to speak for God. And Jesus faults them for this, for imputing their will to God.

In our day and age, the Pharisees of old no longer hold sway, ready to impose their nostrums upon us as coming directly from God. But heaven knows there is a host of others ready and eager to fix on us their way of life or their slant on reality. The media sometimes subtly, sometimes blatantly is there every day to "enlighten" us as to what we must do, feel, and think.

We who are committed to live by Gospel values must first of all develop a keen eye and ear so as to discern the blandishments which the world reaches out to us so as to get us to deviate from the Way, the Truth, and the Life.

The importance of God in the pursuit of truth and success cannot be minimized. Jesus employs a devastating analogy to illustrate this: the plant that the Father has not planted will be uprooted. The devoted Christian must not be taken in.

It is only what originates with God and is grounded in his truth that can have meaning and value for us. Too often that which the media trumpets proves to be disastrous. The world apart from God regularly conceives of projects and solutions that prove to be chaotic. Another notable instance would be war. Removed from God, one cannot expect less than disaster and disappointment.

In every one of life's situations, dear Father, make your will known to me. Let it guide me through the thick and thin of life.

And God Said: Let There Be Light…

Monsignor James Turro

"Let them alone; they are blind guides [of the blind].
If a blind person leads a blind person,
both will fall into a pit." (Mt 15: 14)

At any point in time there are trendsetters. They propose themselves as models which every thinking person should imitate. This is as true in modern times as ever it was in antiquity when the Pharisees without warrant presented themselves for emulation. Their presumption was as laughable – not to say as tragic – as a blind man offering himself as guide to another blind man. Though these men proposed themselves as leaders and guides, the Gospel urges people to ignore them.

Eye diseases in antiquity were the bane of life and were not rare. For a person afflicted with blindness to have as his guide another blind man is to court disaster – both are sure to end up in a ditch. Of course this saying of Jesus is a metaphor. The blind guides aimed at were the Pharisees who took delight in their "enlightenment" and proposed themselves as mentors for the common man. Jesus' designation of them as "blind leaders of the blind" is devastating.

Not to be pedantic, but perhaps note should be taken of the fact that in the sentence we have under study, the future tense is used: "both will fall into a pit." This gives the expression the feel of prophetic certainty.

In these times there are not wanting persons and institutions the media notably – which seek to mentor us and shape our lives. When viewed against the background of the Bible and the Church's teaching, these self-proclaimed guides are seen to be "blind guides of the blind." As with the Pharisees, not only does their hypocrisy blind them to their own defects, but in their blindness they lead others astray.

Our behavior in these our times should be shaped by the words of the Gospel as proclaimed and construed by the Church. Let the Gospel light the way for us as we make our way through life.

Father of light, illumine my way through life that I may not be lured away from the beauty and strength of your truth and your Church.

In All Things to Do Your Will, O God

Monsignor James Turro

"The things that come out of the mouth come from the heart, and they defile. For from the heart come evil thoughts, murder, adultery, unchastity, theft, false witness, blasphemy. These are what defile a person, but to eat with unwashed hands does not defile." (Mt 15: 18-20)

Some people almost make of Jesus an anarchist – uncongenial to law in every instance. In point of fact, however, Jesus' attitude toward the law as delineated by Matthew is quite positive. At one point Matthew quotes Jesus as encouraging the crowds to obey the appointed teachers of the law of Moses – "do and observe all things whatsoever they tell you" (Mt 23: 3). What is more, Jesus upheld the validity of the law up to the time of its fulfillment in his life. As Paul conceives it, the old law served a very exalted purpose: it brought Israel to the Messiah – as a household slave might bring a child to its tutor. What Jesus was unfriendly to was the ballooning oral tradition surrounding the law and promoted by the Pharisees. To cite one instance – eating with unwashed hands.

The list of sins alluded to by Jesus in these verses is a sampling of the various ways that one can offend God. The order in which these offenses are noted follows the order in which they occur in the Decalogue.

Even in our world and in our times, it is seldom that people underestimate the gravity of certain sins. God in his expressed will, as attested to by Scripture and the Church, all too often carries no weight in their thinking. And what is sadly lacking in some Christians is an awareness of the Church's teaching – lacking too is a certain degree of courage and humility to stand by the Church's positions, come hell or high water.

Grant me the strength, dear Father, to observe your commandments, generously and with love. May this be the main drive of my life – to do your will.

The Sound of Silence

Father Joseph Torchia, O.P.

*Behold, a Canaanite woman of that district came and called out,
"Have pity on me, Lord, Son of David! My daughter is
tormented by a demon." But [Jesus] did not say a word
in answer to her. (Mt 15: 22-23)*

When a loved one is ill or hurting, we're willing to go to great lengths to make things right again. We turn to those best qualified to render assistance and provide a means to healing. This is the situation of the Canaanite woman. She does the natural thing: she reaches out to the very one she knows can free her daughter from the grip of evil. The irony is that this woman is a complete outsider who would not ordinarily be receptive to Christ at all. But the sincerity of her plea outshines the tepid responses and skepticism of his closest followers. In this way, she exemplifies that spirit of unconditional trust of everyone in need who looks to Jesus in the most trying circumstances.

But Christ's silence immediately puts a new spin on the story. It highlights one of the greatest challenges for believers, and more specifically, the challenge of maintaining our faith in the course of our prayer life. The lack of a response on Christ's part by no means points to an absence of concern on his part. We know that he hears and that he will respond in a decisive way. But for the moment, his silence poses a severe test to that woman's faith.

How do we deal with seemingly unanswered prayers, and those dry spells when the silence can be deafening? Do we assume that God is oblivious to our needs? Do we give up or persist in our intercessions? Sometimes those periods of apparent silence occur when we are able to hear the voice of the Lord with the greatest clarity and discern his will. Those are the moments when he draws us into the deep waters of faith, out beyond the breakers, when we can no longer touch bottom and understand things from our limited perspective. That's when we surrender completely to his care and enter into the profound mystery of his abiding presence.

God, my Father, help me to listen to the promptings of your will, those gentle words that manifest themselves as a whisper in the night. But help me to persist in prayer even when all I hear is that empty sound of silence.

Can You Hear My Voice?

Father Joseph Torchia, O.P.

His disciples came and asked [Jesus], "Send her away,
for she keeps calling out after us." (Mt 15: 23)

A striking feature of life in any large city is the sight of homeless persons begging for spare change. Some merely extend their hands, waiting for a kind gesture from passersby. But others take the initiative and openly ask for assistance. And if people ignore their presence, they might even call after them. While it can be jarring to those on the receiving end, there's something poignant in this that can prick the conscience of the most self-absorbed pedestrians. There's an insistence in such appeals. You have to admire the sheer determination of those in the most desperate straits who refuse to be denied. It's as if they're saying, "I'm here, I'm a person, can you hear my voice?"

Those people remind me of the Canaanite woman calling out after Christ and the disciples. The disciples' response is so typical. She clearly makes them uncomfortable and they express the kind of annoyance that many of us experience in similar circumstances: "Leave me alone," or "Don't intrude on my privacy," or "Just go away." But in a very real sense, that Canaanite woman provides the ideal inspiration for us all when we raise our hearts and minds to God in prayer.

Now, there are people who pray and people who really pray. The latter group does not merely mouth the words but speaks to the Lord with a passionate conviction that demands to be heard. This woman's example motivates us to pray in that same manner, with passion, with urgency, with our whole being. In this context, the disciples' words "she keeps calling out" are crucial. Because that's precisely what we must do: call out to God with the implicit willingness to conform ourselves to his will. And that presupposes the trust that he does hear us and that he will respond, even if it's not when or how we expected.

God, my Father, I hear the voices of those in need all around me.
May I never send them away, but rather recognize in their voices
the call of my brothers and sisters in Christ.

A Great Teaching Moment

Father Joseph Torchia, O.P.

[Jesus] said in reply, "I was sent only to the lost sheep of the house of Israel." But the woman came and did him homage, saying, "Lord, help me." He said in reply, "It is not right to take the food of the children and throw it to the dogs." She said, "Please, Lord, for even the dogs eat the scraps that fall from the table of their masters." (Mt 15: 24-27)

In the course of his earthly ministry, Christ finds many occasions for exercising his role as teacher. He teaches by his example; by expounding on Scripture; by means of parables; or by posing hard-hitting questions to his followers and opponents alike. By and large, Jesus teaches by challenging people to a new vision of things. His encounter with the Canaanite woman provides a case in point. On the surface, Christ's words seem rather harsh, as if he wishes to exclude her from membership in the kingdom of God. But the ensuing dialogue offers the opportunity for a profound teaching moment that not only expands the woman's horizons of faith, but that of Christ's disciples as well. In this context, however, he teaches in a somewhat indirect manner, eliciting the right responses, and in so doing, demonstrates something vital about the scope of his redemptive mission.

Christ's mission is not confined to a single people. It embraces everyone in need of his message of love, forgiveness, and hope. So the mere fact that this woman is not an Israelite does not prevent her from imploring Christ's assistance. By the same token, Christ's proclamation of the Good News allows no room for the insider/outsider mentality so rife among the scribes and Pharisees. Even Christ's own disciples are not immune to this exclusionary attitude. How about us? Are we susceptible to that all too human tendency to view God's plan through our own restrictive lens? Do we lose sight of the perennial relevance of the truth of the Gospel to all people at all times? If we love in the manner of Christ, in the way he commands us to love, we must recognize our solidarity with all the members of his extended family on earth. Let us, then, never lose sight of that other command he gives his followers: "Go… make disciples of all nations" (Mt 28: 19).

God, my Father, you call all people into your family. Help me to recognize the reach of your love, so that I never exclude anyone from your fellowship. May my witness be directed to the whole world.

Wanting to Believe

Father Joseph Torchia, O.P.

Then Jesus said to her in reply, "O woman, great is your faith!
Let it be done for you as you wish." And her daughter
was healed from that hour. (Mt 15: 28)

Faith is a wonderful gift enabling us to accept God's will. But faith also presupposes freedom. In order to believe, we must want to do so. This isn't just stating the obvious. Because there's a dynamic element of choice involved in belief. And it's especially challenging to believe when we can't anticipate the outcome in advance.

In the Gospels, what accounts for the disparity in outlook between believers and non-believers? The evidence is there for all to see in the person and deeds of Christ. Why does the Canaanite woman believe when those who might have known better (like the Pharisees) simply do not? The non-believers, it seems, are unable to accept the truth and its challenge. So when Jesus tells the woman that it would be done as she wishes, he's neither reducing faith to wishful thinking, nor saying that people dictate their own terms to God. But in healing her daughter, he responds to the very faith which opened her to God's will in the first place. By requesting Christ's help, she entered a sphere that transcends ordinary doubt and uncertainty.

In point of fact, faith entails much more than an intellectual assent on our part. It also requires the receptivity of the heart allowing one to say (in the manner of the Blessed Mother), "May it be done to me according to your word" (Lk 1: 38). This kind of response entails tremendous risk. How different from that hardness of heart which closes us to the very possibility of God's action in our lives. In practical terms, believing demands an openness to the possibility of what seems utterly impossible from our limited perspective. It's to surrender to something beyond our ken. If we conform ourselves to God's will, completely and without reservation, then it will be done for us as we wish. Because then we'll accept whatever he grants us, in his own way, in his own time.

God, my Father, grant me a perspective which attunes me to your perspective, and a willingness to say yes to whatever you will.

Standard of Care

Father William M. Joensen

Great crowds came to [Jesus], having with them the lame, the blind, the deformed, the mute, and many others. They placed them at his feet, and he cured them. The crowds were amazed when they saw the mute speaking, the deformed made whole, the lame walking, and the blind able to see, and they glorified the God of Israel. (Mt 15: 30-31)

Jesus, fully human and divine, draws near to us. He wants to make contact, to unleash the reserves of goodness and lovability that should not be submerged by human frailty, or physical or mental illness. He wants to restore us and draw us to the source of glory. Amazing things happen in persons touched by Jesus; he bestows healing, instills hope, and helps us believe that heaven is open to us.

There is a tendency among medical students in this country to gravitate toward residencies in higher paying specialties such as dermatology, plastic surgery, and otolaryngology. It is not the case that these specialties are inherently more sophisticated or complex; in fact, fields such as obstetrics/gynecology, pediatrics, internal and family medicine – which are relatively less competitive – might in fact require greater intellectual agility, since the potential scope of practice is greater. One cannot presume selfish motives of persons going into higher paying specialties (some have huge student loans; others feel genuinely called), but it does seem that the need of some healers determines the form of treating persons who need healing.

Jesus and we who bear his name as a priestly people allow the predicament of others to orient our own choices and posture. We participate more and more in God's goodness as we approach God; if others have to help us draw close, this is an additional factor in our favor, rather than a liability. With Jesus, we become progressively unafraid to observe and be examined, to see and be seen, hear and be heard. We claim the capacity to bear and transmit grace, to grasp hold of others in our own right. We cannot keep amazement under wraps; we help reveal, rather than conceal, the Christ who comes to us. We are willing to be recognized just as we are: beloved in God's sight, and, hence, worthy to glorify the God of Israel.

God of Israel and healer of humanity, I am amazed each time I am able to approach your Son. May I always bring with me another hurting member of Christ's Body, so that together we may glorify you.

Perpetual Motion

Father William M. Joensen

Jesus summoned his disciples and said, "My heart is moved with pity for the crowd, for they have been with me now for three days and have nothing to eat. I do not want to send them away hungry, for fear they may collapse on the way." (Mt 15: 32)

Jesus has served as field medic who treats the crowds presented to him. And when he observes their hunger of three days' gestation, he soon becomes the master chef who fills the vacuum that nature cannot stand. Jesus is "moved with pity"; the hunger of others is a source of suffering for him. His mercy is a most active passion prompting him to do what he must to make whole. Jesus is ready to place himself in the void opened up by our own failing reserves. He overcomes the survival instincts that are part of our animal nature, that would scatter us in different directions and leave the least among us like so much road kill in the collapse of charity.

If God has been characterized as aloof or indifferent, we first need to take stock of ourselves. We humbly acknowledge that we have sometimes glutted our capacity to feel by quick and easy satisfactions that deliver some sense of mattering amidst the mundane. We know frustration in the face of a family member, acquaintance, or colleague whose imposition upon our fragile co-existence reveals a heart that desires some sense of connection. And yet we fear "going there" – because if another's heart is exposed as a spiritual pothole, it is likely that we will mistakenly regard our own hearts as a drain on a God who surely must be worn out by now.

But we dare not surrender to spiritual fatigue. Jesus, rich in kindness and for ever moved to pity in an unfavorable human climate, should become ever more familiar to us. We take heart in the daily acts that are a compact between ourselves and the Holy Spirit to let persons hungry for our attention claim us. In the process, we recognize that our own hearts are being formed and filled by God's mercy. We are relieved that God does not shrink from our hunger, but puts on an apron and gets to work.

Father of great compassion, you move toward us by sending us your Son, who shows us your paternal pity. Grant me the steadfastness of your Spirit that I may not shrink from those who hunger for you.

Stock Answers

Father William M. Joensen

The disciples said to [Jesus], "Where could we ever get enough bread in this deserted place to satisfy such a crowd?" Jesus said to them, "How many loaves do you have?" "Seven," they replied, "and a few fish." (Mt 15: 33-34)

Jesus' taking stock of available resources should not be likened to King David's census of the people (see 2 Sm 24). David numbered the Israelites in order to assess their military strength; his trust in God flagged. Christ's question about how many loaves and fish the disciples possess is an invitation to witness that God alone can transform their meager means and satisfy the crowd. Every Christian must be able to do the math and be a prudent steward through both bullish and bearish market seasons. But our flourishing depends on the ability to count on God rather than on our personal portfolios. One resource we dare not ration is faith.

A gifted young man tended to procrastinate and then claw himself out of stressful spots. He became increasingly addicted to smoking and other vices, reducing his mental agility and triggering a long dormant autoimmune disease. His once active faith fell by the wayside as he became locked into a spiral of debilitating behavior until finally, prompted by a few strategic questions that exposed his arid state of soul, he was led to take stock of his life. He began to pray again and participate in Mass with a newfound acceptance of who he was, and who he was not. His reliance upon God did not bring an immediate physical cure, but opened him to resources of consolation and encouragement as he counted more on God than on himself. He now recognizes that seeking certain professional careers would further erode his health and his hope of spiritual satisfaction; he has reoriented himself to become an alcohol and drug counselor, working especially with young people. He has laid hold of the holy prudence that recognizes the startlingly small scale of what we possess in proportion to the exponentially greater grace of God, and is well poised to participate in the abundance that God's power brings forth.

Lavish, loving Father, you share the life of your Son by enlisting what so often seems inadequate. May the faith that is your gift free me to count on you, and to place all I am at your disposal.

Ground for Hope
Father William M. Joensen

[Jesus] ordered the crowd to sit down on the ground.
(Mt 15: 35)

So often Jesus' words are directed to an individual person for the sake of healing, rebuke, or other purpose – and only then are the many meant to share in the ripple effects of those words. Here Jesus lands people on the plain by a direct order to a crowd meant to become a communion. Their fitful hunger would scatter them in different directions: persons of means back to their secure pantries; others to scrounge for whatever discarded morsel they might obtain by their own devices. In a social food chain absent faith, there is no mandate for civic friendship. In the wild where the Word has yet to be digested, there is no "reclining at table" in relative ease.

When an event is standing-room-only, advantages in height or the willingness to wield sharp elbows will prevail. But a crowd remains a crowd. Yet in this moment, the Word is beginning to transform lives, shifting the axis of association from vertical to horizontal. If persons sit down, the space they occupy expands and greater contact inevitably ensues. Restlessness might then yield to recognition of common hunger; the tension of sandwiched shoulders can yield to an even greater spread in which the Spirit can operate. The rigidity attending unchosen contact can be displaced by the decision to trust the persons next to us. When we receive God's word in common, we are no longer merely an obstacle to one another in the drive-through lane of life. We sense the breathing of those around us, we unplug ourselves from our electronic cocoons instead of from each other, we suffer the familiar conversation starters, and suddenly, our words are mingling with the Word, our story is being shared. In the moment when Christ orders on behalf of a dining party no longer pitted against each other, the first course of faith and mutual support is set; there is well-grounded reason for hope.

Father of heaven and earth, the ground we walk upon is also a classroom of charity and blessing. May I support those with whom I come in contact today as together we are ordered to your Word.

Happier Meal?

Father William M. Joensen

Then [Jesus] took the seven loaves and the fish, gave thanks, broke the loaves, and gave them to the disciples, who in turn gave them to the crowds. They all ate and were satisfied. They picked up the fragments left over – seven baskets full. (Mt 15: 36-37)

When bruised bodies and egos, broken hearts, and gnawing hunger seem to be the way of the world, how remarkable are those moments when our bodies are salved, our hearts stilled, our hunger satiated. Few and fleeting are the times when we can declare ourselves satisfied, for soon the rumblings of our infinitely capacious souls return. But in the precious moment of communion, we taste heaven; we slip beyond the fragmentation induced by our desire for more. Yet sustained satisfaction eludes us, and a preoccupation with extending the encounter can even thwart the sublime instant of realizing that for which we longed. We humans intuit the greatness of our nature in the experience of the glimmering half-life of earthly goods. Every meal we eat reflects the yoke of our mortality and intimates that the Eternal One beckons us. We come to know that nothing less than God himself will satisfy us.

Jesus the priest takes the seven loaves and few fish provided him, and before they can grow stale or smelly, he acknowledges their source, and accelerates their "death" by transforming them and those who enable their shared consumption. Jesus beatifies all who participate in this eucharistic exchange by confecting a holy stillness that supplants crowded appetites. Yet even this momentary satisfaction is but a premonition of the perpetual sacrifice that will ultimately overcome the fragmentation of our disparate pursuits to find the Love that has set our hearts in motion. We will that Jesus enlist us to gather fragments, and then our persons can become the baskets carried into the desert of human desires, to places where love is not yet present – between us, within us. The Lord who multiplies seven by infinite orders of magnitude alone is capable of leaving us for ever filled.

I do not seek, Father of the heavenly banquet, to be for ever satisfied in this life; what I do ask is that you would help me recognize you as the source of satisfactions by which you draw me to yourself.

Counting on Women and Men

Father William M. Joensen

Those who ate were four thousand men, not counting women and children. And when [Jesus] had dismissed the crowds, he got into the boat and came to the district of Magadan. (Mt 15: 38-39)

One of the prominent cruise lines in the world has the advertising slogan "Escape completely." This is a bit ironic, given that on some of their ships there are thousands of passengers and crew members on board. The ship-sharing denizens might find "escaping" to be more of a state of mind than a physical fact.

When Jesus dismisses the multitude of men, women, and children who have enjoyed a precursor to a eucharistic-style feast, he is not trying to escape from a gathering that has tapped out his power to keep track of the guest list, let alone to put food before them. Jesus leaves the premises with a certain evangelical energy that is inexhaustible. His passage by way of boat suggests the missionary cruise of the Church to both familiar and unfamiliar ports. Jesus does not abandon the mass of persons of modest means with whom he has broken bread; there is a shared mission to fulfill, fueled by the miraculous power to bring forth abundance where before there was only scarcity. To hang around shore waiting for the next meal is to miss the boat; to be fed by Christ is to be soon "dismissed" as at the end of Mass: Go in peace to love and serve the Lord.

There is an appointed time to be together, to commune as God wills. In contrast, couples who cohabit prematurely without marital commitment retain a mental "escape" clause that stymies Christ's power to deepen and sustain spiritual unity whether physically present or absent. Couples sealed in marriage are called to enhance our sense of the evangelical mission to go forth and multiply and then return home, all the while remaining faithful. Our share in Christ's mission repeatedly brings us together to celebrate, and takes us temporarily apart. Persons consecrated by Christ are able to quiet any inclination to escape; love endures, even if the seas sometimes turn rough.

Loving Father, you are always turned toward me, and I never want to escape your watchful gaze. Grant that I may be true to the commitments you have sealed in your Spirit, and fulfill the mission you have set before me.

Confrontage Road

Father William M. Joensen

The Pharisees and Sadducees came and, to test [Jesus], asked him to show them a sign from heaven. He said to them in reply, "[In the evening you say, 'Tomorrow will be fair, for the sky is red'; and, in the morning, 'Today will be stormy, for the sky is red and threatening.' You know how to judge the appearance of the sky, but you cannot judge the signs of the times.]" (Mt 16. 1-3)

The Pharisees and Sadducees are savvy interpreters of appearances, but they are prevented from penetrating below the surface of things into the deeper meaning of the signs before them – signs that indicate the time is right to turn and adhere to the Christ. They pose a test where, no matter what signs Jesus might supply in response, they would change both the questions and the evaluative standards on the spot. The portents of earth and sky pale in comparison to the radiant evidence of God's handiwork in the person of the Son. But we must first prostrate our pride and let God dispel our feckless efforts to live at the level we prescribe.

A young man sensed he had reached the time where he needed to step forward in faith and make a more significant life commitment. Through the turmoil of indecision, in the context of Eucharist, he sensed an interior voice that could only be Christ's, saying, "All I ask is that you trust in me." The message only partially stilled his roiling heart, and so he responded to the voice by saying, "Lord, all I ask for is one more little sign." Driving home on a familiar freeway, within thirty minutes he passed a bridge abutment on which was spray-painted the word "Trust." The young man's heart was stilled; a new peace and freedom to move forward dawned within him.

How many times had he passed that bridge before – that particular word already there?! But now he was attentive, receptive, ready to let Jesus point the way and decipher the signs that already surrounded him – in word and sacrament and the whole palette of personal actions and appearances that God deploys on a daily basis. Pope Benedict XVI comments that God may not send us our own personal star, but God does give us all sorts of signs, seen often in retrospect – in the rearview mirror that Christ adjusts for us.

I do not want to live only on the surface, Father of all times and seasons, but to be constantly alert to the signs of your Son that reveal the depth of your love – today and always.

Sign Language

Father William M. Joensen

"An evil and unfaithful generation seeks a sign, but no sign will be given it except the sign of Jonah." (Mt 16: 4)

Consider two signs: The first is a roadway sign perched near the peak of a mountain in New Mexico that reads "Gusty winds may exist." Not exactly a decisive indicator! The motorist is warned of natural forces that may be encountered – if they in fact even exist. The experience of others who have traveled the same path before may be diagnostic, but is hardly determinative for what one's own experience will bear. Conditions merit caution and may alter speed, but will not likely cause any major change in direction.

The second sign is the sign of Jonah recalled by Jesus. His learned audience should be quick on the uptake, but they seem deliberately slow to grasp his message, let alone act on it. Jonah was the initially unwilling conductor of a mass transit conversion. He found his words taken to heart by a people for whom the living God was no mere speculative possibility, but a bedrock truth. Buffeted by winds issuing from a tentative prophet, they heeded the call to change course, to convert their ways and take up the path of righteousness and truth. And in the process, their example overcomes Jonah's own sluggishness and propels him in the direction of God's Spirit.

For those who resolutely resist Christ's call to consume his bread, to interpret and heed the sign standing right before them, Jesus will not comply by invoking some further miracle to suit their fancy. Even then they would temporize and look for some force that would coax the "may" into a "must" believe. Their false "safe zone" stymies the freedom and respect God affords individuals who must act in faith if they are to reach the destination they seek. Plenty of people are turning to the Messiah who has brought them bread, but their numbers will never be enough for those who prefer to meander in affected indecision. Even Jonah knows that is no way to exist.

Righteous and real Father, convert my attention; guide my conscience; give me the courage to heed the sign of your Son and follow the direction of your Spirit, who blows where you will me to go.

Kneaded Preparation

Father William M. Joensen

*Then [Jesus] left them and went away. In coming to the other
side of the sea, the disciples had forgotten to bring bread.
Jesus said to them, "Look out, and beware of the leaven of the
Pharisees and Sadducees." They concluded among themselves,
saying, "It is because we have brought no bread." When Jesus
became aware of this he said, "You of little faith, why do you
conclude among yourselves that it is because you have no bread?
Do you not yet understand?"* (Mt 16: 4-9)

Matthew's regard for the children of Israel includes
measures of compassion and criticism. In this episode,
we have a perverse sort of passover where those in transit forget both the bread and the leaven of Spirit that would help
them understand God's most recent mighty deed in Christ. In effect,
they "despoil" themselves before departure. The disciples' lapse in
short-term memory leaves them too ripe to turn to that savvy someone who will be all too glad to make the soul pain go away. The
leaven of worldly presumption mingled with careless amnesia has
a certain soporific effect. We are left with a bloated feeling that
deceives us into thinking we have no room left over for God – at
least, until the gaseous bubble within us bursts and we are panic-
stricken that God has left us to starve on the other side of the sea.

We do not enter into this world with a blank slate. Our history
is mingled with those who preceded us, for whom God inscribed
his words on the tablets of their minds and hearts. The Word who
gathers all words unto himself intends that the leftovers of previous gatherings are to be the starter that sweetens, rather than sours,
the next moment of encounter. We are not entitled to proceed with
the presumption that we can passively, vacantly wander about with
naïve trust that God will protect us from all evil with no cooperation on our part. We are to attend to the words of Scripture, take
stock of what God has done in both distant and recent past. Our
conscientious, prayerful preparation triggers both long- and short-
term memories that are appropriate provision for the next phase
of the journey. The Holy Purveyor of Spirit and Life will in fact
supply the missing ingredients, but first honors us by asking us both
to empty our sacks and to recite something of the recipe God has
already entrusted to us.

*Father, dispel my amnesia, by stirring the Spirit who reminds me
what you have done on my behalf, that I may be leaven of the
kingdom in a world longing for you.*

The Provocative Question

Father Donald Haggerty

When Jesus went into the region of Caesarea Philippi he asked his disciples, "Who do people say that the Son of Man is?" They replied, "Some say John the Baptist, others Elijah, still others Jeremiah or one of the prophets." He said to them, "But who do you say that I am?" Simon Peter said in reply, "You are the Messiah, the Son of the living God." (Mt 16: 13-16)

Every teacher knows that one way to restore the attention of students in a class is to ask a sudden question – and the more unexpected and probing the better. The Gospel shows a certain analogy to this. Whenever Jesus places a question before his listeners, he is clearly intent on drawing the human heart to a deeper awareness in faith. The first words of our Lord to any of the apostles, for instance, were a question to Andrew and presumably John, when Jesus turned around to them at the Jordan River and asked, "What are you looking for?" The question was not a casual remark. It was meant to pierce their souls at once and to remain a provocative challenge for a lifetime.

Indeed Jesus will ask us the same question in the silence of our prayer if we are ready to hear him. This possibility of Jesus addressing a challenge to our soul is true also of the questions placed side-by-side in Matthew's sixteenth chapter. "Who do people say that the Son of Man is?… But who do you say that I am?" These questions ought to be heard together at times in our prayer. We might say that the first is answered properly whenever we assent in Catholic faith to the revealed truth of the divinity of Jesus Christ. We renew this assent in reciting the Creed each Sunday at Mass. Yet even while publicly proclaiming our faith, it is profitable spiritually to hear privately in prayer the very personal second question from Jesus – "But who do you say that I am?" Our Lord is asking each of us, in effect, who am I in your life? How important am I in your daily choices? Do you seek my presence each day of your life? Ultimately our answer to this question must echo the response of Thomas after the resurrection – "My Lord and my God!" – for indeed he must become everything to us.

Heavenly Father, grant me the grace in prayer to know that Jesus addresses my own soul in the words spoken in the Gospel, so that I might answer him with a gift of my whole heart and mind and soul.

The Gift of Faith

Father Donald Haggerty

Jesus said to [Simon Peter] in reply, "Blessed are you, Simon son of Jonah. For flesh and blood has not revealed this to you, but my heavenly Father. And so I say to you, you are Peter, and upon this rock I will build my church, and the gates of the netherworld shall not prevail against it." (Mt 16: 17-18)

The response of Jesus to Peter's proclamation of faith recalls certain truths about the nature of Christian belief. First Jesus praises Peter and calls him blessed for his conviction that Jesus is the Messiah, the Son of the living God. Then Jesus states that the knowledge Peter possesses of our Lord's divinity has not been acquired in any strictly human manner, but is a divine gift revealed by the heavenly Father.

The same is true in our own lives of faith. Our capacity to believe that Jesus is God in the flesh has not come from any natural effort of human learning. Instead we receive a supernatural grace to know the indisputable certainty of this truth, a truth that blesses our life with its most essential conviction. Once we possess this gift of faith, the reality of God's plan of love to save humanity through the suffering and death of the incarnate Son can become a kind of ever-present truth permeating our daily awareness.

This is so very different from a non-religious notion of conviction or belief. A man might be full of conviction, for example, that his favorite horse is going to win at the racetrack on Saturday. Another man might possess an unshakeable belief when he looks in the mirror that he is related to Babe Ruth. These examples are of course caricatures of faith. Rather, we believe because we are responding to a sacred gift of the God who has spoken to us in Jesus Christ.

When our Lord proclaims Peter as the rock upon whom he will build his church, we are reminded, moreover, that it is our faith in a divinely instituted Church that continues to assure us of remaining in this truth. The Church is the rock of all ages, and our docility to it will always be inseparable from our love for our Lord.

Father, I know well that my faith is your gift, and I thank you for this immense privilege of belief. Help me always to deepen my trust in you and to keep my desires turned toward pleasing you in all things.

The Petrine Keys

Father Donald Haggerty

"I will give you the keys to the kingdom of heaven. Whatever you bind on earth shall be bound in heaven; and whatever you loose on earth shall be loosed in heaven." (Mt 16: 19)

Saint Peter is often depicted in religious paintings as holding in his hand a set of keys given to him by Jesus after Peter's proclamation of faith in our Lord's divinity. A more humorous tradition imagines that these keys to the kingdom of heaven allude to Peter's job description in eternity as the guardian of the gate of heaven, assigned the task of checking the credentials of all who seek entry. But we know that the phrase Jesus uses is a deeper metaphor for the spiritual power of leadership that the first pope, Peter, and every subsequent pope exercises in the Church. Designated personally by our Lord for this particular service, Peter will be the first to hold the Petrine office named after him.

In performing this unique role, each pope, in history to the present day, receives both a divine command to maintain fidelity to the tradition of revealed faith and a divine promise that he will be protected in his task by the Holy Spirit. Jesus' words to Peter are in effect repeated again to every man who sits in the chair of Peter: whatever you bind or loose on earth is bound or loosed in heaven. The words do not imply that arbitrary decisions by the popes can take place regarding doctrinal matters. Their meaning is more profound. They invite us to understand God's constant presence in his Church guiding the pope in his office as the primary teacher of doctrinal truth. This is a promise from God not always acknowledged. Indeed the Church always suffers internal disunity when there is diminished respect for the teaching office of the Roman pontiff. Our own era has been a case in point. Yet it is equally true how blessed we have been in the Church for many decades now by a succession of saintly, courageous men as popes. Let us keep the Holy Father always in our daily prayers.

Almighty Father, in divine wisdom you have established your Church to be guided always by your Holy Spirit. Grant to me a great love for the office of the pope and a steady remembrance to pray for him each day of my life.

Our Lord's Foreknowledge

Father Donald Haggerty

From that time on, Jesus began to show his disciples that he must go to Jerusalem and suffer greatly from the elders, the chief priests, and the scribes, and be killed and on the third day be raised. (Mt 16: 21)

Our Lord does not speak to the apostles of his passion before Peter's acknowledgement in faith of his divinity. Only after his divine identity has been accepted does he reveal the mission of suffering he must complete as the incarnate Son. A principle of faith is shown here: once the reality of Jesus as God is known, all other mysteries of Christian revelation become accessible and joined to this singular truth. Nonetheless, a gradual process is always at work in deepening one's faith. The difficulty does not entail simply the act of faith in the divinity itself of Jesus. Peter recognizes the divine presence in Jesus, but this knowledge is partial and limited. The suffering that awaits our Lord is a truth still far from Peter's awareness. Even after his act of faith, Peter is like someone who gives a correct answer while deaf to the next question that demands response.

Jesus of course knows this and alludes to what is contained in the prophecies of the Old Testament. The Messiah has to undergo contempt and revilement, and suffer death at the hands of hostile men. We know that the apostles never manage to comprehend these predictions of Jesus' passion. They are shocked at the eventual arrest, trial, and execution of Jesus. Only after his death and resurrection do they come to understand the destiny of suffering that is in the divine plan for the incarnate Son.

Our vantage is the reverse. We know already the completion of the Gospel account. Indeed, our faith deepens as we perceive the entire life of Jesus, including his death, within a foreordained plan of God. A poignance and depth enters the words of Jesus and the scenes of the Gospel when we realize on every page that Jesus is speaking always as one who is preparing to offer himself for us on the cross at Calvary.

Eternal Father, help me to ponder the mystery of Jesus' awareness of his passion prior to his death. Allow me to see that throughout his life he longs for that day, that I may comprehend more fully his love.

The Thoughts of God

Father Donald Haggerty

Then Peter took [Jesus] aside and began to rebuke him, "God forbid, Lord! No such thing shall ever happen to you." He turned and said to Peter, "Get behind me, Satan! You are an obstacle to me. You are thinking not as God does, but as human beings do."

(Mt 16: 22-23)

We may be inclined at first to commiserate with Peter for the stern rebuke he receives from Jesus. When Peter attempts to reassure our Lord that no suffering would come Jesus' way, he perhaps sounds like a man trying to calm another man's fear in the face of uncertain dangers. But Jesus was not expressing anxiety in predicting his future passion. He was alerting the apostles to a prophetic truth about his destiny. Peter had it right in his earlier response to the question about Jesus' identity. But if Jesus was indeed the Son of the living God, as Peter declared, should it be surprising that our Lord would know what lay ahead in his path? Jesus' announcement of his passion, while certainly disturbing, ought to have been received with a simple acceptance – and then pondered more deeply in silence.

We can learn from Peter's mistake. Sometimes our quick negative reactions to God's ways are an obstacle to a deeper understanding of the divine purpose in events. And there is something else to notice in Peter's impulsive correction of Jesus. It is possible he felt a bit too elated and specially favored after Jesus' promise to build his Church on the rock of Peter. In taking Jesus aside in a kind of protective gesture, Peter's presumption seems bold. He may assume he is showing his loyal friendship and offering his own strength to Jesus, and his words no doubt are well-intentioned. But intentions alone do not always please God. Jesus' reprimand is severe – "Get behind me, Satan! You are an obstacle to me." Peter receives it for failing to realize that a much deeper mystery exists in Jesus than he suspected. It may be that we also do not reflect enough on the deeper mystery of love witnessed in Jesus' suffering for us. Perhaps only in the presence of his cross do we approach more closely the boundless love of God for our lives.

Merciful Father, forgive me when I, too, like Peter, become an obstacle to you and in any way resist your plan for my life. Help me to seek always your designs, that I may fulfill your will in my life.

Finding by Losing

Father Donald Haggerty

Then Jesus said to his disciples, "Whoever wishes to come after
me must deny himself, take up his cross, and follow me.
For whoever wishes to save his life will lose it,
but whoever loses his life for my sake will find it."
(Mt 16: 24-25)

These words spoken soon after Jesus' prediction of his passion place before us the challenge of sanctity: to give away one's life for love in a complete sense, without reserve, holding nothing back. This entails a willingness even to die for love of our Lord. The saints, the martyrs, are the great exemplars of this truth. In renunciation and self-abnegation, they found not pain and onerous burden but an exhilarating answer to their soul's passion. Dying to self in heroic generosity was inseparable from an intense commitment of love to Jesus Christ crucified. On the other hand, we may look at ourselves as fit only for the ordinary path. But does Jesus speak these words just to martyrs and saints, or to all who want to pursue him in love?

We have to assume that no one is exempt from this instruction. Renunciation to some degree is a requirement of love. Every soul will find that a deeper love for Jesus Christ brings exacting, even intimidating demands. Indeed there is a mysterious and quite personal nature to this. The road to Calvary is repaved and replicated in countless new ways for the chosen friends of Jesus. But this is not all that is discovered according to Jesus. An ultimate promise accompanies the demanding heroism of love. "Whoever loses his life for my sake will find it." The promise is not a reward simply in the next life. Even now a union with God by grace is possible. In this we ought to remember that it is often the small self-denial, the hidden sacrifice, that is the next step of deeper entry into the heart of our Lord Jesus Christ. Small actions done with great love have always marked saintly lives, and have always prepared saintly lives for the day of greater offering that still awaited them.

Father, grant to me a greater love for self-abnegation, and a
realization that in giving up myself in any sacrifice, I open my soul
to a deeper love for you.

Enduring Wisdom

Father Donald Haggerty

"What profit would there be for one to gain the whole world and forfeit his life? Or what can one give in exchange for his life?"
(Mt 16: 26)

Many people later in their lives can recount the memory of a single significant remark made to them in youth by a parent, a teacher, an athletic coach, which transformed their life. The combination of respect for the speaker and real wisdom in the remark allows the words to strike to the heart and remain a permanent truth affecting the remainder of a life. I remember at about twelve years old, for instance, my father commenting on his conversion to Catholicism during World War II after being raised Protestant that one's conviction in faith has not been tested until we have to choose it over the affection of a friend or a family member. A reason why remarks of this nature exert a strong influence is their evident truth once we allow them in time to become our own experience of life.

Jesus' words in the Gospel can be regular examples of this kind of penetrating wisdom about life. Jesus speaks about the ultimate truths we often face in our choices. His words may confront us with something like a crossroad of options. They urge us to perceive clearly what it is we intend to pursue in our lives. They warn us that a mistaken turn can be tragic and leave us regretful at the end of life. Jesus offers such a statement in these words: "What profit would there be for one to gain the whole world and forfeit his life? Or what can one give in exchange for his life?" Can one think of a better question to engrave in the stone frontispiece of every university gateway? And yet it is so very easy in a culture increasingly detached from religious truths to ignore the question of faith's conviction upon our choices in life. Nonetheless, Jesus' words invite us to remember once again the transitory nature of our lives. Life is short indeed, and we have our one opportunity to seek a life of faithfulness to God's purpose.

Father of all goodness, grant me the wisdom to know what is of eternal value and what is merely passing. May I always have the grace to choose those things which are upright and pleasing in your sight.

Heaven's Appeal

Father Donald Haggerty

*"The Son of Man will come with his angels in his Father's glory,
and then he will repay everyone according to his conduct. Amen,
I say to you, there are some standing here who will not taste
death until they see the Son of Man coming in his kingdom."*
(Mt 16: 27-28)

After exposing in previous verses the profound choice that
faces every follower of our Lord – in effect, how much really
do I want to give him of my life? – Jesus concludes with
divine words that promise untold happiness to the degree we accept
the challenge of full discipleship. There is indeed a stunning reward
that awaits those who are faithful and generous with God –
eternity with God and with all the angels and saints. It is true that
heaven cannot be conceived except in imagination, but it is most
certainly a place of uncontained joy and wonderful companionship.

At various times in history it has been cynically said that Christianity turned people's eyes toward the next life while leaving them
to their human miseries, rather than showing them how to improve
their earthly lot. This caricature of our faith ignores of course the
historical record of the immense charitable works of the Church
over centuries to relieve the sufferings of the poor. It also misses
the true stimulus to faith and works that comes when a life is
animated by a desire for an eventual union with Jesus Christ in the
next life. It is well said that those who do the most for others in this
life – the saintly personalities so dedicated in their heroic
self-giving – are those who long for the day when they can see our
Lord. Jesus says at the end of this passage that there are some who
will not taste death until they see the Son of Man coming in his
kingdom. He refers surely to his own resurrection appearances.
But the words remind us that death need not be feared. It is not
a bitter cup that our Lord will ask us to drink then. If we are
generous in our love during this life, he and his Mother will be our
companions at that hour.

*All-powerful Father, grant to my soul a deep longing to spend
eternity with you in heaven, that I may direct all my choices
during life with this end in view.*

Climbing God's Mountains

Father Aquinas Guilbeau, O.P.

After six days Jesus took Peter, James, and John his brother, and led them up a high mountain by themselves. And he was transfigured before them; his face shone like the sun and his clothes became white as light. (Mt 17: 1-2)

Throughout his public ministry, Jesus exhibits an obvious fondness for the mountains of Palestine. With his disciples often in tow, he repeatedly scales their slopes and rests atop their peaks. Those familiar with Palestinian geography can understand why. Though low and arid by Western standards, the heights of Israel possess a stunning beauty.

The Savior's love for Palestine's peaks centers on more than their natural appeal, however. Jesus draws near to these hills for the same reason as did Abraham, Moses, and David. Their summits are holy. On these favored heights, the Father of creation chose to collect his scattered people, to receive their prayers and sacrifices, and to reveal to them his wise and loving providence. For the Israelites, these peaks stood as witnesses to the Lord's salvific work, reminders of their own election. Traveling among these same mountains, Jesus imitates more than once his Father's actions toward Israel. At their summits, he speaks divine truth to the world. On one such occasion, in anticipation of his impending death, our Lord chooses a mountaintop on which to reveal his divinity and offer comfort to his disciples. At that moment, Christ adds Mount Tabor to the highest rank of Israel's hallowed peaks. Its honor would be surpassed only by Calvary's.

By their very nature, mountains present a challenge to man. Climbers must sacrifice a great deal to reach their summits. Perhaps this is why in the Old and New Testaments God reveals himself on mountaintops. He wishes to indicate that his word requires effort to hear, and sacrifice to understand. That is to say, his revelation does not adapt itself neatly to the contours of this valley of tears. Instead, it calls us to the heights, to something challenging and transformative. On Tabor, Jesus teaches this lesson anew to Peter, James, and John.

Heavenly Father, draw us safely up the mountain of faith, so that at its height we may see your truth and accept your transforming love.

Mount Tabor: Heaven on Earth

Father Aquinas Guilbeau, O.P.

And behold, Moses and Elijah appeared to [Peter, James, and John], conversing with [Jesus]. Then Peter said to Jesus in reply, "Lord, it is good that we are here. If you wish, I will make three tents here, one for you, one for Moses, and one for Elijah."
(Mt 17: 3-4)

For Peter, James, and John, the mystery of the Transfiguration marks a final step in their formation as apostles. They have been chosen by Jesus to witness the horror of his cross, but they require one last lesson in grace before confronting its terror. On their way to Jerusalem, Christ strengthens these men to endure his passion by offering them a deep look into the grace of the incarnation. On Mount Tabor, Jesus reveals to them the glory of his divinity by allowing it to shine for an instant through his transfigured humanity. In a glory hitherto unseen by the disciples, everything changes around them. Without leaving this world, they are enveloped by the life of the world to come.

When examining this mystery we can appreciate how on Tabor Christ brings together, seemingly for the first time, the constitutive elements of the future kingdom. First, we see the Blessed Trinity, the source of all life. All three Persons of the Trinity manifest themselves to the disciples and exhibit their divine communion. Second, Holy Israel is there in the figures of Moses and Elijah, who announce the salvation of the chosen people by acknowledging Christ as the fulfillment of their messianic hope. Finally, the Church is present in the figures of the disciples themselves. They complete this triptych by representing the new and universal people of God, which exists even before Pentecost in the communion of Jesus, Mary, and the apostolic band. In the mystery of the Transfiguration, therefore, the disciples see what we will behold in heaven: the old and new people of God brought graciously into the communion of the Blessed Trinity.

It is no wonder then that Peter, James, and John do not want to leave the mountain. For a moment, in its prefigurement, they find themselves already in heaven. But only for a moment. Calvary still awaits them.

Heavenly Father, you console us in every distress and strengthen us for every trial. Make our hearts docile to this work of your love.

Faith's Brilliant Darkness

Father Aquinas Guilbeau, O.P.

While [Jesus] was still speaking, behold, a bright cloud cast a shadow over them, then from the cloud came a voice that said, "This is my beloved Son, with whom I am well pleased; listen to him." (Mt 17: 5)

We all know the adage: "It's always darkest before the dawn." Like other similar maxims, it attempts to draw a lesson about life from the rhythms of nature. In this case, the lesson taught is simple. Because the sun must set in the west before it can rise again in the east, its absence at night offers us no real cause for concern. Aware of the sun's natural course, we rest assured that the darkest part of night acts to herald the approaching dawn. When repeating the adage, therefore, we encourage others to find within life's difficult moments something like the hope of dawn contained within night's darkest hour.

The Transfiguration reveals, however, that grace possesses a rhythm somewhat different from nature's. If in the natural world night's darkness merely foretells the light of dawn, in the Christian life light can be found in darkness itself. This mystery is revealed on Tabor. As the disciples are basking in the glow of Christ's transfigured face, another light shines upon them. Issuing from its own bright source, this light possesses a brilliance that casts a shadow over them, enveloping them in stunning darkness. Here natural phenomena are stretched to communicate accurately the realities of grace. Within this brilliant darkness, the disciples see light, as it were. They hear the voice of the Father confirm the identity of Jesus: "This is my beloved Son; listen to him."

The Christian learns on Mount Tabor that faith creates a darkness in us that purifies earthly life. Its brilliance, which our physical senses cannot detect, disciplines the senses and corrects our overreliance on them for lasting peace and security. Within the shadow of faith, our spiritual vision is awakened and given room to develop. Therefore, only in the darkness of faith can we grasp the divine truth conveyed to us through the spoken word of the Father.

Heavenly Father, may the grace of Tabor strengthen us to penetrate faith's darkness, in which the truth of your Word is clearly seen.

The Cloud of Knowing

Father Aquinas Guilbeau, O.P.

When the disciples heard this, they fell prostrate and were very much afraid. But Jesus came and touched them, saying, "Rise, and do not be afraid." And when the disciples raised their eyes, they saw no one else but Jesus alone. (Mt 17: 6-8)

God manifests his divinity not once but twice on Mount Tabor. In the first display of power God enlightens the disciples' eyes, whereas in the second he fills the space of their ears. The three disciples react differently to each display, however. They register joy in seeing the transfigured face of Christ, but fear grips their hearts when they hear the voice of the Father. What explains the difference between these two reactions?

The answer may lie in a weakness we exhibit when reading the signs of divine providence: we often recognize the divine origin of providence more easily when it appears to us in miraculous form, and less easily when it unfolds through human agency. In other words, the fewer human hands – the fewer mediations – we see involved in God's work for us, the more easily we recognize its supernatural source. Throughout his public ministry, Jesus confronts this weakness in his followers. The crowds constantly ask him for a sign, some divine trick, to prove his divinity. They crave extraordinary, nature-bending manifestations of God's power over the ordinary graces Jesus is giving them every minute. These include his teaching, mercy, and friendship, each of which is communicating the divine to them. On Tabor, we see this weakness at play again. The disciples recognize the awesome power of God more easily in a talking cloud than on the human face of his Son.

Still, the Father's witness changes the disciples' regard for Jesus. The Father's testimony reveals to them that the sound coming from the cloud and the light emanating from Christ's face share a common source. Therefore, Peter, James, and John learn that day the truth Christ would later elaborate in a prayer offered at the Last Supper: "I have given them the glory you gave me, so that they may be one, as we are one" (Jn 17: 22).

Heavenly Father, as you revealed your Son's identity to Peter, James, and John on Mount Tabor, speak that same word of witness in our hearts, so that we may cling to Jesus and follow him to your glory.

The Mountain and the Crowd

Father Aquinas Guilbeau, O.P.

When they came to the crowd a man approached, knelt down before [Jesus], and said, "Lord, have pity on my son, for he is a lunatic and suffers severely; often he falls into fire, and often into water. I brought him to your disciples, but they could not cure him." (Mt 17: 14-16)

As Jesus and the three disciples descend Mount Tabor, they immediately encounter the needs of the fallen world. A frantic father with a sick son approaches them and pleads with the Lord for help. We see how quickly the graces of quiet contemplation prepare us to hear the cries and supplications of those in need.

Ancient thinkers struggled to reconcile the demands of the active and the contemplative lives, believing that both the goals and the means of leisured thought and manual labor stood together in mutual opposition. Early Christians, too, struggled with the apparent antinomy between action and contemplation, resulting in a popular view of a split between the two. It quickly became commonplace to distinguish the active laity in the world from the contemplative monks in their monasteries. It was held that "ne'er the twain shall meet." This strict separation of the two lives finds an early correction in the writings of the Church's first monk-pope, Saint Gregory the Great. After his election, Gregory came to discover how his ascetical training and monastic prayer served to strengthen his pastoral service. In the life of the preacher especially, he observed, contemplation and action – the *ora et labora* of the Benediction tradition – necessarily join in the preacher's proclamation of the Word. Saint Thomas would later incorporate Saint Gregory's wisdom in his very positive views of the "mixed life."

Of course, Jesus himself lives a "mixed life" of contemplation and action. The juxtaposition of Mount Tabor, the great symbol of contemplative prayer, and the manifold needs of the crowd on the plain suggests how easily Jesus passes from prayer and contemplation to preaching and compassionate service. The two lives of action and contemplation are not opposed in him. Rather, they join to shape his singular life and messianic mission.

Heavenly Father, you have made us to pray and to work. In our imitation of your Son, may the Holy Spirit bring both activities to perfection in us.

Praying the Perfect Petition

Father Aquinas Guilbeau, O.P.

Jesus said in reply, "O faithless and perverse generation, how long will I be with you? How long will I endure you? Bring him here to me." Jesus rebuked him and the demon came out of him, and from that hour the boy was cured. (Mt 17: 17-18)

At certain points in the Gospel text, the narrative advances quickly, and we do not find mentioned every detail of the sacred action it is describing. The Gospels give believers what they need to believe, however. The meaning of Christ's words and works emerge sufficiently without our knowing, for instance, what Christ took for breakfast or the exact hour he was baptized. Still, when reading this Gospel shorthand, we can be left scratching our heads. The meaning of Jesus' words might be clear, but they can appear unexpectedly or surprisingly passionate within the narrative as written. The two verses above give us an example of this Scriptural puzzle.

At first glance, Christ's reaction to the father's plea for healing appears without warning. What fault elicits Christ's just anger? What prompts his quick and forceful condemnation of this generation's faith? Is it the negligent faith of his disciples, whose apparent weakness renders their prayers ineffective? Or is it the undeveloped faith of the father, who might have reduced faith to its utility? Clearly, it is appropriate to pray for the healing of the sick. This father in fact draws near to the very source of healing grace. But could the man have made the mistake of loving the hoped-for effect of grace, that is, the healing of his son, more than its source, Jesus? Although ready to employ faith for the good of his son, was the father ready to take upon himself the responsibilities of a personal relationship with Christ?

Saint Augustine teaches that the greatest change effected by prayer is the conversion of the pray-er himself. The real goal of prayer is not to change God's mind, but to align the heart of the supplicant to the divine will. Therefore, the prayer of both the disciples and the father may have lacked the one petition necessary to all Christian prayer: Thy will be done.

Heavenly Father, make us perfect in prayer. May our hearts align with yours as we seek your face and work for the salvation of our brothers and sisters.

The Powerful Source of Faith

Father Aquinas Guilbeau, O.P.

Then the disciples approached Jesus in private and said, "Why could we not drive it out?" He said to them, "Because of your little faith. Amen, I say to you, if you have faith the size of a mustard seed, you will say to this mountain, 'Move from here to there,' and it will move. Nothing will be impossible for you."
(Mt 17: 19-20)

After reproaching the crowd for its weak and undeveloped faith, Jesus turns to the distraught father and consents to his request. He rebukes the unclean spirit, and the man's young son is healed. As the reunited father and son return home, Jesus is left with his disciples, who still suffer the sting of his reprimand. They possess an illness as serious as the boy's. Their faith is lacking. To cure their weakness, the Lord confers on them an important lesson. He teaches his feeble disciples what in fact faith requires.

Like the father, the disciples approach the Lord and admit their helplessness to him. Humiliated both by the inefficacy of their prayer and by the Lord's scolding, the disciples pose a specific question to Jesus. It appears that they already know its answer – "O faithless and perverse generation!" – but they ask it in such a way so as not to concede defeat. They feign ignorance over the cause of their weakness: "Why could we not drive [the demon] out?" Jesus' response is loving but forthright: "Because of your little faith." This is the saving truth that begins to heal the disciples' weak souls.

Jesus instructs his disciples that faith's real power lies not in its effects but in its source. In other words, the most important truth contained in Christ's instruction on faith is not the virtue's ability to move mountains. Rather, the lesson teaches that the source of faith introduces a mountain-moving power into the world. "Nothing will be impossible for you." Still, faith's real purpose is not to impress us with its effects. Faith conforms us to its divine cause.

Faith becomes weak when belief seeks results without some manifest attachment to the source of faith and the genuine benefits of faith. What comfort does this divine teaching reveal? The Source supplies all we need, even in the absence of hoped-for results.

Heavenly Father, in baptism you bless us with faith. Keep our faith in the revelation of your Son rooted in your truth and in the power of your love.

The Diverse Unity of Providence

Father Aquinas Guilbeau, O.P.

As [Jesus and his disciples] were gathering in Galilee, Jesus said to them, "The Son of Man is to be handed over to men, and they will kill him, and he will be raised on the third day." And they were overwhelmed with grief. (Mt 17: 22-23)

When Christ ascended Mount Tabor, he selected three of his disciples to accompany him: Peter, James, and his brother John. His choice predestined this trio to receive a unique grace. They basked in the glory of the Transfiguration. In privileging these three men, however, does Jesus fail to love the rest of his followers? Are these the only disciples he readied for the horrors of his upcoming passion? Not at all. As Matthew tells us in the verse above, Jesus prepares all of his disciples in due course, though in a less spectacular manner. To the rest, he simply makes known the treachery awaiting him in Jerusalem. So why the Transfiguration for only a few?

The Transfiguration's fuller purposes do not become apparent until after the events on Calvary, when two of the three privileged disciples fail to recall Tabor's grace. John, who remains faithful to the end, is the first to believe in the resurrection (Jn 20: 8), and he is the first to recognize the risen Lord standing on the shore (Jn 21: 7). Later on, James will be the first apostle to shed his blood for Christ (Acts 12: 2). And for his part, Peter, who denied the Lord, will rely on the grace of Tabor to fortify his witness to the resurrection when preaching and writing to various Christian communities (2 Pt 1: 17).

It remains one of the inscrutable mysteries of God's providence that he freely deals differently with his creatures, even when they find themselves in similar situations and with similar needs. In drawing us with our neighbor to himself, God reveals no equality of treatment, though he gives each what he needs. This disparity of treatment is for our benefit. Because God grants different graces to different parts of his Church, the whole is brought together in mutual dependency. In the diversely gifted *ecclesia*, love finds opportunity for its perfection.

Heavenly Father, you know the needs of all and you supply for them in abundance. May we put your gracious gifts at the service of our brothers and sisters.

Peter's Pence

Father Lawrence Donohoo, O.P.

"What is your opinion, Simon? From whom do the kings of the earth take tolls or census tax? From their subjects or from foreigners?" When he said, "From foreigners," Jesus said to him, "Then the subjects are exempt. But that we may not offend them, go to the sea, drop in a hook, and take the first fish that comes up. Open its mouth and you will find a coin worth twice the temple tax. Give that to them for me and for you."
(Mt 17: 25-27)

What the temple tax collectors don't know won't hurt them, but it helps us who overhear Jesus' instructing Peter. He solves not only his own problem, but also Peter's, who just told the collectors that his teacher pays taxes. And so the fisherman who proclaimed the Master's justice is exonerated by his mercy. Peter, now made fisher of money, opens the fish's mouth so that he and his Lord might remain silent.

During a summer of ministry with the Lakota Sioux, I was invited one evening to a small gathering of elders. Excited by this opportunity to get answers about tribal life and history, I mentally prepared my interrogative wish list. But when I arrived I almost saw the aura of silence, and I quickly gleaned that age mattered here. After a long stillness, the chief elder ventured a sentence, and then all fell silent again for another embarrassing eternity. A second elder responded with a terse remark, and all was silent again. And so it continued. Before long I came to see that I came to hear a silence that gives weight to the words and distinguishes them from each other.

Print too much money and it becomes worthless. Blather on and words become cheap. If we really took human speech seriously, there would be a good deal less of it. And it would likelier penetrate human hearts than escape through the other ear. Does another really need to hear this or know that? Less is more. In the Gospels, there is more to this than meets the ear, for there we find the silence of decision and action, the silence of Mary at the feet of Christ, the silence of Jesus praying through the night. The Word himself is spoken out of the silence of the Father. We must be still to hear them both.

God, our Father, help us imitate your silence and your speech. You have spoken only one Word. Let us hear him, and speak words that will truly help others hear your peace.

Who Cares?

Father Lawrence Donohoo, O.P.

At that time the disciples approached Jesus and said, "Who is the greatest in the kingdom of heaven?" He called a child over, placed it in their midst, and said, "Amen, I say to you, unless you turn and become like children, you will not enter the kingdom of heaven. Whoever humbles himself like this child is the greatest in the kingdom of heaven. And whoever receives one child such as this in my name receives me." (Mt 18: 1-5)

In my childhood, a familiar verbal ritual began with my father's asking: "Who's the greatest man in the world?" "You are!" my sisters and I would respond in unified chorus. Even at that tender age we knew along with him that he wasn't even close to winning that title. What his question really expressed was that we were the greatest children in his life. What our answer was really saying was that he was the greatest man in our lives.

"Vanity of vanities, says Qoheleth" (Eccl 1: 2). "Vanity of vanity," one might add, with respect to honor. What difference does it actually make if others render me honor? Long ago Aristotle argued from common sense that it is excellence that human beings truly admire, so why not pursue excellence instead of admiration? Why not avoid the "middleman" of honor since I can't assure I'll receive it, but I can determine whether I should? Aristotle taught that our chances of being happy dramatically increase to the degree that we free ourselves of the need for laurels.

But as Christians, shouldn't we seek God's approval? In fact, we don't need it because we already have it in the form of divine love. We pursue holiness (Christian excellence) not because we try to impress God, but because he's already impressed us – with his grace. If I honor the source, my pursuit for honor can stop. When I recognize God's power and love, the limelight shifts to him. "With a little child to guide them" (Is 11: 6), Jesus makes humility a requirement for the kingdom. Perhaps there we'll hear God saying: "Your humility looks great to me." That's the humility that folds its own tent and disappears. I'm only the greatest when I'm busy proclaiming God's greatness. Even if and when it's recognized, my greatness will not matter.

Heavenly Father, you call me to the greatness that is able to worship you for your infinite greatness. Help me to see that true greatness is recognizing that I'm your creature, your child.

May I Have Your Attention

Father Lawrence Donohoo, O.P.

"Woe to the world because of things that cause sin! Such things must come, but woe to the one through whom they come! If your hand or foot causes you to sin, cut it off and throw it away. It is better for you to enter into life maimed or crippled than with two hands or two feet to be thrown into eternal fire. And if your eye causes you to sin, tear it out and throw it away. It is better for you to enter into life with one eye than with two eyes to be thrown into fiery Gehenna." (Mt 18: 7-9)

So it comes to this. Of course, it doesn't come to this. That's the whole point. Long before reporting to the amputation center, I would deal with my issue. But because I don't take Jesus' teaching here seriously, I'm not likely to take my temptation too seriously either. The point of the violent language here is to put the problem in imperative mode, to shake me up. If this won't, what will? What am I waiting for? How much longer do I have to wait for myself?

There are lots of reasons to wait. For one thing, it's worked so far. Sure, I carry the damage with me, but I judge it's easier to live with the devil I know than to venture out into an unknown domain of grace. Further, I can't solve this problem anyway: I came this way, or the events of life crippled me and I simply have to live with this. Comparative studies are a help here: you think I'm bad, just look at my neighbor. Besides, is it really that important? I agree I'd be better off without this sin, but I'm too busy ministering to others to deal with this…

If we could expend just a fraction of the effort needed to design and sustain such elaborate excuses on devising a plan for making a frontal assault on our temptation, we would be off and running. Fine, but shouldn't we wait for grace? Grace is waiting for us! His name is Jesus Christ, and he just said cut it off, cut it out, send it away! We have met the enemy and he is us – or rather, the part of us that wages this interminable guerrilla campaign against the other part – our conscience – anxious to get on with conversion. With Jesus' help, we need lose nothing but our sin.

God, my Father, I've not taken my sins seriously enough, which is another way of saying I've not taken your Son's redemptive work seriously enough. Help me to end this now!

So There You Are!

Father Lawrence Donohoo, O.P.

"If a man has a hundred sheep and one of them goes astray, will he not leave the ninety-nine in the hills and go in search of the stray? And if he finds it, amen, I say to you, he rejoices more over it than over the ninety-nine that did not stray. In just the same way, it is not the will of your heavenly Father that one of these little ones be lost." (Mt 18: 12-14)

The numbers are on my side. They give me comfort that I have remained faithful, and my mind quickly ranges far and wide to pick out those unfortunates in my world who I conclude are among the lost. But what do the Scriptures report? "All have sinned and are deprived of the glory of God" (Rm 3: 23). It is the ninety-nine who have scattered. Excluding the Shepherd himself, there is one – and only one – who has not strayed: the fair ewe, Mary. The numbers, then, are exactly wrong. By offering completely fallacious statistics, this parable forces me to face the unpleasant fact that I'm the one caught in the briar patch, and that it's high time that I start bleating for my Lord.

But this is not the critical point in this parable. Jesus tells us what it is: the Father's will is that none of his "little ones" be lost. Strictly speaking, we are all little; strictly speaking, we are all lost. The Father means to do something about this. This parable, then, is about him. So let's picture this Good Shepherd, charged to go off in search of the stray, setting out on foot in ninety-nine different directions through the verdant pastures and the dark valleys of our world. And let's picture the same Good Shepherd searching high and low through the hills and dales of our minds and hearts in hot pursuit of us wandering in countless ways. Let's take time to appreciate the fact that we keep this Shepherd very busy. And never was he busier than on that dark afternoon when he was helpless to pursue us: "'I will strike the shepherd, and the sheep of the flock will be dispersed" (Mt 26: 31). Yet never was salvation closer than when we seemed so far away.

Heavenly Father, we have wandered far from you, but we are your people, the sheep of your pasture. We will give thanks to you for ever, because we were lost but now we are found.

It Goes with Saying

Father Lawrence Donohoo, O.P.

"If your brother sins [against you], go and tell him his fault between you and him alone. If he listens to you, you have won over your brother. If he does not listen, take one or two others along with you, so that 'every fact may be established on the testimony of two or three witnesses.' If he refuses to listen to them, tell the church. If he refuses to listen even to the church, then treat him as you would a Gentile or a tax collector."

(Mt 18: 15-17)

What startles us here is that forgiveness doesn't always require that we simply take it on the chin. Yes, sometimes we turn the other cheek, but that doesn't mean we can't file a protest. In fact, we have a clear precedent. When Jesus was struck by one of the temple guards, he objected and asked: "Why do you strike me?" (Jn 18: 23). Of course, in small matters it's better to forgive and forget since making a fuss is more work than it's worth and does more harm than good. But other times reconciliation, and the forgiveness it implies, requires that I confront my offender, and that takes courage.

Actually, there is something to do even before this. I must first admit I've been hurt – to myself, and hopefully to my Lord. For forgiveness is a response to injury. If I have not been hurt, I cannot forgive. And to be wounded implies that I have a capacity to be hurt, whether physically, psychologically, socially, or spiritually. It is not always easy to admit my vulnerability. Under the guise of a deceitful forgiveness, I can parade around as the Iron Man or Woman who just doesn't feel pain. Nonsense. If I can't get over it, I need to get over to my brother or sister and file a complaint. It's not simply a matter of being just to myself, but also of being just to the offender. When people make mistakes, they need to be accountable for them. How can they repent or improve if they receive no feedback on their actions? No use lying to myself by saying it doesn't matter. If it doesn't matter, I need not bother to forgive. Forgiveness is only necessary when it *does* matter. And precisely because it does, I'm meeting my brother to complain and to forgive.

My heavenly Father, give me the courage to confront my weakness and admit my wounds. Then help me over to my brother and sister to let them know about it so that we can start over.

The Power in the Kingdom

Father Lawrence Donohoo, O.P.

"Amen, I say to you, whatever you bind on earth shall be bound in heaven, and whatever you loose on earth shall be loosed in heaven." (Mt 18: 18)

Jesus speaks similar words to Peter in Matthew, chapter 16, but here he is addressing all his disciples. If the formal teaching is about imposing and lifting the ban of excommunication, the practical tidings are that the Lord gives his followers permission to arrange certain matters freely. By ratifying their actions, Christ gives his Church the right and responsibility to help shape his Father's kingdom. We shouldn't then expect, like workers on a construction site, that everything is to follow some preordained blueprint. The divine management style allows the Church to fill in many of the details. And this she has done over the centuries in her liturgy, sacraments, devotions, and pastoral teachings.

What is true for the Church is true for us as well. God's intention to share responsibility is seen in the way he runs his creation. Animals are empowered to seek their own good and raise their young. Even though they aren't strictly free, their spontaneity allows them to respond flexibly to their environment. All the more should we expect our human freedom to include the power to bind and loosen our talents, desires, and relationships in a variety of ways. True, sometimes the Lord makes it clear how he wants things tightened and relaxed, whether through Gospel teaching as the Church presents it or through personal inspirations that enlighten our conscience. But other times he allows us to bind and to loose by standing back and giving us permission to shape our lives in the details according to good common sense. "Come up with a plan and give it your best shot," he seems to say. "And let me know what it is." So we stay closely in touch with him to know when he wants us doing it his way, and when he allows us to do it our way and makes our way his.

Our Father, you are big enough to let us be big too. You have empowered us to share the kingdom's power. Help us to use it carefully since our actions have eternal consequences.

227

Strength in Numbers

Father Lawrence Donohoo, O.P.

"If two of you agree on earth about anything for which they are
to pray, it shall be granted to them by my heavenly Father.
For where two or three are gathered together in my name,
there am I in the midst of them." (Mt 18: 19-20)

Jesus makes two promises when we come together. If we unite in a common petition, our prayer will be granted. If we unite in person, Jesus will be granted. In the first promise, the Lord says, "I'm glad you asked"; in the second, he's saying, "I'm happy to be here." In either case, the startling revelation is that we're important. God wants to do our will and to be with us.

In the Our Father we pray, "Thy will be done," but here the heavenly Father is saying, "Your will be done." But why is this surprising? If being with God is basically relational, shouldn't we expect some give and take? Consider the talk between God and Abraham, God and Moses, God and David, God and Jeremiah, Gabriel and Mary, Jesus and the apostles. God loves interaction. He wants people really engaged with him – to care enough to come to him, to come together, to figure things out, to talk it out.

In a mature relationship, I conform to your will on occasion and you conform to mine. Even better is agreement: you and I make our will one. Instead of your doing my will or my doing yours, we do *our will*. Each of us becomes this new will now shared in common. What's true of us should also be true of God. Better than doing his will, we *become* it – having the same plans, desires, goals, visions, loves. And the Father is glorified by becoming this common will as well. Which means that all this talk about his will or your will or my will breaks down. It's ours. God wills, then, that we will, that we desire, that we desire aright – with him. He and we are in this together, even if he remains first among unequals. Small wonder, then, that when our wills are joined, Jesus shows up. Wherever the Father's will is present, you can expect him to be just around the corner.

Gracious Father, you have given us wills that we might use them
wisely, uniting them to yours and each other's. Help us become
more willful so that our obedience is the same as our love.

Seven, Eight, Nine, Ten

Father Lawrence Donohoo, O.P.

Then Peter approaching asked [Jesus], "Lord, if my brother sins against me, how often must I forgive him? As many as seven times?" Jesus answered, "I say to you, not seven times but seventy-seven times." (Mt 18: 21-22)

Let's note at the outset that it's a brother in question, not a cruel tyrant or serial killer. It's the repeated fault that drives us crazy. We've observed it some seven hundred and seventy-seven times, with no change in sight. Our job now is to outlast him: to put up with this sin longer than he can. We've reprimanded him, called in witnesses, the Church, the police, and still nothing. Then we called our brother a tax collector – and now we get only a vague apology as automatic as the repeated sin. So why should we forgive if everything remains the same, including our brother's stubbornness? Can we forgive someone uninterested not only in reform but even in forgiveness?

Yes, by distinguishing forgiveness from reconciliation. Forgiveness is a power I possess that doesn't depend on my brother's response. "I recognize that you have injured me, either deliberately or not caring enough not to. I know you've hurt me and I want you to know it as well. Though I've been hurt, I want to liberate both of us from your action. I free myself from anger, hatred, and revenge. I free you, not *from*, but *for* responsibility. I invite you to take whatever actions are needed to restore the situation or make matters even better than before." If my words are heard, restitution is offered, changes made, reconciliation achieved, and together we leave the past behind. If my words are ignored, reconciliation is jettisoned, but forgiveness remains possible. I can go it alone. Perhaps I must depart from my brother for a day – or a lifetime. Perhaps we can hobble along, trying to pick up pieces that keep breaking. Not one size fits all in the commerce of forgiveness. To forgive is not to pretend that it never happened. It's to convert what did happen from a curse into a blessing one way or another. That's what Jesus does for us, seven thousand seven hundred and seventy-seven times.

Lord, I see from the numbers game that forgiveness requires patience, and patience is love in slow motion. Help me patiently to forgive my erring brothers and sisters as you forgive my erring ways.

The Divine Debt Reduction Program

Father Lawrence Donohoo, O.P.

"That is why the kingdom of heaven may be likened to a king who decided to settle accounts with his servants. When he began the accounting, a debtor was brought before him who owed him a huge amount. Since he had no way of paying it back, his master ordered him to be sold, along with his wife, his children, and all his property, in payment of the debt." (Mt 18: 23-25)

The total American debt is nearly fifty-five trillion dollars, thirteen trillion in government debt and forty-two trillion in corporate and individual debt. As bad as that is, we know this debt *could* be paid off over time if we choose. But the servant, despite his good intentions, "had no way of paying it back." Even with the best of intentions, the king knows this can't happen. So he forgives the servant's debt.

Yet our situation is far worse than that of the American economy. Like the servant, we can't pay off our debt because any investments we make are done with money loaned from the King. More troubling yet, the human race, imprisoned in sinfulness, has no real earnings capacity.

The parable then only loosely portrays our predicament, and there are critical ways in which it cannot – but to our advantage! There are no buyers out there to whom the King can sell us. And we can be grateful that the King doesn't really need the money anyway. Most importantly, he doesn't want to sell us. In fact, he has a better plan that at first glance looks quite foolish. Instead of *selling* us, he plans to *buy* us back. That's right. With the human race steeped in debt beyond reckoning and without the capacity to earn, God puts himself up as surety for us. "For you have been purchased at a price" (1 Cor 6: 20). The new currency is mercy; its denomination is divine blood. We have been ransomed "not with perishable things like silver or gold but with the precious blood of Christ" (1 Pt 1: 18-19). And who benefits from this? Not the King, but we. For the first time I learn what my fellow debtors and I are really worth. So I'll forget the money.

God, heavenly Father, I thank you sincerely for creating me and then saving me through Christ, your Son and my brother. Through his redemptive work I learn that I have been saved by Love.

I'm Glad I Asked

Father Lawrence Donohoo, O.P.

"At that, the servant fell down, did him homage, and said, 'Be patient with me, and I will pay you back in full.' Moved with compassion the master of that servant let him go and forgave him the loan." (Mt 18: 26-27)

Absolutely overjoyed to hear that his debt was forgiven, the servant was seen singing and leaping as he left the master's palace. A fellow servant indebted to him seized the moment to ask that his own debt be forgiven. The answer was as expected as it was wondrous: "No problem! Go free! Let's keep a good thing going!" And the same response was given to the woman indebted to that servant, who responded likewise to the servant who owed her much. In the end, everyone forgave everyone for everything and everyone started over.

Okay, so things didn't quite work out that way. What went wrong went wrong at the very start. The first task of forgiveness is to accept it, which the servant was unable to do. For accepting forgiveness means not only accepting that the debt *need not* be paid, but that it *can't* be paid. Not now, not later, not ever. Accepting God's forgiveness requires as my first response not to go out and do contrition, or perform good works, or even proclaim his marvelous deeds. It requires that I simply sit – or better, kneel – down and let this mystery sink into my head and my heart.

After I get up, there's more to do. If I can't give back to the Lord for all – or anything – that he has done for me, I can give forward. Here it should be noted that the debts we owe are more than sins. The very structure of our world bespeaks indebtedness. How can I pay back my parents, or they theirs, for the gift of life? No matter how we try, we always "pay back" with the life we've received from others. Or how can I pay back a friend for saving my life? Only by saving someone else's. Procreation (creating forward), whether biologically or spiritually, is passing on the life I've received. And forgiveness (giving forward) of debts or injuries is passing on the freedom I've gained.

My Father, help me to keep your forgiveness in play by granting it to my fellow servants. I give back to you by giving forward to Christ's brothers and sisters in need like me of you and yours.

He Doesn't Get It

Father Lawrence Donohoo, O.P.

"When that servant had left, he found one of his fellow servants who owed him a much smaller amount. He seized him and started to choke him, demanding, 'Pay back what you owe.' Falling to his knees, his fellow servant begged him, 'Be patient with me, and I will pay you back.' But he refused. Instead, he had him put in prison until he paid back the debt."

(Mt 18: 28-30)

A man in a large South American city placed an ad in the local newspaper for his estranged son: "Juan, meet me at the Grand Plaza Hotel on Thursday at 6:00 p.m. All is forgiven. Love, Your Father." His son saw the ad and arrived at the hotel at the appointed time. But he found himself lost in a desperate crowd: hundreds of young men named Juan were looking for their father.

Since waiting for forgiveness can be interminable, spiritual despair can set in. For this reason, God wastes no time in offering it to us. He wants us to start immediately on a life of freedom and joy. And he wants us to waste no time extending this same life to others. Forgiveness loosens the past, steadies the present, and opens the future. It lies at the core of the Gospel because it defines Christ's redemptive work. If God's forgiveness redeems my past, I'm now free to disown who I was and become someone new, whether in large ways or small. With respect to past sins, I am no longer there. And neither are you. But if I do not forgive you, I continue to define you by an ossified past marked by ineradicable deeds – a case of mistaken identity. By denying you the possibility of being the person you have since become, I also deny myself the possibility of meeting you in the present. If there is no forgiveness, there is no encounter.

But when I forgive you, I not only find you in the present, I help you to shape a future built on the present. For your present, like everyone else's, is still in the process of redemption. And when my forgiveness frees you for an ampler future, I receive more of the divine forgiveness I've just given away.

Heavenly Father, help me to be diligent in continuing the work of freeing your children from their past. The dross in my past turns to gold when I give my brother or sister a fresh start.

It Tolls for Thee

Father Lawrence Donohoo, O.P.

"Now when his fellow servants saw what had happened, they were deeply disturbed, and went to their master and reported the whole affair. His master summoned him and said to him, 'You wicked servant! I forgave you your entire debt because you begged me to. Should you not have had pity on your fellow servant, as I had pity on you?' Then in anger his master handed him over to the torturers until he should pay back the whole debt. So will my heavenly Father do to you, unless each of you forgives his brother from his heart." (Mt 18: 31-35)

I learned the English meaning of "forgive" by learning its German equivalent. Stepping into another language, I discovered that "for" is an old Germanic intensifier. By adopting another linguistic viewpoint, I learned that to forgive is to "overgive" – to give too much. And this means, as we learn from the parable, to give just the right amount. For we, like the once-forgiven and unforgiven servants, need this excess. We need something far more generous than the demands of justice – something unearned and undeserved. We need an extravagant Father who gives us not what we deserve, but what we don't.

Note that the only One with propriety rights over the whole universe is the One most lavish, and that we human beings with everything on loan are so tightfisted in "our" forgiveness and possessions. So how do I avoid this stinginess? By taking on another viewpoint and learning the language of mercy.

The parable doesn't teach that the king took his forgiveness back, but that the pitiless servant never received it in the first place. We can know that we've truly received forgiveness only when we pass it on. We can only receive the divine mercy if we are able to extend it. Forgiveness in some sense is this wonderful, wild privilege of playing God. The Pharisees were all in a tizzy because Jesus forgave sins. In fact Jesus gives us all a share in this power. If we understood what a privilege it is to forgive as God forgives (the Our Father), we would hasten to show mercy. By stepping into another's debts and feeling the abyss and the chasm, I discover my own debts and their dissolution.

God our Father, help us to pass on your forgiveness, for we can receive only what we have extended. If we see others in debt, we'll erase it. If we see there's no hope, you'll see joy.

233

God Answers Our Questions with Truth

Douglas Bushman

*Some Pharisees approached [Jesus], and tested him, saying, "Is it
lawful for a man to divorce his wife for any cause whatever?"
He said in reply, "Have you not read that from the beginning the
Creator 'made them male and female' and said, 'For this reason
a man shall leave his father and mother and be joined to his
wife, and the two shall become one flesh'? So they are no longer
two, but one flesh. Therefore, what God has joined together,
no human being must separate." (Mt 19: 3-6)*

Saint Teresa of Ávila wrote that we ought to be most grateful
for the truths that we find most difficult to accept and to live
by. These are the truths we need most, truths that address the
areas of our lives still imprisoned by falsehood and self-deception.
"The truth will set you free" (Jn 8: 32).

Do I really want the freedom of truth? Do I grasp that liberating
truth entails the cross, the death-to-self of conversion? Or do I hope
for redemption without a price, for salvation without penance?
That would be to deny the cross, to prefer a god who winks at sin,
remaining aloof and uninvolved. Jesus answers our questions with
the truth, but his truth leads to the cross, and the cross makes his
teaching credible.

Jesus does not negotiate, provide alternatives, or offer what is
next best if I fail to accept his truth. If he did there would be no
need for the cross, but then, neither would I know God's love, the
love that makes it possible to receive his truth. Jesus knows that
with God set aside, every consideration of what is next best and
every calculation for minimizing evil are moral Towers of Babel
that cannot reach to heaven. He knows that without reference to
God moral truth is readily compromised in the name of every kind
of right thinking and avoiding extremes, of being understanding,
non-judgmental, and tolerant.

There is so little conversion in the world because the outlines of
truth have become fuzzy. Why should I make sacrifices for something
that perhaps, maybe, possibly, might be true? So long as the truth is
in question there can be no conversion, no liberation from sin. To
hear him we must "belong to the truth" (Jn 18: 37) and be ready for
conversion. He appeals to our consciences: "Whoever has ears ought
to hear" (Mt 11: 15; 13: 9, 43). Do I really want to hear what he says?

*God, my Father, today I thank you more than ever for the truths
I have found most difficult. Give me ears to hear your Son's
freeing truth in the teachings of his Church.*

Let the Children Come to Jesus

Douglas Bushman

Then children were brought to [Jesus] that he might lay his hands on them and pray. The disciples rebuked them, but Jesus said, "Let the children come to me, and do not prevent them; for the kingdom of heaven belongs to such as these."
(Mt 19: 13-14)

Saint Matthew does not relate the words of Jesus' prayer, but there is no doubt that they were words of blessing, words of divine love expressing the desire of Jesus' Sacred Heart to impart to these children the gift of God appropriate for them. By his prayer he opened to them his relationship with the Father, the source of all love.

The children were brought to Jesus, implying that their parents played an active role. The apostles rebuked these adults, and Jesus corrected them with words that resound through the ages as encouragement for parents to bring their children to him: "Let the children come to me." "Man cannot live without love," wrote Pope John Paul II, because everyone is made in God's image, and God is love. Bringing children to Jesus is bringing them to life-giving love, to the Father of love who has sent his Son to reveal his love.

Parents bring their children to Jesus because they realize that there is something that only God can give to their children. Only he can give himself, only he can give his love. The highest love that parents can have for their children is to bring them to Jesus to receive God's love. This is accomplished whenever parents lead their children in prayer, in opening their hearts to Jesus, the Father's only Son. It happens when reading the Bible (the Spirit's witness to Christ) and studying the Catechism (the Church's understanding of Scripture). Most especially, by having their children baptized, by bringing them to Mass, to pray before the Blessed Sacrament, and to the sacrament of penance, parents fulfill the Lord's exhortation: "Let the children come to me." Every day, amid the hustle and bustle of life, parents act as Jesus' ambassadors, as the first apostles he sends to his children, as his trusted collaborators in bringing his love to the "little ones" who cannot yet approach him without the help of their parents.

Lord God, my Father, thank you for those who brought me to your Son when I was young. May I love others as I have been loved, and bring many little ones to Jesus.

Ask Jesus the Important Question

Douglas Bushman

Now someone approached [Jesus] and said, "Teacher, what good must I do to gain eternal life?" He answered him, "Why do you ask me about the good? There is only One who is good. If you wish to enter into life, keep the commandments." (Mt 19: 16-17)

The movement of this passage is subtle, but profound. The young man asks about a good to be done to gain eternal life. Jesus moves the perspective from doing to being, stressing that God alone is good. Then Jesus answers the question about the good to be done by identifying it with keeping the commandments. This is Jesus' way of revealing that our doing is rooted in God's being.

Coming from God, who is love, the commandments are his wisdom for all made in his image and who are therefore made for love. They specify what must be done and what must be avoided in order for our actions to be acts of love. By affirming the commandments, Jesus sets us free with the truth about love. It is his way of saying that we must define good and evil as God does. This means that we must be persons of conscience, for conscience hears God's voice and his commands. To keep the commandments of God brings about communion with the God of the commandments.

One wonders how often people ask God about eternal life and what the content of their conscience should be. Preoccupied with earthly concerns like health, prosperity, security, and success in our endeavors, prayer of petition risks being reduced to turning to God as though he were nothing more than a supernatural vending machine to dispense what we think we need to live a full life. God is love, and this is what he most desires to speak to us about. How pleased he must be when those he loves turn to him to inquire about his love, to ask him what his vision for a full life is, and to ask what we must do to live it. Such questions, such prayer, are already the beginning of eternal life, for eternal life is to know the only true God, and Jesus whom he has sent (Jn 17: 3).

Loving Father, thank you for the gift of conscience and the gift of prayer. Forgive me for turning to you so seldom to ask about eternal life and love, and help me to keep the commandments.

Lord, Free Me from All Attachments

Douglas Bushman

The young man said to [Jesus], "All of these I have observed.
What do I still lack?" Jesus said to him, "If you wish to be perfect,
go, sell what you have and give to [the] poor, and you will have
treasure in heaven. Then come, follow me." (Mt 19: 20-21)

How many people identify "being religious" with keeping commandments? Certainly, religion entails knowing God's will and conforming to it. Thus, religion entails observing commandments. Yet the young man's question reveals an awareness that there is more to the life of faith than commandments. Jesus' response opens him, and all of us, to the dimension of total self-giving in love, the dimension of personal vocation.

Commandments concern the objective content of our actions, but they do not go to the inner source, the motives, of our actions. One can keep the commandments of love and yet not be a loving person. Sensing this, the young man's concern that he lacks something is a desire for perfect love. "If you want to be perfect in love," Jesus says, "then you must find the total meaning of your life in following me. Let nothing prevent you from hearing my voice and following me." Many decisions do not fall under the commandments, but they should still be God-centered. Personal vocation is not a matter of precept; rather, it is the way for us to give ourselves totally to Jesus. From among the multitude of good things we can do we have to discern what we should do. Are we free from all attachments to things to hear God's voice, to discern his will, to respond to the prompting of the Holy Spirit?

Perfect love requires that we be poor and humble, pure and chaste, submissive and obedient. The vow and spirit of poverty assure that no possession diminish the gift of self in love. The vow and spirit of chastity assure that pleasures do not impede the total gift of self in love. The vow and spirit of obedience assure that our own will does not create an obstacle to the perfection of love.

Indeed religion, the life of faith, entails more than commandments. Jesus leads us to understand that it is not something more, but Someone more.

Father of my Lord, Jesus, for the sake of perfect love I give to you
my freedom. Let me love you above all things, so that I might
fulfill the vocation you have entrusted to me.

He Left in Sadness, but Did He Return?

Douglas Bushman

When the young man heard this statement, he went away sad,
for he had many possessions. (Mt 19: 22)

It is sobering to realize that this young man, though having kept all the commandments, still could not embrace the Lord's call to follow him. Following Jesus goes beyond keeping commandments. It means to accept God's plan for one's life, one's vocation. Observing commandments does not assure detachment from good things. It is often not something evil that separates us from Christ, but loving good things too much.

Jesus did not compromise. He did not reconfigure God's will for this man. He told him the truth. God's love is based on the truth embodied in the commandments *and* in personal vocation. So, Jesus' words to this man are truth and love. This is why his departure must have anguished Jesus. Jesus is God, and God is love, and love desires to give of itself. By turning away from Jesus, the young man turned away from his vocation, from God's truth and love for him. This could only pierce Jesus' Sacred Heart.

With supernatural hope in God's mercy, an optimist might imagine that one day this young man returned. In truth, he had no place to go, no one else to turn to, as Peter well understood: "Master, to whom shall we go? You have the words of eternal life" (Jn 6: 68). Perhaps the young man came to this realization and returned. Perhaps this prompted Jesus' teaching about the son who at first said no to his father but later changed his mind (Mt 21: 29). No one understands divine mercy and conversion better than Jesus. What joy it would give Jesus to see the young man among the crowds! Might Jesus have taught about the son who changed his mind to affirm the young man's return?

We cannot know. But we do know that Jesus rejoices over conversion. For he is the Father's Son, and the Father rejoices when his children return (the Prodigal Son). Have I returned as many times as I have left?

Praise to you, eternal Father, for your truth and love and mercy.
Never let me be parted from Jesus. With the help of your grace, may
I always embrace his call to follow him.

Christ Became Poor that We May Be Rich

Douglas Bushman

Then Jesus said to his disciples, "Amen, I say to you, it will be hard for one who is rich to enter the kingdom of heaven."
(Mt 19: 23)

In itself wealth is not evil. So if Jesus warns that it can impede entering God's kingdom, it is because, like most accomplishments, normally acquiring wealth is the result of determination and hard work. One must be focused on this goal to achieve it.

Jesus already taught: "Do not store up for yourselves treasures on earth... But store up treasures in heaven... For where your treasure is, there also will your heart be" (Mt 6: 19-21). It is a question of priorities, of one's definition of fulfillment and happiness. The desire to become rich stems from a vision of human fulfillment in terms of earthly prosperity. "You cannot serve God and mammon" (Mt 6: 24). This means: you cannot have two definitions of happiness, two visions of fulfillment. Jesus takes this personally: "Whoever is not with me is against me" (Mt 12: 30). We decide for or against Jesus when we decide what our priorities are.

The old saying that you cannot take money with you, that is, across the frontier of death, is pertinent here. The only thing that we will take with us beyond death is our conscience. We cannot dispossess our conscience. Eternity is the conscience's true home, since it makes eternal truths known to us. It is, so to speak, an earthly home for eternal truth, the place of hospitality extended to God, who is eternal truth. To obey this innate law of hospitality by seeking and acknowledging truth, and by conforming to it, is to welcome eternity into time, and to possess true and lasting wealth. Rich indeed are those who "belong to the truth" (Jn 18: 37), who have sold everything else in order to possess the truth, Jesus himself, the "pearl of great price" (Mt 13: 46). We must dispossess all things to possess the truth, to imitate Jesus, who "for your sake... became poor although he was rich, so that by his poverty you might become rich" (2 Cor 8: 9).

Eternal Father, by your grace and the love of Jesus, may I prize above all things the gift of a conscience and make it a home for your eternal truth.

God's Kingdom: Having More, or Being More?

Douglas Bushman

"Again I say to you, it is easier for a camel to pass through the eye of a needle than for one who is rich to enter the kingdom of God." (Mt 19: 24)

When Jesus teaches that a camel passes through a needle's eye more easily than a rich person enters God's kingdom, we must realize that he knows what he is talking about. We can only enter the kingdom by way of forgiveness of sins. This forgiveness can only come from Christ, and Christ can only forgive us from the depths of his love poured out for us in his suffering and death on the cross. We must keep this in mind to understand another teaching of Jesus on something being "easier": "Which is easier, to say, 'Your sins are forgiven,' or to say, 'Rise and walk'?" (Mt 9: 5). Indeed, is it easier for Jesus simply to call upon the Father's power to make weak legs strong, or to endure rejection, mockery, slander, torture, and death in order to restore spiritual health to our diseased souls?

It has always been a temptation to see material prosperity as a sign of God's favor, but the only kind of wealth that can be directly attributed to Christ's mission is having a purified conscience (Heb 9: 14). As Pope John Paul II put it, the kingdom of God is not a matter of having more but of being more. A conscience purified by the blood of Christ's love is a conscience that acknowledges its spiritual poverty and turns to him for mercy. This is the first beatitude: "Blessed are the poor in spirit,/ for theirs is the kingdom of heaven" (Mt 5: 3).

Here we are close to the Lord's words about the Eucharist: "Do not work for food that perishes but for the food that endures for eternal life" (Jn 6: 27). The "work" that he encourages and approves is not the striving for earthly wealth but believing in Jesus (Jn 6: 29). This means believing that in him the revelation of divine mercy makes those who are poor in spirit rich in love.

God, Father of Jesus, help me to see the emptiness of earthly riches and to count my wealth in terms of your love and the gift of a purified conscience.

Only Say the Word, and I Shall Be Healed

Douglas Bushman

When the disciples heard this, they were greatly astonished and said, "Who then can be saved?" Jesus looked at them and said, "For human beings this is impossible, but for God all things are possible." (Mt 19: 25-26)

There are moments when God grants great clarity regarding the demands of entering his kingdom, doing his will, and being saved. A flash of heavenly insight leads to grasping the seriousness of the Lord's sayings: "How narrow the gate and constricted the road that leads to life. And those who find it are few" (Mt 7: 14); "Many are invited, but few are chosen" (Mt 22: 14). These texts echo in what Saint Peter wrote, that "the righteous one is barely saved" (1 Pt 4: 18).

Insight into the arduousness of receiving God's love to become a new person and the terrible toil of penance and conversion ultimately derives from the realization of the price of Christ's redeeming love. Biblical language is graphic; it is a question of a death-event. What is earthly and sinful must be put to death, the "old self" crucified (Rom 6: 6; Gal 5: 24).

By God's grace this truth excavates the deepest recesses of a soul and establishes there the most profound humility. Humility is based on the realization that what God calls us to is beyond our ability to attain by our own effort. This would lead to despair were it not for the integrity of the One who calls us. He calls us out of love and with power. Jesus is God, and when God calls out, "Let there be light," there is light. When Jesus calls the lame or paralyzed to walk, the blind to see, and the leprous to be pure, it all happens according to his word. It is no different when he bids us enter his Father's kingdom. For the spiritually lame, paralyzed, blind, and leprous, the only hope is that Jesus should "only say the word, and I shall be healed."

In the power of his healing love, our hope is certain, and we can say with Saint Paul: "I have the strength for everything through him who empowers me" (Phil 4: 13).

God, my Father, grant that at every Mass I may pray with ever-increasing insight and devotion: "Lord, I am not worthy to receive you, but only say the word and I shall be healed."

Let Us Approach the Throne of Mercy

Douglas Bushman

Jesus said to [his disciples], "Amen, I say to you that you who have followed me, in the new age, when the Son of Man is seated on his throne of glory, will yourselves sit on twelve thrones, judging the twelve tribes of Israel." (Mt 19: 28)

The throne symbolizes the king's role as judge. Perhaps the most memorable judgment is when Solomon discerned who the true mother of an infant was (1 Kgs 3: 16-28). He judged truthfully, and this makes it a just judgment, one that is neither deceived nor biased, but true. Jesus reveals his authority as Judge by referring to his place on a throne, both here and in a later verse (Mt 25: 31). He is the just Judge, whose judgments are true because he himself is the truth. He is the truth about God's merciful love. This is why we are reassured: "So let us confidently approach the throne of grace to receive mercy and to find grace for timely help" (Heb 4: 16).

Jesus judges from a throne of mercy to dispense God's grace! The truth guiding his judgments is the truth that God is love, that his Father is "rich in mercy" (Eph 2: 4). He was faithful to this truth unto death, and he is faithful to it in every judgment he makes.

Christ entrusted his authority to judge to the Church. While awaiting the final judgment, we already submit to his merciful judgment when we confess our sins in the sacrament of penance. "In this sacrament, the sinner, placing himself before the merciful judgment of God, *anticipates* in a certain way *the judgment* to which he will be subjected at the end of his earthly life" (CCC 1470). The apostles' successors, the bishops and their priest-collaborators, exercise Christ's office as Judge every time they give absolution. And it is the dignity of every one of the faithful to participate in this judgment, so that it does not come as something imposed from the outside, but as the truth that sets us free from the inside. By identifying and confessing our sins, we are one with the just Judge, seeing what he sees. We see the truth about sin, but above all we see the truth about God's mercy.

Father of mercy, I give you my greatest thanks for the death of your Son, who revealed the depths of your mercy, and for the bishops and priests who hear my confessions.

Leave All Things to Find All Things

Douglas Bushman

"Everyone who has given up houses or brothers or sisters or father or mother or children or lands for the sake of my name will receive a hundred times more, and will inherit eternal life. But many who are first will be last, and the last will be first."
(Mt 19: 29-30)

God is the source of any goodness in things and people that make them loveable. This is why everyone must love God more than home, property, and even family. This fulfills the precept: "You shall love the Lord your God with all your heart, with all your soul, with all your mind, and with all your strength" (Mk 12: 30). We must certainly love all of God's works, especially all human beings whom he loves in a special way, thereby endowing them with a unique goodness and dignity. By the gift of grace in Christ, our love for all of God's creatures is actually a participation in God's own love. Charity is the supernatural love by which we love God as he loves himself, we love all men and women as he loves them in Christ, and we love all of creation as God does. By this properly ordered love, by this charity, God's will is done on earth as it is in heaven. It is eternal life begun on earth. In this way every Christian is called to leave behind all possessions and even family. Yet, just as losing our lives for Christ is the way to find them (Mt 10: 39; 16: 25), so giving up all things for Christ is the truest way to have and to love them.

Throughout the Church's history, God has called some to live out this priority of love of God by the literal and actual dispossession of all goods and familial relationships, by consecrating themselves to the evangelical counsels of poverty, chastity, and obedience. Their mission is to bear witness to the priority of love of God over all other loves, and to the transcendent values of the kingdom of God. This is a gift to the whole Church, a sign from heaven to strengthen our faith so that every day in the life of every Christian God's will may be done on earth as it is in heaven.

Heavenly Father, I thank you for the gift of those in consecrated life and for the sign of your kingdom of love that you give us through them. Keep them faithful to your call, and may their witness inspire me to love you more perfectly.

No One Left Out

Father Joseph Torchia, O.P.

"The kingdom of heaven is like a landowner who went out at dawn to hire laborers for his vineyard. After agreeing with them for the usual daily wage, he sent them into his vineyard. Going out about nine o'clock, he saw others standing idle in the marketplace, and he said to them, 'You too go into my vineyard, and I will give you what is just.' So they went off." (Mt 20: 1-5)

In the movie classic *On the Waterfront*, there's a grim scene involving the morning hiring of longshoremen for a day's work on the docks. The process is obviously rigged. The foreman only selects the ones willing to "play ball" and pay their requisite "kickbacks." The rest must fend for themselves, or submit to an ongoing cycle of exploitation. In either case, they will lose, and be consigned the heavy burden of injustice. Such a fate is radically different from that of the laborers in Christ's parable, the ones standing idle in the marketplace. The landowner not only gives them work, but insures a just compensation for their efforts.

In a very real sense, those laborers represent everyone in need of divine grace and all who benefit from its abundance – people like us. This grace flows from an unconditional love with no strings attached. It offers us an ironclad contract sealed in Christ's own blood, in which he does all the giving and we gladly receive. And what we receive is not only just, but more than anything sinners like ourselves deserve.

Christ completely redefines the meaning of justice. The justice he provides is not a matter of fairness or equality or some *quid pro quo* with a neat and tidy balancing of interests. Jesus owes us nothing. But by his crucifixion and death, he pays a debt that we can never begin to pay on our own. This is the act of the God made man who freely "emptied himself,/taking the form of a slave" (Phil 2: 7) for our redemption. This is a giving that knows no restrictions. It neither diminishes nor varies in its intensity. It allows no one to remain idle and unfulfilled in its capacity to transform people's lives. And it leaves absolutely no one standing out in the cold.

God, my Father, I thank you for drawing me into your service, for putting my talents to good use, and for the abundance of your love and mercy.

Untapped Potential

Father Joseph Torchia, O.P.

"[The landowner] went out again around noon, and around three o'clock, and did likewise. Going out about five o'clock, he found others standing around, and said to them, 'Why do you stand here idle all day?' They answered, 'Because no one has hired us.' He said to them, 'You too go into my vineyard.'"

(Mt 20: 5-7)

In the competitive world of sports, there's something especially inspiring about certain athletes. These players were never recruited; they received no lucrative scholarships; they had no guarantee of a place in next season's lineup. They're the "walk-ons" who simply make the team through natural talent, a honing of skills, and sheer determination. Some become stars or even legends.

This is the kind of success story we all enjoy hearing, because it's wonderful when raw potential finds its appropriate outlet and comes to fruition. But what about countless others whose potential remains untapped? They might accomplish so much if they could only find an opportunity to actualize their latent abilities. For this reason, they're like those idlers in Jesus' parable, the ones with nothing to do but wait for a chance. Their searing reply to the landowner's question affirms their frustration: "No one has hired us." Yet, in hiring them on the spot, the landowner makes no assumptions about their inactivity. Are they lazy, unreliable, or just so many shiftless malingerers? The landowner saw something else here. Anyone willing to wait all day in the heat must really want to work! So he puts their potential to good use.

The vineyard of evangelization also requires laborers. In his bountiful goodness, God has invested us with everything we need to do his work in the contexts of our lives. He gives us an intellect to grasp truth, a free will inclined to the good, and a capacity for unselfish love. He endows us with many other gifts unique to each of us as persons. And because he made us, he knows what we can do in a way that exceeds anything we can comprehend. But those to whom so much is given cannot be idle bystanders. The call we received at baptism is a call to serve, and to be all we were created to be in furthering God's kingdom on earth.

God, my Father, take whatever I can offer and put it to good use in carrying out your will.

245

The Great Reversal

Father Joseph Torchia, O.P.

"When it was evening the owner of the vineyard said to his foreman, 'Summon the laborers and give them their pay, beginning with the last and ending with the first.' When those who had started about five o'clock came, each received the usual daily wage. So when the first came, they thought that they would receive more, but each of them also got the usual wage."

(Mt 20: 8-10)

Our culture is fond of phrases that implicitly extol preeminence, whether in regard to scholastic achievement, professional success, athletic prowess, or biological survival: head of the class; inner circle; upper echelon; top notch; prime candidate; front rank; leader of the pack, etc. Our very status as *homo sapiens* seems geared to an exaltation of being first, and a corresponding disdain for anything less. This isn't necessarily bad; there's nothing wrong with striving for excellence. The problem arises when we interpret salvation on the basis of human criteria of greatness.

Christ's disciples aren't above this kind of vanity. A few even jockey for position in the kingdom of God (see Mk 9: 33-34). So we shouldn't be surprised by the reaction of the disgruntled laborers in Christ's parable. It simply proceeds from the common premise that those who show up first have certain entitlements and the last should wait their turn. But the landowner's salary policy turns this reasoning on its head. And in this way, it's paradigmatic of the value system endorsed by Christ.

Jesus teaches that those who wish to be first shall be last (see Mk 9: 35). This isn't the way of the world, in Christ's time or in our own. But it's wholly consistent with God's plan of redemption. God draws upon the weak and lowly ones for his saving purposes. As Saint James' Epistle reminds us, God chooses "those who are poor in the world to be rich in faith and heirs of the kingdom" (Jas 2: 5). Jesus himself sets the tone for this way of living by assuming the role of the suffering servant, even unto death. By entering into the pattern of Christ's way of living, we learn to die a little each day: a slow dying to our interests that frees us to love God and neighbor in a richer manner. This is the key to our fulfillment, the means to true greatness, the end for which we are made.

God, my Father, grant me the humility to accept my creaturely status, and in so doing, to be willing to assume the role of the servant, in the way Christ does for our redemption.

An Even Break

Father Joseph Torchia, O.P.

"And on receiving it [the laborers] grumbled against the landowner, saying, 'These last ones worked only one hour, and you have made them equal to us, who bore the day's burden and the heat.'" (Mt 20: 11-12)

Now, that's the kind of man I would want for an employer! Not a bad pay scale, is it? This memorable parable can easily be read in such terms, as a commentary on fair labor practices or the need for an equitable wage for services rendered. But Christ's message really tells us something crucial about God. It highlights the unlimited generosity of divine love. This is a love that makes no distinctions between people based on their backgrounds, or social status, or previous moral track record. This is a love as receptive to repentant sinners as it is to devoted, lifelong believers. Remember the good thief on the cross who "steals" his way into heaven after appealing to Christ's mercy? This is God's way; it's the mark of his dealings with sinful humanity in the gift of his only-begotten Son for our redemption. He does this out of the sheer gratuity of his own nature.

God's love is all-encompassing enough to embrace saints, aspiring saints, and outright sinners. Perhaps that's too hard for seasoned, inveterate sinners to imagine, that God can be so loving and forgiving. Or, perhaps it's a bit disgruntling to those who feel they've already "run the race" and paid the price of discipleship to see those lost sheep so easily welcomed home! But most of us, I suspect, readily identify with those laborers hired at the end of the day – those waiting for an even break, just trying to slip under the wire. We wouldn't deny them, because that's precisely the way we would want to be treated. But we know that God gives us far more than an even break. He gives us the greatest gift imaginable. He offers us the chance to become new persons, restored to what we were intended to be, his children. And for this reason, we can all rejoice and be glad.

God, my Father, I thank you for the generosity of your love and forgiveness. May I be generous in my spirit of charity and always willing to forgive in imitation of you.

Hitting the Jackpot

Father Joseph Torchia, O.P.

"[The landowner] said to one of [the laborers] in reply, 'My friend, I am not cheating you. Did you not agree with me for the usual daily wage? Take what is yours and go. What if I wish to give this last one the same as you? [Or] am I not free to do as I wish with my own money? Are you envious because I am generous?'" (Mt 20: 13-15)

I imagine winning a dream lottery jackpot worth about two hundred million dollars, tax free. While such a windfall seems like the greatest boon anyone could ever receive, it would present an immense challenge. How will you use this newly acquired wealth? Will you save, spend, or share it? Many friends, no doubt, would happily advise you on these pressing questions (along with suggestions of worthy beneficiaries). But suppose you were to surprise everyone by giving away the whole lot to some needy people you just happened to meet? For starters, you'd probably lose some of those friends, but not before they soundly berated you for what they perceived as your utter foolishness. In exasperation, you might well echo the words of the landowner in Christ's parable: "Am I not free to do as I wish with my own money?"

But that landowner raises another question suggesting something unsettling about human nature. Are people really prone to envy at the generosity of others? If so, why? Whether they realize it or not, such envy would have to extend to the most generous one of all, God himself. Do we begrudge God for having brought us into being, for sending his only-begotten Son for our redemption, and for the depth of his love and mercy? Surely, no one could be jealous of the sheer graciousness of God's love. This unlimited generosity sets the standard for any unselfish giving on our part. If we can give in this way, it's because we have an incentive that flows directly from our Creator. And if we know anything about him, it's that he's a giving God, intimately involved in every aspect of our lives. So we take our lead from the exemplar of generosity. Our call is to be "good stewards of God's varied grace" (1 Pt 4: 10), who use our gifts in service to others. In this way, our giving will bear fruit abundant enough to enrich all the earth.

God, my Father, we rejoice in your generosity that knows no bounds. Grant us the grace to be generous to those around us, to give until it hurts, and to lose ourselves in the very act of giving.

Sharing the Passion of Jesus

Father Donald Haggerty

As Jesus was going up to Jerusalem, he took the twelve [disciples] aside by themselves, and said to them on the way, "Behold, we are going up to Jerusalem, and the Son of Man will be handed over to the chief priests and the scribes, and they will condemn him to death, and hand him over to the Gentiles to be mocked and scourged and crucified, and he will be raised on the third day." (Mt 20: 17-19)

On three occasions Jesus speaks of his approaching passion. If we ask how he knows, the answer may not be simply by a divine awareness of the future event. We can assume he understands quite clearly from the prophetic testimonies of the Old Testament that he will undergo rejection and suffering. Isaiah fifty-three is the most striking example, a chapter that Saint Thérèse of Lisieux memorized and often pondered in prayer. One wonders if Jesus did likewise. But if we ask further whether Jesus already realized much earlier that those closest to him would abandon him at the hour of his ordeal, the answer is surely that he did. We will hear this explicitly in his words to the apostles at the Last Supper. Why, then, we may ask, does he take his apostles aside in a particular way and speak of his passion? If his purpose is to forewarn them so that they might not be shocked and scandalized when that day arrives, it would make no sense to do so if they would not in any case respond with courage.

Perhaps there is another reason for these predictions of his suffering and death. Jesus wants the apostles to reflect after his resurrection that while knowing what awaited him – the mockery, the scourging, the nailing to a cross – he still walked ahead without hesitation to face his terrible last week. His act of supreme love at Calvary to offer his life to an ignominious end was a choice he fully embraced, a completion of his divine mission which filled his whole life with longing. When we hear our Lord speak in the Gospel of the future event of his passion, we might also realize that we, too, have to pass through our own unique sharing in our Lord's passion, but never alone. Jesus promises his close presence always, even as he prepares us for the self-offering still awaiting us.

Father, let your Son's passion give me courage. May I perceive any suffering in my life as an invitation to unite myself to him and to join my own offering to his sacrifice at Calvary.

The Bitter Cup

Father Donald Haggerty

Jesus said [...], "Can you drink the cup that I am going to drink?" [James and John] said to him, "We can." He replied, "My cup you will indeed drink, but to sit at my right and at my left [, this] is not mine to give but is for those for whom it has been prepared by my Father." (Mt 20: 22-23)

"Can you drink the cup that I am going to drink?" The cup of suffering which Jesus is soon to embrace in his passion can never be thought his alone. If we aspire to close relations with him, we will never be able to stand off to the side at Calvary as observers, merely offering Jesus our compassion. Over a lifetime he will beckon us to the foot of the cross, until we too become sharers in his suffering. A threshold of courage must be passed if we are to know our Lord more intimately, the threshold of affliction. Blessed Mother Teresa of Calcutta sometimes told those in physical pain that their suffering was the kiss of Jesus from the cross. But she also at times recounted the story of one ill woman who asked that Jesus stop then from kissing her so much. The truth of a union with our Lord through suffering is not easily accepted. No doubt it is more common to seek a companionship with him protected from unpleasant trials.

Like James and John, we may even want signs of favor to confirm our closeness to God. Nonetheless, the holy one who is dishonored at Calvary asks us not to avert our eyes from his passion – and to expect immolation in our own life. Jesus' question to James and John is a challenge to perceive the cost of union with him. When they answer somewhat naïvely with a resounding "we can," this response draws from our Lord a promise that they will indeed drink that cup one day. The promise reminds us not to desire a different form of intimacy with our Lord. Suffering is always a difficult burden – but it is also a blessing extended to those who seek greater oneness with our Lord. We ought not to anticipate an alternative path of union. The cup we will be asked to share with Jesus cannot but open us to greater love for him.

Merciful Father, with your grace may I never refuse the cup of suffering which your Son asks me to offer in my life, and may every offering I make be for the salvation of souls.

The Servant

Father Donald Haggerty

When the ten heard this, they became indignant at the two brothers. But Jesus summoned them and said, "You know that the rulers of the Gentiles lord it over them, and the great ones make their authority over them felt. But it shall not be so among you. Rather, whoever wishes to be great among you shall be your servant; whoever wishes to be first among you shall be your slave." (Mt 20: 24-27)

The brothers James and John, in their request for seats of honor beside Jesus, have strayed from a proper grasp of true honor with God, allowing a desire for privilege to seduce them. Jesus' correction occurs in the question whether they can drink the cup he is to drink. He points to his own passion and reminds them, whether or not they realize it at the time, that there is no true spiritual greatness except in a willingness to drink with him the cup of suffering.

Their fellow apostles apparently do not listen well. They immediately rise up in indignation, taking offense at what they view as the brothers' gambit to secure a promise of favor from Jesus. All this draws from our Lord a further instruction, once again linked to the words he has just spoken of his approaching passion. Now he addresses himself to all of them as men destined to occupy positions of leadership in the Church. The authority he exercises finds its culmination in the ignominy of the cross. Must there not be a parallel in their own lives? His power is the strength of one who bends down beneath the weight of a cross. Must they not be willing to bow down in service? His leadership is the example of self-immolating love. Must they not be ready for their own passion? We do not have to bear the burden of any office in the Church to realize that Jesus proposes this for all of us to some degree. Those great in the eyes of God are those who serve the rest. Often this may be a person unknown and concealed from any public view, a largely hidden life of holiness enriching the Church by selfless service to others. It has always been a distinctive trait of Christianity that we discover frequently only after a person's life how many hidden acts of goodness filled their days.

Heavenly Father, keep me humble, always ready to be a servant to the needs of others, that I may please your Son and imitate his own willingness to humble himself as a servant.

The Price of a Ransom

Father Donald Haggerty

*"The Son of Man did not come to be served but to serve
and to give his life as a ransom for many."*
(Mt 20: 28)

One of the fitting titles that has been given to Jesus from the prophetic testimony of the Old Testament is that of the suffering servant. Isaiah in particular writes of the Messiah as a servant who will be crushed in pain as he offers himself for the transgressions of the many. We have an endless source of meditation in this image when we realize the revelation into the heart of God it provides. The divine choice of the Son of God to enter this life of our own human flesh only to conclude it by suffering a Roman crucifixion points to a fathomless mystery of love in God. Divine love unites itself to the marred features of a man suffering a criminal's execution. Yet despite the devastating appearance, the redemption of humanity is taking place at Calvary. This central truth of Christianity is prophesied as Jesus proclaims that he came into the world "to give his life as a ransom for many."

It is true that the ransom Jesus pays as a price for sin by his suffering on the cross is uniquely his offering as the Son of God. But we ought to hear as well in these words an invitation to join our own personal self-offering to that of our Lord. It may be that we have lost somewhat in the Church the importance that sacrificial reparation once held. The meaning of this is essentially to offer up for the sake of another, to make reparation for the sins of others. On more than one occasion I have heard bishops tell gravely ill priests that their life at that time of struggle is more fruitful than ever. Throughout our lives Jesus will ask us to join renunciation and sacrifice to his offering, to unite our suffering with his on the cross as a providential means of filtering grace to souls in need. Let us be courageous in accepting this request from him.

Father, grant me the grace to realize more deeply the immense generosity of your Son's passion, and for my part to seek always to unite my life to his offering at Calvary.

Passing By

Father John Dominic Corbett, O.P.

As they left Jericho, a great crowd followed [Jesus]. Two blind men were sitting by the roadside, and when they heard that Jesus was passing by, they cried out, "[Lord,] Son of David, have pity on us!" The crowd warned them to be silent, but they called out all the more, "Lord, Son of David, have pity on us!"
(Mt 20: 29-31)

The blind men sitting by the roadside must have felt at a standstill. Nothing much was happening for them. They could hear hustle and bustle, but it never really seemed to concern them. Life seemed to pass them by without calling them into its stream. The routine of begging seemed to be as it was in the beginning, is now, and ever shall be.

Then something stirs. These blind men would have the advantage of especially sensitive hearing. They would know the sound of crowds. They could tell the difference between the sorrowing shuffle of a funeral procession and the leisurely stroll of a group on their way to synagogue. This crowd is different. The air is electric. Someone important, someone very important, is passing by. Who? Jesus of Nazareth. They had heard that he was a wonder worker, this Jesus. But he is coming closer and closer and then he would pass them by and then be gone and they would never have the chance to speak to him. How could they arrest the flow of time? How to get him to stop and speak with them?

They shout out his title, "Son of David." This is the same as calling him their king because the Son of David was indeed the king of Israel. They acknowledge his royal authority. They name Jesus as the one who in God's name ruled God's people.

They shout out their desperate prayer, "Have pity on us!" Pity is the property of the mighty. It is the virtue of the strong. It is a kingly virtue. Calling on the king's pity reminds him of his true identity and of the true purpose of his power.

It is a prayer that can arrest the almighty in his tracks. It is a prayer that can attract the awesome and Kingly pity of Christ to our own souls, to our friends, to our country, and to our whole world.

Father, you sent your only Son into this world to be its King and merciful Savior. Help us to call upon him with confidence and by so doing cooperate in his kingly rule over our lives.

A Simple Question

Father John Dominic Corbett, O.P.

Jesus stopped and called [the two blind men] and said,
"What do you want me to do for you?" They answered him,
"Lord, let our eyes be opened." (Mt 20: 32-33)

When one is very young one doesn't have words for what one wants. A child may need and cry for warmth, a change of clothes, milk, but the mother or father has to guess the need until they grow accustomed to the varying pitches of the baby's voice which serves as its rudimentary language.

Later, one's words and one's needs come closer together, and we have an improved capacity to ask for what we want. It might be an admission to a school or department. It might be a date with someone very attractive to us. The more concrete the desire, the easier it is to put into words.

But there remain desires in the human heart that elude easy description, though we have code names for them. Happiness, integrity, joy are among them. We have some knowledge of what these words mean, and yet the better our knowledge the better we know its incompleteness. The realities these poor words suggest are within and yet somehow always outside of or beyond our experience. They are ordinary words which open out into meanings somehow beyond our grasp.

Is sight one of those words? Jesus asks the blind men what they want from him. Can they know what they are asking? They have never been anything but blind. They have nothing to contrast blindness with, so they can't even fully know what it is to be blind. What can they mean when they ask to see? "Lord, let our eyes be opened. Let us know our world. Let us in on the secret which everyone else is somehow in on and which eludes us." Fortunately we don't have to understand fully our own prayers before we make them. Jesus knows the full import of what they are asking, and so he grants their deepest desire. When their eyes are opened for the first time – they see him.

Father, send your Spirit to us and teach us to pray for the things that we need but do not understand. Let the Spirit pray in us "with sighs too deep for words."

Follow Travelers

Father John Dominic Corbett, O.P.

Moved with pity, Jesus touched [the blind men's] eyes.
Immediately they received their sight, and followed him.
(Mt 20: 34)

The Spirit of God hovered over the formless chaos. Suddenly a word was spoken. "Let there be light," and there was light. The light shined in the darkness not, we may assume, as a gradual brightening but as an all at once fact. Once there was nothing. Then there was something. Before there was only darkness, and then, without interval, there was light.

Something like this is going on with the two blind men sitting by the road. Life is passing them by. They are going nowhere. They see nothing and only hear rumors of the lives that others lead. They have heard that there is a colored and textured world, but they themselves know nothing if it.

Then Jesus passes by. They hear him passing by and they cry to him as to their only chance of salvation. "Have pity on us. Open our eyes." Suddenly, at his touch – and as sudden as the appearance of light on the first day – there was light. Then their world was no longer a world of shadows enveloping shapes but a real world, colored, three-dimensional, beautiful, full of promise, and full of menace.

But however beautiful and terrible their first experience is of seeing the world, it is overshadowed by their experience of seeing Jesus. "They received their sight." They see the real purpose of seeing anything – that is, they see him and see what he is about. When they receive their sight the first thing they do is not to explore their world. Rather they use their sight to follow him. They follow him all the way up to Jerusalem to his crucifixion. They see. They see that their seeing and living and dying will be centered upon following this mysterious figure all the way into his own mysterious destiny. "What do you want me to do for you?" "We want to see." They do indeed see. And therefore they follow.

Father, let there be light in our souls. Let us see Jesus as he passes by in our lives. Let us not let him pass in vain. Let us follow in his footsteps.

The Beasts of Bethlehem and Jerusalem

Father Aquinas Guilbeau, O.P.

[The disciples] brought the ass and the colt and laid their cloaks over them, and [Jesus] sat upon them. The very large crowd spread their cloaks on the road, while others cut branches from the trees and strewed them on the road. The crowds preceding him and those following kept crying out and saying:/ "Hosanna to the Son of David;/ blessed is he who comes in the name of the Lord;/ hosanna in the highest." (Mt 21: 7-9)

The Judean cities of Bethlehem and Jerusalem are not particularly welcoming to Jesus. In the former, the place of his birth, he is ignored by some and nearly killed by others. A few lowly souls – and three wise ones – come to adore his infancy, but already the plottings of evil men threaten his safety and force his family to flee. In the latter city, the royal home of the Jewish kings, enthusiastic crowds will eventually welcome Jesus out of seclusion and hail him as a conquering king. Soon, however, they will demand his death.

Nazareth, the city of Jesus' hidden life, stands in stark contrast to Bethlehem and Jerusalem. Tucked in between the hills of Galilee, Nazareth provides Jesus and his family a quiet and secluded life. For years the Lord does not draw attention to himself, but only labors with Joseph, receives the motherly ministrations of Mary, and enjoys the religious and social rhythms of small-town life. When it comes time for him to move from Nazareth to Jerusalem, however, on a divine and public journey that will take him nearly three years to complete, the evil forces he first contends with in Bethlehem return to pursue their wicked task.

The shouting crowds waiting for Jesus in Jerusalem are not strong enough to resist repeating Bethlehem's reception of him. They too move from indifference to Jesus' presence, to recognition of his divine majesty, and finally to rejection of his truth and love. Scripture heightens our sense of their treason – and it indicts our own – by pointing out a certain irony. The actions of the beasts of Bethlehem and Jerusalem are juxtaposed to those of their peoples. The ox and ass of Bethlehem find their parallel in the ass and colt of Jerusalem. The former keep him warm in the manger while the latter quietly bear the weight of his majesty. Dumb beasts! And they act more wisely than men.

Heavenly Father, all creation praises your Son. May we never ignore his truth, nor remain indifferent to his love.

The True Enthusiasm of Faith

Father Aquinas Guilbeau, O.P.

And when [Jesus] entered Jerusalem the whole city was shaken and asked, "Who is this?" And the crowds replied, "This is Jesus the prophet, from Nazareth in Galilee." (Mt 21: 10-11)

What is it about Jesus that captivates the entire city of Jerusalem? It remains difficult for us to say. Not being Jews of first-century Palestine, we cannot appreciate fully how Christ's triumphal entrance into the city ignites the political, cultural, and religious hopes of God's oppressed people. For centuries the Israelites had been told to await a Messiah who would save them. Now he is finally in their midst, seated on a donkey, entering the city of the temple and of the kings. From the viewpoint of Israel's enthusiastic hopes, Jesus is about to begin something new. The old powers of the world will soon find themselves overturned. Of course, the Jews of Jerusalem are not completely wrong about Jesus' mission, but their enthusiastic reception will take a dramatic turn.

The tragic lesson of Israel's enthusiasm – its volatility results in Good Friday – contains a lesson for faith. Faith can stir up in us tremendous excitement, an enthusiasm about life, and even about eternal life that we might find hard to contain. We all know the compelling and even contagious fervor of the new convert. Common also is the experience of desiring to rekindle this initial fervor once its flame has lost its heat. In many hearts, the hearth of faith can grow cold. We must remember, however, that while faith can elicit these emotions, it can never be rooted in them. Even absent all emotion, faith remains what it is, the trusting assent of the mind to God's revelation. Faith receives its power and truth, therefore, from its divinely given content and not from our human sentiment. The Israelites welcoming Jesus seem to understand this lesson. Matthew tells us that many ask as Jesus passes by, "Who is this?" There has to be a reason for their enthusiasm.

Heavenly Father, your Son has come into the world to set it on fire. May our enthusiastic reception of his revelation achieve perfection in true faith.

O Wonderful Exchange!

Father Aquinas Guilbeau, O.P.

Jesus entered the temple area and drove out all those engaged in selling and buying there. He overturned the tables of the money changers and the seats of those who were selling doves. And he said to them, "It is written:/ 'My house shall be a house of prayer,'/ but you are making it a den of thieves." (Mt 21: 12-13)

During Christmastide, the Church's liturgy sings the beautiful antiphon, "*O admirable commercium,*" O wonderful exchange! This verse announces the Church's wonder at the mystery of the incarnation. "O wonderful exchange, the creator of the human race, taking our flesh upon him, deigned to be born of a virgin; and, coming forth without the seed of man, bestows his divinity upon us." As the verse explains, man stands as the beneficiary of God's merciful initiative. The incarnation contains a double action, or a type of exchange: a divine person takes up into himself man's nature from below, and at the same time man is taken up into God's life above. As God moves down into his creation, man moves up into eternity.

Accomplishing this great exchange required Christ to make many other, smaller exchanges over the course of his ministry. For example, Jesus prepares for the final consummation of the *commercium* by cleansing the temple. With the one who embodies the divine exchange now active in its precincts, the criminal exchange there of money and animals can no longer be tolerated. Consequently, Christ drives out the money changers and personally restores, with his very presence, the honor of the temple as a place of pure sacrifice. Unknown to those who witness this cleansing, however, Jesus' action presages another exchange that affects the temple. On Calvary, Christ brings to an end the Old Testament prescriptions to offer animal sacrifice. His own self-immolation in obedient love for the sins of the world renders the temple sacrifices unnecessary. To replace them, Christ exchanges his own eucharistic sacrifice, which perpetuates in space and time the grace of the *commercium*. To the end, therefore, through the priests standing at every Christian altar, Christ renews the work of his great and wonderful exchange.

Heavenly Father, in the incarnation your Son exchanged his heavenly glory for an earthly mission. May our surrender to his humble work elevate us to you.

The Freedom of Christ

Father Aquinas Guilbeau, O.P.

The blind and the lame approached [Jesus] in the temple area, and he cured them. When the chief priests and the scribes saw the wondrous things he was doing, and the children crying out in the temple area, "Hosanna to the Son of David," they were indignant and said to him, "Do you hear what they are saying?" Jesus said to them, "Yes; and have you never read the text, 'Out of the mouths of infants and nurslings you have brought forth praise'?" (Mt 21: 14-16)

"For freedom Christ set us free; so stand firm and do not submit again to the yoke of slavery," writes Saint Paul in his Letter to the Galatians (5: 1). In the temple area, Christ announces this promised freedom to mere children. They rejoice. We sometimes hesitate. Is it not true that obstacles to the full exercise of freedom abound in this fallen world? Hindrances to the free activity of the spirit affect the interior and the exterior of the human person. They include slavery and coercion or illness and disability. Freedom's most paralyzing foe, of course, is sin. In saving us from sin and restoring us to friendship with God, Christ concerns himself with freeing men and women from a whole host of enslaving afflictions: the blindness and lameness that constrict movement, as well as the jealousy and sinful pride that strangle love. Christ frees his disciples in both body and soul. The Church continues this work of divine emancipation. And like Christ, Christians can suffer for the liberation they win for the poor and sinners.

The healed man is in a certain sense the freest man. This is not to say that sin and sickness are necessary for freedom to flourish. But the one who has his body or soul (and often both together!) freed of some affliction knows not only the great value of freedom restored, but more so because of his knowledge of the one who restores it. Freedom is most free when it is lived close to its source. The freed disciple is freest when he lives close to Christ. Those healed in the temple, therefore, acclaim Christ immediately as the living source of their freedom. Little do they know, however, that the work of liberation is not yet complete. Leaving them in the temple, Christ is moving steadily to Calvary.

Heavenly Father, your Son's passion and death has freed us from sin. Through conversion and penance, may we come to the perfect knowledge of Christ's freedom.

Bearing Fruit

Jack Sacco

When [Jesus] was going back to the city in the morning, he was hungry. Seeing a fig tree by the road, he went over to it, but found nothing on it except leaves. And he said to it, "May no fruit ever come from you again." And immediately the fig tree withered. (Mt 21: 18-19)

There is a fig tree in my backyard. Like many fruit trees, it sits idly by for most of the year, only producing fruit for a few weeks during the hottest part of the summer. Figs are in abundance for those weeks; so much so that it's difficult to harvest them all before they are eaten by birds or other animals. However, for the remainder of the year, there's not the slightest trace of bud or fruit to be found… in fact, there is nothing on it except leaves.

Surely Jesus must have known when a fig tree would or would not bear fruit. So why would he even look for figs when they were out of season? And why would he be so harsh to the tree, which was simply fulfilling the cycle of life as designed by God?

There are many times in my life when I've felt the time wasn't right for something, that the opportunity had already passed or that it would be better to wait awhile, that I was too young for this or too old for that. In addition, I was always instructed that patience was a virtue, and that we should not seek immediate gratification.

But the lesson I garner from the story of the fig tree is that God's timing is perfect, no matter what I might think. And when he asks us to bear fruit, we should do so despite the circumstances in which we find ourselves.

How often do you pull out the good china, or open that special bottle of wine, or go on an adventure simply for the thrill of it? How often do you tell the special people in your life how much they mean to you? How often do you risk everything to follow your dreams? How often do you bear the fruit of a life well lived?

Heavenly Father, grant us the wisdom to know and appreciate our talents and gifts, and the wisdom to use them in such a way that they bear good fruit that will be pleasing to you.

Unlimited Power

Jack Sacco

When the disciples saw this, they were amazed and said, "How was it that the fig tree withered immediately?" Jesus said to them in reply, "Amen, I say to you, if you have faith and do not waver, not only will you do what has been done to the fig tree, but even if you say to this mountain, 'Be lifted up and thrown into the sea,' it will be done. Whatever you ask for in prayer with faith, you will receive." (Mt 21: 20-22)

Ever wonder what you would do if you had unlimited powers? Would you wither up a fig tree? Would you toss a mountain into the sea? Would you heal the sick and comfort the afflicted? Would you amass great fame and fortune for yourself?

Most of us assume that the world would be a much better place if we could somehow achieve omnipotence. At least it would be better for us. There would be no wars, no hunger, no illnesses, no injustices, and, I suppose, no fruitless fig trees. And we'd all be wealthy beyond measure. But the truth is that there are many times when we feel rather helpless, as if life's situations and events, grand and small, are simply beyond our control.

Jesus offers some interesting advice. He says that if we have faith and do not waver, we will be able to work wonders. Throwing a mountain into the sea certainly sounds impossible (and isn't recommended since it would most likely cause a tsunami), and yet we have assurance that an unwavering faith can accomplish this and more.

I realize that it's easy to pray for nebulous things like world peace and an end to hunger, but how often do we have the faith actually to ask for something concrete, even if it sounds impossible? If Jesus has assured us that we will receive that for which we ask, then why are we so hesitant to ask? If he has truly granted us such awesome power, why do we so rarely use it? Is it that we don't want to appear selfish? Or is it that we don't really have sufficient faith in Jesus' words or the power and intentions of God?

And if we lack faith, then how can we hope to bear the good fruit which we are called to share with the world?

God the Father, it is so easy to surrender to what seems impossible or inevitable. Please take and transform our lack of faith, so that we will feel confident enough to ask for anything, knowing that the promises of your Son will be honored.

The Expert's Authority

Jack Sacco

The chief priests and the elders of the people approached [Jesus] as he was teaching and said, "By what authority are you doing these things? And who gave you this authority?" (Mt 21: 23)

We like experts. We trust them. We assume that their word is definitive. But truth is truth, whether it comes from the mouth of an expert or an amateur. Some people can be quite territorial about their field of expertise. And they're not happy if anyone else makes a statement that trespasses onto that field. If their knowledge and authority are questioned, they will often resort to attacking the credentials of the non-expert as opposed to the arguments he or she is making. I have heard it said that a specialist, that rarest form of expert, is someone who learns more and more about less and less until he eventually knows everything about nothing. What is sometimes missing from their limited vision is the overall picture, and what is often lacking in their analysis is the simple, the obvious, and even the profound. You'd think that with all the "experts" in Washington regulating the economy and governmental affairs, everything would be running smoothly. And yet difficulties not only abound, but seem to be ever increasing. While the experts are yelling at each other and touting their brilliance, the problems keep getting worse. Finding actual solutions often seems secondary to placating the egos and maintaining the stature of the experts.

Another issue is the underlying agenda of the supposed expert. Is it to further the truth regarding their chosen subject? Is it to help others? Or is it to protect their own positions in society? The chief priests were far less concerned with the truth of what Jesus was doing and saying than they were with the fact that he seemed to be usurping their authoritative domain. They viewed him not as a harbinger of truth, but as a threat. Whereas the words and deeds of Jesus would reveal the Truth of the Almighty, the accusatory questions of the chief priests revealed their arrogance, their jealousy, their anger, and their pettiness.

God the Father, grant us the desire to seek the truth and the wisdom to recognize it, no matter the source. Grant us the humility to listen to others, even if they trespass on our assumed area of expertise.

Walking the Walk

Jack Sacco

"What is your opinion? A man had two sons. He came to the first and said, 'Son, go out and work in the vineyard today.' He said in reply, 'I will not,' but afterwards he changed his mind and went. The man came to the other son and gave the same order. He said in reply, 'Yes, sir,' but did not go. Which of the two did his father's will?" (Mt 21: 28-31)

The proclivity of people to say one thing and then do another is not a recent development, nor is it the exclusive domain of politicians and snake oil salesmen. Humankind has been doing it since we first walked the planet.

I'm sure we've all run across people who are great at talking the talk, but not so proficient at walking the walk. It's not simply a matter of bragging or padding a résumé, but of preaching one message, and then living another, or of making grand promises that one has no intention to keep. This behavior is as easy to detect as it is despicable. And yet it's quite likely that we've all been guilty of it from time to time.

Just as the lie is often worse than the original offense it is meant to cover up, the passive aggressive nature of the one son breaking his promise is worse than the other one refusing to go work in the vineyard in the first place.

Notice how Jesus doesn't ask, "Which of the two gave his father the right answer?" He asks, "Which of the two did his father's will?" In another passage, when describing the final judgment, he says, "I was hungry and you gave me food." He doesn't say, "I was hungry and you promised me food." It is the doing, not the talking, that redeems us. In fact, one could make the argument that the talking without the corresponding action condemns us.

How many times have you been disappointed by someone who had promised to help you? How many times have you disappointed others? Would you rather someone say yes and then not do what you asked, or say no and then acquiesce?

Jesus' lesson is simple and profound. When it's all said and done, it will be what was done that will far outshine what was said.

God the Father, help us to be honest enough to say what we mean, and to mean what we say. May our words and actions align so that we always set a good example as we seek to do your will.

Holier than Thou

Jack Sacco

"Amen, I say to you, tax collectors and prostitutes are entering the kingdom of God before you. When John came to you in the way of righteousness, you did not believe him; but tax collectors and prostitutes did. Yet even when you saw that, you did not later change your minds and believe him." (Mt 21: 31-32)

Have you ever known anyone who was so holy that it made you sick? I'm not talking about real sacrificial holiness, but rather the artificial, saccharine type that is specifically designed to let everyone know how pious they are. You know the type… they are quick to quote Scripture or to let you know how many rosaries and novenas they say in a given day, and they're ready to pass judgment on those who don't quite match up to their prayer regimen.

But it's not the prayers or the piety or even the propensity for judgment that's the problem. In all likelihood, our queasiness in the presence of such people often stems from their "holier than thou" attitude ironically coupled with their hypocrisy.

Hypocrisy in the form of saying one thing and doing another is both incredibly transparent and offensive. And it's especially abhorrent in those who call themselves followers of Christ. Have you ever been in need, only to be ignored by certain self-righteous people, but eventually to be helped by someone who didn't even claim to be Christian?

I once knew a man who had been involved in some pretty sketchy situations, most of which were completely his fault. Drugs, infidelity, violence, and scams were all part of his daily routine. But somewhere along the line, through a set of almost miraculous circumstances, he underwent a rather remarkable conversion experience. Despite a destructive lifestyle that had been ingrained in him from an early age, the message of Jesus inspired him to change his life completely.

His friends and associates – and even his wife – told me that his newfound faith had produced a profound change in every aspect of his being. Unlike many who simply claim holiness for the sake of impressing others, this man took the Word of God to heart, and it transformed his life.

God the Father, shine your light on our path as we journey toward true holiness. May we not only recognize your Word, but may it transform our lives.

Trust

Jack Sacco

"There was a landowner who planted a vineyard, put a hedge around it, dug a wine press in it, and built a tower. Then he leased it to tenants and went on a journey." (Mt 21: 33)

It feels good to be trusted, to be put in charge. And it feels good to be able to trust others, to be able to allow them to handle your affairs with confidence that they will act in your best interest with aptitude, integrity, and honor.

Though we have ample evidence that fraud, corruption, apathy, and laziness abound, we still have both a need to be trusted and a desire to trust others.

It is therefore not difficult to imagine that God the Father has a desire both to trust those to whom he's bequeathed his kingdom on earth and to be trusted by us. This kingdom, much like the vineyard in the parable, has been planted by God and built up by those who've come before us. Now, as we take our place at the front row of history, the Father must trust us just as he has trusted those who came before us.

The challenge of being true to this calling has been around as long as the calling itself. In Jesus' time, social, political, and theological circumstances provided a myriad of distractions that could easily serve to undermine the trust that God had placed in his people.

Today, with modern technology, twenty-four hour news cycles, the constant bombardment from advertisers, and an almost cult-like fascination with the lifestyles of the rich and famous, there is undoubtedly much more competition for our attention than ever before.

And so, like every generation, we must ask ourselves the following questions: How trustworthy are we to be put in charge of the vineyard? How knowledgeable and prepared are we to assume control of the property, and to harvest a bountiful crop worthy of the trust that has been placed in us? How willing and able are we to block out the many distractions of the world in order to be true to our calling?

God the Father, may we always be worthy of your trust in us as stewards of your vineyard. May we thus reap a bountiful harvest, using your gifts to enrich the world.

Betrayal

Jack Sacco

"When vintage time drew near, [the landowner] sent his servants to the tenants to obtain his produce. But the tenants seized the servants and one they beat, another they killed, and a third they stoned. Again he sent other servants, more numerous than the first ones, but they treated them in the same way."
(Mt 21: 34-36)

I have a cousin who is a rock star. Throughout his career, he has sold millions of records and has been a featured performer in concerts around the world. I've been backstage at several of his concerts, and I've seen the adulation and love his fans pour out on him. As one might imagine, his success has not only afforded him fame and prestige, but a great deal of wealth. He had a manager who, in keeping with his title, was in charge of managing his affairs, including his finances. It so happened that this particular man was also the manager for several well-known performers. He convinced my cousin, along with his other clients, to invest a great deal of money in a new venture that he promised would redouble their accumulated wealth. One morning, they discovered that the manager – along with their money – had disappeared. They rushed to his office, only to find that the place had been cleaned out. The manager had betrayed them all, and had escaped with millions of their dollars.

I feel safe in assuming that we've all had experiences in which we trusted someone who ultimately betrayed us. Perhaps we didn't put them in charge of millions of our hard-earned dollars, but still we trusted them to some degree, and they interpreted that trust as an opportunity to take advantage of us. Since we can't control the actions of others, the more important questions are these: How many times have we betrayed a trust that someone placed in us? How many times have we squandered the gifts and talents God has given us, or used them in the service of evil as opposed to the service of good? All gifts, large and small, are bestowed upon us by the Creator. When he asks for the fruits of those gifts, will we show that we can be trusted, or will we be willing to betray?

God the Father, grant us an appreciation for your generosity in bestowing your gifts, and in trusting us to manage them here on this earth. May we always use them in the service of good, and may they bear much fruit that will be pleasing to you.

Greed and the Mob Mentality

Jack Sacco

"Finally, [the landowner] sent his son to [the tenants], thinking, 'They will respect my son.' But when the tenants saw the son, they said to one another, 'This is the heir. Come, let us kill him and acquire his inheritance.' They seized him, threw him out of the vineyard, and killed him." (Mt 21: 37-39)

Sometimes the person who is worthy of the greatest respect is shown the least. The motives for this can be plentiful, but often boil down to a combination of fear, jealousy, greed, and that powerful yet irrational impetus known as the mob mentality.

Fear of change, of any deviation from the status quo, can motivate people to distrust the perceived agent of that change. Such distrust can manifest itself in the form of ridicule and character assassination.

Jealousy of the stature and accomplishments of another can sow deep seeds of resentment and anger. It's not that the other person has done anything to warrant our antipathy… it's simply that they possess something we feel they do not deserve.

Greed, jealousy's cousin, can deceive our minds into fantasies of how much better life would be if we only had this or that possession. Greed unchecked can become a fire that no amount of water can ever quench.

Any one of these can motivate us to irrational behavior toward another. But when you couple any or all of them with a mob mentality, then logic, ethics, and even decency can be dramatically reduced. And the results can be lethal. Politicians, aware of these tendencies in the population at large, often fan the flames of class warfare in an effort to bolster their own agendas. Many realize that if they can inspire fear, jealousy, or greed – and can then somehow work the mob into a frenzy – they can suspend rational behavior and achieve their otherwise unattainable goals. What would you have done had you been part of the crowd in the parable? Would you have peacefully given the landowner's son his rightful share even if it meant calling down the wrath of the mob on yourself? Or would you have joined the others in their revolt, mistreating the son, throwing him out of the vineyard, and killing him?

God the Father, grant me the clarity of mind and the courage of conviction to see fear, jealousy, and greed for what they are, and not to use them as motivations to attack others. May my respect for you and your Son – and not a desire to conform to the mob – always be my primary motivation.

Retribution

Jack Sacco

"What will the owner of the vineyard do to those tenants when he comes?" [The chief priests and elders] answered [Jesus], "He will put those wretched men to a wretched death and lease his vineyard to other tenants who will give him the produce at the proper times." (Mt 21: 40-41)

It's easy to become arrogant and bold when there are no consequences associated with one's misdeeds. But payback can come in a variety of ways, and at a time most inconvenient. For some, the fear of retribution is the only reason to behave in a civil manner toward others. For others, not even that threat is taken seriously. Most laws are based on social norms that should be obvious: don't murder, don't steal, don't harm others, etc. And each law has a penalty associated with it. We even have highly-trained police forces charged with catching those who, despite the threat of punishment, insist on breaking the law. And yet there is no shortage of criminals who plan and carry out illegal acts on a daily basis. They understand that what they are doing is wrong and that they will likely be punished for their deed, but they do it anyway.

The tenants in the parable had to know that stealing from the landowner, and then murdering his servants and his son would not be dealt with lightly. But they apparently had no respect for the owner or the law. To make matters worse, they had no fear of reprisal for their acts. Jesus asks the question, "What will the owner of the vineyard do to those tenants when he comes?" in order to illustrate the irrationality of the tenants, and to teach his followers not to act in the same way. It's easy to see the big picture from a distance. It's simple to understand that if we break the rules, there will likely be unpleasant consequences. But sometimes, in the heat of the moment, or faced with circumstances that breed temptation, we can ignore what we know to be true, and we can act in ways that betray our own morality and sense of decency.

God the Father, grant that we may do what is right for the sake of goodness and justice, not merely out of fear of retribution. May we act fairly toward our neighbors, and produce the good fruit that you expect from us.

Justice

Jack Sacco

Jesus said to [the chief priests and elders], "Did you never read in the scriptures/ 'The stone that the builders rejected/ has become the cornerstone/ by the Lord has this been done/ and it is wonderful in our eyes'?/ Therefore, I say to you, the kingdom of God will be taken away from you and given to a people that will produce its fruit." (Mt 21: 42-43)

We love the underdog, the guy who has been mistreated, misunderstood, and cast aside. We want to see him overcome the odds. We want to see him rise up and succeed. The downtrodden hero or heroine who somehow makes an unlikely comeback to achieve victory has been the theme of story and song for centuries. One of the main components in the appeal of such rags-to-riches narratives is the honor and goodness of the protagonist. If protagonists acted despicably, then they would likely neither attract sympathy for their predicament nor inspire the cheers of others. It is, in part, their decency in the face of injustice and overwhelming odds that causes us to want to see them succeed, and to feel vindicated when they ultimately do so.

The young Giuseppe Verdi was rejected for admission to the famous Milan Conservatory of Music. The examiners told him that he lacked the requisite talent, but that if he was determined to study musical composition, he should seek out a local conductor who would be willing to act as a mentor. Verdi eventually found a maestro willing to teach him, and over the next few years, despite setbacks, adversity, and personal tragedy, he honed his musical talent into a formidable force. Soon he was composing some of the most famous operas in all of Italy. His body of work is still recognized as among the most moving and powerful in all of opera, and he is viewed by many as the greatest of all the operatic composers. Today the Milan Conservatory – the very school that had rejected the young composer – is named in his honor: the Giuseppe Verdi Conservatory of Music. The divine justice of the rejected stone becoming the cornerstone reminds us of the nobility of those who, despite adversity, walk with faith in God, and are ultimately rewarded with victory.

God the Father, give us the courage and strength to fight the good fight, despite the odds, the adversity, and the opinions of others. May we recognize the talent and value of our neighbors, so that we will not reject them unjustly.

You're Invited

Jack Sacco

*Jesus again in reply spoke to [the chief priests and the Pharisees]
in parables, saying, "The kingdom of heaven may be likened to
a king who gave a wedding feast for his son. He dispatched his
servants to summon the invited guests to the feast, but they
refused to come. A second time he sent other servants, saying,
'Tell those invited: "Behold, I have prepared my banquet,
my calves and fattened cattle are killed, and everything
is ready; come to the feast."'"* (Mt 22: 1-4)

I once heard a priest say that Jesus' greatest desire for us is to be
happy here on earth, and then to live eternally with him in
heaven. This model – being happy on earth and then being eternally happy in heaven – is, in every respect, the best of both worlds.

Such optimism, as welcome as it may be, is in direct contrast to
the outright doom and gloom that some people preach. For them,
one can never hope to get to heaven unless he or she is miserable
here on earth.

But Jesus himself, much like my priest friend, is much more positive in his outlook. For him, heaven is like a marvelous feast that
the Father invites us to attend. Even when we refuse his invitation,
as we often do, he extends it again and again, revealing to us the
wonders and majesty that await each of us in our heavenly home.

The question remains: How does one go about accepting that
invitation? It seems as if the answer is contained within the parable itself. If the allegorical king is God the Father, and his son is
Jesus Christ, then the bride, though only implied, must be the
Church. It is therefore through that relationship of Christ to his
Church that we are invited to partake of happiness, both in this life
and in the life to come.

As my priest friend pointed out, we are not only invited to attend
the feast, but to journey to the banquet hall in the company of our
fellow invitees. The encouragement we receive and the friendships
we make along the way are themselves part of the benefit of attending. Through good times and bad, the Church provides us with the
means of accepting the invitation and the vehicle to transport us
safely and happily to our destination.

*God the Father, may we always appreciate your invitation, and
may we look forward to the feast and fellowship you have prepared
for us. Nothing could ever be more fulfilling than being with you
at the heavenly banquet.*

Thanks, But No Thanks

Jack Sacco

"Some ignored the invitation and went away, one to his farm, another to his business. The rest laid hold of his servants, mistreated them, and killed them." (Mt 22: 5-6)

How would you feel if you had a party and no one showed up? Everyone likes for their invitations to be accepted, and for their invited guests to enjoy themselves at the scheduled event. But the prospect of people ignoring the invitation can be daunting, not only because of the assumed expense of the party, but because such a snub would indicate that those invited clearly had no desire to be associated with the host.

Not accepting an invitation is one thing. Ignoring it is quite another. But actually killing the person who delivered the invitation is extreme to say the least.

Biblical stories abound of prophets charged with delivering messages to God's people, only to be mistreated and killed for their trouble. It seems that whenever the message involved people changing their lifestyles – and it almost always did – the prophet knew that he or she could expect resistance and even martyrdom.

Faced with the prospect of your own murder at the hands of the ungrateful masses, would you be willing to accept the job of inviting them to the feast? But if we are called to evangelize others through our actions and words, then isn't extending that invitation precisely what we are called to do?

And what about the invitations that are extended to us by others? Do we ignore them? Do we simply say no? Or is our reaction a bit harsher?

In the end, most invitations call us to some type of change. Perhaps it's simply an opportunity to change our routine, to share a meal with friends, to visit a new place, or to meet new people. Or perhaps it's an opportunity to change the way we approach life itself.

The invitations we accept and reject as we journey through life – and the changes we make as a result – will guide us in our discernment of the ultimate invitation... the one from Christ to join him in his kingdom.

God the Father, may we not be cavalier in our rejection of your invitation. May we appreciate the immeasurable honor you bestow on us by asking us to attend your feast, and may we always say yes.

The Worthy Guest
Jack Sacco

"The king was enraged and sent his troops, destroyed those murderers, and burned their city. Then he said to his servants, 'The feast is ready, but those who were invited were not worthy to come. Go out, therefore, into the main roads and invite to the feast whomever you find.'" (Mt 22: 7-9)

I once heard an impassioned homily in which the priest explained in great detail how no one was actually worthy to receive the Eucharist. He spoke at length about mankind's sinful nature, and powerfully made the case that no one deserved to approach the altar and partake of the body of Christ. The only problem was that when it was time for communion, no one in the congregation moved.

I completely understand the point the priest was making. However, it was obvious that his homily had backfired. Now, instead of humbly acknowledging the majesty and goodness of God, the people were hesitant to move from their seats and to accept Christ's invitation to share in his feast. After several awkward seconds, the priest finally said, "It's okay, you can come up and receive the body of Christ. None of us are worthy, but we have been invited by Jesus." The people in the congregation looked relieved, and slowly made their way to the altar.

It's interesting to note that, in the parable, the king didn't say that those who were invited simply did not want to come. He claimed that they were "not worthy" to come. But if they were *not worthy*, then why had they been invited in the first place? The distinction is subtle, but it points to the deeper truth that sometimes our worthiness (or lack thereof) is simply a function of our willingness to accept the invitation.

Jesus knows all about our unworthiness. And yet he still extends to us an invitation. By putting our own insecurities and worries aside and by answering yes to his invitation, we open up a new world of possibilities… a world prepared by Christ from the beginning of time. After all the sacrifices he made on our behalf, the act of not accepting his invitation would truly make us unworthy.

God the Father, grant that we may demonstrate our worthiness to be called to your Son's feast by responding to your invitation. May we be for ever grateful for the goodness you show by inviting us despite our sinfulness.

The King's New Best Friends

Jack Sacco

"The servants went out into the streets and gathered all they found, bad and good alike, and the hall was filled with guests."
(Mt 22: 10)

This wedding feast is starting to sound like a free-for-all. The invitations to the original guests were rejected and ignored, so now the servants – at least the ones who haven't been killed – have gone out again, grabbing all manner of people off the streets, and inviting them to the party. It's not hard to imagine that the hall would soon be filled with guests of all types. It almost seems as if the king's desperation has doomed the party to failure. After all, would you be happy if the invitations to your wedding were rejected, and if strangers were simply plucked off the street to fill seats at the banquet hall? But, as intended by the parable, there emerge from this one short passage a couple of deeper issues to consider.

One is the inclusiveness of the current invitation. There is no longer an exclusive guest list. The feast is now open to all, good and bad. The prime factor in being invited is not one's previous status or relationship with the king, but one's willingness to say yes to the invitation itself. This inclusiveness, though perhaps a direct result of the rejection and apathy of the previous invitees, turns out to be a windfall for those on the street who presumably would never have been invited to the wedding feast. The notion that the "bad and good alike" were ultimately invited to attend was certainly good news to those who happened to be on the street that day, and it should be good news to all of us living in the twenty-first century.

The second issue is the fulfilled desire of the king to have a hall filled with guests who actually want to be there, who are excited about the prospect of celebrating the occasion and sharing a hearty meal with royalty. In this way, all of humanity, and perhaps God himself, benefits from the inclusiveness of the invitation.

God the Father, thank you for including me on your guest list. May I not only say yes to your invitation, but may I be open to all people regardless of their race, creed, or economic status, and may all of my relationships be mutually uplifting.

Appropriate Attire
Jack Sacco

"But when the king came in to meet the guests he saw a man there not dressed in a wedding garment. He said to him, 'My friend, how is it that you came in here without a wedding garment?' But he was reduced to silence. Then the king said to his attendants, 'Bind his hands and feet, and cast him into the darkness outside, where there will be wailing and grinding of teeth.' Many are invited, but few are chosen." (Mt 22: 11-14)

Having gone through so much trouble to invite everyone to his feast, it seems somewhat incongruous – and almost rude – that the king would then cast out one of the guests for not being properly dressed. At the same time, the seeming inconsistency in the allegory serves notice to us that there may very well be a story behind the story.

Jesus himself made a point of inviting everyone, good and bad, to follow him. His message was one of inclusion, sometimes over the objections of his closest friends. But even though his invitation has been extended to all, a simple acceptance of that invitation is not good enough.

Like the son who had promised his father that he would work in the field, but then decided not to do so, those who simply pay lip service by saying yes to the invitation without properly preparing themselves are ultimately unworthy to attend. What would you think if you hosted an elegant formal dinner, and one of your invited guests showed up in swimwear, flip flops, and a straw sun hat? Chances are that you would feel disrespected, perhaps even mortified. And your other, more properly attired guests would very likely feel uncomfortable and embarrassed.

Acceptance implies that one is willing to prepare oneself appropriately for the event. In some cases, that preparation might involve something as simple as putting on the proper apparel. In others, it could mean completely changing one's way of life. Christ has invited us to the feast. Our acceptance of that invitation implies that we will be willing to prepare properly for the banquet by "putting on Christ." Not to do so reveals a lack of respect for our host, and a lack of appreciation for the majesty of the event. In this way, many are indeed invited, but only a few – those who have made the decision to change their lives by living in accord with God's message – are chosen.

God the Father, may we gratefully accept your invitation to the heavenly feast, and may we arrive prepared, cloaked in purity and grace, worthy of admittance into your kingdom.

The Image of God

Father Joseph T. Lienhard, S.J.

*Knowing [the Pharisees' and Herodians'] malice, Jesus said,
"Why are you testing me, you hypocrites? Show me the coin that
pays the census tax." Then they handed him the Roman coin.
He said to them, "Whose image is this and whose inscription?"
They replied, "Caesar's." At that he said to them, "Then repay
to Caesar what belongs to Caesar and to God
what belongs to God." (Mt 22: 18-21)*

"Whose image is this and whose inscription?" "Caesar's."
Jesus asks the Pharisees for a coin, and they show him
a Roman coin, which has the image of the Roman
emperor on it. He does not ask them for another coin, one that has
the image of God on it – for there was no such coin, and there never
could be. The Jews never made an image of God, not only because
the law forbade it, but also because they knew that the image of
God was to be found elsewhere – namely, in human beings.

In Genesis 1: 26 we read, "Let us make man in our image, after
our likeness." Interpreters point out that this verse is an answer to
the idolatry of the people who surrounded the Israelites. Those
people all made statues of themselves and said, "These are our gods."
But the Book of Genesis teaches something very different: God
made little images of himself and said, "These are you." The Fathers
of the Church were intrigued by what the Bible said about images
and developed the theme further. In the Letter to the Colossians,
Saint Paul called Christ "the image of the invisible God." The Fathers
read Genesis 1: 26 not as "in the image" but "after the image" – that
is, Christ is the image of God and we are made after the image: God
modeled man on Christ.

And so we come back to the coin with Caesar's image on it: "Then
repay to Caesar what belongs to Caesar and to God what belongs
to God." God's image is not on a coin, but in us, and it means that
we owe all that we are to him. In a way, the phrase says, we should
become what we are: if we are made after the image of God, who
is Christ, we ought to bring the image of Christ to fullness within
ourselves.

*God our Father, Lord of all creation, all things come from you; make
us grateful, we pray, for your gifts, and call us back to yourself.*

A Marriage Made in Heaven?

Father Joseph T. Lienhard, s.j.

Jesus said to [the Sadducees] in reply, "You are misled because you do not know the scriptures or the power of God. At the resurrection they neither marry nor are given in marriage but are like the angels in heaven." (Mt 22: 29-30)

We find three stages in the biblical approach to marriage. In the Old Testament, the children of Israel were a small tribe, often threatened by their enemies with extinction. The rabbis found six hundred and thirteen commandments in the Torah, the first five books of the Bible, and they pointed out that the first of these commandments was "increase and multiply." Celibacy was not valued in the Old Testament, and childlessness was adjudged a curse.

With the coming of Christianity, tribal borders vanished, and the faith could spread throughout the world. Survival was no longer a problem. And further, Jesus offered his disciples a new ideal: voluntarily foregoing marriage as an anticipation of his kingdom. Tradition has it that Saint John the apostle and evangelist remained unmarried. And Saint Paul proposed the same ideal as Jesus had: for those who can accept it, there is a higher way. Jesus never prohibited marriage, and the early Church rejected anyone who wanted to make celibacy obligatory. But still, the Church encouraged foregoing marriage as an anticipation of the life to come. That higher way anticipates in the present what the future kingdom of God will be.

It is that kingdom that Jesus speaks of when he says, "At the resurrection they neither marry nor are given in marriage but are like the angels in heaven." In the final state, the number of human beings will be complete. The love of those raised from the dead will be directed wholly to the living God who saved them, and the sacrament of marriage will be fulfilled in the union of Christ with his bride, the Church. The Sadducees did not believe in the resurrection of the dead; hence they could not understand the progression from a tribe struggling to survive to the fulfillment of God's everlasting kingdom. By his own resurrection, Christ showed us how our hope will be fulfilled.

Eternal God and Father, you have called us to the fullness of life in Christ; bring us, we pray, safely to your eternal kingdom.

The Mystery of Loving God

Father Joseph T. Lienhard, S.J.

*One of them [a scholar of the law] tested [Jesus] by asking,
"Teacher, which commandment in the law is the greatest?"
He said to him, "You shall love the Lord, your God, with all
your heart, with all your soul, and with all your mind. This is
the greatest and the first commandment. The second is like it:
You shall love your neighbor as yourself. The whole law and the
prophets depend on these two commandments." (Mt 22: 35-40)*

Have you ever reflected on how mysterious the command to love God is? We all know what it means to love another human being – spouse, parents, children: we want to see them safe from all harm; we want them to have good things; we want them to respond to us, to acknowledge us, to love us in return. But what does it mean to love God?

At the end of his *Spiritual Exercises*, Saint Ignatius Loyola has a final meditation, entitled "Contemplation to Obtain the Love of God." At the beginning of the meditation, Saint Ignatius makes two points. The first point is that love is proved by deeds rather than by words. We have all heard the phrase, "Promises, promises," and we know what it means: all words and no action. True love fulfills its words in actions. Saint Ignatius' second point is that lovers demonstrate their love by giving each other gifts. A bouquet of flowers, a box of candy, a silk necktie – these are the simplest kinds of gifts, but still they can mean a great deal. There are higher sorts of gifts, reaching up to the total gift of self in marriage. One old ritual for the sacrament of marriage has the haunting phrase, "with my body I thee worship," a beautiful expression of total love and commitment.

Saint Ignatius' next step is to ask us to contemplate God's gifts to us: first in creation itself, then in his presence and activity in the world and in us. Finally, we are to apply the two principles to our love for God. First, if I love God, I should show that love by deeds and not only by words. And then, my love for God should be demonstrated by the gifts I return to him, for all that he has given me. What those gifts are to be, each one of us must know.

Eternal Lord of all things, you have given me all that I am; I offer myself to you, and I consecrate my life to serving you in truth and in charity.

Practice What You Preach

Father Joseph T. Lienhard, S.J.

Jesus spoke to the crowds and to his disciples, saying, "The scribes and the Pharisees have taken their seat on the chair of Moses. Therefore, do and observe all things whatsoever they tell you, but do not follow their example. For they preach but they do not practice. They tie up heavy burdens [hard to carry] and lay them on people's shoulders, but they will not lift a finger to move them. All their works are performed to be seen." (Mt 23: 1-5)

How often have we heard the phrase "Practice what you preach"? Perhaps we've said it to others, with a certain edge in our voice, a certain sense of superiority. Or perhaps someone else has said it to us, implying gently, ever so gently, that there is something hypocritical about us. And if that happens, we are annoyed, and quite rightly so. For to hear "Practice what you preach" implies that there is some lack of integrity in us, some lack of honesty. "You don't live up to your own ideals. What gives you the right to tell me how to live?" Hypocrite, hypocrisy, hypocritical – those are nasty words. And yet, who of us can say, for all of our lives, "not guilty" to the accusation, "hypocrite"?

Only one, really, can say that. Why? No one of us lives up to his ideals. With each sin, with each fault, I am being a bit of a hypocrite. It was Jesus Christ, and he alone (the Blessed Virgin Mary aside) who lived a life of perfect integrity. "God was reconciling the world to himself in Christ," Saint Paul writes (2 Cor 5: 19). In Christ, all the disorder brought about by original sin, and by all the sins that followed it, is overcome, at least potentially. With Christ, and in Christ, the great victory has been won; all that is left is a mopping-up operation, as the idiom has it.

Saint Augustine describes the Christian life after baptism as a life-long convalescence, a gradual healing of the effects of original sin. Healing is a coming together of what has been parted, cut, separated. As we grow in the grace of Christ, we will come, more and more, to practice what we preach. The wounds of sin are healed, and in our lives we grow more like Christ. The remnants of hypocrisy gradually fall away, and we are free in Christ.

God our Father, you sent Christ your Son to heal the wounds of sin; help us to live his words as we put them into effect in our lives.

What Is a Servant?

Father Joseph T. Lienhard, S.J.

"The greatest among you must be your servant. Whoever exalts himself will be humbled; but whoever humbles himself will be exalted." (Mt 23: 11-12)

What would it mean to be someone's servant? Most of us, I suppose, did not grow up with servants in our household; and none of us ever experienced slavery. A slave is owned by his master; he is no more than a useful piece of property. A servant is free; he is paid to work, and he can leave. But for much of human history, people had little choice except to work as servants. Even in the United States in the nineteenth century, servants were common. If you tour President Franklin Delano Roosevelt's summer home in Hyde Park, New York, for example, you are shown the servants' quarters, a large part of the house.

What did servants do? A maid cleaned the house, did the laundry, set the table, washed the dishes. The butler supervised the family meals, answered the door, received guests. If you think about it, servants appear frequently in Jesus' parables. A servant works in the fields. He cooks dinner for his master, and he eats only after the master has eaten. Servants are to wait up, even half the night, until the master returns. Sometimes servants are told to invest money, and they are punished if they do not make a profit. And, after all else, they are to say, "We are unprofitable servants."

The life of a servant can be unpleasant; yet Jesus tells us, "The greatest among you must be your servant." But he does more than tell us. He himself takes the role of a servant, in a dramatic gesture. At the Last Supper he lays aside his outer garment, the sign of a master, and puts on an apron. He undertakes the lowliest of servants' tasks: he washes the feet of his disciples. Here is a parable in action. On the following day, Good Friday, he will fulfill what the prophet Isaiah foretold in the Servant Songs: he will offer the ultimate act of service.

Almighty God and Father, you sent Christ your Son to give himself for us; help us to serve you faithfully all the days of our lives.

Jerusalem, Jerusalem

Father Joseph T. Lienhard, S.J.

"Jerusalem, Jerusalem, you who kill the prophets and stone those sent to you, how many times I yearned to gather your children together, as a hen gathers her young under her wings, but you were unwilling! Behold, your house will be abandoned, desolate. I tell you, you will not see me again until you say, 'Blessed is he who comes in the name of the Lord.'" (Mt 23: 37-39)

The passage proposed for contemplation is mysterious, even baffling. Jesus addresses Jerusalem – is it the inhabitants of the city, or the Jewish nation? Whoever it is, they have killed the prophets, itself a mysterious phrase. One would expect Jesus to say next, "You ought to welcome the prophets and those sent to you; you ought to welcome me." But he doesn't say that. Instead, he speaks of gathering the children together, of protecting them and guarding them in their helplessness. Jesus does not ask them for a change of heart; instead, he offers them protection and shelter – in other words, the gift of grace. But they were unwilling to accept this gift. Jesus then prophesies the destruction of their house, the destruction of Jerusalem. Sullen persistence in ignorance, in sin, has its consequences, just as all of our free actions have consequences.

Jesus' hearers have had their last chance, or almost their last chance. "You will not see me again," he says, "until you say, 'Blessed is he who comes in the name of the Lord.'" Jesus quotes Psalm 118: 26. As often in the New Testament, the quotation of one verse of a psalm invokes the whole psalm. Psalm 118 is the last of the five psalms of the "Egyptian Hallel" (Psalms 113 to 118), which were sung at Passover: the first two before the meal and the last three after it. Matthew may well allude to this practice when he writes that, after the Last Supper, Jesus and his disciples sang a hymn; it may have been Psalm 118. If so, then Jesus' words are fulfilled in a mysterious way, as his disciples sang, "Blessed is he who comes in the name of the Lord!" In Psalm 118 the speaker is afflicted on every side, but God's steadfast love saves him, and he enters the temple. The mystery of the verses from Matthew is resolved in Psalm 118, a psalm we might pray attentively.

God our Father, make us, we pray, attentive to your words in the Holy Scriptures, and break open their meaning for us.

The True Temple

Father Joseph T. Lienhard, S.J.

Jesus left the temple area and was going away, when his disciples approached him to point out the temple buildings. He said to them in reply, "You see all these things, do you not? Amen, I say to you, there will not be left here a stone upon another stone that will not be thrown down." (Mt 24: 1-2)

The Gospels seldom mention works of art or architecture. We read of the stable Jesus was born in. We also read of some houses, like the house of Peter's mother-in-law, and the houses of Zacchaeus, Martha and Mary, and Simon: but in each of these cases, the mention of a house is incidental. What is important is the meal that takes place in the house, and the people Jesus dines with. The temple in Jerusalem was different. It was primarily the house of God. At its center was the Holy of Holies, in Jesus' time an empty room. In the first temple, destroyed centuries before Jesus, the ark of the covenant had been kept in the Holy of Holies. The temple was a place for worship and sacrifice, not for the assembly of the community. We know that the temple that Jesus saw, the one he cleansed of buyers and sellers, was destroyed in the year 70 A.D. by the Roman army. Jesus' disciples are amazed at the size and the beauty and the architecture of the temple in Jerusalem.

Jesus' prediction is twofold: yes, this building will be destroyed. But this destruction will also be a liberation, a freeing. Even before the temple was destroyed, Jesus had said to the woman at the well, "The hour is coming when you will worship the Father neither on this mountain nor in Jerusalem" (Jn 4: 21). The true worship of God will no longer take place only on one mountain on earth, or in one temple. The true worship of the one true God will spread to every corner of the earth. No longer will animals be offered to God. Rather, from the most magnificent cathedral to the tiniest chapel in a little convent, the Holy Sacrifice of the Mass will be offered each day. The stones of the earthly temple are pulled down, but the temple of the body of Christ is being built up.

God our Father, hear us, we pray; help us to worship you rightly, in spirit and in truth, all the days of our lives.

Trust in the Name

Father Joseph T. Lienhard, S.J.

"Nation will rise against nation, and kingdom against kingdom;
there will be famines and earthquakes from place to place.
All these are the beginning of the labor pains. Then they
will hand you over to persecution, and they will kill you.
You will be hated by all nations because of my name."
(Mt 24: 7-9)

Nation against nation, kingdom against kingdom… famines and earthquakes… labor pains… persecution, hatred, death, because of my name. This is a frightening series of pictures. Jesus predicts disaster, but he also offers hope. Jesus gives us two things to trust in. One is the name; the other is labor pains.

To know the name of Jesus is to enjoy his protection. In the Old Testament, the name of God is uncertain. "I am who am" (Ex 3: 14) is as much the refusal to give a name as the revealing of a name. In Genesis, God will not disclose his name to Jacob (Gn 32: 23-31). Later, the Jews would no longer even attempt to pronounce the name of God. But Jesus is God's definitive self-revelation, and he has entrusted us with his name. To know someone's name is to have power over that person. What is the function of a name in society? We have some trivial uses of names, such as, "Hi, my name is Scott, and I'll be your server." But the reality is much deeper. To know someone's name is to enter into a relationship with that person, to be human for each other, as opposed to being a thing. To reveal one's name is an act of trust. Jesus has a name, and he has titles, like "Christ." Ironically, it was Pontius Pilate who made the most profound use of Jesus' name, and of his title, when he wrote the sign for the cross: "Jesus of Nazareth, King of the Jews." Pilate, you make only one mistake: this is the king not only of the Jews, but of the whole world.

As for the labor pains that Jesus spoke of, they may designate our very lives. We do indeed struggle, but our struggles have a purpose, and they will have a marvelous result: the fullness of life.

Eternal Lord and Father, we thank you for sending us Jesus Christ
as our Savior and King; may we always glory in his name, in which
we find our only hope, and our salvation.

The Power of the Creed

Father Joseph T. Lienhard, S.J.

"Many will be led into sin; they will betray and hate one another. Many false prophets will arise and deceive many; and because of the increase of evildoing, the love of many will grow cold." (Mt 24: 10-12)

The words of Jesus predict the coming of a sad state for the Church. To sin is bad; to lead others into sin is worse. Jesus predicts treachery and hatred within the community, and the extinguishing of the flame of love. But his most serious prediction is the rise of false prophets, those who will lead others away from the truth that God has revealed. A beautiful nineteenth-century hymn, known by its first line, "The Church's One Foundation," expresses the same sad thoughts:

> Though with a scornful wonder, men see her sore oppressed,
> By schisms rent asunder, by heresies distressed,
> Yet saints their watch are keeping, their cry goes up,
> "How long?"
> And soon the night of weeping shall be the morn of song!

There are false prophets enough in our day, prophets who want to make Jesus Christ only one of many saviors, prophets who want to import pagan practices into Christian worship, prophets who want to reshape the Bible to meet their own tastes.

But we have a weapon that enables us to recognize false prophets. Archbishop Timothy Dolan of New York, in his book *Priests for the Third Millennium*, recounts a dramatic use of this weapon. In the 1970s, an auxiliary bishop of Saint Louis was made administrator of the archdiocese. At that time, the seminary was in revolt, and this bishop – a country pastor, really – had to face down an angry group of faculty. The bishop told the faculty that there were clear, consistent Catholic truths that they had to teach the seminarians. The faculty spokesman sneered at the bishop and dared him to state one truth that had not changed. The bishop's mouth went dry; he probably wished that he were back in his parish in the hills. Then, after a long pause he looked up and began, "I believe in God, the Father almighty, creator of heaven and earth…" Our weapon is the Creed.

God, our eternal Father and Lord, confirm us in the truth that you have revealed through Jesus Christ, and help us to live the truth in charity.

Perseverance to the End

Father Joseph T. Lienhard, s.j.

"But the one who perseveres to the end will be saved."
(Mt 24: 13)

Saint Augustine of Hippo wrote at length about the gift of perseverance, which he calls "a divine gift by which an individual perseveres in Christ to the end of this life." Each day of our lives, we pray, "Lead us not into temptation, but deliver us from evil," acknowledging our need for God's grace. The gift of perseverance in Christ is the grace of graces, the gift that confirms our salvation in the last moments of our lives. A fall from perseverance may be despair, which means giving up hope, rejecting the gift of hope. But more often we are tempted by another sin, one that early monks in Egypt reflected on. These monks pondered a sin they called *acedia*.

The word is hard to translate; it can mean "boredom" or "tedium"; it has also been called the noonday devil, a phrase that the monks found in Psalm 91, verse 6, as translated into Greek. They understood this noonday devil – an intriguing phrase – as the temptation that afflicts a monk in the middle of his day. The sun does not seem to move; the monk tries prayer but soon thinks of some little task that needs to be done; he tries to do his work, but soon wonders why he is doing this useless task. He begins to think that his life as a monk is pointless; he could do more good if he returned to the city. It seems that even a single hour will not pass. He is tempted to acedia, to boredom, to the noonday devil. He wants to give up the Christian life that he has dedicated himself to. In other words, he is tempted against perseverance.

There are high points in our lives as Christians, moments of sacramental joy, moments of intense prayer. But many of our days seem to be plodding repetitions of each other, with tepid prayer and trivial sins. Do we need to fight our own noonday devils?

God our Father, give us the gift of perseverance; make us faithful in our lives as Christians and bring us safely, we ask you, to our goal.

The Son of Man

Father Joseph T. Lienhard, S.J.

"Just as lightning comes from the east and is seen as far as the west, so will the coming of the Son of Man be." (Mt 24: 27)

Perhaps Jesus' most intriguing designation for himself was "Son of Man." We need not be concerned here about the source of the title. We can reflect, rather, on what the title implies, and how Jesus uses it. "Son of Man" is a generic term, equivalent to "human being." When Jesus calls himself the Son of Man, he is affirming the fullness of his human nature. In a marvelous teaching, the Council of Chalcedon in 451 spoke a clear and solid word about who Jesus was. To paraphrase the council's words, it said that he is God in the same way that God the Father is, and man in the same way that we are. In other words, he is not some intermediate being, some demigod or superman. The Son of Man is the son of Mary, human in just the way that we are. But more: the Son of Man is the archetypal human being, the exemplar of what all of us strive to be. If we want to know what we ought to be, what we ought to become, what we hope to be, we need only look at the Son of Man.

Jesus used the title Son of Man in two distinctive ways: the Son of Man would suffer, and the Son of Man would die and rise again. Any one of us could make a list of what we have suffered, and surely of what other people have suffered. To suffer seems to be part of the human condition, but to understand that suffering has a meaning is part of Christian revelation. It is because the Son of Man suffers that we see the meaning of suffering. And finally, the Son of Man not only suffers; he dies, and he rises from the dead. Thus the Son of Man represents victory over the final enemy, death. The Son of Man reveals to us, in his own person, who we truly are.

God our Father and Lord, you have revealed yourself in Christ your Son. Through his suffering and death, bring us, we pray, to the fullness of life.

The End of the World?

Father Joseph T. Lienhard, s.j.

"The sign of the Son of Man will appear in heaven, and all the tribes of the earth will mourn, and they will see the Son of Man coming upon the clouds of heaven with power and great glory. And he will send out his angels with a trumpet blast, and they will gather his elect from the four winds, from one end of the heavens to the other." (Mt 24: 30-31)

The description in the New Testament of the "end of the world," as it is often called, or the Last Judgment, can be confusing, even frightening. Michelangelo's great fresco in the Sistine Chapel is one depiction of that judgment. Part of the reason for the confusion is the fact that the evangelists used details from the destruction of the city of Jerusalem in 70 A.D., which some of them, at least, knew about, to illustrate the final judgment that Jesus proclaimed. The passage from Saint Matthew that we meditate upon has three elements: first, the coming of the Son of Man; then, a cataclysmic event, symbolized by a trumpet blast and causing grief and mourning; and last, the gathering of the elect. Grief, fear, and mourning – yes. But when one reflects further on this passage, it can be an occasion for hope, for confidence, for joy.

The heart of this message is the triumph of the Son of Man, Christ the King. Each year, on the last Sunday of the Church's calendar, we celebrate the solemnity of Christ the King. We can phrase it this way: we Christians know, and know for certain, how the Great Story is going to end. Yes, it is true: we experience suffering and death, wars and destruction. But they are not the end. Finally, Christ will triumph over all death and all sin; Saint Paul writes that God will put all enemies under Christ's feet (see 1 Cor 15: 25). In many Byzantine churches, the mosaic image in the apse over the sanctuary is a depiction of *Christos Pantokrator*, Christ the Ruler over All – a most appropriate image for our Gospel reflection. Looking upon that image of Christ, the serene ruler, we understand what the end will be. And we are part of that picture, for as we affirm in the Creed, "We look for the resurrection of the dead, and the life of the world to come."

Eternal God and Father, strengthen our faith in the universal kingship of Christ; and make us, we ask, his loyal and trusting subjects.

The Word Abides For Ever

Father Joseph T. Lienhard, S.J.

"Heaven and earth will pass away, but my words will not pass away." (Mt 24: 35)

Jesus' words here are, at first, startling. After all, if heaven and earth pass away, where would his words abide? But Jesus is not speaking about time, but about the very nature of his words, God's words. We see the power of God's words in the very first verses of the Book of Genesis: "God said, 'Let there be light,' and there was light." God needed only to speak a word, and the world came into being. Later, in the New Testament, we read that "the word of God is… sharper than any two-edged sword" (Heb 4: 12). The power of God's word is also the power of Jesus' words. The phrase we are pondering, "my words will not pass away," ought to give us the right approach to reading and hearing the Gospel. Each day at Mass, the Gospel is proclaimed, and we stand to hear it, in honor of the words of Jesus. But we need to do more than hear them, more than just admire their wisdom and their beauty. The words of Jesus have the power to transform our lives.

As we hear the Gospel each day, or each Sunday, it ought to shake us up, threaten us – but also console us, encourage us. "Take up your cross and follow me." "Do not be afraid, little flock." "Unless a man loses his life…" "I will send you another Paraclete." "I am with you always." Think of how a lover listens to every word of the one he loves. That ought to be our attitude, as we hear Jesus' words in the Gospel. Those are not words spoken long ago that are now only historical curiosities. Jesus, raised from the dead, lives for ever, and his words are addressed to us, now. They are the best guide we could find for our lives, for our hope. Jesus lives, and his words will never pass away.

God our Father, open our hearts to the words that Christ, your Son, spoke to us; and give us the strength to put them into effect in our lives.

Is the Thief Coming?

Father Joseph T. Lienhard, S.J.

"Stay awake! For you do not know on which day your Lord will come. Be sure of this: if the master of the house had known the hour of night when the thief was coming, he would have stayed awake and not let his house be broken into. So too, you also must be prepared, for at an hour you do not expect, the Son of Man will come." (Mt 24: 42-44)

Jesus here uses a short parable that surely attracted the attention of every listener. No one wants to have his home broken into. Not only does a burglar take our property; he violates our privacy. Someone comes home after a burglary: drawers have been opened, closets have been rifled, jewelry boxes have been overturned. For months afterward, the owner thinks, "If only... if only... if only..." That is Jesus' point: be prepared, so that you don't have to say, "If only..." What should we be prepared for? The coming of the Son of Man, the coming of Christ. Jesus' comparison of himself with a thief is striking. For a thief to break in is a bad thing; for Christ to come is surely a good thing. But it is also a moment of judgment. Christ is clear on this point: it is our responsibility to be prepared.

And how are we to be prepared? Christ has already given us the means. We are to be free of the guilt of sin; for this, we have the sacrament of reconciliation, confession. We are to be united with Christ, as far as we can be; for this we have frequent Holy Communion. We are to know Christ, and to love him; for this we have the Gospels, and the whole of Scripture, by which we hear the voice of Christ; and we have prayer, by which we converse with him. We are to grow like Christ, by the practice of virtues: the infused virtues of faith, hope, and charity; and other virtues like patience in the face of adversity, courage in the face of opposition to our beliefs, and prudence in making the right choices. Our entire lives ought to be a preparation for the coming of the Son of Man; if that is the case, he will find us awake.

God our Father, help us, we ask you, to be ready to receive Christ our Lord when he comes to us in glory, and make us worthy of everlasting life in your kingdom.

Rest and Responsibility

Father Anthony Giambrone, O.P.

"Who, then, is the faithful and prudent servant, whom the master has put in charge of his household to distribute to them their food at the proper time? Blessed is that servant whom his master on his arrival finds doing so. Amen, I say to you, he will put him in charge of all his property." (Mt 24: 45-47)

Most of us already feel like we have quite enough to do. Is it really such a blessing, then, when the Lord promises his faithful servants the reward of more responsibilities? Is it so enticing to bear total responsibility, *for everything*? Our obligations often enough seem the very source of our fatigue. So, why would the Lord offer a metaphor of more work as work's reward? Where is the comfortable retirement package? "Well done, good and faithful servant. Come, and enter your master's joy."

Such questions usually bring us to an impasse. We find ourselves trapped in sterile hope, wishing after illusory contentment: a state of peace finally free from any imposition on our wills. In reality, however, the rest we long for is not (as we like to imagine) a kind of unending bliss of uncommitted idleness. The true refreshment and repose that comes from God arises from making his concerns our own. This is why the right reward for vigilant devotion is a deeper immersion in the affairs of the Lord – not a generous severance.

Jesus' image of the dutiful servant's "super-promotion" is not meant as a cruel extension of his drudgery. The servant here is not like that unprofitable (and abused) worker who must scramble to fix his master's meal after trudging in from the field (Lk 17: 7-10). That, perhaps, is a case for the unions. Here, however, our servant stumbles into another scene altogether. Busy about his business – making his master's will his own – he is abruptly overtaken by the huge weight of beatitude: covered with the ensigns of power and prestige. The lowly servant suddenly becomes the functional equal of his master: like Joseph in Egypt (to whom Jesus likely alludes). The concerns of the lord and his servant are now perfectly one. The tale is an allegory for our final divinization in grace, when our will at last rests perfectly in God's.

Father, make me faithful in your service. Visit me in my labors and expand my concerns. By the inducement of your grace make me truly devoted, until every interest of my will conforms perfectly with yours.

The Chaste Fire of Wisdom

Father Anthony Giambrone, O.P.

"Then the kingdom of heaven will be like ten virgins who took their lamps and went out to meet the bridegroom. Five of them were foolish and five were wise. The foolish ones, when taking their lamps, brought no oil with them, but the wise brought flasks of oil with their lamps." (Mt 25: 1-4)

A poet of our age has written: "Genius is the fire that lights itself." The idea, it would seem, is that a sudden flash of insight – a moment of genius – comes like an illumination from nowhere. It is no deduction, not the sum of acquired learning or some product of experience. It is a spontaneous combustion, a lightning strike in the mind, a virginal conception.

Faith is such a fire. It erupts with light in our souls, yet springs from no natural seed. It is a grace the Church Fathers pictured as a virgin bearing a lamp.

In Jesus' parable, all ten virgins have this fire of faith, for all go out to meet the Lord. The line Jesus draws between wisdom and folly, then, is not like the line which separates the wheat from the weeds, believers from unbelievers. The great test of wisdom and folly – dividing the virgins, five against five – tries the endurance of faith itself.

We have all often felt this trial. Whenever the challenge of rising above our senses presses upon us – whenever, namely, we find ourselves dispirited from attending on a Lord whom we neither can see with our eyes nor hear with our ears – then the light of faith within us threatens to flicker and die and leave us quite lost. Like the virgins awaiting the bridegroom in the darkness, we require new fuel for the flame.

Wisdom is the fire that carries its own fuel, the chaste flame that burns through the night. It lives by a savor attuned to the Spirit – beyond the sleep of the senses – from a source inexhaustible and divine. Wisdom judges and guides us aright by the rule of faith when we feel lost in the darkness. It is the unction and oil which fires with living ardor the failing embers of belief. Wisdom is practical and concrete: like a sensible bridesmaid; like the works of charity, without which all faith is dead.

Father of lights, from whom every good blessing and perfect gift comes, give me the gift of wisdom. You give liberally and without regret to all who ask in faith; grant me, too, the grace truly to wait on you.

Wake-Up Call

Father Anthony Giambrone, O.P.

"Since the bridegroom was long delayed, they all became drowsy and fell asleep. At midnight, there was a cry, 'Behold, the bridegroom! Come out to meet him!' Then all those virgins got up and trimmed their lamps. The foolish ones said to the wise, 'Give us some of your oil, for our lamps are going out.' But the wise ones replied, 'No, for there may not be enough for us and you. Go instead to the merchants and buy some for yourselves.'"

(Mt 25: 5-9)

One of my college friends was an unusually resilient and talented sleeper. A few of us, noticing his gifts, decided to put them to the test. One night, as he snored blissfully away, we hoisted the four corners of his mattress, folded him up like a taco, and carried him outside where we displayed him – still asleep – on a picnic table in front of the dorm.

What he was in the order of nature, we can often be in the order of grace. We can nod off into a state of complete, spiritual numbness asleep to the living world around us and unresponsive to the gentle (or even forcible) prodding of grace. We might sink into a dream world, an illusion of our own creation; or, we might be lost in a blank stupor. Either way we lose touch with what is most vibrant, living, and real: God's providential action in our lives.

To a certain point this is an inescapable effect of the fall. Spiritually, we all have a touch of narcolepsy. As willing as the spirit might be, we all at times (often the worst times) bow under the heavy weight of the flesh. As in the case of the ten virgins, and like Peter, James, and John, untimely drowsiness will press sleep irresistibly upon us. It is then that we become captive to our own lower nature – overcome by nightmares of unfounded worry, vain dreams and preoccupations, or the plain fatigue of surrendered despair.

The good news is this: The Lord will always provide us with the grace of a wake-up call. The virgins are roused by an anonymous cry, and the three in the garden are stirred by Jesus' hand. However and whenever it comes, the question for us is this: When God seeks to wake us from our slumber to open our eyes and lift them to heaven, are we ready to rise? Or do we just roll over?

Father, now is the time to wake from sleep, for our salvation is closer than when we first believed. Dispel the darkness of my dreams and open my eyes to see you as you truly are.

The Light of His Face

Father Anthony Giambrone, O.P.

"While [the foolish virgins] went off to buy [oil], the bridegroom came and those who were ready went into the wedding feast with him. Then the door was locked. Afterwards the other virgins came and said, 'Lord, Lord, open the door for us!' But he said in reply, 'Amen, I say to you, I do not know you.' Therefore, stay awake, for you know neither the day nor the hour."

(Mt 25: 10-13)

Did the foolish virgins ever get their oil? We never hear that they did. In fact, we might catch a glimpse of Jesus' subtle playfulness here. Being a little *dim*, the silly girls run off shopping for oil at midnight. One might rightly smile. True, the end is not so funny: the girls return and the bridegroom coldly calls out, "I do not know you." Still, the connection between the bridegroom's stinging words and the virgins' folly is there. He doesn't recognize them because they are standing outside *in the dark*.

What, then, is the virgins' ultimate folly? That they forgot to bring oil in the first place, or that they ran off to buy some at the last minute and thus missed the barring of the door? It's all of a piece, of course; the girls are foolish from beginning to end. There is, nevertheless, a particular lesson in this pitiful scene before the locked gate. It is the folly of not recognizing the moment that renders the virgins themselves unrecognizable. Had they appreciated the urgency of the call – "Behold, the bridegroom!" – they would have cut their losses and been there for his coming. That would have changed everything, however; for the arrival of the bridegroom itself provides the light that the virgins are wanting. His very presence illumines their identity and gives them their purpose.

Who has not seen an acquaintance out of context and looked right past their face? When the bridesmaids miss the marriage, they have lost their proper context. Their role has passed away, and they vanish into the darkness.

The coming of the Lord on the last day is our true context, the setting of our deepest identity. The brilliant presence of Jesus Christ, radiant in glory and risen from the dead, will, on that day, shine pure light on our faces. He will recognize us and call us by name – provided we are waiting to welcome him.

Father, you want your banquet hall filled with rejoicing. Give me the grace to answer your call. Prepare me for the feast that I might enter in through the door at the marriage of the Lamb and his bride.

Spiritual Mattress-Stuffing

Father Anthony Giambrone, O.P.

"It will be as when a man who was going on a journey called in his servants and entrusted his possessions to them. To one he gave five talents; to another, two; to a third, one – to each according to his ability. Then he went away. Immediately the one who received five talents went and traded with them, and made another five. Likewise, the one who received two made another two. But the man who received one went off and dug a hole in the ground and buried his master's money." (Mt 25: 14-18)

Diversification is a basic strategy in wealth management. Still, we might wonder why the master – obviously an accurate judge of ability – didn't simply entrust all his talents to the *first servant*. That would have been the obvious way to maximize the prospects of gain. We can infer that perhaps the master is not interested above all in the *raw accumulation of wealth*. Perhaps the master's parceling out of his talents is something more than mere economics.

In fact, the word "entrusted" is more literally translated "handed over" or even "gave." This is important; for a close reading of the parable reveals that *the master never takes back his talents*. He will indeed call his servants to account – but that is a mere matter of reporting. The end of the story assumes that the first two servants retain their little fortunes. Or better put, the question of ownership simply becomes irrelevant; the servants are initiated into the world of their lord. From all evidence, the master's desire is only to lavish upon his servants an ever greater share in his prosperity – as much as they can handle and enjoy.

With this munificent master in view, we can consider the third servant. His behavior betrays a character governed by fear. He fears losing the money because, quite simply, he fears his master. His apparent failure in "industrious responsibility" thus belies a deeper failure. He has mistaken his master for a miser; and in so doing, miserliness – joyless fear of loss – has mastered him.

We all have our own image of God. If it is false, it will govern us like a tyrant. May we see the Lord as he is: joyful and generous with all his creatures.

Father, you wish only to lavish the riches of your grace upon me. I now hold your Holy Spirit as a first installment, and you have not given a cowardly Spirit. May I profit by your gifts and your Spirit of joy.

The Master's Joy

Father Anthony Giambrone, O.P.

*"After a long time the master of those servants came back and
settled accounts with them. The one who had received five
talents came forward bringing the additional five. He said,
'Master, you gave me five talents. See, I have made five more.'
His master said to him, 'Well done, my good and faithful
servant. Since you were faithful in small matters, I will give you
great responsibilities. Come, share your master's joy.'"*

(Mt 25: 19-21)

The parable of the talents is, in some ways, like the parable of the vineyard and the wicked tenants as it should have been. The master goes away and puts his property in the hands of others. The moment of reckoning comes for those entrusted with his goods… and… his servants obstinately, violently refuse to hand over the talents? No. They come peaceably forward one by one, laying before their lord the fruits of the labor: "See, I have made five more."

What is remarkable is the absence from the servants' mentality of the tenant's deadly avarice: "Come, let us kill him and acquire his inheritance" (Mt 21: 38). The servant who has prospered his master's money to double has not acquired a higher opinion of himself in the process. He has not made himself equal and heir to his master. There is no slave revolt, no proletariat resentment, no indignant, covetous right to the fortune. This is all the more interesting when we observe that Luke's version of the talent story (which is really quite different and might simply be another parable) does include a revolt: "We do not want this man to be our king" (Lk 19: 14).

Matthew's account, however, is quite clear. It is the lord who makes the servant his equal: "Come, share your master's joy." Whereas Luke speaks about governing cities, Matthew promotes the faithful servants into the master's own lordly ease. Entrance into this sphere of sovereign joy is by invitation only – not by forced entry.

We are all servants and tenants, stewards of the gifts of God; and sedition tempts us all. Always before us is the lie that if we only reach, struggle, and stretch out our hand, we can be gods. But the paradoxical truth is this: happiness, rest, satisfaction, and the ease of joy come only when we hand over everything we hope might be ours.

Father, what am I that you are mindful of me? You have put everything under my feet. By your grace may I humbly subject all things to you, the one who has subjected them all to me.

The Second Servant

Father Anthony Giambrone, O.P.

"[Then] the one who had received two talents also came forward and said, 'Master, you gave me two talents. See, I have made two more.' His master said to him, 'Well done, my good and faithful servant. Since you were faithful in small matters, I will give you great responsibilities. Come, share your master's joy.'"

(Mt 25: 22-23)

A dose of mediocrity can be like medical dye before a spiritual MRI. It brings all the vanity in our system out of hiding, glowing in self-advertisement.

The middle servant is prepped for such a procedure. One can imagine his every last thought of envious pride now bubbling to the surface. Being less talented, he has been given less than his confrere, made less than his confrere, and received only a form-letter word of appreciation. His spirit is set for a vicious, psychological tailspin.

The interior monologue is predictable enough: "What makes Mr. Five Talents so great? I earned the same 100 percent profit, and I obviously could have done the same with more talents. Giving me two was below my dignity. As for my 'master's joy,' what's that worth? *Everyone* gets 'great responsibilities.'" The pattern is clear, though it runs a thousand permutations: comparisons become a sterile fixation; dubious assumptions manufacture self-flattering syllogisms, and a morose pathology suggests the insincerity and insufficiency of one's treatment.

This is an imaginative intrusion into the story, yes; but the spiritual situation is quite real. What's more, the master's action serves as an antidote to this unhappy affliction. By offering the same reward to both servants, the master makes one thing very clear: the measure of our dignity does not rest upon our share of native ability. It is based upon our fidelity. The indiscriminate reward also reveals the full wealth of glory at the master's disposal. This is clearly that same lord who doled out equal wages to all the workers in the vineyard – however many hours they'd worked. His scandalous generosity combats the lie of our vain and indignant envy. He shows that true greatness and glory is so unmerited and immense that there can be no peer struggle or shortage of resources in the realm of eternal joy.

Father, there is no limit to the resources of your eternal joy. Help me to be at peace with the lot you have given me, so that I might be welcomed into your presence as a good and faithful servant.

Fear of the Lord

Father Anthony Giambrone, O.P.

"Then the one who had received the one talent came forward and said, 'Master, I knew you were a demanding person, harvesting where you did not plant and gathering where you did not scatter; so out of fear I went off and buried your talent in the ground. Here it is back.'" (Mt 25: 24-25)

It is generally wise to be diplomatic with one's boss. As a rule, calling him "demanding" and waxing metaphoric about his oppressive expectations is bad policy – the sort of office etiquette designed to get one *fired* (i.e., promptly tossed into Gehenna).

If the final servant takes this suicidal nose dive, it is because he has already ceased to enjoy his employment. He has ruminated and brooded until the image of his master strikes terror and disgust in his mind. That the servant should thus shrink in paralyzed fear is no wonder. His lord has become for him a greedy and usurious task-master, an unforgiving Shylock bent on his pound of flesh. The monster in his mind is simply too much for the servant to bear.

As the master will momentarily expose, the poor wretch is quite literally *demented*, deprived of his mind. Gripped and driven by fear, he has lost all orientation and has acted against his own (and the master's) self-interest: "Should you not then have put my money in the bank?" The foolish servant's head is apparently buried in the sand along with his talent.

The problem is not that the servant fears his lord. Fear of God is the beginning of wisdom. We *should* direct our lives in fear of "the one who can destroy both soul and body in Gehenna" (Mt 10: 28). If we mature properly as spiritual children of God, this wholesome but provisional servile fear will eventually pass over into a holy and filial fear which does not tremble at the thought of punishment, but at the thought of wounding the beloved. If our spiritual growth is stunted, however, we risk developing a crippling anxiety disorder like this servant: a sub-rational, inhibiting fear which distorts and resents the face of God and no longer orients us toward our proper end. The moment the master's joy appears as a cruel farce, we are on a collision course for Gehenna.

Father, help me to guide my actions in wisdom and holy fear. Let me not be trapped by slavish anxiety, but mature as your true child, concerned only to please you.

Freedom and Responsibility

Father Anthony Giambrone, O.P.

"His master said to him in reply, 'You wicked, lazy servant! So you knew that I harvest where I did not plant and gather where I did not scatter? Should you not then have put my money in the bank so that I could have got it back with interest on my return?'" (Mt 25: 26-27)

If the master had been intent on having his money in the bank, he could have managed it easily enough. A word at his departure would have sufficed. Why then put a lump sum in the hands of a servant and walk away with no hint of instruction?

The master apparently relies on the sheer force of his own character to guide things aright. The servant knows what sort of man he is. The rest should simply be obvious. Thus, rather than lay down a constraining command ("put my money in the bank"), the master prefers to elicit a free response. This is the true sense behind the master's description. He harvests where *he* did not plant – not because he is a monomaniacal usurer. He harvests where he did not plant, because, quite simply, he allows his servants the freedom to plant and scatter as they like. He prefers, that is, to leave things in the hands of others (as the whole business with the talents makes clear). This master is anything but a micro-manager.

The final servant, of course, has rather twisted this lordly freedom into an oppressive burden. He has distorted the motives of the master, so ready to share the joy of the harvest. The servant is thus a kind of existentialist-quietist, tormented by the cruel fate of being handed a charge and answering with indolent inaction. What is curious is that he still presents his inert failure as an act of faithful service. It takes the master's rebuke to point out that the lazy bum really should have done something.

Freedom can be a terrifying gift, and we often seek to escape it. Like the third servant we might even paint our *inaction* as dedicated service to the Lord: "discernment" perhaps or "prayerful consideration." It is right and good to wait in reverent stillness; but fear must not masquerade as piety and prevent us from ever offering the Master our free response.

Father, help me respond to your goodness with generous creativity. May I have the energy and courage to act tirelessly in your service, and may I glorify you in accepting the full freedom of the children of God.

Haves and Have-Nots

Father Anthony Giambrone, O.P.

"'Now then! Take the talent from him and give it to the one with ten. For to everyone who has, more will be given and he will grow rich; but from the one who has not, even what he has will be taken away. And throw this useless servant into the darkness outside, where there will be wailing and grinding of teeth.'"

(Mt 25: 28-30)

The divine economy is no socialist utopia. "To everyone who has, more will be given and he will grow rich; but from the one who has not, even what he has will be taken away." As ever and always, the rich get richer and the poor get poorer.

It may at first sight seem strange that such an unforgiving and non-egalitarian principle should prevail in the realm of God's grace. If the third servant makes out badly in this system, however, it is because he has rendered his portion from the Lord *closed to growth*. Not only has he failed to trade actively to expand his little treasure as the other two servants did. He has not even left the talent to increase in the bank – a thing requiring no effort from him. His hole-in-the-ground investment strategy has positively cut off all possibility of increase.

This is significant when we watch how money moves in the dispensation of divine giving. Like a mustard seed, it grows. It expands and blossoms until its breaks all bounds. "To everyone who has, *more will be given*." The master wants only to pile riches upon riches: "a good measure, packed together, shaken down, and overflowing" (Lk 6: 38).

This is the real rule in the realm of God's grace. Unless we introduce an obstacle, the riches of divine favor will expand in our lives. It is like the gravity of love in Dante's universe, where anyone unimpeded by sin floats upwards faster and faster, rising like fire toward the celestial height. If this is the way when merely left unimpeded, imagine when one actively works with grace!

The stripping of the third servant's talent is not an act of violence against him; it is simply a consequence of this universe where God's favor in our lives seeks to grow more and more. Grace cannot abide where it is smothered. Its own inner force prevents it.

Father in heaven, break down every obstacle I have put to your grace. Let your generous kindness overwhelm me with good favor that I might become ever richer and richer in your blessings.

The Christian Meaning of Solidarity
Michele M. Schumacher

"When the Son of Man comes in his glory, and all the angels with him, he will sit upon his glorious throne, and all the nations will be assembled before him. And he will separate them one from another, as a shepherd separates the sheep from the goats." (Mt 25: 31-32)

It is striking that the Good Shepherd who "lays down his life for the sheep" (Jn 10: 11) and leaves the ninety-nine in search of one sheep who has gone astray (Mt 18: 12) is presented here as separating these sheep from the goats with the specific intention of welcoming the ones into "the kingdom prepared... from the foundation of the world" (v. 34) and of sending the latter "into the eternal fire prepared for the devil and his angels" (v. 41).

More striking still, perhaps, is the fact that these sheep and goats are portrayed as the nations, for we are accustomed to thinking of judgment as rendering an account of personal responsibility and personal sin. Here, however, we are invited to recognize the social dimension of both grace and sin: what the Church presents as the communion of saints, on the one hand, and a communion in sin, on the other hand. To be sure, this is not an excuse for complacency; for there is no sin – however seemingly insignificant or "hidden" – that does not have consequences for the rest of humanity. Similarly, there is no one, as the saying goes, who goes to heaven alone.

More important than recognizing our personal responsibility vis-à-vis the moral climate of humanity, however, is recognizing our solidarity in Christ, in virtue of which we are – each one of us – accountable to one another. "If, because of one man's trespass, death reigned through that one man, how much more will those who receive the abundance of grace and the free gift of righteousness reign in life through the one man Jesus Christ" (Rom 5: 17, RSV). In him we were chosen "before the foundation of the world": not so that our sin might be overlooked by his goodness, but so that in him we might – each and every one of us – "be holy and without blemish" (Eph 1: 4) in service of the "least" ones.

Heavenly Father, grant that I might partake of the grace of your Son so as to care willingly and lovingly for the needs of my brothers and sisters, and simultaneously to encourage others to do the same.

The Heavenly Prince and the Pauper

Michele M. Schumacher

"He will place the sheep on his right and the goats on his left. Then the king will say to those on his right, 'Come, you who are blessed by my Father. Inherit the kingdom prepared for you from the foundation of the world. For I was hungry and you gave me food, I was thirsty and you gave me drink, a stranger and you welcomed me, naked and you clothed me, ill and you cared for me, in prison and you visited me.'" (Mt 25: 33-36)

S triking is the contrast of this king who reveals himself as the "least" of God's little ones: the one who is hungry and thirsty, the one who is naked and ill, the one who is estranged and imprisoned. In all of its dramatic quality, this passage is reminiscent of the tale of "The Prince and the Pauper": not that this "prince" (Christ the King) would seek freedom from all the difficult responsibilities of "royal life" by clothing himself in a poor child's attire. On the contrary, he wears rags so that the poor child might be robed in the princely attire of grace: so that the pauper might be recognized as the king's own son and welcomed into the kingdom prepared for him "from the foundation of the world" (v. 34). Indeed, the Son of God became man, the Fathers of the Church teach, "so that man might become a son of God."

It is precisely to this end – our salvation – that Christ reveals himself as both "prince" and "pauper," for we might discern in this revelation a heavenly invitation – almost in the form of a plea – to conversion. This, more specifically, is an invitation to be counted among those "blessed" by the Father of the heavenly Prince. As such, it is a revelation of us to ourselves – as paupers called to princely glory – and this, precisely in the revelation of Christ as true God and true man. As we come to recognize this heavenly king as the one who "emptied himself," who took "the form of a slave... in human likeness," the one who "humbled himself... to death on a cross" (Phil 2: 7-8), and the one who thereby identifies with all the lowly, we are simultaneously invited to recognize our own selfishness and vainglory (see v. 3). This, however, is good news, indeed: it constitutes our first step toward the kingdom of heaven.

Heavenly Father, grant that I might turn from the lowliness of sin to embrace the riches of glory awaiting those who share the humility of your Son.

The Faith That Acts

Michele M. Schumacher

"Then the righteous will answer [the king] and say, 'Lord, when did we see you hungry and feed you, or thirsty and give you drink? When did we see you a stranger and welcome you, or naked and clothe you? When did we see you ill or in prison, and visit you?'" (Mt 25: 37-39)

This powerful scene of the final judgment reveals the true meaning of faith that saves (see Jas 2: 14). This, our Lord suggests, is not so much the act of recognizing him in the humble ways in which he reveals himself to us: in the infant child of Bethlehem, in the poor carpenter of Nazareth, in the humble preacher of Galilee, in the crucified one of Calvary, in the tiny host of the tabernacle, in the least of our brothers and sisters, in – that is to say – the "poorest of the poor," as Blessed Teresa of Calcutta would have it. Why not? Because even the demons acknowledged this poor itinerant preacher as the Son of God (see Mt 8: 29; Lk 4: 34, 41; Jas 2: 19). And thus judgment cannot simply concern our acknowledgment of Christ's divinity and sovereignty, or even of his littleness. "Not everyone who says to me, 'Lord, Lord,' will enter the kingdom of heaven," Jesus teaches; "but only the one who does the will of my Father in heaven" (Mt 7: 21).

Hence, Saint James rightly reasons, "What good is it… if someone says he has faith but does not have works? Can that faith save him? If a brother or sister has nothing to wear and has no food for the day, and one of you says to them, 'Go in peace, keep warm, and eat well,' but you do not give them the necessities of the body, what good is it? So also faith of itself, if it does not have works, is dead" (Jas 2: 14-17). Faith that saves is, in short, manifest as *faithfulness*: as obedience to the love command in virtue of which Christ's own love is "brought to perfection in us" (1 Jn 4: 12). In the end, we shall be judged according to our love, "the greatest" of what is eternal (see 1 Cor 13: 13).

Heavenly Father, grant that I might allow your gift of faith to become a well-spring of good works in my life.

Giving from the King's Treasury

Michele M. Schumacher

"And the king will say to [the righteous] in reply, 'Amen,
I say to you, whatever you did for one of these least brothers
of mine, you did for me.'" (Mt 25: 40)

The human heart is naturally moved to respond before the evils of poverty, pain, and injustice. One man's suffering is somehow the suffering of us all, and all of us rightfully wish to alleviate it. Most of us are thus likely to react to this Gospel passage as enthusiastic and well-intentioned philanthropists. As such, we are perhaps much too quick to respond to these challenging words by acting to remove our neighbor's poverty without considering our own.

To be sure, nowhere in the Gospels – perhaps least of all here – can we discern an encouragement of self-interest or an invitation to self-indulgence, selfishness, or egoism in its many ugly forms. On the other hand, we are sadly deluding ourselves if we think that we can feed others if we have not first of all eaten of the King's banquet. "All you who are thirsty,/ come to the water!/ You who have no money,/ come, receive grain and eat;/ Come, without paying and without cost,/ drink wine and milk!/ Why spend your money for what is not bread;/ your wages for what fails to satisfy?" (Is 55: 1-2). Every one of us has need of this water, this milk, this wine, and this bread, in virtue of which we might, in turn, administer to the hungry and thirsty, the poor and suffering. It is therefore with good reason that Saint Paul asks: "What do you possess that you have not received?" (1 Cor 4: 7). If we have something to give, it is because we have received from this King of kings, who alone can satisfy the deepest needs of the human heart. Let us all grant that he might fill us, so that we in turn might fill others. Or better said: let us grant that he – the Bread of Life – might remain ever present within us so that in us, through us, and with us, *he* might feed the least of our brothers.

Heavenly Father, grant that I might humbly seek to be filled with
your gifts in prayer and the sacraments in virtue of which I might
be rendered capable of administering to others.

Judging God or Allowing His Judgment to Reign in Us?

Michele M. Schumacher

"Then [the king] will say to those on his left, 'Depart from me, you accursed, into the eternal fire prepared for the devil and his angels. For I was hungry and you gave me no food, I was thirsty and you gave me no drink, a stranger and you gave me no welcome, naked and you gave me no clothing, ill and in prison, and you did not care for me.'" (Mt 25: 41-43)

It is not God who will not receive us into his kingdom. It is not he who judges us. It is we who will not receive his kingdom into our hearts. We do not judge him worthy of kingship in the humble form in which he presents himself: as this "least one" (see Mt 25: 45) who identifies himself with poverty, chastity, and obedience; who seeks no vain glory; who clothes himself with humble human flesh and fulfills his mission by way of death by crucifixion (see Phil 2: 6-8). We might in fact appreciate the idea of a king who does not come "to be served but to serve and to give his life as a ransom for many" (Mk 10: 45), but when his way of humility is presented as the only path leading to eternal glory, we often prefer the glory of this passing world. When entering the kingdom means becoming "like children" (Mt 18: 3), when a rich man can access it only with great difficulty (19: 23), when it is said to belong to those "who are persecuted for the sake of righteousness" (5: 10), we might well say to this king: "Depart from me!"

Thankfully, however, God does not give up on us as quickly as we give up on him. As Saint Paul expresses it: "If we are unfaithful, he remains faithful, for he cannot deny himself" (2 Tm 2: 13). Even when we turn our back on him, he earnestly seeks after us. Far from condemning us for every time that we fail to serve him in the hungry and the thirsty, in the naked, ill, and imprisoned, he invites us in this Gospel passage to conversion: to recognize that his is a kingdom wherein to serve is to reign, and that heavenly glory awaits those who serve with love.

Heavenly Father, grant that I might constantly accept your invitation to conversion so as to willingly embrace your way of humility and love.

Christ's Recognition of Us as His Own

Michele M. Schumacher

"Then [those on his left] will answer and say, 'Lord, when did
we see you hungry or thirsty or a stranger or naked or ill or
in prison, and not minister to your needs?'"
(Mt 25: 44)

It is not our vision that is called into question here: our willingness, or our capacity, to see Christ in "the least" of his brothers. After all, those who are judged righteous and invited to enter the kingdom did not recognize the Lord in his "least brothers" any more than did those judged unrighteous. Indeed, the question posed by the unrighteous in this verse is almost an echo of the questions posed by the righteous: "When did we see you hungry and feed you, or thirsty and give you drink? When did we see you a stranger and welcome you, or naked and clothe you? When did we see you in prison, and visit you?" (Mt 25: 37-39). We might therefore conclude that the final judgment does not concern *our recognition of Christ*, especially as he is hidden in the persons of his "least brothers" (v. 40). It concerns, rather, *Christ's recognition of us* as those who attended (or not) to him.

We are judged, in other words, according to whether or not the Lord recognizes us as having ministered to him in the "least ones" (v. 45) with whom he identifies. Perhaps more profoundly still, it concerns *Christ's recognition of himself as serving in and through us*. As such, it is a question of our having granted him the possibility of using us to minister to the "least" of his brothers and sisters. Christ does not merely judge us, therefore, for having served him (in others) or for having failed to serve him. He judges us most especially for allowing him (or not) to accomplish the Father's will in the very works of mercy that he has given us to do in his name.

Heavenly Father, help me to open my heart generously to others so that Christ might effectively achieve his saving works of mercy in and through me and thereby recognize me as his own.

The Mystery of "One Christ Loving Himself"

Michele M. Schumacher

"[The king] will answer [those on his left], 'Amen, I say to you, what you did not do for one of these least ones, you did not do for me.' And these will go off to eternal punishment, but the righteous to eternal life." (Mt 25: 45-46)

In examining our consciences, we often tend to reflect upon what we have done that is unworthy of a child of God. But the Lord invites us to dig deeper, as it were, so as also to uncover our sins of omission: what we have not done. As in the penitential prayer of the Mass, I am invited to confess having sinned "in my thoughts and in my words, in what I have done *and in what I have failed to do.*" It is this failure to do God's will – to look after the needs of the hungry and thirsty, of the naked and estranged, of the ill and the imprisoned; of all of those, in short, with whom Christ identifies – that is addressed here.

Precisely because Christ identifies with them, moreover, what is expected of us is not simply that we do to others as we would have them do to us, as the Lord revealed earlier in this Gospel (see Mt 7: 12). More profoundly still, it means doing to others as we would do *to Christ.* Such, after all, is the measure he has given to our love for him: "You are my friends," he teaches, "if you do what I command you... This [is what] I command you: love one another" (Jn 15: 14, 17). He who "did not come to be served but to serve" (Mt 20: 28) nonetheless wills to be so present in our love for one another, that his presence might be discerned both in the one who serves and in the one who is served; in the one who loves and in the one who is loved.

That is why Saint Augustine rightly addresses the mystery of Christian love in terms of "one Christ loving himself." Those who partake of this mystery thereby experience, even now, union with Christ, and thus also something of the promise of eternal life.

Heavenly Father, grant that I might be so faithful in my love for the "least" of Christ's little ones that I might thereby be united to him and in him to you.

Christ's Final Preparation for Calvary

Father Aquinas Guilbeau, O.P.

When Jesus finished all these words, he said to his disciples, "You know that in two days' time it will be Passover, and the Son of Man will be handed over to be crucified." (Mt 26: 1-2)

Having completed his final teaching on the kingdom of heaven, Jesus reminds his disciples of a most sobering theme – his upcoming passion. Even after receiving months of instruction, those following Jesus to Jerusalem apparently kept these two subjects miles apart in their minds, for they did not see – or did not want to see – any link connecting them. Christ again tries to correct their error in the hopes of strengthening them to endure the mystery of Calvary. Anxious for their salvation, he once more reveals to them the very source of the grace that will heal them. He explains their life in the future kingdom. But to draw them close to the kingdom, Jesus again explains the meaning of his cross.

This conceptual union of cross and glory is what Christ taught Peter, James, and John atop Mount Tabor. Jesus manifested to them the splendor of his divinity as he discussed his passion with Moses and Elijah. The union of cause and effect, merit and reward – cross and glory – were revealed to these three disciples in one miraculous moment. But the Christian lesson of the cross is a long one to learn. Only one of the three who witnessed the Transfiguration would remain with Christ all the long way to Calvary. Are we surprised to discover that Christ's lesson in Jerusalem, two days before his death, still meets up with failed comprehension? We shouldn't be. Does Christ therefore offer this teaching in vain? Not if we understand Christ's mercy.

Like the grace of the Transfiguration, the effect of this final announcement of the passion will have its desired effect after the completion of the paschal mystery. That vision atop Tabor, like this teaching in Jerusalem, will serve the disciples best when they hear on Easter Sunday the announcement of the resurrection. Herein is established the Christian rhythm of hearing, remembering, and believing.

Heavenly Father, your Son foretold the mystery of Calvary, and thus prepared his disciples for its horror and glory. Confirm our surrender to the mysteries of your providence, which you prepare us with your grace to receive.

Evil's Emptiness

Father Aquinas Guilbeau, O.P.

Then the chief priests and the elders of the people assembled in the palace of the high priest, who was called Caiaphas, and they consulted together to arrest Jesus by treachery and put him to death. (Mt 26: 3-4)

Saint Augustine was among the first Christian teachers to shape the world's understanding of evil. The fifth-century bishop of Hippo argued the bold claim, based on the teachings of Genesis, that evil is not a presence in itself but rather an absence of goodness. Through writing and preaching, the holy Doctor explained that evil appears only wherever a due good is lacking. Augustine thus exposed the error of conceiving evil as something positive and existing alongside goodness as its equally powerful foe. In so doing, Augustine helped the Christian world to overcome a popular, longstanding belief, that an evil god of matter contends with a good god of spirit. We know from his *Confessions* that Augustine himself fell under the influence of this view when he was a young man. Then Augustine saw the light. God reveals himself in Genesis as the One and All-good, the Creator of heaven and earth and all that dwells therein. This Good God shares his own goodness with his creatures. He also makes his intelligent creatures free so that they can freely embrace this goodness and bring it to perfection.

Augustine's teaching that evil results from a privation of the good continues to inform the Christian understanding of the moral life. When we sin, not only do we fail to attain what is good for us, but we also work actively against it. Herein lies the destructive pathology of sin. It is not enough for the one hardened by sin to avoid pursuing what is good. Eventually, he becomes inclined to destroying it. Because he prefers the absence of goodness to its presence, he works to ensure that goodness disappears around him. Thus, the sinful man undertakes the futile task of trying to rid goodness from creation. More than most, the chief priests and elders display this crazed logic when they plot to destroy Jesus.

Heavenly Father, creator of heaven and earth, conform our minds to all that is true, and our hearts to all that is good.

The Order of Love

Father Aquinas Guilbeau, O.P.

Now when Jesus was in Bethany in the house of Simon the leper,
a woman came up to him with an alabaster jar of costly
perfumed oil, and poured it on his head while
he was reclining at table. (Mt 26: 6-7)

The nineteenth-century Flemish missionary, Saint Damien de Veuster, chose to live – and die – in Hawaii. Forsaking sun and surf, Father Damien served for nearly two decades as the pastor of a community of lepers quarantined on the island of Moloka'i. Through word and sacrament, the "leper priest" brought the love of Christ to bear on a community defined by disease and despair. Pope Benedict XVI canonized Father Damien on October 11, 2009.

Father Damien found an example for his priestly life in the practice of the Lord. After all, Jesus, just before his death, spent an evening in the home of a leper named Simon. Herein lies a powerful lesson regarding the Christian life. The fraternity and affection Jesus offered Simon that night provided Father Damien sufficient inspiration and grace to sustain his entire priestly vocation. And how did that happen, we might wonder? How could a single action of Christ inspire an entire Christian vocation? Another figure in Simon's house, the woman with the alabaster jar, reveals the answer.

The unnamed woman arrives with a jar of oil, which in the ancient world was used to anoint sores. But upon entering Simon's house, she does not tend to his illness. Instead, something else present in Simon's home, other than his disease, requires her attention. It is Christ's divine and royal majesty, cloaked beneath his flesh, which would soon be mocked by a crown of thorns. The woman anoints Jesus' head in anticipation of those wounds, and in honor of the sacrificial death they will signify. The woman reminds us, therefore, that Christ always remains deserving of our first devotion. Even before the poor and the sick, whom we must serve, Christ deserves our first affections. Father Damien knew this, and his affection for the Lord sustained his many years imitating one simple mystery of his life.

Heavenly Father, purify our hearts, that we may love you above all things and our neighbors as ourselves.

Love's Extravagance

Father Aquinas Guilbeau, O.P.

When the disciples saw this, they were indignant and said,
"Why this waste? It could have been sold for much,
and the money given to the poor." (Mt 26: 8-9)

Does the Church's wealth undermine her witness to the poor? This question surfaces periodically, especially among those who view the Church's temporal holdings – her gilded churches and art collections, for example – as sinfully prodigal in light of the world's poverty. Centuries of Christian practice, however, confirm that the demands of both charity and justice require the Church to manage an earthly treasure.

The Church retains wealth for three reasons only: to order divine worship, to provide for her ministers, and to engage in acts of the apostolate and of charity (*Code of Canon Law*, 1254.2). It is interesting that the Church mentions worship first as a reason for her possessing wealth. This is no accident, and among all biblical figures the woman with the alabaster jar teaches us why.

The disciples took the woman's extravagant anointing of Christ to be sinful and unjust. In leveling their critique, however, the disciples unwittingly created a false opposition between two obligatory loves: the love we must show to Christ as God and the love we must show to the poor as his brothers. Christ's answer to the disciples' rebuke corrects their error and establishes the true ordering of the Church's love. In effect, Christ reveals that charity is not a zero sum game. To the contrary, worship given to God is related to the charity shown to the poor as perfections of the same virtue – justice. And these two perfections of justice are hierarchically ordered: "Seek first the kingdom [of God] and his righteousness," Jesus says in the Sermon on the Mount (Mt 6: 33), which command he confirms in his reaction to the disciples' critique. "The poor you will always have with you" (Mt 26: 11). Therefore, like the woman with the jar, the Church bestows her extravagant love upon God first. Then Christian love redounds extravagantly to all, especially the poor.

Heavenly Father, source of all life and love, draw us with our neighbor into the divine communion you share with the Son and the Holy Spirit.

Christ, Poor and Humble

Father Aquinas Guilbeau, O.P.

Since Jesus knew this, he said to [the disciples], "Why do you make trouble for the woman? She has done a good thing for me. The poor you will always have with you; but you will not always have me. In pouring this perfumed oil upon my body, she did it to prepare me for burial. Amen, I say to you, wherever this gospel is proclaimed in the whole world, what she has done will be spoken of, in memory of her." (Mt 26: 10-13)

At the beginning of his Letter to the Philippians, Saint Paul reflects on Christ's humility. To express his thoughts, he quotes an early Christian hymn that couples Christ's humble poverty with his self-sacrificial love. "He emptied himself,/ taking the form of a slave," the hymn proclaims (2: 7). Accordingly, Saint Paul explains that the Word first reveals his humility in the renunciation of his right to divine glory, which was prerequisite to his assuming our human nature and living as man. Thus, in the words of the hymn, the Word's incarnation is akin to his becoming a slave. Therefore, Paul concludes that, even before his shameful death on the cross, the Word humbles himself for us. As his divine power becomes dependent upon his human powers, the Word willingly bears the humiliation of the incarnation. In Christ, the eternal Word speaks with a human tongue, the omniscient Word thinks with a human brain, the omnipresent Word moves with human feet. As a result, Christ is truly the Poor One, for as the incarnate Word he among all men has set aside the most.

Because he is the poorest of all, Christ can claim the extravagant anointing by the woman with the alabaster jar as a righteous act that renders no injustice to the poor. In truth, the woman draws close to the Poor Christ to perform a corporal work of mercy. With the anointing she gives him, the woman unites herself to Christ in light of his impending death and consequent need for burial. With her costly oil, the woman pours out everything she has in honor of the very mystery that will give her life. She gives all in exchange for everything that Christ gives for her. The payment is just, and it shows no injustice to either rich or poor. We can learn from the woman's extravagant outpouring of love. At that table, she imitates the self-sacrificial love of Christ.

Heavenly Father, your Son humbled himself to save us. May we imitate his humility and conform our daily lives to your good and loving will.

The Cost of Betrayal

Father Aquinas Guilbeau, O.P.

Then one of the Twelve, who was called Judas Iscariot, went to the chief priests and said, "What are you willing to give me if I hand him over to you?" They paid him thirty pieces of silver, and from that time on he looked for an opportunity to hand him over. (Mt 26: 14-16)

In the house of Simon the leper, Judas makes his final decision to abandon Jesus. That night, he cuts the last thread of his will connecting him to the apostolic band. The scene of Christ's anointing by the woman with the alabaster jar is altogether too much for him. It constitutes the last straw, the final offense against his loyalty to Jesus. In earlier days, Judas had looked forward to the liberation Jesus promised to win for Israel, which he took to mean freedom from the domination of the Romans. But as the months passed, the Master never took up arms. He failed to confront the governor and his forces. Instead he traveled from town to town, preaching mercy and compassion and love for one's enemies. Did Jesus not care that the Romans remained in Jerusalem?

And now, in the home of an unclean man, the purported Messiah, the Promised One, receives what Judas considers scandalous pampering at the hands of an anonymous woman, an act that, to his eyes, offends both decency and justice. Judas loses faith. Jesus has not become what he expected. Where did the reputed Messiah fail in his mission? How could anyone expect this man to overthrow the Romans?

Still, for all of Judas' sad misunderstanding of Jesus, his betrayal comes down to money. Judas is a man who views life through the lens of dollars and cents. Naturally, he carries the money purse for the apostles (Jn 13: 29). But his calculating greed clouds his judgment. Matthew tells us that all of the disciples object to the woman's anointing of Jesus, but John offers the further detail that Judas sanctimoniously leads the protest (Jn 12: 4). Misunderstanding and greed then combine to turn Judas' abandonment to betrayal. That night he recoups something of his loss: thirty pieces of silver. Judas sells his loyalty to Jesus for a fraction of what he would have asked for the woman's oil.

Heavenly Father, your love cannot be measured in dollars and cents. Help us not to calculate the return we owe for your gifts of life and love.

In Your House

Father Anthony Giambrone, O.P.

On the first day of the Feast of Unleavened Bread, the disciples approached Jesus and said, "Where do you want us to prepare for you to eat the Passover?" He said, "Go into the city to a certain man and tell him, 'The teacher says, "My appointed time draws near; in your house I shall celebrate the Passover with my disciples."'" The disciples then did as Jesus had ordered, and prepared the Passover. (Mt 26: 17-19)

I s there a Quartering Act written somewhere in the divine law? Twice in the Gospels we find Jesus taking hospitality by force. In the first case, the Lord acts with abrupt and arresting authority. "Zacchaeus, come down quickly, for today I must stay at your house" (Lk 19: 5). Here, on the eve of his passion, the manner is different. The arrangements are mediated and mysterious. The appointed time draws near, and a "certain" unnamed host is drafted to supply the Lord his furnished upper room. In a rendezvous worthy of a spy novel, the disciples (as the other Gospels relate) track a man with a water jar and reserve the place with a cryptic message from "the Teacher."

What is curious in these scenes is that the Son of Man who "has nowhere to lay his head" acts in the home of another as at once *both host and guest.* Jesus orchestrates the evening, but the others provide him a place. There is a mystery here of the Lord's humble accommodation. The great God whom heaven and earth cannot hold welcomes creatures into *his presence* by bowing to enter *their homes.* It is the mystery of Mary, who, as Hopkins sang, "gave God's infinity dwindled to infancy welcome in womb."

We experience this mystery of *hosting* the one *in whom* we live and move and have our being each time the Lord comes to us in Holy Communion, each time he says to our soul, "In your house I shall celebrate the Passover." It is awe-inspiring to share this dignity with the unnamed householder of Jerusalem. Our hearts, blessed and filled with the real presence of Christ, become, of every hallowed spot on earth, the Lord's *chosen site* for that true Passover around which all history for ever turns. As the appointed time draws near, in each and every communion, let us prepare a place fit for the Lord.

Father in heaven, what kind of house can I build for you? Earth is your footstool and heaven your throne. Give me the grace to welcome you into my life, not as a guest, but as the owner and host of my heart.

Loyal to the End

Father Anthony Giambrone, O.P.

When it was evening, [Jesus] reclined at table with the Twelve.
And while they were eating, he said, "Amen, I say to you,
one of you will betray me." (Mt 26: 20-21)

"Amen, I say to you, one of you will betray me." These sudden words shatter the focused mood of the Passover, as suspicion and indignation agitate the room. But what exactly distresses the disciples so deeply?

It is not the prospect that Jesus has reached the dread moment of his passion. That they already know. Three times the Lord predicted the fate awaiting him in Jerusalem; and on this eve of his final ordeal, Jesus has solemnly announced the meal as his last before he suffers (Lk 22: 15). No, it is not the fate of Jesus, but *their own fate* that shocks them; for the disciples all suffer from illusory confidence – sinfully scandalized by the unthinkable thought of their failure. "Surely it is not I?"

What breeds such misguided self-assurance? Perhaps a false sense of the end. The Twelve suppose that they know Jesus' plans and are committed to the last drop of their blood. They know that he has come here to die; and they have said, "Let us also go to die with him" (Jn 11: 16). But in this sentiment, wrought in real loyalty, there lurks a hidden vainglory unworthy of the Lord. The apostles know Jesus will die, but they expect the death of a hero. Now the Lord reveals an ugly truth. He will fall like a thing thrown away. There will be no final stand. This is the line where all loyalty halts. Swords in Gethsemane are easily drawn; but a betrayed Messiah – content with his fate – is a Messiah even I can betray.

We who vow to die with the Lord in our baptism are like these disciples. Even in our most fervent self-oblations and our warmest sentiments of surrender, a lust for glory may be hidden. If we would follow the Lord loyally to the end, we must first be humble enough to see that his end is humbler than any death we've imagined.

Father in heaven, apart from your grace I cannot remain true to the path of your Son. Give me the gift of fortitude to follow him to the end and stand by his cross with Mary and John.

Better for That Man

Father Anthony Giambrone, O.P.

Deeply distressed at this, [the disciples] began to say to [Jesus] one after another, "Surely it is not I, Lord?" He said in reply, "He who has dipped his hand into the dish with me is the one who will betray me. The Son of Man indeed goes, as it is written of him, but woe to that man by whom the Son of Man is betrayed. It would be better for that man if he had never been born." Then Judas, his betrayer, said in reply, "Surely it is not I, Rabbi?" He answered, "You have said so." (Mt 26: 22-25)

If any Gospel passage chills, this is the one. "It would be better for that man if he had never been born." One could hardly imagine a curse more sober and unrelenting. Admittedly, as scholars remind us, we must account for the exaggerations of "Semitic hyperbole." Still, by any reckoning, we stand here face to face with a grim and frightening image of the Lord.

Such an image is disturbing enough – sufficiently apocalyptic and untamed – that if a Jesus like this came too close, we would likely put up some defense and seek cover. This, perhaps, gives us a psychological insight into Judas' response. He knows very well that he has been caught red-handed; yet we misunderstand him if we see only his clumsy lie. The slimy, two-tongued lie is there, yes; but his self-preserving dishonesty rings with an undertone of horrified and half-serious protest. For Judas, Jesus cannot *really mean* what he says. The betrayer speaks to his own conscience as much as to Jesus and the others: "Surely it is not I, Rabbi?" "What I'm about to do cannot possibly be so grave." "If you understood…"

A world of rationalization hides in those fateful words: "Surely it is not I?" The tragedy is that here, at the final hour, Jesus reveals to Judas in plain sight the eternal horror awaiting him, yet Judas chooses not to believe. With full consent, he ratifies his mortal folly; and Jesus solemnly grants his betrayer that freedom: "You have said so."

It is easy to consider Judas a singular species of sinner – and he was. Still, we are warned from feeling too immune. We must at times let the Lord speak *to us* with horrible honesty; for often the last grace given to a sinner – great or small – is a shudder of fear. And it is better for that man to tremble. After all, can I imagine Jesus cursing me? Probably no more than Judas.

Father in heaven, give me the humility to accept the horror of my sins. Give me the grace of contrition. Let me be repulsed by my evil that I might turn back to you.

Behold the Lamb

Father Anthony Giambrone, O.P.

While they were eating, Jesus took bread, said the blessing, broke it, and giving it to his disciples said, "Take and eat; this is my body." (Mt 26: 26)

Why would Jesus identify himself with the unleavened bread of Passover, rather than with the paschal lamb? It is interesting to ask. The roasted lamb, after all, was the center of the meal; the bread and bitter herbs were mere side dishes. It was the lamb whose flesh was sacrificed in the temple and whose blood was the guard against death. In atoning death and sacramental communion it was the Passover lamb which foreshadowed the living Lamb of God.

Obviously, the bread possessed its own rich symbolism. It was the sign of the Israelites' haste, and spoke of their liberation from slavery. Echoes of the miraculous manna in the desert were naturally present as well. The unleavened loaf was thus a truly fitting element to embody God's gift of spiritual nourishment to *homo viator*, itinerant humanity marching on the road to salvation. Still, we may wonder at Jesus' choice to make present his body, not in the form of true flesh, but in the inanimate "work of human hands."

Saint Thomas Aquinas offers us light on this mystery in speaking of the utter failure of our senses to perceive Christ's presence in the Eucharist. The species or appearance of bread *demands* of us a pure and rational apprehension of Christ's true flesh. We are forced to rise entirely beyond our senses and humbly bow our intellect in a submission of sheer faith. Were the Lord's body to be present to our senses with physical flesh and blood, our act of faith would be weakened and earthly.

But there is a cosmic level to this mystery as well. "Let all former rites surrender to the Lord's New Testament." The Lord comes under the veil of bread precisely because he has replaced the lamb as the victim. What could not be accomplished by the blood of bulls and goats, Jesus accomplished by his obedience – and in the bread, he has left the unbloody memorial of his offering.

Father, Jesus Christ your Son, our Pasch, has been sacrificed. By your grace may we clear out of our hearts all the leaven of hypocrisy and insincerity, and worship him as Lord in spirit and in truth.

Blood of the Covenant

Father Anthony Giambrone, O.P.

Then [Jesus] took a cup, gave thanks, and gave it to them, saying, "Drink from it, all of you, for this is my blood of the covenant, which will be shed on behalf of many for the forgiveness of sins." (Mt 26: 27-28)

When Jesus says his blood will be "shed" (literally "poured out") he is using resonant Old Testament language. On the one hand, "shedding blood" was code for the height of violent crime. As idolatry was the great sin of man against God, spilling innocent blood was – from the murder of Abel – the archetypal sin of humanity against itself. The gravity of such violence, which attacked the image and likeness of God, put an impossible strain on relations between God and humanity. Thus, the "violence" which filled the earth in Noah's day warranted the destruction of the whole world order (Gn 6: 13).

On the other hand, "pouring out blood" was the sacrificial act which undid the effects of sin. After the flood, as part of the new covenant establishing peace between the Lord and his creation, Noah was instructed to pour out the life-blood of every slaughtered animal; and this practice became the way Israel atoned for her sins (Lv 17: 11-13).

The shedding of Jesus' innocent blood is the supreme fratricide, the violent murder of the Image of the Father. Jesus' death absorbs in itself all the self-inflicted wounds of humanity – all the blood shed since the foundation of the world (Lk 11: 50). At the same time, the pouring out of his precious blood is the ultimate act of sacrificial atonement. It institutes a new covenant and new creation, an everlasting pact of peace between God and humanity.

We all do violence to ourselves. Destructive patterns of thought and habits of vice assault and mar God's image within us. Our self-inflicted wounds bleed like open sores, crying out for vengeance. At every Mass, however, the resonant words of the Lord immerse us in the mystery, as the old world order is washed away and a new creation is born. Jesus' blood, which speaks more eloquently than that of Abel, is a flood poured out for the forgiveness of sins.

Father, restore in me your divine image through the precious blood of your Son. Help me to drink worthily from his wounds that I might be washed and remade inside and given a pure and contrite heart.

New Wine in the Kingdom

Father Anthony Giambrone, O.P.

"I tell you, from now on I shall not drink this fruit of the vine until the day when I drink it with you new in the kingdom of my Father." (Mt 26: 29)

In heaven there will be no sacraments. There will be no need. The mysterious veil of signs and symbols which now shields our weak eyes from the blazing glory of Christ and the Spirit will be lifted, and we will see God as he is, for we shall be like him.

Jesus here lifts our minds to the contemplation of this reality beyond and behind the sacraments. We are led to consider the true messianic banquet: hinted at in Jesus' table fellowship with sinners, boldly foreshadowed in his feeding the multitudes, mystically tasted at the Last Supper, but now at last in sight.

What will it be, that great banquet in the kingdom of the Father? How will we feast upon and share in the fruits of Christ's passion, the *res tantum* of the Eucharist, the reality itself – *directly* and no longer filtered through the weakness of our faith? What will it mean for hope and faith to pass away as we taste and see the goodness of the Lord in the full possession of perfect and abiding charity?

That unending day sustained in perfect love will be the great marriage of the Lamb. It will be the moment when the bride in glistening white is finally taken into the bridegroom's home; when all of us sullied and soiled are made for ever clean, to enter the king's hall in our white wedding garments. Tasting the wine anew in the kingdom of the Father will be that joyous moment when the Son of the King and heir to all things takes himself a bride – through whom he will pass on the heritage of his own royal dignity.

At present, our sensible and intellectual perception is constrained by the weakness of our desire and belief. In truth, we are already there, but like men blindfolded, darkened in sense and spirit. Already we drink this very wine, but to our numb lips it tastes like any other.

Father, bring me into your kingdom. Grant me the grace to enter your banquet hall, with my baptismal garment unstained. Keep me within your holy Bride, the Church, that through her I might be made an heir of your Son, Christ Jesus the Lord.

Your Faith Will Be Shaken

Father Anthony Giambrone, O.P.

Then, after singing a hymn, they went out to the Mount of Olives. Then Jesus said to [the disciples], "This night all of you will have your faith in me shaken, for it is written:/ 'I will strike the shepherd,/ and the sheep of the flock will be dispersed';/ but after I have been raised up, I shall go before you to Galilee."
(Mt 26: 30-32)

Every disciple of Jesus must endure this terrible night and see the shepherd struck. It is no easy thing to watch, of course. The full-frontal revelation of Jesus' path of weakness is scandalous. There can simply be no preparation. Indeed, even though we all know of the promise of the cross – as the disciples had heard Jesus' three passion predictions – the reality is always and unavoidably destabilizing. We never quite imagine it as it really is.

One way or another, types of suffering enter our lives that we cannot comprehend, cannot believe to be our predestined path to divine glory. Often our suffering is too mundane. Daily annoyances like crying children, a slow internet connection, or having to borrow an embarrassingly under-sized suit coat (a real example) somehow fail to impress our sense of importance – despite our pious devotion to the Little Flower. We may better sense the cross in our personal, interior struggles – social, emotional, psychological – which press down on us with real weight. But inevitably these feel so shameful that we are hardly prepared to celebrate them like Saint Paul as the sign of our heavenly election. External afflictions have more the look we expect, but our pain might easily swell too great or continue too long for us to recognize and rejoice in the saving hand of the Lord.

Whether this night falls upon us gently or with cruel violence, the abandonment we experience is real. It is this very abandonment, this weak sense of an absence of a divine plan, which scandalously makes God present before us: as a beat-up and abused god with little aura of a Savior. Our faith – intractably romantic – is disappointed by this epiphany, as our esthetic taste is disaffected by the unimpressive Christ of a Georges Rouault painting.

Yet, should we make it through this night, the crucified Lord will surprise us once more in Galilee.

Father, you reveal yourself through your Son as one abused and despised in this world. Help me to hold fast to my faith through all the scandals of my life, that I might find you there revealed.

A Cathartic Cock-Crow

Father Anthony Giambrone, O.P.

Peter said to [Jesus] in reply, "Though all may have their faith in you shaken, mine will never be." Jesus said to him, "Amen, I say to you, this very night before the cock crows, you will deny me three times." Peter said to him, "Even though I should have to die with you, I will not deny you." And all the disciples spoke likewise. (Mt 26: 33-35)

There is a fine line between being faithful and being stubborn. Both can be doggedly blind and tenacious. When Peter answers Jesus' prophecy with a bullheaded refusal to listen, he fancies himself supremely faithful and devoted. The rock is already cracking, though, on the order of trust and reliance.

Peter's mulish insistence is touching, of course. It is born of endearing loyalty – impetuous and tragically weak though it is. He is Sancho Panza with more bluster: earnestly committed to his lord, however uncomprehending and timid at root. The rugged *piscatore* from Galilee is less a puppy dog, though, and certainly no comic foil. Peter warrants pity and fear – more Oedipus than Argus (Odysseus' faithful hound).

Horrified at the oracle forecast for him, Peter strains to avoid it. It is not fate, however, that circles back to haunt him when he wakes to what he has done. His tragic flaw lies elsewhere. In counting upon himself Peter takes account only of himself – to the shameless neglect of his master and friend. Peter supposes that his own stubborn will-power can fend off moral failure; and when his manly resolutions crumble before an inquisitive girl, he is blind to the wider drama around him.

This is what is so remarkable about Peter's denial: he utterly forgets Jesus' prophecy. His self-reliance so excludes denial as a prospect, that he actually misses it as it slowly overtakes him. It takes the cock-crow to snap him from his Pelagian trance. Peter's cathartic tears will wash him, but not as an act of self-redemption. It is the sudden remembrance of Jesus' word which will penetrate Peter's heart and heal him.

Apart from God's grace we can be only stubborn and never truly faithful. Yet whenever we fall into blind self-reliance, the divine Word which understands and foresees our weakness will wake us like a cock-crow to heal us.

Father, apart from you I can do nothing. Help me to accept the scandal of my own weakness, so that I will not rely upon myself but upon you. When I fall, wake me by your word and heal me from my sins.

Loneliness and Solitude

Father George William Rutler

Then Jesus came with them to a place called Gethsemane, and he said to his disciples, "Sit here while I go over there and pray." He took along Peter and the two sons of Zebedee, and began to feel sorrow and distress. Then he said to them, "My soul is sorrowful even to death. Remain here and keep watch with me."

(Mt 26: 36-38)

Peter, James, and John were the same three Jesus took up the mountain to witness his Transfiguration, just as he took them into a house to see him raise the daughter of Jairus from the dead. Now he takes them to the Garden of Olives to be with him in his agony. The three names flow together like Abraham, Isaac, and Jacob. Our Lord strengthened this trio in the theological virtues, so that they might encourage the rest of the apostles. He gave them faith by showing his radiant glory. He gave them hope when he raised the dead girl. When he sweat blood in Gethsemane, he showed them the divine love which passes all understanding. His human nature, through which he worked these acts empowered by his divine nature, was perfectly human, which is why he wanted human friendship. The more human we are, the more we shrink from loneliness. As the Son of God, Jesus was never alone, as the Father was always with him; but as our brother, he wanted Peter, James, and John to stay with him. Dread of loneliness is not weakness: it is a declaration that, from the beginning, God did not want us to be alone. A priest is often with people as they are dying. When other senses fail, there is a mutual consolation in holding hands. Jesus the Light of the World would have approved the dying words of the writer O. Henry: "Turn up the lights. I don't want to go home in the dark." Jesus wanted human friends so that he might unite them with his Father in heaven. Sometimes we need to be alone to learn the difference between loneliness and solitude. Loneliness is separation from God, and solitude is private friendship with him. What we do with solitude reveals how far our desire for friendship reaches all the way to heaven.

Almighty Father, by whose will Christ took our human nature and became our friend, grant to us an increase of faith, hope, and love, so that we might rejoice in the knowledge that you are always with us.

For the Needs of the Whole Church
Father George William Rutler

[Jesus] advanced a little and fell prostrate in prayer, saying, "My Father, if it is possible, let this cup pass from me; yet, not as I will, but as you will." When he returned to his disciples he found them asleep. He said to Peter, "So you could not keep watch with me for one hour? Watch and pray that you may not undergo the test. The spirit is willing, but the flesh is weak." (Mt 26: 39-41)

The same apostles who were offended that Christ seemed to be sleeping in their boat during a storm without care for their safety, slept through his agony in Gethsemane. During the storm, Jesus was in control even though his human nature was asleep. It was not that way with the apostles in the garden. When they were asleep, they were oblivious to what was happening. Perhaps their sleep was the kind of slumber into which one slips as a refuge from an impending crisis. It is tempting to doze as God is doing his most splendid works. Has anyone never wool-gathered once in a while during Mass? Perhaps Peter, James, and John could be patrons of the distracted. As they slept, Jesus was in a duel with Satan who would tempt his followers all their lives. Jesus won. We cannot do that without him. Jesus knew that we need his help: "Watch therefore, and pray." As members of the Church, we have the support of our fellow Catholics throughout the world, and the saints in heaven who are on the lookout for us even when we are neglectful of our own spiritual safety. By the same token, our prayers for others strengthen them more than we know. In Gethsemane, Jesus was teaching his Church the efficacy of offering our confessions and prayers for the needs of the whole Church. "So you could not keep watch with me for one hour?" An hour before the Blessed Sacrament is more powerful than the work of parish committees and church meetings, useful as they may be. The three apostles slept during history's first Holy Hour. That does not excuse our laziness, but it inspires us to work through our weakness, just as those three men later did. Strengthened by hard experience, Peter, wide awake, says to all the faithful through his successors the popes: "Be sober and vigilant..." (1 Pt 5: 8).

God our Father, I pray in my weakness for your strength. If I have the blessing one day of seeing you face to face, it will be because of you and not of me. That is my inspiration and joy.

Two Kinds of Will

Father George William Rutler

Withdrawing a second time, [Jesus] prayed again, "My Father, if it is not possible that this cup pass without my drinking it, your will be done!" (Mt 26: 42)

Belaboring the obvious, the difference between God's will and mine is that God's will is his and my will is mine. When God became a man in Christ, there were two wills at work. There was no conflict between his divine and human wills. But as he was perfectly human, he constantly had to make an act of will to do what his Father wanted. Obeying God's will is "surrender to divine Providence." Unlike earthly surrenders which involve loss, this surrender to God's plan for us brings immeasurable gain. If we only do what we want, we will be little different from other creatures. A preacher once said that a man wrapped up in himself becomes a very small package. Any day you can read the latest best-selling book about "how to be number one," and the advice turns out to be gossamer, like a sparkler instead of sharp lightning. But doing our own will is not a harmless self-indulgence. "My will be done" is civilization's unfailing recipe for disaster. In 1925, an author published a book in which he said: "In my hand a suitcase full of clothes and underwear; in my heart an indomitable will, I journeyed to Vienna." The book was *Mein Kampf* and Hitler's battle was a dark one. Jesus also engaged a battle when he did his Father's will and journeyed to Jerusalem. As Hitler opened a crack into hell, Jesus opened one into heaven. When he rose from the dead, Jesus invited us to enter heaven with him. We give God our will in baptism and strengthen that gift in confession, and unite with his will in Holy Communion. It is easy to attract attention by singing, "I did it my way." But celebrity turns into celebration only when we can pray, "May it be done to me according to your word" (Lk 1: 38).

Eternal Father, through union with your Son in baptism I can become what you want me to be, and by your Holy Spirit I can do what you want. May I always be grateful for such a privilege and promise.

Sublime Repetition

Father George William Rutler

*Then [Jesus] returned once more and found [his disciples]
asleep, for they could not keep their eyes open. He left them
and withdrew again and prayed a third time, saying
the same thing again.* (Mt 26: 43-44)

Jesus repeated his prayer. There are those who criticize repetitious prayers. The rosary is repetitious and the liturgy itself is collective repetition. The angels keep repeating, "Holy." There is something problematic about trying to make worship "innovative." In worshiping the mystery which Saint Augustine called "ever ancient, ever new," there is no need for novelty. Christ makes all things new. We can only make new things, and they get old fast. Wise people have said that the liturgy should feel like a comfortable old shoe, and not like a new one that has to be broken in. Jesus returned "once more" and found the apostles asleep. His solution? He "prayed a third time, saying the same thing again." He had warned against vain repetitions (see Mt 6: 7), but the complaint was against vanity, not repetition. Breathing is repetitious, and so are heartbeats. Vanity would twist the arm of God, like spinning words on a prayer wheel. That is why those false prayers, which guarantee your request if you say them so many times, offend the virtue of religion. An individual in my church refused to stop distributing such prayer cards, so I told her that I would pray nine times that she stop. But in a parable (Lk 18: 2-8), Jesus praised another woman who "importuned" a judge until her case was heard. That is why we have great litanies and novenas. He keeps "knocking" at the door of each soul. Either he is Our Annoyer or Our Savior. I cannot think of a more gracious protocol than the way Jesus did not annoy the sleeping apostles by waking them, but groaned alone as they snored. If we give up, Jesus does not. The next day he will fall under his cross not once or twice but three times, and in the name of love he will get up not once or twice, but three times, and all for us.

Almighty Lord, I thank you for your persistence when I lack endurance. My strength is not mine but yours, and my faith in you is your faith in me, working in spite of me.

The Clock on the Wall

Father George William Rutler

Then [Jesus] returned to his disciples and said to them, "Are you still sleeping and taking your rest? Behold, the hour is at hand when the Son of Man is to be handed over to sinners. Get up, let us go. Look, my betrayer is at hand." (Mt 26: 45-46)

In 2007, a NASA satellite probe seemed to support Einstein's theory that space and time "bend." Gravity is the result of a distortion of space and time and, as the world spins, stars warp space-time. If we are not physicists, we still have the mental image of Dali's painting of clocks melting. God created time as "kronos," which is the chronological measure of the passing of our lives. There is also a quality called "kairos." It is the purpose behind "kronos." Chronologically, Jesus was about thirty-three years old. In "kairos" he is the Alpha and Omega, the beginning and the end. Time often "bends" for us: an hour of pleasure may seem like a moment, while a moment of pain can seem interminable. Physically, it is time to wake up in the morning. Morally, it is time to change my life. At a wedding in Cana he said that his "hour" had not yet come (Jn 2: 4). In Gethsemane his "hour" had come. As man and God, Jesus combines "kronos" and "kairos." The purpose for which he had come into time and space was about to be fulfilled. In the rear of my church, a clock faces me as I stand in the pulpit. Some may think that the preacher does not pay proper attention to the arms on it. In front of the church is God's clock: the crucifix. The arms on it belong to Jesus showing eternal love. Minutes and hours only make sense when the arms of Christ embrace us. A few moments of distracted prayer often seem very long, and at other times God bends us in a way that seems unaware of time. God is patient with us as he was with his dozing disciples. Time spent in prayer is a gift from heaven, even if we do not realize it when we glance at the clock on the wall.

Holy Father, "a thousand ages in thy sight are like an evening gone." Help me to make the most of every moment, so that I may be your steward of the days you have given me, and then rejoice with you for ever.

The Worst of Friends

Father George William Rutler

While [Jesus] was still speaking, Judas, one of the Twelve, arrived, accompanied by a large crowd, with swords and clubs, who had come from the chief priests and the elders of the people. His betrayer had arranged a sign with them, saying, "The man I shall kiss is the one; arrest him." Immediately he went over to Jesus and said, "Hail, Rabbi!" and he kissed him. Jesus answered him, "Friend, do what you have come for." (Mt 26: 47-50)

Sentimentality, which is emotion without sacrifice, mocks love. Carl Jung said that "sentimentality is a superstructure covering brutality." Tyrants have wept for their family pets while slaughtering people, and demagogues persuade others that they are acting "for our children." Judas betrayed Jesus not with a slap but with a kiss. Having custody of the apostles' treasury, he thought he was in control of them and Christ himself. He became bitter when Christ did not dance to his tune. He sentimentally claimed to be concerned for the poor (Jn 12: 5) when he only cared about himself. Without love for Christ who instituted the Church, some may substitute the visible institution for Christ, and use charity as a means of control. That distortion corrupted Ananias, Sapphira, and Simon Magus (Acts 5: 1-10; 8: 9-24). Judas was the first to betray Christ in exchange for a government grant.

A sentimentalist cannot be a real friend. Friendship has two characteristics. First, friends share a common love for something outside themselves. Judas would not join Jesus in loving the Father in heaven. Second, friends are honest with each other. The Arabic word for "friend" is *Sadeeq*, which means one who tells the truth. Saint Basil said, "The flatterer speaks to give pleasure, but the friend refrains from nothing, even truth which gives pain." Sentimental Judas tried to flatter Jesus instead of worshiping him. Jesus responded by calling him "Friend" in an evocation of what Judas might have been if he had been honest. Jesus cured demoniacs who were possessed. He could not cure Judas who wanted to possess. When religion is used for self-promotion and worship lapses into entertainment, they give Jesus a false kiss. The saddest enemies of Christ are those he called to be holy and then who go their own way, haunted by him.

Almighty Father, grant me the faith to know that the same Love that made all the universe to delight in it, came into that creation and called me your friend. May I never take for granted this mystery you have granted me.

Handling the Lord

Father George William Rutler

Then stepping forward they laid hands on Jesus and arrested him. And behold, one of those who accompanied Jesus put his hand to his sword, drew it, and struck the high priest's servant, cutting off his ear. (Mt 26: 50-51)

In the science of DNA, "Human Accelerated Regions," or HARs, are forty-nine segments of the human genome which mark the radically different vertebrate development in humans contrasted with chimpanzees. HAR2 controls the development of the wrist and thumb which paved the way for our ability to play a Chopin sonata, needlepoint a cushion, and perform neurosurgery. The prehensile thumb is not the key to the difference between a man and a monkey; but humans, in God's image by virtue of the ability to know and love God, can raise the twenty-seven bones of each intricate hand in praise of the Creator who enabled us to handle creation. When the Word that made all things became flesh, he had human hands, but the human mind that moved them was united with the divine mind which designed life. The hands that hammered nails into wood in the carpentry shop in Nazareth could heal the sick when placed on a feverish head, and could warm the cold hand of a corpse. In Gethsemane, the soldiers "laid hands on Jesus and arrested him." Jesus knew that he would be abused, to paraphrase Pascal, until the end of the world, for as "you did for one of these least brothers of mine, you did for me" (Mt 25: 40). Christ permits the world to handle him, and the world responds by manhandling him. The hands of the carpenter that nailed wood were nailed to wood by human hands capable of the finest surgery and the worst butchery. Saint John wondered at the condescension of God: " ...what we looked upon/ and touched with our hands/ concerns the Word of life" (1 Jn 1: 1). To receive Holy Communion with such awe, we should joyfully be reconciled with him first in confession. Saint John Mary Vianney said that when we confess sin, our hands take the nails out of the hands of Jesus.

Heavenly Father, grant to me the gifts of discernment and reverence, that I may receive the Blessed Sacrament with the awe of my First Communion, and that your mercy may make the humility of my last communion.

Watching and Waiting

Father George William Rutler

Then Jesus said to him, "Put your sword back into its sheath, for all who take the sword will perish by the sword. Do you think that I cannot call upon my Father and he will not provide me at this moment with more than twelve legions of angels? But then how would the scriptures be fulfilled which say that it must come to pass in this way?" (Mt 26: 52-54)

Jesus had ordered his apostles to carry swords (Lk 22: 36). Next, he orders one of them, presumably Peter, to put his sword away. Saint Augustine reconciles that by saying our Lord's command was a warning against assault "without the command or sanction of any superior, or legitimate authority." Jesus could use angels to protect him. Saint Jerome calculated that he meant seventy-two thousand of them. Peter's violence did not prevent his appointment as leader of the Church on earth, just as Moses would lead the Jews although he had killed an Egyptian. Augustine nicely says that "both transgressed the rule not through hardened ferocity, but through a warmth of spirit capable of good." The anger of both was misguided love. As "deep waters cannot quench love" (Sg 8: 7), God chose not to drown their passion, but to channel it toward a greater good. Divine love has a purpose higher than revenge for sins: he was intent on redemption from original sin. Salvation is the only "liberation theology" that really liberates from death. After the human race betrayed God, a flaming sword blocked man's return to paradise. Innocent Christ must die to put that sword away. God's plan was to fulfill the prophets he had inspired. I still remember the words of a guide on the Mount of Olives many years ago, who said to me that Jesus watched the guards crossing the Kidron Valley with torches in the bright moonlight, a walk of at least twenty minutes: "He saw them coming and he waited." It is no surprise that he was not surprised, and so nothing that we do surprises him who knows what is in the heart of man. So he waits for us, whether we are coming to worship him by grace or attack him by sin. His sovereignty over history watches to see what we are going to do with the freedom he has given us.

Heavenly Father, as your Son waited to do your will as you would have it, so give me the patience to serve him as he commands and when he commands, so that in all that I do I may honor the Holy Spirit who lives and reigns with you and the same Son, one God for ever.

Running the Wrong Way

Father George William Rutler

At that hour Jesus said to the crowds, "Have you come out as against a robber, with swords and clubs to seize me? Day after day I sat teaching in the temple area, yet you did not arrest me. But all this has come to pass that the writings of the prophets may be fulfilled." Then all the disciples left him and fled.

(Mt 26: 55-56)

In 1938 the aviator Douglas Corrigan was supposed to fly from New York to California, but instead his flight ended in Ireland. He blamed it on defective instruments and heavy clouds, but he probably did it deliberately to spite the government which forbade a transatlantic flight. Despite his skill, history remembers him as "Wrong Way Corrigan." In Gethsemane, the apostles fled from Jesus not by calculation and spite, but by sheer lack of courage. They had been with the Master, day and night, for three years and heard him say, "I am the Way." So when they turned their backs to him, it was more shameful than the false bravado of the armed mob who came by night with swords and clubs because they could not contradict Christ's logic by day. The mob was like the officers who, having been defeated by Wellington at Waterloo, turned their backs to him at a reception in Vienna. Their conqueror said with biting disdain, "I have seen their backs before." Christ expected the cowardliness of a mob, but saw with sadness his own men flee. They did not go down in history as "the Wrong Way Apostles" because eventually they returned and gave their lives for him. Everyone has moments of courage, which is a natural virtue, but steady courage all through life, in the daily trials of suffering and discouragement, is a supernatural virtue. Aquinas links that kind of courage with the virtues of munificence and magnificence, which are forms of generosity. It takes courage to give God all we are, when only he notices it. Monsignor Ronald Knox spoke once of those who "have turned their backs upon their country and now have the effrontery to say that they have their country behind them." To flee from Christ, even if it seems a way of preserving one's life, is to lose the way, truth, and life itself.

Blessed Lord, may I stay with you day and night, in good times and in bad, even when a weak world thinks I am foolish. For you have promised that if I do not flee from you, I shall one day behold you face to face.

In the Grandstand

Father George William Rutler

Those who had arrested Jesus led him away to Caiaphas the high priest, where the scribes and the elders were assembled. Peter was following him at a distance as far as the high priest's courtyard, and going inside he sat down with the servants to see the outcome. (Mt 26: 57-58)

The difference between stage plays and what theologians call the "drama of salvation" is that, in the Christian drama, the audience and the players are the same. Only by getting up on the stage of history with Christ is it possible, as Pope John Paul II said, to "become what you are." Peter became a shadow of himself when he followed Jesus "at a distance." Yet this was part of his formation as Prince of the Apostles: by the humiliation of his behavior in the passion, he began to perceive his weakness. The "*Quo vadis?*" legend of Peter retreating from Rome at the prospect of his martyrdom has psychological substance: he learned from his first failure in Jerusalem that he could not rely on himself in Rome. "Simon, Simon, behold Satan has demanded to sift all of you like wheat, but I have prayed that your own faith may not fail; and once you have turned back, you must strengthen your brothers" (Lk 22: 31-32). Jesus cannot be known from a distance. The spiritual dilettante, who squints at him as a curiosity, will never know what to make of him. Jesus enlisted Peter in his drama when he said, "Follow me." Christianity is not a spectator sport. Christians are in the arena, not in the grandstand. Those "motivational" speakers, who dabble in Jesus as one source of inspiration among many, come and go, replaced on television quickly by clones of themselves. There is a kind of spiritual bulimia which tastes the Lord but does not "inwardly digest" him in the heart. Cardinal Newman described those who "put on a new religion every morning" as if religion were only "spiritual thoughts and feelings" without doctrine. Peter "sat down with the servants to see the outcome." But from their point of view they could see nothing true. Only when Christ is "all in all" (Col 3: 11) can we be anything at all.

Father in heaven, may your Son fill me with his love that I desire him above all things and, by so doing, come to understand that without him I am nothing, and that it was for him that I was made.

Hearing but Not Listening

Father George William Rutler

The chief priests and the entire Sanhedrin kept trying to obtain false testimony against Jesus in order to put him to death, but they found none, though many false witnesses came forward. Finally two came forward who stated, "This man said, 'I can destroy the temple of God and within three days rebuild it.'"
(Mt 26: 59-61)

The word "torture" means to twist, and to lie is moral torture because it twists the truth. The Prince of Lies twisted God's words. Satan has no imagination, and can invent nothing except the deadly art of the twisting of what already exists. When Jesus was on trial, there were any number of people willing to perjure themselves for a price. Whether the reward be some social advantage or financial gain, it cheapens the one who sells out. Thus we have the example of Saint Thomas More's true sorrow for Richard Rich who lied about the saint on trial in order to receive the chancellorship of Wales. More problematic is the individual who does not twist the truth, but who thinks the truth itself is a lie. Two men testified, accurately, that Jesus said he could destroy "the temple of God" and rebuild it in three days. They were right: he did say that; but they were also totally wrong, because they did not understand that Jesus was speaking of himself as "the temple of God" and was predicting his resurrection. They heard but did not listen. We can misunderstand the voice of God in the Church if we hear only the words but not the Word behind them. Then we are tempted to think that we can change them or dismiss them if they do not match our understanding of how things should be. Thomas Jefferson made himself small when he tried to shorten the Bible. The Gospel is "of" our Lord Jesus Christ; it is only "according to" Matthew, Mark, Luke, and John who were inspired to write the Word's words. This is why liturgical reading of the sacred texts should be done reverently, but not dramatically in an attempt to "give it meaning." That usually means giving it our meaning. So chanting the texts has anciently been used both to hear and listen. And the song goes on.

God our Father, may I never try to make you into my image. In all things may I tell others the truth of your Son, so that each day I may grow into his image, whom I did not choose but who chose me.

The Sound of Silence

Father George William Rutler

The high priest rose and addressed [Jesus], "Have you no answer? What are these men testifying against you?" But Jesus was silent. Then the high priest said to him, "I order you to tell us under oath before the living God whether you are the Messiah, the Son of God." Jesus said to him in reply, "You have said so. But I tell you:/ From now on you will see 'the Son of Man/ seated at the right hand of the Power'/ and 'coming on the clouds of heaven.'" (Mt 26: 62-64)

I had a friend who controlled the conversation by pausing in mid-sentence. It was a clever device: one was less likely to interrupt him in that brief silence than when he had finished the phrase. There are deliberate pauses called "caesuras" in poetry. Both Homer and Virgil use them to add drama to the opening lines of their *Iliad* and *Aeneid*. In music a conductor can stretch a caesura for full effect. There were times when Jesus paused and did not speak. The silent caesura of Jesus unnerved the high priest: "Have you no answer?" The silence cut the man's conscience: "I order you to tell us…" So Chesterton called such silence "the unbearable repartee." From those refusals to speak we can learn as much about the Word of God as we can from his spoken words. It is a clue to Jesus, rather like "the curious incident of the dog in the night-time" which Sherlock Holmes noticed in the story "Silver Blaze." The curious incident was precisely that the dog did not bark. To the woman of Canaan, at first "he did not say a word" (Mt 15: 23). Instead of answering the men who brought to him the adulterous woman, he wrote something on the ground in silence (see Jn 8: 6). Pontius Pilate "was greatly amazed" at his silence (Mt 27: 14), and when Herod questioned him, Jesus "gave him no answer" (Lk 23: 9). Each time, after the pregnant caesura, he burst out with wonderful words. There was one exception. When Jesus was taken before Herod, he was silent and remained silent. Jean-Pierre Camus said, "Wisdom consists in knowing when and how to speak and when and where to keep silent." Jesus knew that decadent Herod's sensual life was one of amusing diversions. He wanted Jesus to join his retinue of entertainers and "perform some sign" (Lk 23: 8). He even lacked the high priest's capacity for outrage. For Herod, silence had no sound.

Dear Lord, who went to the cross in silence "like a lamb led to the slaughter," let me hear you in what you do not say, so that when you do speak, I may understand.

Heads but No Brains

Father George William Rutler

Then the high priest tore his robes and said, "He has blasphemed! What further need have we of witnesses? You have now heard the blasphemy; what is your opinion?" They said in reply, "He deserves to die!" Then they spat in his face and struck him, while some slapped him, saying, "Prophesy for us, Messiah: who is it that struck you?" (Mt 26: 65-68)

At the trial of Jesus, a mob mentality took over. The high priest forgot the Mosaic law (Lv 21: 10) that said his garments should not be torn. The Talmudic commentary prescribed the tearing of clothing as a sign of outrage at blasphemy, but the high priest must remain above the sway of emotion. To this day, judges wear special robes in respect for laws which transcend personal sentiments. The court in Jerusalem also broke the law by shouting rather than voting one by one, the youngest voting first so as not to be influenced by those of senior rank. A mob claims to want justice, but its existence as organized chaos contradicts that. A proverb says that the mob has many heads but no brains. Thomas Jefferson knew the dangers of a majority, and opted for a republic over mere majority rule: "A democracy is nothing more than mob rule, where fifty-one percent of the population may take away the right of the other forty-nine." Mob rule is not always wild. More often, it is subtle and outwardly civilized, in the form of fashion and moods, and "political correctness." But if we believe something because "everybody says" or "as most people know," we are nodding with heads and not thinking with brains. At a cabinet meeting when Lincoln was unanimously opposed by his cabinet, he said, "There are eight nays and one aye. The aye has it." After Cardinal Montini became Pope Paul VI and rejected the majority opinion of some consultors, he was asked, "What does Montini think?" He replied, "The Pope is no longer Montini." No one wants to be unpopular, but it will happen if we follow Christ who was punched and spat upon. "If I were still trying to please people, I would not be a slave of Christ" (Gal 1: 10). It is very hard to be a Christian if it is easy.

Almighty Father, give me the courage to follow the great multitude of angels and saints praising your Son, rather than the earthly crowds that crucify him.

Cold by the Fire

Father George William Rutler

Now Peter was sitting outside in the courtyard. One of the maids came over to him and said, "You too were with Jesus the Galilean." But he denied it in front of everyone, saying, "I do not know what you are talking about!" (Mt 26: 69-70)

A wit said of a woman that she had all the qualities of a peacock, except beauty. Without beauty, the screeching peacock's strutting is absurd. After Christ was arrested, Peter began to resemble the peacock without beauty, and it was a miserable sight, and most miserable to Peter himself. Still ringing in his ears was his proud boast, "I will not deny you" (Mt 26: 35). All the disciples had said the same. It is easy to be brave in a crowd. And it is easy to chant the Creed with a thousand other singers: much easier than saying it alone in the face of cynics. But now by the fireside, when one of the maids recognizes him as a companion of Jesus, Peter's dashed pride makes him look foolish, and the voice that once was inspired by the Father in heaven to declare Jesus the Christ, now screeches: "I do not know what you are talking about!" Of course he knew, but he feigned a kind of deafness. The Latin word "for deaf," *surdus*, gives us "absurd." Suddenly everything seemed absurd to Peter, and Christ in chains made no sense at all. The chill he felt was not from the night air, but from his soul. He tried to warm himself by the fire, but no material consolation can cancel the chill that only love can warm. "Yet I hold this against you: you have lost the love you had at first" (Rv 2: 4). Matthew does not mention the fire in the courtyard where Peter tried to stop shivering, but Mark and Luke do, and John speaks specifically of a charcoal fire, *athrakian*. He will use the same word once more. After the resurrection, on the shore in Galilee, Peter will see Jesus standing by a charcoal fire, asking him if he loved him (Jn 21: 9). While Peter had humiliated himself, Christ humbled him. And Peter was never cold again.

Lord my God, may I love all things because of you and not in place of you, for without the fire of your love, all things grow cold.

Face to Face

Father George William Rutler

As [Peter] went out to the gate, another girl saw him and said to those who were there, "This man was with Jesus the Nazorean." Again he denied it with an oath, "I do not know the man!"
(Mt 26: 71-72)

Another serving girl recognized Peter. She must have seen Jesus, and may have paused to listen to him long enough to register the faces of at least some of his apostles. Developmental psychologists say that, between seventeen and thirty weeks, babies become able to distinguish a smile from a frown, and are attracted to the smile. Those who believe in God will know that the smile is the expression of love, and God's loving gift of love makes man desire to love and to be loved. Pope Benedict XVI has called Jesus "the face of God." When Peter first saw that face, he followed the Master. Peter's denial that he knew Jesus was betrayed by the anguish on his face. Like the girl in the courtyard, people study our faces throughout our lives. Through what they see, they may be drawn to Jesus or discouraged from seeking him. Peter pretended that he did not "know the man," but he was too honest a man to be a good actor. Peter's simple humility could not keep his disguise for long. Aquinas says, "The beings that possess the highest degree of nobility must also possess the highest degree of simplicity." This is the state of "sanctifying grace" which lets the face of Christ shine through our own faces. Apart from God, the smiles on our faces can be insincere and even cynical like the Cheshire Cat. We cannot truly smile if we live a lie. Cosmetic surgery can make it harder to smile. Saint Paul must have had a most genuine smile as he wrote: "At present we see indistinctly, as in a mirror, but then face to face. At present I know partially; then I shall know fully, as I am fully known" (1 Cor 13: 12). George Orwell said that everyone at fifty has the face he deserves. So long as we acknowledge Christ, our faces will be ageless.

Blessed Lord, may I confess my sins and do penance for the lies I have lived, so that on the day you promised, I may see you face to face, and not as a stranger.

What Cannot Be Denied

Father George William Rutler

*A little later the bystanders came over and said to Peter, "Surely
you too are one of them; even your speech gives you away." At
that he began to curse and to swear, "I do not know the man."
And immediately a cock crowed. Then Peter remembered the
word that Jesus had spoken: "Before the cock crows you will deny
me three times." He went out and began to weep bitterly.*
(Mt 26: 73-75)

It was said of a statesman that whenever he struggled with his
conscience, he emerged the victor. When Peter struggled,
his conscience won. He could have sympathized with Marlon
Brando's guileless character, Terry Malloy, in the film *On the
Waterfront*, who moans to Father Barry: "This conscience stuff can
drive you nuts." Because Peter was honest, his attempts to deny
Christ were half-hearted, and half-hearted lies can break the heart.
Peter wept. The bystanders had known that he had been with Christ
by his accent. The Galileans were casual with their gutturals
and snobbish Judeans mocked what they considered an inferior
Aramaic pronunciation.

In our day there are so-called "cultural Catholics": people who
claim no longer to walk with Christ, but their "speech" gives them
away. Our culture itself, with all its inheritance of Catholic art and
philosophy and moral law, cannot be denied even if Christ himself
is denied. But soon those cultural institutions, from higher education and human rights and benign science, and trust in the existence of truth, begin to decay without Christ as their cornerstone.
But those who once walked with Christ speak with his accent and
cannot be rid of him, however much they deny his existence. It is
true of individuals and nations. Either Christ will inspire or he will
haunt, but he cannot really be denied. Often those who claim to be
"liberated from Catholic guilt," curse and swear like Peter, in vain
pretense that they never knew Jesus. It is an act, and one ruinous
to souls and entire cultures. Some of the most violent despisers of
Christ have the potential to become his greatest champions, if only
they would remember that they "speak" like him through the remnants of the Christian civilization they still retain. Then, like Peter,
they could begin to speak "through him, and with him, and in him."

*Heavenly Father, strengthen my conscience by the power of your
Holy Spirit, that I may never forget what I was or what you have
called me to become.*

The King of Tides

Father George William Rutler

When it was morning, all the chief priests and the elders of the people took counsel against Jesus to put him to death. They bound him, led him away, and handed him over to Pilate, the governor. (Mt 27: 1-2)

Canute was one of the greatest medieval kings ruling England and much of Scandinavia. There is a much misunderstood story of him setting his throne up on a shore and commanding the waves to roll back. They did not. The shore may have been in Bosham in West Sussex or, more likely, along the Thames on Thorney Island where the Houses of Parliament now stand. Whether by ocean waves or river tides, Canute knew he would get wet. He was instructing his courtiers that flattery would get them nowhere: "Let all men know how empty and worthless is the power of kings, for there is none worthy of the name, but he whom heaven, earth, and sea obey by eternal laws." Then he placed his crown on the crucifix in Winchester Cathedral. Earthly rulers come and go. "The King is dead. Long live the King." Christ has no successor: "Christ has died. Christ is risen. Christ will come again." The local religious leaders bound Jesus and handed him over to the secular power, accusing Jesus of having set himself up as an earthly king. Pilate's cynicism was more professional than theirs: he may actually have studied under Cynical philosophers, and he saw through the scheme. There are attempts in every age to bind Christ's Body, the Church, and subject it to human governments, as if courts and congresses can undo the laws of God and nature. But the tides of history will not be held back. Christ was not bound by his shroud nor is he bound by human governors. Like any people of superficial piety, the high priests and elders indicted themselves when they said they had no king but Caesar. But Christ will not be bound by opinion or fashion or the ballot box. Human institutions can bind his body but they cannot cover his eyes which stare at us as they stared at Peter.

Heavenly Father, help me to worship you in the mystery of the Holy Trinity, and to seek only your heavenly kingdom which has no end.

After It Is Too Late

Father Michael Nolan

Then Judas, his betrayer, seeing that Jesus had been condemned,
deeply regretted what he had done. (Mt 27: 3)

A few years ago, I traveled through what is described as a developing country. We visited some remote areas where people follow the traditional ways of their ancestors. Whatever children learned in these areas was taught to them at home. Formal education for children was just being introduced to the area. As we traveled to one of these new schools, the parish priest described the educational challenges. He explained how difficult it is to combat truancy. As I listened to him describe these problems, I could not help but think that we have the same problems in my "advanced" country. Only after seeing the school could I grasp the depths of their problems. The school was a clay hut without windows or electricity. The only light for the room came from the empty doorway. A few magazines were the only teaching materials available to the teachers. That depressing sight has never left me.

Our minds often work this way – through our eyes. So do our consciences. Judas learned this the hard way. Judas hatched a plot betraying Jesus for money. He had left everything to follow Jesus, but covetousness followed him. Later on Jesus warned of his betrayal in earshot of Judas. Judas even denied it. But the sight of what resulted from his betrayal could not be denied. Only seeing what he did to Jesus finally got through to him. We can hear warnings about the gravity of our sins. We can be told why our sinning is so destructive. Unfortunately, the effects of our wrongdoing aren't usually understood until the deed is done. Only after it is too late. Satan has known this ever since the man and the woman ate the fruit of the forbidden tree. "Then the eyes of both of them were opened, and they realized that they were naked." This is why he finds it so easy to tempt us. It has worked that way since the very beginning.

Father in heaven, who created all things as a reflection of your glory,
help me to trust that, through your Son, I have everything I need.

Confession with Forgiveness

Father Michael Nolan

[Judas] returned the thirty pieces of silver to the chief priests and elders, saying, "I have sinned in betraying innocent blood." They said, "What is that to us? Look to it yourself." (Mt 27: 3-4)

Years ago the parish priest learned how to minister to the parishioners by sitting in the confessional. Today, he picks up his dry cleaning. He stops by the bank. Most importantly he gets his hair cut. Confession may be out of fashion in the present period, but there is no lack of confessions. Television and radio have capitalized on the phenomena. The bestseller lists are littered with the tell-all books of notorious figures and wannabe celebrities. Nail salons, hairdressers, and the local coffee shops have tapped into the market and take advantage of our need for confession. The empty confessional coupled with the sacrament's limited availability has coincided with the huge growth of a counseling industry. Yet this is nothing new. It is part of the human condition. For many people regret what they have done. They share their transgressions with others. Sadly they don't unload them on the one who can forgive them. For only the priest has the power to grant God's forgiveness. Only through the sacrament of penance can the sinner receive mercy.

Judas regretted what he had done. In fact Saint Matthew tells us he deeply regretted what he had done. Yet where did he turn after examining his conscience? He ended up confessing to his collaborators. He didn't turn back to Jesus. He went to those who could not forgive him, as they were also guilty of transgression. Jesus commanded us to forgive those who trespass against us, but only after we first ask God, the giver of mercy, to forgive our trespasses. Judas confessed to those who didn't care what happened to him. And they said, "What is that to us? Look to it yourself." This is what many people face if they make confession to everyone except the priest. They end up facing it themselves, never knowing the mercy and love that endures for ever.

Father of mercy, call me back whenever I stray from the help you give me through your Church.

Capable of Falling

Father Michael Nolan

Flinging the money into the temple, [Judas] departed and went off and hanged himself. The chief priests gathered up the money, but said, "It is not lawful to deposit this in the temple treasury, for it is the price of blood." After consultation, they used it to buy the potter's field as a burial place for foreigners. That is why that field even today is called the Field of Blood. (Mt 27: 5-8)

The Lord chose twelve men and made them his apostles. He made these men apostles to be a blessing for all the nations. He first sent them to the lost sheep of Israel. Judas Iscariot was one of the Twelve. He was the apostle who betrayed him. Yet before he betrayed his friend, Judas, like the other eleven, was given great powers. "As you go, make this proclamation: 'The kingdom of heaven is at hand.' Cure the sick, raise the dead, cleanse lepers, drive out demons" (Mt 10: 7). Yet when the time came for the Last Supper, Judas couldn't live up to his calling. He could not sustain the friendship. None of those special powers could save his vocation. His betrayal speaks to anyone who has committed to a religious vocation or marriage. If an apostle can engage in treachery then so can each one of us.

All Christians ignore the treachery of Judas at their peril – especially Jesus' priests. Mother Church is aware of the dangers her priests face daily. She seeks to save them each time they offer the Holy Sacrifice, aware that the best of them is capable of falling. The Church requires her priests to say certain prayers before they receive the Eucharist. The faithful don't hear these prayers as they are said sotto voce. Yet it is helpful to be aware of these priestly prayers. "Lord Jesus Christ, Son of the living God, by the will of the Father and the work of the Holy Spirit your death brought life into the world. By your holy body and blood free me from all my sins, and from every evil. Keep me faithful to your teaching, and never let me be parted from you. Lord Jesus Christ, with faith in your love and mercy I eat your body and drink your blood. Let it not bring me condemnation, but health in mind and body." May these prayers save all priests today.

Holy Father, protect your priests this day, so they may grow in holiness and remain set apart.

A Church That Is Attractive

Father Michael Nolan

Then was fulfilled what had been said through Jeremiah the prophet, "And they took the thirty pieces of silver, the value of a man with a price on his head, a price set by some of the Israelites, and they paid it out for the potter's field just as the Lord had commanded me." (Mt 27: 9-10)

There is great pressure today on bishops and pastors to raise money for their churches. Globalization and the information highway have increased the number of requests. Pastors write checks to foreign missions in between answering the door to hand someone a food voucher. There is also a greater need to emphasize almsgiving in richer cultures. Almsgiving covers a multitude of sins. It assists the poor in this life while aiding the rich in the next life. Yet almsgiving does not, like philanthropy, judge a gift greater based on more zeros. Almsgiving helps us with God only when the gift comes from righteous means. Even the chief priests who paid Judas for his betrayal knew they would dishonor themselves if they put those coins in the temple treasury. For the Lord does not honor anything connected to falsehood or sin.

The Church of today grows by remembering the following ancient lesson. Once a prominent man named Marcion arrived in the city of Rome. He made a great donation to the Church. Later on he was shown to be a heretic. Marcion believed the God of the Old Testament is different from Jesus of the New Testament. He attracted a following. The bishops recognized the seductiveness of this heresy and the dangers it was causing to the unity of the Church. They excommunicated Marcion. They also returned his donation. Unlike the thirty pieces of silver, the donation was returned not because it was blood money. Yet it was similar in that it came from someone who worked against God's mission. Recalling this lesson will help us today.

The Church's bankbooks must honor her treasure in heaven. Remembering that the account balance does not reflect the Church's true wealth is a must for leaders and donors. It is the source of righteous donations that reflects our inner beauty. This makes the Church attractive and successful.

Father of all that is good, let me not cling to what I have but give in a way that reflects your great beauty.

Speaking by Way of Silence

Father Michael Nolan

*Now Jesus stood before the governor, and he questioned him,
"Are you the king of the Jews?" Jesus said, "You say so." And
when he was accused by the chief priests and elders, he made no
answer. Then Pilate said to him, "Do you not hear how many
things they are testifying against you?" But he did not answer
him one word, so that the governor was greatly amazed.*
(Mt 27: 11-14)

Who has not regretted remaining silent when something
needed to be said? Who hasn't regretted talking when
silence might have accomplished more? Developing the
art of when to speak and when to be silent comes with practice
and experience. It begins when we allot time for prayer and holy
reading.

In the sight of his enemies, the one who had told his disciples
they will be given what they ask for, refuses to give his enemies the
information they need to condemn him. Even when he speaks,
Jesus' answer shows he is not afraid to stand up to them. Pilate questions
him. Jesus responds by telling him nothing. The chief priests
and elders make accusations, but he remains silent. A lack of
responses to interrogators is often interpreted as proof of guilt or
an attempt to conceal information. That is not the case with Jesus.
His refusal to answer the governor's second round of questioning
shows us it is different. Jesus' silence is a form of resistance against
this exercise of evil. More often silence is understood as weakness.
This time it reveals God's power and goodness. In fact, criminals
and despots have always maintained power by threatening the person
who considers going public. The silence of many individuals,
as well as whole nations beset with corruption, abuse, and widespread
injustices, speaks to the high level of fear present in today's
world. Yet the silence of Jesus has nothing to do with fear. It comes
from divine courage. It comes from who he is.

He is the Lamb of God who has been led to the slaughter, and
the Good Shepherd who does not run from the wolf. As the silent
lamb he proved his innocence. As the Good Shepherd, he chose to
speak to those who recognize his voice, and not those who address
him for evil purposes.

*Father of all ages, let me hear once again the call to follow your Son
even though I have resisted in times past.*

Don't Ignore the Wife

Father Michael Nolan

While [Pilate] was still seated on the bench, his wife sent him a message, "Have nothing to do with that righteous man. I suffered much in a dream today because of him." (Mt 27: 19)

Pilate's wife instructs her husband not to pass judgment after a night of bad dreaming. She suffered in the dream just before the trial so her husband might not suffer the rest of his waking days. She sent word of her bad dream so he might do the right thing. The timing of her dream confirms that God's mercy is always at work. For she dreamt about Jesus before Pilate made his final decision. The dream confirms the breadth of God's mercy, for she suffered in a dream from which she could awake instead of suffering permanently for the rest of her life.

The Lord offered salvation through the dream just as the Lord had used dreams in the past. Before Jesus, God saved Israel by giving Joseph the power to interpret the dreams of Pharaoh. Pharaoh gave Joseph responsibility over the whole land of Egypt. The Lord appeared to King Solomon in a dream inviting him to ask for something. Solomon asked God for an understanding heart so he could judge the people and distinguish right from wrong. The Lord was pleased to give him his wisdom. Daniel could describe the dream of King Nebuchadnezzar as well as interpret it. This led the Babylonian king to worship the God of Israel.

While the baby Jesus was saved numerous times through the dreams of Joseph and the Magi, the wife's dream failed to guide Pilate toward making the right decision. A dream from God does not insure men will trust its message. For Pilate represents all who think a real God is incapable of suffering. Pilate stands with those who lack compassion when someone suffers. Pilate ignored his wife who tried to help him in his ignorance. May this help us prepare to stand in front of the final Judge. May Pilate's mistake make us approach judgments in a different way. May this remind us that our thinking always needs wisdom inspired by God.

Father of mercy, help me not to run from the suffering you have given me so that I may grow in compassion for those around me.

Living the Passion

Father Michael Nolan

The chief priests and the elders persuaded the crowds to ask for Barabbas but to destroy Jesus. The governor said to them in reply, "Which of the two do you want me to release to you?" They answered, "Barabbas!" (Mt 27: 20-21)

Since medieval times the passion and resurrection of our Lord has been transmitted to audiences through re-enactment. These passion plays aren't performed as regularly as they were in times past, but the genre isn't entirely dead. It has moved into the churches. On Passion Sunday and Good Friday certain congregations have adopted the practice of assigning parts to the reading of the passion. Often times a narrator is assigned, the priest takes the part of Jesus, and the assembly takes the part of the crowd. The lay faithful take the part of the angry crowd shouting, "Crucify him" and, "We want Barabbas." The wisdom of proclaiming the Gospel in this manner escapes me. For unlike a passion play that is performed for entertainment, everything we say and do in worship has real effects and consequences. Just walking into a church can mean you want Jesus in your life that very moment. And it can happen.

This is the great challenge for the preacher who speaks just after those present have said they prefer Barabbas to Jesus. The challenge for the preacher can be made a bit more difficult. For the reading of the passion is read to show all of us how much our Lord loves us. The proclamation of the passion allows the death of our Lord to enter deeper in our hearts. The passion shows us how to take up our cross and follow so we might be disciples. So we can live like Simon of Cyrene who helped Jesus carry his cross. So we might look on from a distance like those women of Galilee. So we can look to Joseph of Arimathea who insured the Lord received proper burial by giving him his tomb. So we might emulate Mary Magdalene and Mary the mother of James and John who remained facing the tomb even after the huge stone had sealed the entrance.

Father all-powerful, you sent your Son as the fulfillment of our desires. Help me to call on his name whenever I am tested.

They Made Me Do It

Father Michael Nolan

Pilate said to them, "Then what shall I do with Jesus called Messiah?" They all said, "Let him be crucified!" But he said, "Why? What evil has he done?" They only shouted the louder, "Let him be crucified!" (Mt 27: 22-23)

Local teenagers who get in trouble with the law often show up at my church office. The judges at the courts send them out to work instead of sending them to a detention center. They call it community service hours. When someone comes asking for work hours, I sit down and talk with them. We don't assign them work without talking for a while. Sometimes this is helpful for them. Sometimes if they are Catholics they also go to confession. Sometimes these young people are charged as individuals. Sometimes they are arrested and charged with a group of other people. This seems to make a difference when we sit down before they work. If they are convicted of a crime, as an individual, they either defend their innocence vigorously or admit to committing the crime. When they have gone to trial with others the conversation is often very different. Often they say that they were there when the crime took place, but it was the others who were at fault. Sometimes they just happened to be spectators or innocent bystanders. Other times they claim to have been unaware that a crime was taking place. It is easier to shift the blame when others are involved.

It was also easier for that crowd who wanted Jesus crucified. It was easy not to believe, or ignore the question of culpability. Crowds have often been a stumbling block to the mission of Jesus even when they were coming to him in large numbers. Large numbers don't always mean success. The crowd blocked Zacchaeus from seeing Jesus until he climbed that tree. The multitude tried to silence Bartimaeus from getting Jesus' attention, while crowds of people left him after hearing they had to eat his flesh and drink his blood. It is hard to be with Jesus if you travel in a crowd, for it changes without warning and it rarely has a conscience.

Father of all that is true, purify my mind so I may become like a child and enter your kingdom.

No Escape for Pilate

Father Michael Nolan

When Pilate saw that he was not succeeding at all, but that a riot was breaking out instead, he took water and washed his hands in the sight of the crowd, saying, "I am innocent of this man's blood. Look to it yourselves." (Mt 27: 24)

The case against Jesus had fallen apart. Judas, his accuser, had hung himself. The charges lacked evidence for a clear verdict. Jesus shows no interest in making a public defense. Even the governor's wife recommended that he dismiss the trial. The trial takes place on Pontius Pilate's watch. Yet the power to decide what happens to a man's life has shifted to a mob. We know from history that, as governor, Pontius Pilate often considered how his decisions would affect his own power and standing. At a trial where he is expected to judge whether a man is guilty or innocent, Pilate announces that he himself is innocent. "He took water and washed his hands in the sight of the crowd, saying, 'I am innocent of this man's blood.'" Pilate was correct in the sense that he recognized there is only one judge. He was wrong in thinking he was that judge. For none of us has the final say in how we are judged. We are all held accountable by the only one who is truly innocent. But everyone is held accountable by the only one whom we can say was truly innocent.

Pilate's judgment failed, for instead of being deemed innocent, the Roman governor is tied to the suffering of Jesus. The Church makes sure that nobody forgets his cowardice. At every Sunday Eucharist and at each solemn feast the Christian people announce for everyone to hear that the one who washed his hands and claimed his innocence in front of the crowd did so prematurely. We say in the Creed, "He [Jesus] suffered under Pontius Pilate." Only two human beings beside the Son of God are mentioned in the Creeds of the Church – a young Virgin whose yes to God meant life for Jesus even if it brought her condemnation, and a man in power who sent Jesus to death just to escape the pressure of making the right decision.

Almighty Father, you sent your Son among us to reveal your unending mercy. Enlighten my mind and soften my heart so that I may be ready for his coming in glory.

No Limit to God's Mercy

Father Michael Nolan

And the whole people said in reply, "His blood be upon us and upon our children." Then [Pilate] released Barabbas to them, but after he had Jesus scourged, he handed him over to be crucified. (Mt 27: 25-26)

Jesus is held as Barabbas is released. This confirms that the Gospel of Jesus Christ is a witness and teaching on the mercy of God. Jesus' friends abandon him just as he knew they would. The crowd wants him crucified. A notorious murderer is released instead of him. Death by crucifixion isn't even enough. Pilate has him scourged just after asserting his own innocence in the shedding of Jesus' blood. Yet Jesus continues to do his Father's will. For God the Father didn't change his mind even with the indignities imposed on his Son.

It is difficult to find any reason why God would still have mercy on any human being after knowing what Jesus went through. For mercy is given when someone asks for it. Mercy is given when someone promises to make up for his transgressions. Mercy demands cooperation in the future. But Jesus, an innocent man, accepts a death sentence so we can be blessed with the mercy of God. For the mercy of God is that God loves us first. He doesn't love us after we change. He pardons us in advance. His mercy precedes our repentance.

Jesus came to reveal the face of the true God. The truth is reached when mercy is experienced. Take the example of a child. A child needs to experience mercy before he can admit his faults. A little boy not loved by his parents cannot admit his faults. The child, who can only receive mercy by admitting his faults… will never admit his faults. His fear is too great. He will be afraid of how the parents will react toward him. The possibility of rejection is very real for that child. The child does not admit his faults first and then receive mercy from the parents. The opposite is true. It is the same with God's mercy, except for one difference: God's mercy is limitless. There are no limits to the mercy of God.

Loving Father, we know there is no limit placed on your mercy. Soften my heart that my words this day may reflect the mercy and compassion granted to me.

Judgment Day

Father Michael Nolan

Then the soldiers of the governor took Jesus inside the
praetorium and gathered the whole cohort around him.
They stripped off his clothes and threw a scarlet
military cloak about him. (Mt 27: 27-28)

The Roman soldiers delay the procession to Golgotha. They decide to make Jesus king for the day. They perform their mock enthronement behind the walls of power. The crowd outside does not receive an invite. Yet the real protagonist of this drama is the God of judgment and mercy, for the soldiers' senseless actions help us see God's work of salvation.

Stripping him of his garments, the soldiers want to humiliate him. Yet Christ the king accepts the judgment of Adam. Dressing him in a scarlet robe, the soldiers emphasize his empty power. By wearing the color of blood, Christ the king accepts the world's blood. By surrounding their prisoner with the whole cohort, they attempt to intimidate him. In reality they anticipate when Christ will judge all the nations assembled before his throne. On his throne he will bless those who recognized him when he was naked and a prisoner. He will invite them to spend eternity with him. On his throne he will punish those who denied the dignity of the hungry and thirsty, the stranger or the naked, the ill or imprisoned as they did to him in that praetorium. He will send them to eternal punishment prepared for the devil.

Knowing that God was really in charge at this moment helps us learn that everything in the Gospels is recorded for our benefit, unlike most violent scenes produced by the media. The torment of Jesus was done to protect us, by insuring that we care for the least among us. Jesus opted to undergo this torment showing how he is serious about the final judgment. He came in mercy the first time he dwelt among us. He came to offer us life in abundance. This is why we love him instead of fear him. When he returns the second time, pray that we be ready for our judgment.

Merciful Father, your Son brought heaven to earth. Draw my heart into union with your Son so I may be an instrument of healing and communion.

The Light within Darkness

Father Michael Nolan

Weaving a crown out of thorns, [the soldiers] placed it on [Jesus'] head, and a reed in his right hand. And kneeling before him, they mocked him, saying, "Hail, King of the Jews!" They spat upon him and took the reed and kept striking him on the head. (Mt 27: 29-30)

The letters that Blessed Teresa of Calcutta wrote to her confessors and spiritual directors were published after her beatification. They paint a portrait of a mystic engaged in spiritual warfare. Those letters save her life from the biographers who reduce her to being a humanitarian. These documents contribute to her being recognized as a saint. Mother Teresa's writings describe a seeming contradiction in her soul. For after responding to God's call to serve the neediest, she soon felt refused by him. It had brought her into darkness.

Her struggle can help us understand how Jesus survived the torture of those soldiers. "Weaving a crown out of thorns, they placed it on his head, and a reed in his right hand. And kneeling before him, they mocked him, saying 'Hail, King of the Jews!'" Who isn't bothered by the viciousness that accompanied the soldiers' recreation? Who can explain the Father's abandonment of Jesus? Mother Teresa helps us. For in the time of her dark night, this nun came to learn that darkness and pain don't leave you when you serve God. The opposite comes true. The closer you come to those who live without faith in God, the more you come close to pain and rejection.

Mother Teresa stayed with the darkness by staying with those she served. She showed us that our salvation does not come by running in another direction, but rather by abandoning oneself to God, even if it is done in darkness. Jesus was tortured not because he was abandoned; he survived by already abandoning himself to his Father. Mother Teresa discovered this the more she said yes in her darkness. For after spending years in that darkness she discovered a deep joy – that Jesus can't go anymore through the agony – but that he wanted to go through the agony in her; in her experiences. More than ever she wished to surrender herself to Jesus. More than ever she was at his disposal.

Holy Father, even in the darkness your Son's light can find a way to enter. Help me not to despair in my struggles, but to learn to call upon your name more and more.

The Need to Know

Father Michael Nolan

And when [the soldiers] had mocked [Jesus], they stripped him of the cloak, dressed him in his own clothes, and led him off to crucify him. (Mt 27: 31)

The mockery directed at our Lord is not something the parish priest can ignore if he truly desires to offer people hope. There cannot be a resurrection without a person dying. Jesus' death was scandalous as it was preceded by cruelty and ruthlessness. He wasn't just convicted and executed. He first watched his friends betray or abandon him. His trial was fixed. He was scourged, spat upon, stripped naked, taunted and mocked before he even touched the cross. The priest needs to remember how our Lord died and share it with those he meets in his ministry. The sinner who denies the dignity of another person the way the soldiers tortured Jesus needs to know what is sinful. They need to feel guilty if they are to change. The victim of senseless violence or anyone whose human rights are denied needs to know that Jesus stood on the side of those who face intimidation and injustice.

When someone dies an especially difficult death, the family may be carrying in their minds the scandalous images of the body being ravaged. Before they hear that Jesus rose from the dead, that family needs to know what our Lord went though to get to Easter morning. The young woman who struggles to understand why the teachings of her Church don't agree with everything promoted by the rest of society needs to hear how Jesus did not bend or give in just to avoid the mockery. The young man needs to know that a Christian has to be ready to be mocked or punished when he stands up for the truth. Every Christian needs to recall every day the details of how our Lord died so as to understand the true meaning of forgiveness and mercy. For Jesus didn't just die and leave all the cruelties behind. First he asked the Father to show mercy on them. Then he returned to offer peace and spread that peace and mercy.

Heavenly Father, help me to embrace the sufferings placed upon me so I may have greater compassion for those around me.

Getting Ready for Duty

Father Michael Nolan

As [the soldiers] were going out, they met a Cyrenian named
Simon; this man they pressed into service to carry [Jesus'] cross.
(Mt 27: 32)

Jesus did not tell his disciples everything they needed to know on the first day. "Come after me, and I will make you fishers of men" (Mt 4: 19) was all he said to those two brothers who were fishing by the sea. They left everything and followed him. All he said to the man sitting at his desk collecting taxes was two words: "Follow me" (Mt 9: 9). Matthew got up from his desk and followed him.

Over time the teacher continued to show his disciples how to master the art of following. He taught them that following corresponded to their nature. He emphasized that following saves you, but only if you follow by carrying something heavy. Three things make the cross heavy. It is obligatory. It requires self-denial. The cross is encountered daily. "If anyone wishes to come after me, he must deny himself and take up his cross daily and follow me" (Lk 9: 23).

The followers of Jesus resisted these crucial lessons. We know this by how their grief overwhelmed them each time he warned of the cross that awaited him in Jerusalem. We know this from our own experience. We only have to ask ourselves whether denying ourselves and taking up our cross was on our agenda for today. The apostle Paul described the cross as a stumbling block. It was the same for those first disciples, and it is the same for us today.

But the final lesson confirms we can follow Jesus because no one can say the cross is too heavy. We can take up the cross, for it was handed to a guy without any warning, while we have been warned. Simon of Cyrene took up the cross that was forced upon him. He didn't get to choose one more to his liking. Simon was pressed into service to carry his cross. And the remarkable thing about this was he found the strength to do it.

Holy Father, your Son embraced the heavy cross so that we might
be brought to you. Strengthen us so that we might see the cross as
our salvation.

Overflowing Grace

Father Michael Nolan

And when [the soldiers] came to a place called Golgotha (which means Place of the Skull), they gave Jesus wine to drink mixed with gall. But when he had tasted it, he refused to drink. After they had crucified him, they divided his garments by casting lots; then they sat down and kept watch over him there. (Mt 27: 33-36)

The soldiers of Pilate escorted Jesus to his battle site. They weren't just following orders as they continued to torment him on the way. They mocked him. Inexplicable cruelty leads either to more cruelty or opens the way to mercy and compassion. For Jesus, it was the former. His trial lasted long after Pilate washed his hands. We might be tempted into focusing all our attention on the human cruelty of the Lord's passion. We shouldn't! Too much focus on evil can lead us to despair. For the place where the soldiers brought him helps us see that their mockery would fail. In the end their pointless malice and evil gestures would be overturned by God's desire to rescue man. Everything the soldiers did to Jesus helps us see that he was dying to set us free from the very evil lodged within those soldiers' hearts. For the place where the soldiers brought Jesus is Golgotha.

Golgotha means Place of the Skull. It was given this name because some believe Adam was buried there. He was the first to die because he disobeyed God. The rest of us have been dying ever since. Saint Paul wrote, "Where sin increased, grace overflowed all the more" (Rom 5: 20). Sin increased from the place where Adam ate the fruit of the forbidden tree. He then made garments by tying fig leaves together. Then he naïvely tried to hide from God. This earned him a place in the Place of the Skull.

At Golgotha, Jesus was offered something to drink. He tasted it but refused to drink. Then the soldiers tore his garments after stripping him naked. They nailed him to the tree thinking they would see him die. They didn't realize that he was really killing death. For the Lord's passion is not proclaimed to recount senseless cruelty, but rather the victory Christ accomplished by returning us to a place even better than that garden.

Father of wisdom, help me to recognize your abiding presence this day. Let this knowledge inspire me to draw others to your kingdom.

The King of Kings

Father Michael Nolan

And [the soldiers] placed over [Jesus'] head the written charge against him: This is Jesus, the King of the Jews. (Mt 27: 37)

When the Magi arrived in Jerusalem they asked King Herod, "Where is the newborn king of the Jews? We saw his star at its rising and have come to do him homage" (Mt 2: 2). This request for directions set in motion a death threat against Jesus that would last his whole life.

King Herod sent soldiers to kill the baby Jesus. His plan failed, though not before many innocents died instead of Jesus. Jesus and the family escaped before the massacre. After John the Baptist prepared the way for him, Jesus of Nazareth preached the kingdom of God. He announced to the people of Israel that the kingdom of God was in their midst. This question of kingship would lead him into danger soon after entering the city of Jerusalem as a king.

The formal charge that Pilate questioned him on was whether he had made himself a king. He refused to give an answer. For this he was sentenced to death and was nailed to a tree. In death, Jesus was denied royal treatment while mockingly labeled a Jewish king. That sign sought to justify the unjust condemnation. The final answer concerning his identity was not answered until after Jesus defeated his real enemy: sin, and death itself. This is why we call him Christ the King.

The question of kingship is a question for every Christian. For every Christian, male or female, was anointed priest, prophet, and king on the day of their baptism. The kingdom of Christ enters the soul. It remains there as long as we earnestly desire what Jesus taught us to say: "thy kingdom come." We say "thy kingdom come" so the devil will run. We pray "thy kingdom come" so that he who reigns in heaven may reign in us. We always ask for his kingdom to come because when this world comes to an end, we will need his kingdom to come to us.

Loving Father, your Son's presence among us made it possible for us to enter your kingdom. May I find some time for prayer so I may honor you for your gift.

What Did He Actually Say?

Father Michael Nolan

Two revolutionaries were crucified with [Jesus], one on his right and the other on his left. Those passing by reviled him, shaking their heads and saying, "You who would destroy the temple and rebuild it in three days, save yourself, if you are the Son of God, [and] come down from the cross!" (Mt 27: 38-40)

I began to know who God is by picking up a Bible and reading it. On entering the seminary, I was introduced to the world of commentaries. Most of these modern commentaries are written to facilitate the reading and interpretation of the ancient texts. Any interpretation made by the student needed the support of the commentaries. A few years later, the focus shifted back onto the original texts. I can still recall one of my professors saying, "I don't want to know what some expert said about the writing of a Church Father. I want to know what the Church Father actually wrote." I suspect the professor had a bad experience with modern interpretation. So did Jesus.

Jesus had said to his disciples after cleansing the temple, "Destroy this temple and in three days I will raise it up." He wasn't speaking as a terrorist, but some made him out to sound like one. His accusers inaccurately made these claims at his trial. Even after the trial had ended and Jesus was hanging on the cross, those passing by felt a need to repeat the false charges. "You who would destroy the temple and rebuild it in three days, save yourself…"

The Christian can learn something from Golgotha, for it isn't so far from us today. For those who passed by Jesus hanging on the cross represent the ideas shaped by the passing world. They approach but allow no time for contemplation. They repeat what has been said about Jesus over and over again. They shake their heads in frustration since he does not fulfill their expectations. The Christian still encounters this situation today. And it may never change. And there is probably nothing any of us can do about it, except to become like those disciples who "came to believe the scripture and the word Jesus had spoken" (Jn 2: 22), remembering his words with love and affection.

Father all-powerful, grant me the wisdom to discern between all that comes from you and anything that offends you.

Conditions for Believing

Father Michael Nolan

Likewise the chief priests with the scribes and elders mocked [Jesus] and said, "He saved others; he cannot save himself. So he is the king of Israel! Let him come down from the cross now, and we will believe in him. He trusted in God; let him deliver him now if he wants him. For he said, 'I am the Son of God.'"
(Mt 27: 41-43)

Jesus attracted followers throughout his travels. There was something attractive about him. Just the sight of him could give people faith. Those who followed him did it with promises or conditions. Yet this changed when people saw him hanging on the cross. People still came to see him. But on the cross, Jesus was not as attractive as before. On the cross he came off as a failure. They still said they would believe in him, but this time they set up some conditions. Let him come down from the cross now, and we will believe in him.

The coffee shop near my rectory is a great meeting place. It is an easy place to meet strangers and strike up conversations. It is not unusual to get into a discussion of religion often with Catholics who have left the Church. They see me sitting there dressed in clerical garb, and take advantage to ask a question. Many times people want to tell me why they left. More often they feel a need to list for me all that is wrong with the Church. The doctrines of the Blessed Trinity or the resurrection are usually not included on their lists. What tops their lists are the faults of the Christian people. They recount a couple of events in the two thousand years of the Church's history to show that she is tainted. The memory of a bad encounter really sticks with them. A few tell me they never learned the faith.

I enjoy listening and talking most of the time. I just know how to meet their conditions. For most of us share culpability for the Church's failings. Some assure me that they believe in Jesus but not his Church. Others just want the Church and her children to be held accountable. Some say they will return when the Church stops failing. I pray that on their return they don't find the Church empty.

Father of all that is good, your Son never failed or rejected your will. Forgive the sins of your sons and daughters so no one will be lost and all will be one.

354

The New Revolution

Father Michael Nolan

*The revolutionaries who were crucified with [Jesus]
also kept abusing him in the same way. (Mt 27: 44)*

One of the least attractive aspects of confession is recounting the same sins. It can be frustrating. Repeating the same sins can point to a lack of spiritual progress and growth. The same sins can make the sinner ask whether liberation is ever possible. Confessing the same sins can make one wonder whether they are boring. The tedious aspect of confessing the same sins can make one wonder whether going to confession is worth it. In the back of my head, there is also the fear that my confessor might think that I am too weak or not battling hard enough.

Even at his moment of death, Jesus had to deal with the same sins. He was crucified along with revolutionaries, but there seemed to be nothing revolutionary about them. Saint Matthew tells us the revolutionaries abused him. His Gospel records that they "kept abusing him in the same way." The Gospel writer wrote this to describe how these revolutionaries joined those who shouted at Jesus as they walked by. Foolishly they told Jesus to come off his cross as they themselves were hanging on their own. By joining with the crowd in abusing Jesus, these criminals showed that their revolution had failed. It fell like every other revolution that denies the truths of God. Their revolution may have even started with pure motives, but it ended up succumbing to the usual corruption. Their revolution was ending the same way all other false revolutions end – by abusing people.

On the cross, Jesus accepted his suffering. On that cross, the Lord refused to return evil for evil. On that cross, Jesus proposed by his holy silence a new revolution based on the cross. Instead of swords, Jesus used the cross for the revolution that still continues today to change human lives.

Blessed Father, you sent your Son to give us life. May this knowledge save me from ever losing hope.

For What?

Father Vincent Nagle, F.S.C.B.

From noon onward, darkness came over the whole land until
three in the afternoon. And about three o'clock Jesus cried out
in a loud voice, "Eli, Eli, lema sabachthani?" which means,
"My God, my God, why have you forsaken me?"
(Mt 27: 45-46)

Jesus' cry on the cross still shakes us. "*Lema sabachthani?*" It is usually translated as "Why have you forsaken me?" but its literal meaning from Aramaic is "*For what* have you abandoned me*." "For what?" This is the great question roaring forth from our Savior in his extreme suffering. "For what?" We demand an answer, for without one, we feel we might as well not have lived.

I understood this clearly on my grandmother's eightieth birthday. At the end of the party, my mother and I stayed behind to clean up the apartment, and then the three of us sat down to a cup of tea. "Well, Gram, how does it feel to be eighty?" I asked. She answered without smiling, "Yesterday I was eighteen." "Ah, it went by fast, did it?" I responded. Then she smartly smacked the table with her hand and repeated with emphasis, "Yesterday I was eighteen."

She who had led a very interesting and adventurous life, when looking back upon it, could not find *her* life in all those events. That is to say, she could not find *what* it was it had all been *for*. It seemed to her as if she had not done it at all, and that, truly, only the day before she had been just beginning at eighteen.

What I saw in her words was that our lives are not many things, but only one. And if we cannot discover *what* life is *for*, then it is as if it were for nothing. For my grandmother, as if it had not been at all. If my life can manage to express one true thing, then everything in my life, every sacrifice or trial, is worth it. If not, then no success can make up for it. Jesus our Savior came and in his last breaths cried out for us the question to which he himself is the answer.

By your grace, Father, do not let me live my life in vain. Let me
meet again your Son, and so discover the reason for my existence.

Not the Next Thing

Father Vincent Nagle, F.S.C.B.

Some of the bystanders who heard it said, "This one is calling for Elijah." Immediately one of them ran to get a sponge; he soaked it in wine, and putting it on a reed, gave it to him to drink. But the rest said, "Wait, let us see if Elijah comes to save him." But Jesus cried out again in a loud voice, and gave up his spirit.
(Mt 27: 47-50)

This bystander has made a tragic mistake, and missed an occasion of grace. Jesus' manner of suffering has been so unusual, and his cry to his Father is so unexpected that it awakes in him an excitement. "Surely," he thinks, "this must all mean something, it must all be leading up to something." His imagination is alive with possibilities: "Let us see if Elijah comes." He runs to offer Jesus wine, hoping to strengthen him and keep death off a little longer. He wants to see what is coming next, and he doesn't want Jesus to die before it happens. But there is no "next." Jesus cries out and gives up his spirit. And this moment of moments, this sacrificial victory of perfect freedom and loving obedience to our saving God, is missed by this man who is waiting for the "next" thing.

I am tempted to make the same mistake. Even after all these years I can fall into the trap of thinking that being a Christian is fundamentally a path, a getting from point A to point B, a journey to the "next" thing. And I miss the occasion of grace, the opportunity to be with Jesus in what he is doing at the moment, even if that moment looks like failure, darkness, sin, and death. I can become fixated on getting past this or that weakness, on helping someone to solve some problem, or discovering some new insight, that I do not look at him right in front of me and worship him here and now.

Christianity is not first of all about fulfilling an itinerary. It is about the present, not the "next" thing, no matter how distressing. It is keeping company with the Son of God even to the point of sharing in his cross. For he is the Alpha and the Omega and so progress doesn't mean getting to the next thing, but staying with him, the only thing.

Father, I get so caught up in getting ahead that I forget to look for your Son — now. Don't let me miss this present moment, redeemed by Jesus, your Son our Savior.

The Blood and the Veil

Father Vincent Nagle, F.S.C.B.

And behold, the veil of the sanctuary was torn in two from top to bottom. The earth quaked, rocks were split, tombs were opened, and the bodies of many saints who had fallen asleep were raised.
(Mt 27: 51-52)

There can come a moment – and in our hearts we are secretly praying for it – when an event takes place after which nothing for us can ever be the same again. At the same time we fear facing something so powerful and dramatic coming upon us. When it does come, it is something that we cannot but be grateful for.

A girl I know told me of such an event. She was one of two children of a poor single mother living in an economically and socially devastated industrial town of New England. Few of the girls she knew finished high school and most got pregnant early and without a prospect of marriage. She was in a confirmation class, and did not like it or the priest teaching it. When he invited a few students to New York City for a day, she agreed to go, but was regretting it. To her surprise they passed a pleasant enough day. On the way home they were among the first to come upon an overturned car on the freeway. It was bad. There were two victims and blood everywhere. The priest jumped out of the car and ran to do what he could. Eventually he came back with blood on him, and had the children pray for the victims.

She was stunned. She had not respected this man at all, but he had not been afraid. Something new opened up before her. Her world, she saw, was dominated by fear, and this was a free man. How? It seemed impossible. At that moment it was like the veil of her life was rent in two, and many things that were always dead to her suddenly, impossibly, came alive, like "the bodies of many saints." From that moment on the limits of her life began to give way to the freedom of Christ.

The perfect obedience of Jesus' death on the cross is that event for all the world.

Don't leave us here in fear and darkness, Father! Free us and bring us to life through the work of your Son, our Redeemer.

Calling Out the Dead

Father Vincent Nagle, F.S.C.B.

And coming forth from their tombs after [Jesus'] resurrection,
they entered the holy city and appeared to many.
(Mt 27: 53)

A Jewish friend asked me for advice on what to say to a person whose only brother had died. Her friend – a young woman whom we'll call Cheryl – could not get past it. She was riddled by guilt. He had been sick for a while, and she, wanting to live her own life, had put distance between them and avoided having to care for him. One weekend he was alone and asked her to stay with him. She had refused. When she came back home at the end of the weekend, he had died alone. She blamed herself.

Her friends tried to convince her that she had nothing to feel guilty about, and even if she did, he was going to die in any case. They would tell her that she could not have made any difference. They urged her to move on. But for her this was not possible. Life for her had become *impossible*.

I told my friend to speak to Cheryl – a secular Jew – this way: "If you say you are guilty, then I say it, too. You are guilty. Now what? Is your word the final word? Is there another word to be heard on this, more knowing and powerful than yours, full of mercy, capable of reconciling what our sins have put asunder, even beyond the grave? If you think there might be, then go to where you see people who have heard that word of mercy. Be with them and dedicate yourself to the works of mercy they perform for others. In sharing that mercy with others, you might find it for yourself."

The fact is that loss, guilt, failure, violence, and sin are real. There is no getting past them. We are in tombs. We are waiting for a word, an event to bring us out of these tombs through a merciful, reconciling act. May those liberated from their tombs appear to us, giving us hope!

Through sin and guilt life itself can be impossible, Father. Free us, open our graves, through your Son who offered himself as a victim for us.

Assent

Father Vincent Nagle, F.S.C.B.

The centurion and the men with him who were keeping watch over Jesus feared greatly when they saw the earthquake and all that was happening, and they said, "Truly, this was the Son of God!" (Mt 27: 54)

The centurion said, "Truly, this was the Son of God." What did this Roman soldier know about the one, true God, and who might or might not be his Son? Almost certainly, he knew very little about such things. But he did know that this is what people were saying about Jesus, what the Sanhedrin had accused him of laying claim to, that he was "the Messiah, the Son of God" (Mt 26: 63). After having then watched how this man suffered and how he died, the centurion could not find in himself any explanation of what he had witnessed other than what this man himself claimed.

The first time that I acknowledged the power and the holiness of this man Jesus was just such a situation. I was working at a survival camp run by a priest. I was amazed to see how, by sincerely leading my campers to follow the program of the camp, I could notice them change. Arriving full of undirected energy and selfishness, lacking curiousity about each other or what was around them, I observed them over time become cooperative, attentive to one another, obedient, and even pious. I could not explain it. Not a chance that it was me changing them. So I asked the priest, "What is it that is bringing about this change?" He answered, "I guess it must be Jesus Christ." I assented completely, because nothing else could answer. I have never stopped assenting.

The Roman soldier said to himself, "No one has ever suffered and died as this man, with such love and forgiveness. Nothing in me can name what I have witnessed. I will hear what this man says for himself." He was no theologian, but he knew that he either believed this man, or he could no longer believe himself. And he confessed, "This man truly was the Son of God."

Father, your Spirit at work has opened me up to the sacred name of your Son. May that same Spirit allow me always to proclaim him as the Son of God!

Standing with the Women

Father Vincent Nagle, F.S.C.B.

There were many women there, looking on from a distance, who had followed Jesus from Galilee, ministering to him. Among them were Mary Magdalene and Mary the mother of James and Joseph, and the mother of the sons of Zebedee.

(Mt 27: 55-56)

A cousin of mine is a complete materialist and is always trying to point out how what we do is from material drives and instincts. "Life is not about love," he will insist, "but the need to procreate and feel ourselves protected and safe." Besides wondering what his children make of all of this, I have often had to admit that there is a lot of truth in what he is saying. This kind of challenge has made me more than once examine my relationship with God, my discipleship with Christ, my membership in the Church. It has made me ask the questions, "For what do I love God?" and, "Do I actually love him? Or do I love only what it is that he can do for me?"

The presence of those women at the crucifixion of Jesus questions me the same way. There he was, to every observation powerless and, as the bystanders pointed out, not even able to save himself (Mt 27: 42). What could they expect from him anymore? Nothing. What use was he to them now? None. And yet there they were. Most of their sons and other men folk had fled. But there they were. They loved him. Do I love him like that? Do I truly love this Jesus who has filled my life with grace, or is it the graces that I love? Do I love the Lord, or just what I expect him to do for me?

The question brings me to the Blessed Mother, who stood with those women (Jn 19: 25). In her I learn to love her Son not for what he has done, does, and may do for me. With her I learn to love him as she does. She loves him because he is beautiful even in this disfigurement, and in his person itself. Before and without doing anything, he is all her delight. I want to stand with these women for ever.

Father, you know that by myself I am weak and without courage. Do not leave me alone, but keep me in the company of your saints, who glorify your name in love of your Son.

Disciples in the Shadows

Father Vincent Nagle, F.S.C.B.

When it was evening, there came a rich man from Arimathea named Joseph, who was himself a disciple of Jesus.
(Mt 27: 57)

Who is this Joseph of Arimathea? He suddenly pops up, and not in the expected place. How could someone from the Sanhedrin (Lk 23: 50) be a disciple of the Lord? Weren't they the ones that schemed to put him to death? The disciples of Jesus are not always who or where we expect them to be. We rightly have images of people who truly do their best, pray and sacrifice in order to lead good lives, obey the Church, live in chaste fidelity and make real acts of charity toward their neighbors. These are good images, reinforced, thanks be to God, by many wonderful examples.

But the hearts that belong to him sometimes are found back in the shadows where they are unnoticed and unlooked for. I think of Norman, raised in a brutal environment, who started to lash out in violence at a young age, and grew up in reformatories. I met him when he was living on the streets, committing small crimes, and separated from his children and their mother whom he loved with all his heart. I remember seeing the way store owners and police officers would look at him and speak to him as if he were an animal. And indeed sometimes he behaved like one. I recall how little patience I would have for him. Yet, I can also remember when we would pray together how he would cry to Jesus for salvation from the bottom of his soul with a plea so full of agony it would cut through me. Over the years I saw the great many small sacrifices he made to turn from that life to Jesus, and how many times he was humiliated by failure. Norman was a disciple in the shadows, a flawed warrior in the trenches.

Joseph of Arimathea reminds us that those who belong to Christ do not always fit the mold. They are often lost sheep looking for their shepherd.

Oh, Father, let me always be ready to name as "brother" all who cry to your Son for salvation. Do not let me be scandalized by their need for our beloved Redeemer.

It's Not Over

Father Vincent Nagle, F.S.C.B.

[Joseph of Arimathea] went to Pilate and asked for the body
of Jesus; then Pilate ordered it to be handed over.
(Mt 27: 58)

Joseph of Arimathea was a rich and powerful man, and a member of the Sanhedrin (Mk 15: 43). Though he was a disciple of Christ who had not consented to the deed (Lk 23: 51), still it must be asked what he had done to stop it. When we see him come on the scene, it is too late, and there is nothing more to be done than put the body in a tomb.

This fatal tardiness on Joseph's part recalls to me a girl I knew when I was a college chaplain. She was not a top student, but a friendly, sincere girl and one of the few active Catholics on campus. She had trouble walking because of a handicap. One day someone told me that she was sick and that I should visit her. I did not do so right away, though I cannot remember what the reason was, or even if I had one. A few days later I knocked at the door and could see that something was not right. She had died that morning and they had just carried the body away. I did not know anyone there, and they did not seem interested in my presence. I left, aghast at the outcome of my procrastination. At her funeral, I offered myself as her companion of prayer on her journey.

I had not acted in time and now she had passed on without a visit from her priest. Sometimes we fail to act, as the Arimathean. And yet, with Christ, the story has not ended, though that final curtain of death has fallen. Any hope of making a difference seems to have gone, but still the one who conquered death holds all in his hands. It is not over. Joseph is for me the patron of those who did not act until too late. Today, it is the empty tomb he provided that millions of pilgrims come to visit.

Father, you have given us our tasks, and at times we turn away and fail. Do not let this put an end to your victory. Let our penance serve the victory of Christ in the world.

Keeping Vigil

Father Vincent Nagle, F.S.C.B.

Taking the body, Joseph wrapped it [in] clean linen and laid it in his new tomb that he had hewn in the rock. Then he rolled a huge stone across the entrance to the tomb and departed. But Mary Magdalene and the other Mary remained sitting there, facing the tomb. (Mt 27: 59-61)

That man is dead and buried. And they do not depart, these women who loved him. Their work is done, having prepared his body, but they sit staring at the place that holds him. They are waiting, but for what? Something in them says: "It can't be over. I know that his dead body is cold in that hole, but the life that I saw in him, the new life that I received from him, I know that this cannot be the end of it. I remember the truth of that exceptional friendship, the power of his word and deed. I am overflowing with the memory that he died as no one dies. And all of this says to me something I cannot explain, except that it cannot end here. It is still true." And the very presence of each other confirms them in that memory, that certainty. They sit watching.

He who has loved knows that love makes a promise of "for ever." And we believe it because it corresponds to something inside. When a loved one passes, it does not seem real. Still, we know that the people who surround us, though their promises be true, still they are not the ones who can fulfill those promises. But this man in the tomb, he was different. He was the promise keeper! So, in the dark, together, they wait.

In our own lives, when faced not only with death but with so many scandals in the Church, failures in our communities and families, and sometimes confusion even from our pastors, it can seem as if that magnificently alive presence is dead and silenced. But we are like the women. We know the truth of what we have seen and lived, and the presence of the others with us is a living memory. And we, aware that even our failures can serve your plan, sit with these women, facing the tomb, praying and waiting.

Father, let us live in the memory of your Son's loving presence, and his victory in our lives. Do not let our hearts stop looking for him, even in the darkness.

Answering the Violence of Fear

Father Vincent Nagle, F.S.C.B.

The next day, the one following the day of preparation, the chief priests and the Pharisees gathered before Pilate and said, "Sir, we remember that this impostor while still alive said, 'After three days I will be raised up.' Give orders, then, that the grave be secured until the third day, lest his disciples come and steal him and say to the people, 'He has been raised from the dead.' This last imposture would be worse than the first." (Mt 27: 62-64)

How much fear we see in the Pharisees. They willingly appeal to the raw power of a foreign military machine to secure them against these few men and women, Christians. The same fear that makes them request a military guard from Pilate is a sign that they have, in their hearts, understood how exceptional this man Jesus is. And this understanding makes them afraid, since something so exceptional threatens to change everything.

Most of my brothers and sisters are not Christians. I have often been amazed at the extent to which some of them fear Christianity. Once a sister of mine, a very tender hearted woman, burst into tears just thinking that I believed in the immortal soul and prayed to Jesus. How far that put me outside of her world! And how it seemed to threaten it! A brother of mine once remarked angrily at how he hated it when anyone spoke of good works done by Christians. It lent credence to what must be opposed and stopped.

In the end, the only answer to fear is love. Once, shortly after I was ordained, the atheist son of that same sister came to stay with me in Italy. He, a philosophy major at Princeton, accepted the invitation to stay in our seminary and study philosophy in Rome. I called my sister to tell her. She answered, "Good. When you went into the seminary, I thought I had lost a brother, but you love me more now than then. I hope the same for my son." She still fears Christianity, but she no longer fears me, as once she certainly did.

May the power of the resurrection of Christ free us to die in love for those who fear and hate us because of our Lord! May our sacrifice reconcile them to the exceptional nature of that man Jesus, and make them ask for him indeed to change everything.

Father, the presence of your Son threatens to change everything. Let it, for we need nothing less.

Unforeseeable Events

Father Vincent Nagle, F.S.C.B.

*Pilate said to [the chief priests and the Pharisees], "The guard is
yours; go secure it as best you can." So they went and secured
the tomb by fixing a seal to the stone and setting the guard.*
(Mt 27: 65-66)

The power of Rome was the dominant reality of its time. When
the local Jewish authority, the Sanhedrin, won Roman
military backing, this was a very strong move. This was to
insure that the tomb occupied by the dead body of Jesus remain
closed. And yet despite all of this power an event occurred that,
in the end, was unforeseen and therefore uncontrollable. That same
event continues to occur and, like what happened at the tomb,
cannot be secured against.

I know a man here in Israel who was born into a religious
Jewish family in South Africa, immigrated to Israel as a young man,
and then later went to the United States to study. He came back
years later as a Catholic priest and is the vicar for Hebrew-speak-
ing Catholics now. I know a Christian Palestinian who, like so many
others, left to study engineering in Europe, and there married a
European girl. But unlike so many others, they both had a strong
conversion experience, and despite all the obstacles and the poverty
they have had to subject their children to in order to resettle in this
land, they are here and are living a witness to Jesus in the land of
his earthly ministry.

The power can only defend itself against the foreseeable. The
event of the victory of God in Jesus Christ is unforeseeable. Some
powerful social and educational systems seek to "set a seal" against
this event, and much of the mass media deny it, like the power that
first spread the story of the resurrection being faked (Mt 28: 15).
But who can "secure" the world against something that strikes the
heart without warning, and turns people from their fear of the
power to belonging to the love of God in Christ? God's grace is not
the result of an historical process, but the free act of love that our
hearts are waiting for.

*Father, I feel crushed by the powers that oppose the good and deny
the truth. Let me have hope through the unforeseeable grace of your
Son's victory.*

The Eighth Day

Father Romanus Cessario, O.P.

After the sabbath, as the first day of the week was dawning,
Mary Magdalene and the other Mary came to see the tomb.
(Mt 28: 1)

The Catechism explains the significance of the way that Saint Matthew counts the days of the week: "Because it is the 'first day,' the day of Christ's Resurrection recalls the first creation. Because it is the 'eighth day' following the sabbath (cf. Mk 16: 1; Mt 28: 1), it symbolizes the new creation ushered in by Christ's Resurrection. For Christians it has become the first of all days, the first of all feasts, the Lord's Day… Sunday" (CCC 2174). Mary Magdalene and the other Mary, perhaps a relative of Jesus, are the first to observe the Christian Sunday. Of course they still must make this discovery. "The first day of the week was dawning." We who have been given the precious gift of the Christian Sunday realize that we cannot live without this weekly celebration.

No wonder an early bishop of the Church felt compelled to answer the objection that he, one can suppose, had heard from some of his fourth-century parishioners: "You cannot pray at home as at church, where there is a great multitude, where exclamations are cried out to God as from one great heart, and where there is something more: the union of minds, the accord of souls, the bond of charity, the prayers of the priests." Saint John Chrysostom pronounces a warning that applies to Catholics of the twenty-first century. The resurrection of Christ commits us to the celebration of the Lord's Day on Sunday. There is no replacement for going to church on Sunday. There is no substitute for the celebration that occurs within the context of the Eucharist, the Sunday Mass. Moral obligation, however, falls short of explaining why we should hasten to Sunday Mass. Rather the holy women of Saint Matthew's Gospel, the Marys, provide the best reason. Love. Love prompted them to come early in the morning of the first day of the week to anoint Jesus' body. And Love revealed himself to them.

Loving Father, the resurrection of your Son brings joy to the whole world. Grant me the grace to remain steadfast in observing Sunday, the Day of the Resurrection, and thereby merit to obtain the reward of everlasting life that it promises.

A Vision of Angels

Father Romanus Cessario, O.P.

*And behold, there was a great earthquake; for an angel of the
Lord descended from heaven, approached, rolled back the stone,
and sat upon it. His appearance was like lightning and
his clothing was white as snow. (Mt 28: 2-3)*

In order to appreciate the appearance of angels in the New
Testament, one must recall that they come as messengers from
God. Because these spirits speak only what God commands
them to say, the testimony of the angels cannot be refuted. Were
the angels not to be trusted, we would find ourselves in a terrible
dilemma. Think of all the messages that would elicit our puzzle-
ment if not our skepticism. An angel delivers the most important
of all messages at the Annunciation. "The child to be born will
be called holy, the Son of God" (Lk 1: 35). The angels then herald
the birth of the Savior. "Glory to God in the highest" (Lk 2: 14).
The angels "rolled back the stone" of the empty tomb. The angels
confirm the Ascension. "This Jesus who has been taken up from
you into heaven will return in the same way you have seen him
going into heaven" (Acts 1: 11). Angels minister to Christ during
his temptations. If angels are not to be trusted, then all is placed in
jeopardy. All are bereft. Because God sends them, we trust the holy
angels.

They, however, are not the only spiritual creatures to appear in
Saint Matthew's Gospel. Demonic spirits also emerge (see Mt 12:
22-32). These unclean and evil spirits pursue objectives other than
drawing the human race close to the Savior of the world. They
rather seek the ruin and the destruction of our souls. Jesus deals
directly and effectively with these malicious spirits. He also warns
us about their tactics and wiliness (see Mt 12: 43-45). It is comforting to observe that whatever menace the bad angels pose to Christian life, they are reduced to slithering around the universe, capable
only of launching indirect attacks. By contrast, the angel of the
resurrection appears "like lightning" dressed in clothing "white as
snow." The good angels receive their power from God. Only good
things follow in their suite.

*Gracious Father, you send your holy angels to announce Christ's
saving mission and to guard our steps. Draw us into the company
of the angels and the saints so that we may praise for ever the
splendor of your infinite goodness.*

Faith Is a Gift

Father Romanus Cessario, O.P.

The guards were shaken with fear of [the angel]
and became like dead men. (Mt 28: 4)

The modern world exhibits an allergic reaction to the thought of dependence, even to dependence on God. Dependence, they say, characterizes infants and slaves. At the same time, the creature cannot escape being dependent on the Creator. This dependency is inscribed in the order of created reality, the order of being, the order of the way things are. Self-starters enjoy no entrance to the Christian Gospels. No starting point for the self-sufficient. Such as these exclude themselves by their imaginary view of the origin of things. Philosophical arguments conclude to a Creator. However, only the gift of divine faith disposes us to accept the testimony of the good angels. Only divine faith enables us to believe in the resurrection. This does not mean that the resurrection is a religious invention that cunning manipulators foist on credulous believers. The resurrection is an historical event the evidence for which, such as the empty tomb, remains indirect. The guards placed at Christ's tomb even testify to the resurrection. They "became like dead men." The resurrection remains a transcendent mystery. No human being can penetrate its innermost essence. Christian faith in the resurrection recognizes in this transcendent mystery the definitive proof of Christ's divinity and confirmation of the truthfulness of what the Savior did and taught. So we should be grateful to the anonymous guards assigned to prevent the apostles from stealing Christ's body. They were ordinary men routinely fulfilling their assigned duties. Their petrifying fright at the vision of an angel stands in stark contrast with the joyful expectation that would soon fill the hearts of those who, moved by love, hastened to the tomb.

Exalted Father, the resurrection of your Son announces the bright promise of immortality. Keep us faithful to the new life that this mystery introduces into the world, and bring us one day to eternal glory.

The Paschal Proclamation

Father Romanus Cessario, O.P.

*Then the angel said to the women in reply, "Do not be afraid!
I know that you are seeking Jesus the crucified. He is not here,
for he has been raised just as he said. Come and see the place
where he lay." (Mt 28: 5-6)*

At the Easter Vigil that the Church celebrates each year, the
priest sings at the start of the liturgical service, "O happy
fault, O necessary sin of Adam, which gained for us so great
a Redeemer!" No wonder the angel first tells the women who have
come to the tomb, "Do not be afraid." What is better, the angel
addresses these words of comfort to the whole human race. In order
to benefit from the promises of new life that Christ's resurrection
introduces into the world, the Christian commits himself to a life-
long search for Jesus the crucified. As long as one remains on this
earth, Christian living requires an embrace of the passion and death
of the Redeemer.

Two mysteries create one saving action. We call it the paschal
mystery. Calvary and the Empty Tomb stand side by side. Sometimes Christians are wrongly led to imagine that the Christian life
moves from one resurrection moment to another. To attempt to
follow this pattern leads to frustration. Adam's sin retains its necessity until the end of the world. When we forget about "seeking Jesus
the crucified," we find ourselves living a one-sided Christianity. This
one-sidedness can take the form of naturalism. Since the resurrection has enlightened the world, one imagines that the Christian life
requires a continual exertion of our natural energies in order to
measure up to a high moral vision of human life. The other and
more popular alternative is false optimism. We think that the
resurrection introduces a world where human sufferings no longer
figure in Christian living. No sin. No sorrow. No penance. The angel
announces that neither alternative embodies the full meaning of
the resurrection. All still are required to seek the crucified One.

*Gracious God, the resurrection of your Son relieves the world of its
fear. Grant me the grace to remain close to the crucified Savior so
that by the merits of his passion and death, I may come to the glory
of his resurrection.*

The Apostle to the Apostles

Father Romanus Cessario, O.P.

"Then go quickly and tell his disciples, 'He has been raised from the dead, and he is going before you to Galilee; there you will see him.' Behold, I have told you." (Mt 28: 7)

The great teachers of the Church appreciate the special place that Mary Magdalene holds in Catholic devotion. Based on their reading of Saint Matthew's Gospel, they would refer to Mary Magdalene as the Apostle to the Apostles. The Church of course rests on the authority and witness of the apostles themselves. At the same time, God chooses Mary Magdalene, the one forgiven much since she loved much, to announce the resurrection to Christ's apostles. She alerts them to expect the first appearance of the risen Christ. The full realization of what had taken place on Easter Sunday only slowly dawned on Christ's closest disciples. We know that even when the apostles approached the Ascension, "they doubted" (Mt 28: 17).

The angel's instructions to Mary Magdalene establish the pedagogy of the resurrection. We discover how God leads us to make the resurrection the sure basis for daily living. Many of us, however, vacillate between the exuberant enthusiasm of Mary Magdalene and the dubious hesitations of the apostles. Given this occurrence, hope inevitably characterizes our journey toward God. The figure of the Magdalene hastening toward the apostolic band sustains our Catholic hoping. Especially do sinners require the witness of this holy woman so venerated within the Catholic tradition. In fact, since only the Mother of Christ is without sin, the example of Mary Magdalene applies to all believers. She received from the angel the message that Christ is risen. Imagine what strong sentiment filled the Magdalene as she rushed toward the apostles. Her reaction urges us to examine our own enthusiasm for the benefits Christ's resurrection ushers into the world. Each should accept Mary Magdalene as an apostle and friend. Make her the companion of your progress toward the full possession of faith and hope and charity.

Omnipotent God, the resurrection of your Son removes all fear from the world and ushers in a new era of joyful expectation. Keep me close to those who witness to this grace and to those who encourage me to enter fully into its joy.

Mixed Emotions

Father Romanus Cessario, O.P.

Then [the women] went away quickly from the tomb, fearful yet overjoyed, and ran to announce this to his disciples.
(Mt 28: 8)

The holy women do what the angel commands. They run to announce Christ's resurrection to his apostles. This movement toward the apostles, especially toward Saint Peter, establishes a prototype for the constitution of the Church. The witnesses are still human. Saint Matthew likes to remark on their mixed emotions. The apostles worshiped Christ but still doubted. The holy women are fearful and at the same time overjoyed. The sentiments of the holy women who run away bearing the good news of Christ's resurrection should encourage us.

As we progress in the life of faith, we should expect these same sentiments to develop in us. In itself, fear is a holy disposition. Only when fear constrains our spiritual development, for example, when we experience moments of servility – the stultifying kind of fear that restrains us from sinning only because we fear punishment – does the emotion of fear begin to threaten our spiritual welfare. Filial fear, on the other hand, characterizes those persons whose fear includes offending the heavenly Father whom they love. This fear is liberating. Such holy fear also can coexist with joyfulness. Although we usually do not speak this way, we can find ourselves simultaneously overjoyed and fearful. The saints sometimes allude to these states in themselves. They confront something difficult, perhaps a temptation, and a holy fear wells up inside them, for they are resolved to remain close to the One whom they love. Simultaneously, the saints experience joy, even a surpassing joy, inasmuch as they perceive almost immediately that the difficult thing causing them to fear affords also an occasion to turn to Jesus and Mary. Only the resurrection of the Son of God creates this kind of possibility.

Benign Father, instill in me the holy fear that will keep me close to you. Through the resurrection of your beloved Son, grant me the grace to remain joyful whatever adverse circumstances may befall me and one day enter your eternal joy.

From Glory to Glory

Father Romanus Cessario, O.P.

And behold, Jesus met [the women] on their way and greeted them. They approached, embraced his feet, and did him homage.
(Mt 28: 9)

The risen Christ receives a glorified not a resuscitated body. The properties of this glorious body afford the risen Savior great liberty of movement. He is no longer bound by the limitations of space and time. "For this reason," says the Catechism, "the risen Jesus enjoys the sovereign freedom of appearing as he wishes: in the guise of a gardener or in other forms familiar to his disciples, precisely to awaken their faith (cf. Mk 16: 12; Jn 20: 14-16; 21: 4, 7)" (CCC 645). The appearances of the risen Jesus make known the truth of the resurrection. They also manifest the glory of Christ risen from the dead. The truth of the resurrection requires that Jesus exhibit signs of continuity with his earthly state. The actions of the women suggest continuity. They approached him. They embraced his feet. They did him homage. The holy women would never have acted in this way toward someone whom they did not recognize. Saint Matthew in this single verse makes it clear that the risen One is the same as the crucified One.

Today's Christians ordinarily do not enjoy this "familiar" encounter with the risen Lord. We rather meet Christ in faith and in the sacraments of faith. These sacramental encounters compare with that of the women on the road to Galilee. Only the mode of the meeting is different. The holy women beheld a recognizable vision of the risen Christ. We behold the truth of the risen Christ. Christians of all ages enjoy something in common with the women whom Jesus met on the road to Galilee. All must face the mystery of discontinuity. All must live by hope for the new life that flows from the resurrection. No one should cling to what is visible. "For who hopes for what one sees?" (Rom 8: 24). The theological virtue of hope provides a springboard for the Christian life. We find ourselves impelled toward the state that gives meaning to a glorified body.

Mighty God, the glory of the risen Lord sustains those who embrace the way of faith, hope, and charity. May the resurrection obtain for us the merits to behold for ever the vision of your glory.

Messengers to the World

Father Romanus Cessario, O.P.

Then Jesus said to [the women], "Do not be afraid. Go tell my brothers to go to Galilee, and there they will see me."
(Mt 28: 10)

Inclusiveness and egalitarianism so much characterize our everyday values that the Christian believer finds it difficult to appreciate that God loves those whom he chooses. He does, however. As Saint Paul testifies, God chose us in Christ, "before the foundation of the world" (Eph 1: 4). Who can read this account of the resurrection appearance and not come away with the impression that only those chosen to receive the message of Christ's resurrection in fact receive it? The rendezvous in Galilee includes those men whom God has chosen to learn about the greatest "event" in the history of the world. What are we to conclude? God entertains partialities? God plays favorites? God excludes some from his benevolence? None of these replies becomes the God of infinite love and goodness whom Jesus has revealed. So there must be another divine factor at work.

Saint Thomas Aquinas suggests that Christ makes known his resurrection to a chosen few so that these same "brothers" would later become witnesses to others. In other words, from the very start, the Church exhibits the mystery of sanctified mediation that continues to this day in her preaching and sacraments. Salvation remains a free gift of God. No one enjoys a right to anything. No one can claim the right to preach authoritatively the Good News. No one can assert a right to salvation. No one can merit for himself the first grace of baptism. All is grace, as the Little Flower was fond of repeating. God teaches this gratuity by ordaining that all divine graces proceed in an orderly pattern from the center. Christ's apostles visibly occupy this center. From this same center flows a strong movement of grace that we call evangelization. This work falls on the shoulders of all those who embrace personally the merciful and forgiving love of the crucified and risen Savior. As Mary Magdalene did.

Dearest Father, make us joyful in the resurrection of your Son. May the grace that we have received spring up in our souls as a permanent source of energy and devotion to make your holy name known and loved.

Sleeping Witnesses

Father Romanus Cessario, O.P.

*While [the women] were going, some of the guard went into
the city and told the chief priests all that had happened. They
assembled with the elders and took counsel; then they gave a
large sum of money to the soldiers, telling them, "You are to say,
'His disciples came by night and stole him while we were asleep.'
And if this gets to the ears of the governor, we will satisfy [him]
and keep you out of trouble." (Mt 28: 11-14)*

I f *cinema verité* were available to Saint Matthew, then surely one
of his frames would include this episode in the life of the religious authorities of Jerusalem. The holy women whom Jesus
reassures about his resurrection are scurrying off with the luminosity that being overjoyed can create in people. At the same time,
the darkness of mendacity envelops the everyday guards set to watch
over the tomb of Jesus. Something of tragicomedy surrounds this
scene. One wonders what exactly the guards did tell the chief priests
and the elders. No matter. The proposed fix-it has evoked from
Christian apologists the obvious rebuttal: You bring forth sleeping
witnesses! Then there is the bribe to ensure that the guards repeat
the alibi with a straight face. All of this surely reflects the pathos
that Saint Matthew saw developing among those who did not welcome the news that Jesus is the Messiah.

It would be wrong to reflect on this turn of events, and to mutter smugly, "O God, I thank you that I am not like the rest of humanity – greedy, dishonest…" (Lk 18: 11). Rather Christians should
reflect on the gratuity of the gift of faith. What places us among
those who believe in the resurrection of Jesus? Nothing that we have
done on our own. Nothing that we have merited. Only the divine
goodness accounts for our election. When we ponder the utter gratuity of our call and election, then we find ourselves moved to
express gratitude to God for all that we have received. Gratitude
exhibits a specifically Christian character when this virtue moves
us to pray that the Good News of the resurrection reach the ends
of the world. Apathy about the spread of the Gospel or, what is
worse, calculated efforts to thwart the spread of the Gospel work
not only against the good of a religious tradition. These sins also
oppose authentic human development.

*Heavenly Father, grant me a special love for the truth of your
Gospel. Make me enthusiastic to evangelize the whole world in
a way proportionate to my vocation in life. May all that I do
proclaim the resurrection of your Son.*

Dirty Money

Father Romanus Cessario, O.P.

The soldiers took the money and did as they were instructed.
And this story has circulated among the Jews to the present
[day]. (Mt 28: 15)

The soldiers did what soldiers do. Did not John the Baptist warn men of this stripe that they should not look for dishonest ways to supplement their income? "Soldiers also asked him, 'And what is it that we should do?' He told them, 'Do not practice extortion,... and be satisfied with your wages'" (Lk 3: 14). Nonetheless these soldiers took the money and perpetuated a lie. It would be interesting to speculate what would have happened had these soldiers believed the resurrection. And perhaps eventually they did. Saint Matthew resists the temptation to speculate. Instead he notes that the false story continued to circulate.

In the Letter to the Romans, Saint Paul observes that divine predestination unfolds in human history. We become the privileged beneficiaries of divine revelation because God has chosen us. We are "predestined to be conformed to the image of his Son, so that he might be the firstborn among many brothers" (Rom 8: 29). Nothing thwarts the divine plan. Surely not such a lame explanation as the one the soldiers accepted a bribe to propagate. "For the gifts and the call of God," says Saint Paul, "are irrevocable" (Rom 11: 29). On the other hand, falsehoods do not build up the loving communion of persons that God has planned for the human race. One religion's story is not as good as another's. Religious relativism poses a significant threat to the well-being of the human community. Religious truth governs the highest aspirations of the human spirit. When one does not believe that Jesus rose from the dead, something else governs one's outlook on life. We have become accustomed to think about religious liberty as a good thing. At the same time, the freedom to practice the religion of one's choice remains a transitional feature of human life. In the end, there is only one story about the resurrection of Jesus. The true one.

Loving God, you are the source of all truth. Make me a lover of the truth so that my whole life will find its direction and purpose in the joyful resurrection of your Son, our Lord Jesus Christ.

One Is Missing

Father Romanus Cessario, O.P.

*The eleven disciples went to Galilee, to the mountain to which
Jesus had ordered them. When they saw him, they worshiped,
but they doubted. (Mt 28: 16-17)*

Eleven go out to the mountain of the Ascension. One is
missing. Who is he? Judas. By all accounts, Judas was dead
by the time that the good news of Jesus' resurrection had
begun to galvanize the apostles to go out and meet him. Saint
Matthew suggests that Judas met his fate even before Christ's death.
"Then Judas, his betrayer, seeing that Jesus had been condemned…
went off and hanged himself" (Mt 27: 3, 5). Poor Judas. Think about
the drama of his self-condemnation. Psychological explanations
do not provide much help. Who knows what thoughts ran through
this disciple's mind? Theological analysis is required.

Consider an illustrative comparison between Judas and Peter.
Both men were followers of Jesus; both men listened to his
teaching; both men received the same formation in discipleship.
And both men betrayed Jesus. Peter, we know, deeply regretted his
cowardice, but somewhere along the line he had learned the basic
lesson of Christ's teaching: forgiveness. One can only conclude that
Judas had missed this important lesson. Peter affords a model for
the penitent Christian, who no matter what he has done turns to
the Lord. To whom else would one go? Judas sadly illustrates the
lesson that every believer mightily must avoid: the great error that
there is one sin that Christ will not forgive.

It takes courage to admit wrongdoing. On the other hand, who
can read the Gospel of Matthew and not come away with the
impression that Christ makes it a point to show his sympathy for
sinners? For Saint Matthew, the lesson starts with himself. One only
has to study Caravaggio's *The Calling of Saint Matthew* to behold
divine authority overcoming all resistance to its invitation. Even
without this masterpiece before us, it is sufficient to remember that
Peter supplies the example to imitate. Judas sets the example to
avoid at risk of one's life.

*Merciful Father, the gift of forgiveness comes from your crucified
Son. Give me a deep trust in your unconditional love so that I may
always turn to you. Do not let me die without repentance for my
sins.*

The Everything of Our Lives

Father Romanus Cessario, O.P.

*Then Jesus approached and said to [the eleven disciples],
"All power in heaven and on earth has been given to me. Go,
therefore, and make disciples of all nations, baptizing them in
the name of the Father, and of the Son, and of the holy Spirit,
teaching them to observe all that I have commanded you."*
(Mt 28: 18-20)

C onsider for a minute the movements, the men and women, and the shed blood that these words have inspired since Saint Matthew composed them. Missionaries have reached the most remote places of the globe. Monks have constructed monasteries all over the world. Martyrs have faced enormous odds rather than renounce the promises of their baptism or deny even one article of Catholic faith. Think of Antoine Daniel (May 27, 1601–July 4, 1648), who was a Jesuit missionary at Sainte-Marie among the Hurons, and one of the eight North American Martyrs. This heroic Frenchman continued to wring moisture from damp towels in order to baptize his catechumens as ferocious warriors attacked the Huron village where he was saying Mass. Not even the aggressors' arrows that struck his person kept Father Daniel from completing his priestly sacramental ministry. His macerated body was thrown into the wooden chapel that was then set ablaze. And there are many, many more such accounts of everyday and extraordinary heroism in response to the command that Jesus gives his apostles on the mount of the Ascension. "Go, therefore, and make disciples of all nations."

These great monuments to Christian faith do not proceed by happenstance. Implicit in the instructions that Jesus gives is the mediation of the Church. Preaching and sacraments mark the chief activities that the Church undertakes. Today we speak about evangelization. There is no way to count oneself among the followers of Jesus without observing the requirements that he wisely ordains. When we accept the complete truth of the Catholic faith and embrace fully her sacramental life, then we find ourselves in the company of the holy men and women who have made this teaching and worship the everything of their lives.

Gracious Father, your Son Jesus Christ has commanded his apostles to teach, to govern, and to sanctify. Grant me the grace to remain faithful to the Catholic Church until death and to fulfill all that is required of me by her teaching.

The Great Consolation

Father Romanus Cessario, O.P.

"And behold, I am with you always, until the end of the age."
(Mt 28: 20)

We come to the final verse of Saint Matthew's Gospel. People are reluctant to think about Christ as going up into heaven. This hesitation seems rather odd. Where else would Jesus go? The glorified body of Christ escapes the limits established by our time and our place. So heaven is neither up or down or sideways. Heaven is found wherever the glorified body of Jesus exists.

There is another meaning given to the Body of Christ. We speak about the Mystical Body of Christ. The Catechism explains that "Christ and his Church… together make up the 'whole Christ'" (CCC 795). As he returns to heaven, the risen Christ addresses the members of his Body. He announces the great consolation that has kept Christian believers alive and active for more than two millennia. "I am with you always, until the end of the age." The Lord promises to remain with his Church. There is something unique about how Christ remains with us. Christ abides with his Church by making himself one with her. This fellowship is compared to the marriage covenant between a man and a woman. So we image Christ and the Church related to each other as Bridegroom to Bride. Christ, the spotless Bridegroom. We, the members of his Body, the Bride. A spotless Bride, even though individual members of the Church can fall into sin.

The close of Saint Matthew's Gospel prepares us for the life that we live today. At the same time, the divine promise spoken at the Ascension points to a future glory that belongs to those who love Jesus above all things. To love Jesus is not a difficult matter. Within the Church, we find all the means necessary for maintaining our spousal attachment to the glorified Savior. Foremost among these means are the sacraments of the Church, and the liturgy that daily celebrates the mysteries Saint Matthew has recorded for us to ponder "until the end of the age."

Merciful Father, we rejoice in the promise of your Son to remain with us until the end of the world. Grant us the grace to live daily in his love, so that we may attain the happiness of the everlasting age.

Brief Biographies of Contributors

- **Helen M. Alvaré** is associate professor at George Mason University School of Law and a consultor to the Pontifical Council for the Laity.

- **Douglas Bushman** is director of the Institute for Pastoral Theology at Ave Maria University. He received his S.T.L. degree from the University of Fribourg, Switzerland.

- **Father Peter John Cameron,** O.P., is editor-in-chief of MAGNIFICAT and author of *Mysteries of the Virgin Mary: Living Our Lady's Graces.*

- **Father Romanus Cessario,** O.P., serves as senior editor for MAGNIFICAT and teaches theology at Saint John's Seminary in Boston, MA.

- **Father John Dominic Corbett,** O.P., teaches fundamental moral theology at the Dominican House of Studies in Washington, DC. He also preaches retreats and offers spiritual direction.

- **Father Lawrence Donohoo,** O.P., teaches systematic theology and serves as spiritual director at Mount Saint Mary's Seminary in Emmitsburg, MD.

- **Anthony Esolen** is professor of English at Providence College, a senior editor of *Touchstone Magazine,* and a regular contributor to MAGNIFICAT. He is the translator and editor of *Dante's Divine Comedy* and author of *Ironies of Faith.*

- **Father Anthony Giambrone,** O.P., is a Dominican priest of the Province of Saint Joseph currently studying Scripture at the École Biblique in Jerusalem.

- **Father Aquinas Guilbeau,** O.P., writes from Fribourg, Switzerland, where he is pursuing a doctorate in moral theology.

- **Father Donald Haggerty,** a priest of the Archdiocese of New York, teaches moral theology and is a spiritual director at Saint Joseph's Seminary in Yonkers, NY.

- **John Janaro** is associate professor emeritus of theology at Christendom College. He is currently engaged in research, writing, and lecturing on topics in religion and the humanities. He is the author of *Never Give Up: My Life and God's Mercy.*

- **Father William M. Joensen,** a priest of the Archdiocese of Dubuque, is dean of Campus Spiritual Life at Loras College, where he also teaches philosophy and is spiritual director for seminarians.

MAGNIFICAT®

Bringing the Word of God to Life

❧ Every month, you will receive a new issue that will help you participate more fervently in the Mass and will offer you inspirational tools for a constantly-renewed spiritual life.

❧ MAGNIFICAT's convenient "pocket-size" allows you to take it everywhere and pray throughout the day.

❧ Only $3.75 a month!

Every day, the treasures of the Church

THE TREASURES OF PRAYER:
◆ Morning, evening, and night prayers inspired by the Liturgy of the Hours and adapted to your busy schedule
◆ First-rate spiritual and biblical essays

THE TREASURES OF THE EUCHARIST:
◆ Readings and prayers of each daily Mass
◆ Liturgical insights

THE TREASURES OF THE SAINTS:
◆ Every day, the eloquent life of a saint as a spiritual guide for daily living

THE TREASURES OF SPIRITUAL LIFE:
◆ Carefully selected daily meditations drawn from the very best writings of the Fathers of the Church as well as from recent spiritual masters

THE TREASURES OF SACRED ART:
◆ Inspiring award-winning covers to help you lift up your heart to the Lord
◆ Full-color reproductions of great works of sacred art, complete with explanatory notes

To subscribe, call: 1-866-273-5215
or visit our website: www.magnificat.com

MAGNIFICAT is also available in Spanish.

MAGNIFICAT®